CROWOOD METALWORKING GUIDES

SHARPENING

COMMON WORKSHOP TOOLS

DR MARCUS BOWMAN

METABO

CROWOOD METALWORKING GUIDES

SHARPENING

COMMON WORKSHOP TOOLS

DR MARCUS BOWMAN

THE CROWOOD PRESS

First published in 2020 by
The Crowood Press Ltd
Ramsbury, Marlborough
Wiltshire SN8 2HR

enquiries@crowood.com
www.crowood.com

British Library Cataloguing-in-Publication Data
A catalogue record for this book is available from the British Library.

ISBN 978 1 84797 667 8

Disclaimer
Safety is of the utmost importance in every aspect of metalworking. The practical workshop procedures and the tools and equipment used in metalworking are potentially dangerous. Tools should be used in strict accordance with the manufacturer's recommended procedures and current health and safety regulations. The author and publisher cannot accept responsibility for any accident or injury caused by following the advice given in this book.

Typeset by Marcus Bowman
Printed and bound in India by Parksons Graphics

Contents

Acknowledgements

The author would like to thank those individuals and companies who have expended time and effort to contribute photographs and information for this book:

Arc EuroTrade Ltd
John Baguley
R. D. Barrett Small Tools Ltd
David Beattie
Bowland Trading Ltd
Celtic INC
Chronos Ltd
DMT
Eccentric Engineering
W. E. Falck
John Florence
Glendo LLC
Glenn Evans of Glennview.com
Gränsfors BRUK AB
Haskpro LLC
Nigel Hill
Alan Hooper
David Haythornthwaite
Horotec SA
Jack Sealey Ltd
Leon Kirk
Lansky Sharpeners
Lee Valley Tools Ltd
Donald Mitchell
John Moran at gadgetbuilder.com
Morse Flight Systems
Howard at MYFORD-LATHES.COM
Spyderco LLC
Steve Lindsay Engraving and Tools
T D Fitchett Ltd
The Society of Model and Experimental Engineers
Tormek AB
Toulouse Museum
Versalab INC
Niels Vrijlandt of Nielsmachines.com
Warren Machine Tools Ltd
Weald Enterprises

The author wishes to commend those members of bulletin boards, discussion groups and bloggers who have selflessly shared their work, provided solutions to problems and stimulated ideas.
Thanks, too, to the sterling work done by those standards organisations which have laboured long and hard to produce usable and practical standards for tool features, geometry and terminology.

British Standards Institution
American National Standards Institute
ISO: International Organisation for Standardization

But most of all, a very special thanks to my long-suffering personal support team, Hazel and Rachael, whose support made the writing task so much easier.

Every effort has been made by the author and publisher to contact the copyright holders of the works illustrated in this book. Should any omissions have been made and/or the correct source not been acknowledged, the publishers will rectify this at the earliest opportunity upon reprint.

OPPOSITE PAGE: A DMT Diamond Wave Sharpener featuring convex and concave abrasive surfaces. Photo: DMT.

Introduction

The underlying purpose of this book is to give you an understanding of what is involved in sharpening common workshop tools, from scissors, shears and knives, to lathe tools and drills. The range includes screwdrivers, chisels, and punches, along with the more specialist gravers and scrapers. The aim is to equip you with the knowledge of what happens during the sharpening process, and provide practical examples of how to sharpen a range of common tools by using sharpening stones and grinding wheels on a bench grinder.

This is not a book about tool and cutter grinding; and it does not deal with sharpening milling cutters, reamers, taps or dies. Nor is it a book about designing and making your own cutting tools.

Using sharp tools is one of life's great joys. A sharp tool feels right; the job seems that much easier; and the quality of the cut usually means there is less work to do to produce a finished surface on the object. This book is all about sharpening tools; giving them precise cutting edges; and ensuring the tool angles are suited to the way the tool is to be used and the materials to be cut.

The means of sharpening range from using an abrasive stone to sharpen a knife or restore the shape of a screwdriver blade, to using a bench grinder to give more life to a chisel, or put a keen edge on a range of lathe tools.

The tools range from the everyday knives and scissors to punches, clockmakers' gravers and lathe tools, with a substantial section on devices for sharpening drills.

Fig. 1: In this book, sharpening is based around a bench grinder, bench stones, and accessories such as templates and setting gauges. This grinder has a replacement wheel on the right, together with a home-made wheel guard.

Abrasives are essential, and there is information on types of abrasives, grades, grits and mesh sizes, as well as forms of abrasives like stones, wheels and papers.

The equipment is centred around abrasive stones used on the bench, and bench grinders fitted with a range of abrasive wheels, as these are widely available and easy to use. However; buying a stone or a bench grinder is one thing, but looking after abrasive surfaces is another, and many a shed or workshop has a flat stone and a bench grinder which seem ineffective because their abrasive surface has been clogged or damaged and is no longer capable of creating a keen edge on any tool. Restoring abrasive surfaces is a common requirement, so there is information on how to maintain the surface of a flat stone and the face of the wheel on a bench grinder.

Much of the ancillary equipment shown in this book is commercially available, but, to get the best out of any flat abrasive stone or a bench grinder, it helps if you have good metalworking skills and are able to make some simple accessories. These might include simple devices to hold a tool against a flat stone securely and at an accurate angle, or alternative rests (or at least larger platforms for rests), sliding plates and adaptors, and, optionally, some small devices for holding work so that it can be positioned accurately and safely as it is presented to a grinding wheel. There are lots of photos of self-made equipment, but because these are relatively simple items, there are no dimensioned drawings. Instead, the photos give ideas and inspiration, allowing you to make accessories to suit your own grinder and your own ways of working.

There is general advice on bench grinders, and there are examples of the use of readily available tools such as vee blocks, toolposts, collet holders, protractors and gauges.

There is a little maths and a few handy formulae, but there are also tables which can be used instead.

The specific examples included in the book are designed to demonstrate a range of techniques which allow a variety of surfaces and edges to be restored using appropriate forms of abrasive. Although it is easy to dip into the contents to find techniques suited to particular tools, reading through all the examples from beginning to end will provide an ordered sequence designed to help demonstrate a full range of methods; and although you may not envisage sharpening every type of tool, it is worth reading all the examples, because there are usually other applications for the techniques you will learn.

Approached in the right frame of mind, sharpening is a satisfying task, and its end result is to produce a tool well suited for use in the workshop. If taken at an unhurried pace, it is an almost Zen-like way in which to occupy time as you restore the capabilities of the equipment in the workshop, knowing that the tools will be ready for whatever challenge they face. Their owner, too, will be prepared for the next job.

STAY SHARP; STAY SAFE

The workshop is a place of industry but it should also be a place of tranquillity, focus, and the pleasure which comes from creating things. The sharp cutting edge plays an important part in most workshops, but it also represents a source of danger.

Workshops can be dangerous places, for all sorts of reasons, but there are specific dangers associated with sharp edges.

A sharp edge can easily cut flesh, and careless or imprecise use of a sharp tool brings the danger that the cutting edge may penetrate skin, sever sinew and nerve tissue, or slice through bone. A knife which slips, a saw blade which wanders, or a machine with unguarded cutting edges which may allow contact between blade and body parts are all potential sites of serious injury to humans or animals. Take every care to avoid all of these.

A blunt cutting tool is almost as bad, and while it may not cut quite so quickly or effectively, there is the real added danger that a blunt tool must be forced to cut. That forcing action may increase the danger that the tool slips or the work moves under the force, and the unguided cutting edge, blunt though it may be, causes serious injury to nearby parts of the body. Gently stroking a sharp hacksaw over a sheet of thick steel will part the sheet cleanly and accurately, while a blunt blade must be pressed much more firmly into the surface to have any effect. With increased pressure comes loss of accurate control, and the danger that if the blade breaks, hands, head and chest may come down hard on the sharp edge of the work. Whereas a gentle movement can easily be arrested as a sharp blade finishes cutting and drops off the material being cut, the kind of high pressure needed for a blunt blade often means a loss of control as a knife is pulled heavily off the material. The nearest targets then become an adjacent hand, arm, stomach, ribs, or leg.

Material being cut may move unless firmly secured. Cutting steel with a chisel creates sufficient force for lightly clamped work to be pushed out of a vice, at which point it becomes a projectile capable of damaging whatever lies in its path. A blunt chisel requires much more force to make it cut, and even tightly clamped work may move under the pressure. Failing to attend to the condition of parts of a tool which are intended to be struck by a hammer, like the end of a chisel for example, may result in the danger that fragments fly off and cause injury. A misshapen cutting edge on a chisel or a punch may shatter, producing flying projectiles akin to the fragments of a hand grenade.

Sharp cutting edges and well-maintained tools are a basic requirement and the first precaution in the workshop.

Impact-proof goggles are an essential, and good ear defenders are a wise addition where tools make noise. The noise of a grinder sharpening a tool is loud and contains many high frequencies, which are quite capable of causing serious hearing impairment, so you should take precautions to protect your ears. The dust created by grinding gets everywhere, and can cause serious lung problems, so wear a good quality dust mask.

Gloves may be a useful form of protection, but a sharp knife can easily cut cloth or leather, and modern materials such as Kevlar or woven stainless steel wire may be more appropriate, depending on the task.

Abide by appropriate Health and Safety recommendations when using tools, even in the home workshop or craft studio, because those regulations represent good practice, designed for your own protection. When using grinding wheels and grinding machines, obtain a copy of the relevant Health and Safety regulations, particularly in respect of mounting and using wheels safely. These regulations are mandatory in an industrial situation, but are essential for safety even in a home workshop. Skill is an important aspect of safety, and you should take the time to practice using tools.

Many of the photographs shown in this book are of grinders. For clarity, so that you can see as much detail as possible of the various set ups for sharpening tools, many of the photographs show grinders which have had all or part of their protective wheel guards removed. Under no circumstances should you operate a grinder without those protective guards in place.

As with everything else, the best safety equipment is only effective when it is worn; and the most appropriate safe working methods are only useful when they are practised. Take your time; think about what you are doing; and enjoy working safely.

1 Sharpening Media

Any part of a tool may be shaped by rubbing it with an abrasive material. The abrasive rubs and removes material, changing the shape of the tool. In particular, a cutting edge may be rubbed with an abrasive so that some of the material is removed, leaving the edge sharp. Often, the area immediately behind or adjacent to the cutting edge is rubbed into a particular shape with the abrasive, to give the edge particular properties such as a long shape tapering to a thin cutting edge (like a razor blade or a scalpel) which can penetrate material deeply using little force, or a short steep slope to give the edge sufficient strength (Fig. 2) to withstand heavy pressure (like a chisel).

Fig. 2: Cutting edges may have different thicknesses and angles, to suit their purpose and the materials they will cut.

Abrasives were originally naturally occurring materials such as emery, Arkansas stone, corundum, cubic boron nitride (cBN) and diamond, used in their natural state, or refined to give them a relatively uniform structure. Modern abrasives are often man-made synthetic materials which benefit from a consistent particle size and a precise composition designed to remove material at a particular rate or in a particular way. Synthetic materials complement rather than replace the natural abrasives, providing a wider range of choice of materials. Table 1, in the Further Information section at the end of this book, lists commonly available abrasive materials, their relative hardness, and some applications.

An abrasive material contains particles which act like small cutting tools and can remove some of the material being rubbed by the abrasive. As the particles rub and cut, they become blunt, so an important part of the action of an abrasive is to allow the blunted particles to be removed. In some materials this happens naturally as the abrasive rubs away. When sharpening a knife blade on a soft stone, for example, the stone may appear to wear and be reduced to dust as it rubs the knife blade. That dust contains particles which have rubbed the blade and been blunted in the process, and the bond between those particles and the others remaining in the stone is sufficiently weak that the blunted particles separate from the stone. This reveals new, sharp, particles which can then act on the knife blade. In this way, although the stone wears away, it provides a continuously refreshed face to rub the blade, removing material from the blade, changing its shape and sharpening it in the process. Some stones do not degrade as quickly, and retain their particles for longer. This can result in blunt particles rubbing on the work, and the steel of a knife blade will tend to smear on the stone, clogging it and tending to prevent the release of blunt particles. That, in turn, leads to a less efficient cutting action. So there is a balance between the rate at which the stone releases blunt particles, the speed of the cutting action, and the rate at which the stone wears.

> ***FRIABILITY***
>
> A material which can easily be worn away by being reduced to smaller particles (like a soft stone wearing to dust) is termed 'friable'.
>
> All materials have a degree of 'friability', but some are more friable or less friable than others, just as all materials have the property of 'hardness' but some are harder or less hard than others.
>
> A hard material is termed 'indurate', although, as with friability, some materials are more indurate or less indurate than others.
>
> The degree of friability in an abrasive is an important factor in its ability to remove material from a workpiece.

Synthetic abrasives work in the same way as naturally-occurring abrasive materials, but the shape and size of the grains can be accurately controlled, making the cutting action more predictable and consistent. The abrasive particles are mixed with a bonding material, and the mixture is moulded to a useful shape such as a wheel or a flat stone.

The choice of bonding material affects the way in which blunt particles are released from the material, and the strength of the bond can be arranged to suit the requirements of the material being abraded, as well as controlling the economics of the operation. However, just as with the natural stone, a lower release rate may result in contamination of the grinding medium by the material being sharpened because blunt particles are not being released sufficiently quickly. This can lead to clogging of the abrasive material, reducing the effectiveness and the efficiency of the sharpening process.

Abrasives may be classified as 'soft' or 'hard'. Soft abrasives release abrasive particles before they are fully blunt, while hard abrasives hold onto their particles even after they have been made blunt. The most desirable condition would be somewhere in between, with the abrasive neither too soft nor too hard, but just right compared with the material being sharpened. In more recent times, abrasives based on diamonds or cBN have been termed 'superabrasives', because they are effective against hard materials, and their particles stay sharp for a relatively long time.

BONDED ABRASIVES

Abrasive particles can be mixed with a bonding agent, then moulded and/or pressed into shape. This process is used to form flat surfaces (Fig. 3), cylindrical or conical shapes such as wheels (Fig. 4), or other shapes of abrasive (e.g. triangular, tapered or curved) for specific purposes (Figs 5 and 6). Commonly-used bonding materials are listed in Table 2.

Grinding wheel bond types

Bond type	Description	Bond reference letter
Resinoid	Originally obtained from trees, most resins are now synthetic and reinforced by other materials. Resinoid wheels are often suitable for heavy grinding.	B
Shellac	A secretion of the female lac insect. Although the bond is of low strength, shellac wheels can providuce a good final finish on work.	E
Metal	Powdered metal and diamond or cBN particles are sintered (pressed together under high pressure and heat) to form a metal-bonded abrasive for wet grinding, ceramics and glass-based materials.	M
Oxychloride	Magnesia oxychloride cement, made from magnesium oxide and magnesium chloride, produces a relatively soft bonding compound. Oxychloride wheels can create very sharp edges on cutting tools.	O
Rubber	Natural and artificial rubbers create an elastic wheel often used for centreless grinding. Rubber-bonded wheels can provide a very fine finish.	R
Silicate	Sand and sodium carbonate (soda ash) are combined at high temperature to provide a bonding material. A wheel made with silicate bonds generates relatively little heat during grinding.	S
Vitrified	The most widely used bonding agent, made from types of clay. Wheels with a vitrified bond are rigid and strong, and are capable of both high rates of material removal and of precision grinding.	V

Table 2: Common types of wheel bond.

Fig. 3: A range of flat abrasive surfaces.

Fig. 4: Abrasives may be moulded to make wheels.

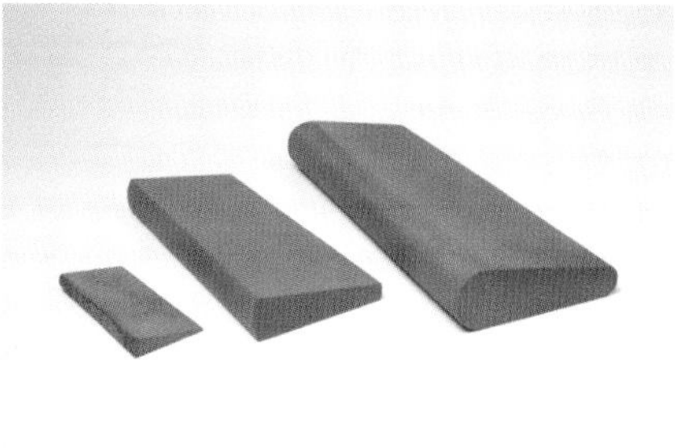

Fig. 5: Abrasives may be moulded in various shapes.

Fig. 6: An Arkansas stone of triangular cross-section.

COATED ABRASIVES

A flat surface can be coated with a bonding agent and abrasive particles. The surface may be flexible or rigid, and typical types of coated abrasives include emery paper (Fig. 7), soft-cored abrasive pads, abrasive belts, tape and string (Fig. 8).

Fig. 7: Emery paper made using corundum powder.

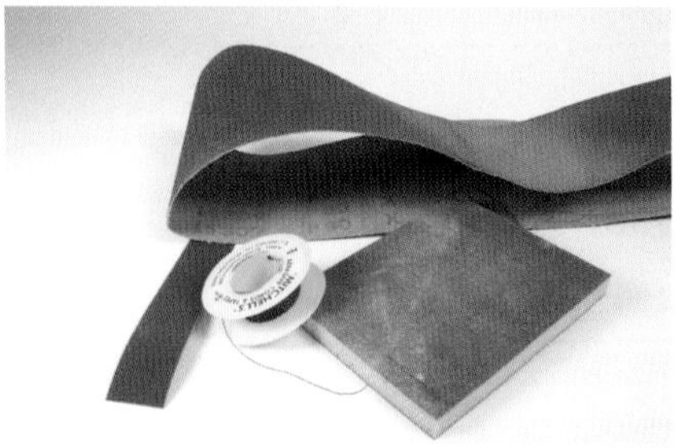

Fig. 8: Abrasive belt, tape (abrasive strip), soft-cored pad, and abrasive-coated string (cord).

For some materials such as diamond, the coating process may be technically complex and include chemical vapour deposition or plating (often involving depositing nickel to hold the diamond particles in place). Coatings are normally applied to metal plates which are either stand-alone or may be embedded in plastic or resin to form a composite plate. The metal plate in a composite plate may be perforated (Fig. 3), and the holes allow the diamond slurry developed during a sharpening session to become trapped but remain active there, or, where the resin substrate is at the same level as the abrasive surface, the particles may become embedded in the resin, enhancing the abrasive action of the plate.

ABRASIVES IN OTHER FORMS

Abrasives are available in paste or liquid form, including products such as grinding paste (often used to grind valves and valve seats), rubbing compounds (often used to burnish paint), polishing pastes, and polishing liquids (Fig. 9).

Fig. 9: Abrasive pastes and liquids.

Fig. 10: Abrasive bars consisting of paste and abrasives, for applying to a hone.

Another approach is to impregnate a soft material such as leather or canvas with abrasive particles, to make a hone or a strop. The abrasive particles may be applied by spraying, but they are often held in suspension in a paste, frequently moulded into the shape of a bar, rather like a bar of soap (Fig. 10), and the bar is rubbed against the hone to transfer abrasive particles. The surrounding paste in the bar is also transferred, and acts as a lubricant. The colour of the bar denotes the grade or grit size of the abrasive particles. Pre-impregnated cloths, wadding, and soft impregnated blocks are also available (Fig. 11) and these are useful for surfaces which feature corners and curves.

Fig. 11: Impregnated cloth and wadding, and soft impregnated block.

GRINDING STONES AND PLATES

A rectangular abrasive block with flat faces (Fig. 3) can be used to sharpen a wide variety of tools. These abrasive blocks are often called stones, whether they are made of naturally occurring or synthetic materials. Flat-faced stones (rectangular blocks) are normally used manually. The stone is most commonly laid on a bench and the tool is held by hand or in a simple guide, and moved over the abrasive surface manually (Fig. 12). In some cases, the size or shape of the tool makes it easier to hold the stone and move it across the edge being sharpened. Sheet metal shears, for example, are too awkward to sharpen if the stone is on a bench, but can easily be sharpened by holding the stone in one hand and rubbing it across the cutting edge of the shears (Fig. 13). Stones are commonly available in a range of sizes and grits, and man-made stones may have a uniform

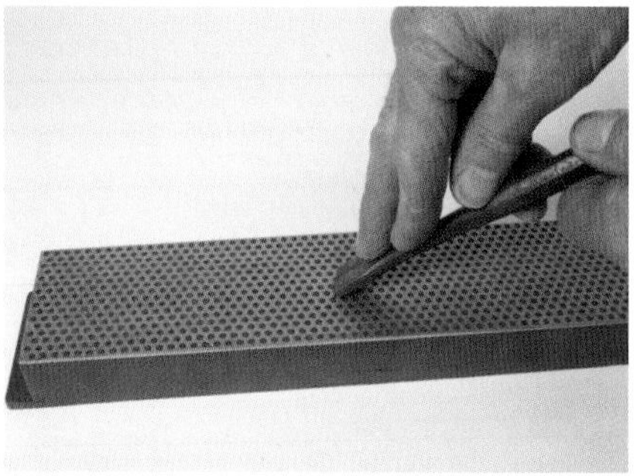

Fig. 12: A tool can be shaped or sharpened by moving it across the surface of an abrasive stone or plate, while pressing firmly.

Fig. 13: A tool can also be sharpened by moving a stone across the cutting edge of a stationary tool.

grit throughout, or may have different grit sizes on two sides, for convenience, like the combination carborundum stones shown in Figs 14 and 15 which have a coarse grit on one side and a finer grit on the other.

Fig. 14: Combination stones have a different grit size on each major face, giving both coarse and fine faces on a single stone.

Fig. 15: A combination stone has two stones of different grades stuck together.

Non-flat shapes of abrasive stones have their uses too, and stones required to sharpen tools which have flat, externally and/or internally curved faces may have a combination of flat and rounded faces (Figs 5, 6 and 16–20). The flat faces of stones with a triangular cross-section may be used in internal

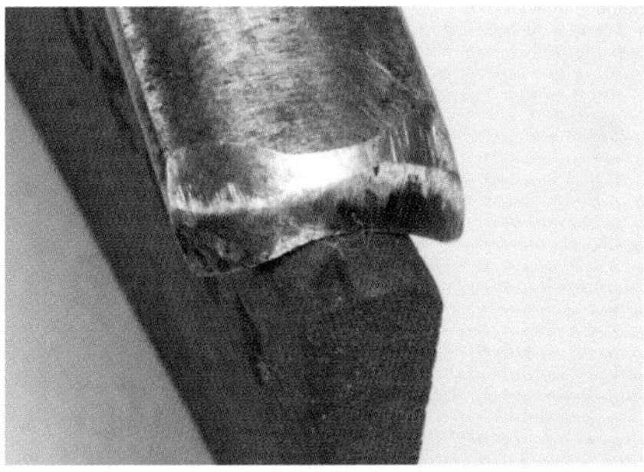

Fig. 16: Shaped stones are useful for sharpening shaped tools.

Fig. 17: A triangular stone is useful for sharpening internal corners with the same angle as the corners of the stone, or larger.

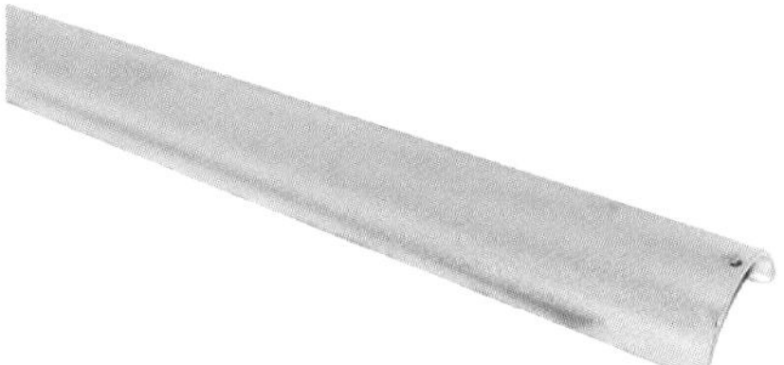

Fig. 18: A Diamond Honing Cone with a convex curve. The diameter changes along the cone. Photo: DMT.

Fig. 19: A DMT Diamond Wave Sharpener with both convex and concave abrasive curved surfaces. Photo: DMT.

Fig. 20: A circular abrasive stone with flat upper and lower faces. Photo: GRÄNSFORS BRUK, SWEDEN.

corners such as on the vee tool shown in Fig. 18. The flat upper and lower faces of a circular abrasive stone (Fig. 19) provide equal access from all angles.

GRINDING WHEELS

Grinding wheels have a central hole and are designed to be mounted on a rotating spindle. One convenient shape of grinding stone is the cylindrical flat-sided stone found on most basic bench grinders (Fig. 21). This is a

Fig. 21: Bench or offhand grinders are normally fitted with cylindrical flat-sided abrasive wheels.

useful shape because if the wheel is rotated at a uniform rate (typically 1400 or 2800 revolutions per minute), all points on the curved face of the periphery travel at the same linear speed (the speed measured as if they were travelling in a straight line on-the-flat), known as the surface speed. That helps provide a uniform rate of grinding. Although the circular flat-sided stone is useful, that basic shape does not suit all tools, so wheels suitable for tool and cutter sharpening are available in a range of shapes depending on the intended purpose of the wheel. As with abrasive stones, the shape of the wheel makes some tasks easier or more difficult than others. A convex surface (curving outwards) allows the creation of narrow angled faces by raising a horizontal tool above the centre height of the wheel (Fig. 22), while a tapered wheel can reach more easily into a flute (Fig. 23).

The basic shapes of grinding wheels are defined in national and international standards documents, available from national standards bodies such as ANSI (American National Standards Institute), BSI (British Standards Institution) and ISO (International Organisation for Standards), and these shapes may be augmented by individual manufacturers, to produce a wide range of useful shapes for general or specific tasks. Fig. 24 and Table 3 contain details of typical wheel shapes for tool and cutter grinders.

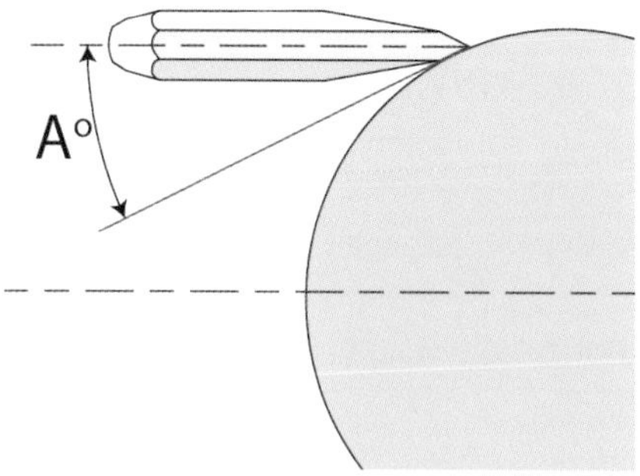

Fig. 22: Raising a horizontal tool above wheel centre height creates an angled face on a tool. The greater the height, the greater the angle A degrees.

Fig. 23: A tapered wheel has clearance at the back, and can reach into a confined area such as a flute.

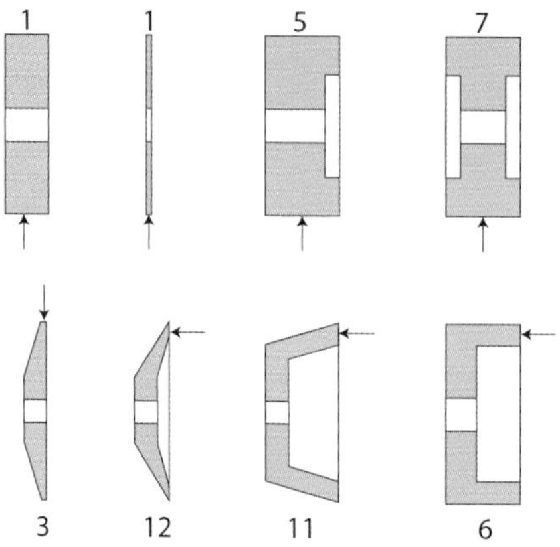

Fig. 24: Cross-sections of common wheel shapes for tool and cutter grinding. Arrows indicate working faces. Reference numbers correspond to wheel types listed in table 3.

Grinding Wheel Shapes	
Wheel type reference number	**Description**
1 (General)	Straight wheel for general applications
1 (Saw)	Thin straight wheel for saw sharpening
5	Wheel recessed on one side
7	Wheel recessed on both sides
3	Wheel tapered on one side
12	Dish wheel
11	Taper cup wheel
6	Straight cup wheel

Table 3: Grinding wheel shapes in common use. Reference numbers refer to Fig. 24.

The linear speed of points on the side of the wheel depends on their radial distance from the centre of the wheel (Fig. 25). Unrolling the red and blue paths and laying them flat shows that the red path is longer, so particles on the red and blue paths travel different distances in the same time (the time taken for one revolution). All points on the red circle travel at a speed of 2 x π x R x RPM metres per minute, and all points on the blue circle travel at 2 x π x r x RPM metres per minute. Because r is smaller than R, points on the blue circle travel more slowly than points on the red circle.

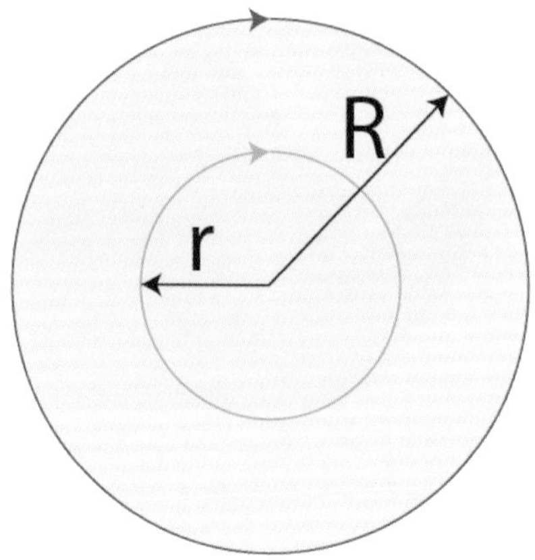

Fig. 25: On a rotating wheel, the linear speed of a particle depends on its radius.

Grinding wheel speed

By law, every grinding wheel must carry a label stating its recommended Maximum Operating Speed (MOS) which is the maximum allowable safe rotational speed (in RPM) of the wheel (Fig. 26).

That allows a match between motor

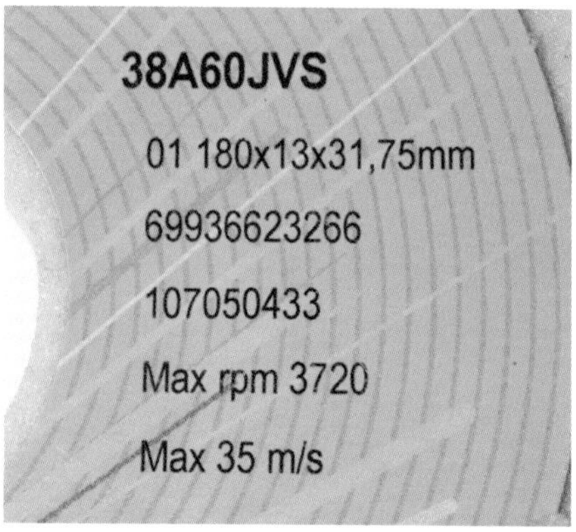

Fig. 26: By law, all grinding wheels must carry a label showing the maximum permissible rotational speed, in RPM. Many also show the maximum permissible linear speed at the periphery, often in metres per second (m/s).

speed, usually expressed in RPM, and the grinding wheel rotational speed. However; the important speed is the linear speed of the periphery of the wheel, in metres per minute (m/min) or feet per minute (ft/min). To distinguish between linear speed and rotational speed (revs per minute), the term 'surface speed' is often used, and the units then become Surface Metres per Minute (SMPM) or Surface Feet per Minute (SFPM). The significance of rotational speed is that the faster an abrasive particle is travelling, especially at the periphery of a wheel, the greater the force attempting to throw the particle off the wheel, and the stronger the bond must be to hold it in place. As rotational speed increases, these forces increase, but the strength of the bond remains constant. When the forces produced by the wheel's rotational speed exceed the strength of the bond, the wheel will shed particles and break apart, endangering everything nearby.

The significance of surface speed is that each abrasive particle is essentially a cutting edge, and there is a range of effective cutting speeds for each material being ground. There is also a balance to be struck between effective cutting and reasonable (and cost effective) wear on the wheel. Ideally, the surface speed should lie in an appropriate range for the material being ground, and that means taking the effective diameter of the wheel into account. Where the face of the wheel is the curved peripheral surface, the effective diameter is the diameter of the wheel, but where type 6, 11 or 12 wheels are used, the effective diameter is the diameter of the point at which the work contacts the wheel (Fig. 27). If the grinding face is wide there will be a range of diameters in contact with different points on the work simultaneously, producing a range of speeds across the work (Fig. 28). For wheels of this type the grinding face is usually relatively narrow (6 to 10mm being common), and it is usually possible to find a method of presenting the work to the wheel so that this variation is minimized. That normally involves the cutting edge of the work being traversed across the face of the wheel, so that only a portion of the cutting edge is in contact with the face of the wheel at any moment.

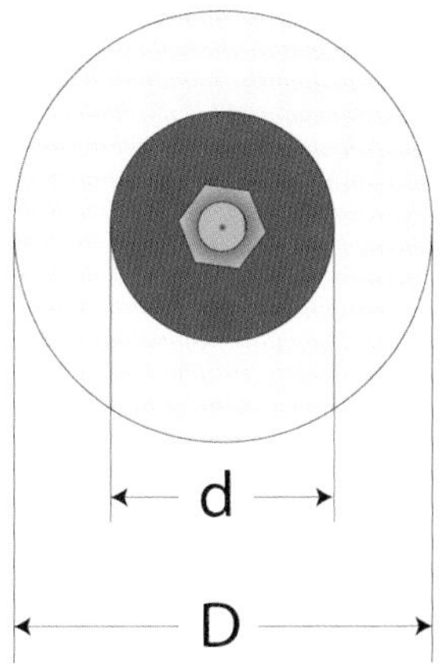

Fig. 27: The effective diameter of a particle depends on its distance from the centre of the wheel.

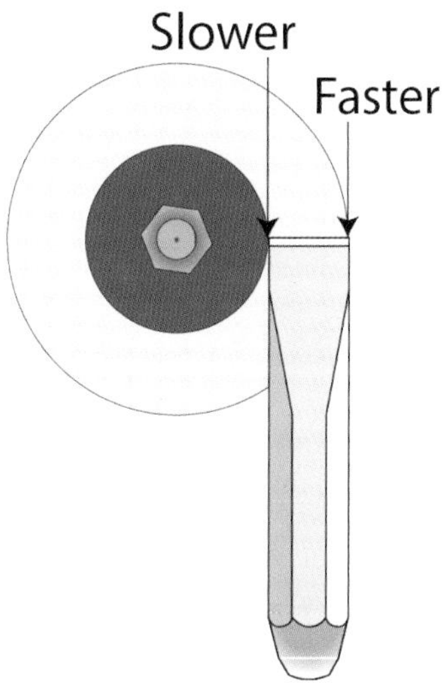

Fig. 28: On this type 6 cup wheel, the chisel experiences different cutting speeds at different points.

Rotational speed, surface speed and wheel diameter are related by the following formulae (where π = 3.14):

Surface speed (m/min) =
rotational speed (RPM) x π x
wheel diameter(mm) / 1000
Rotational speed (RPM) =
surface speed (m/min) x 1000 / (π x wheel diameter (mm))
or
Surface speed (feet/min) =
rotational speed (RPM) x π x wheel diameter(inches) / 12
Rotational speed (RPM) = surface speed (feet/min) x 12 /(π x wheel diameter (inches))

For example:

Wheel diameter 200mm
Rotational speed 1420RPM
Surface speed(m/min) =
1420 x 3.14 x 200/1000 = 891760/1000 = 891.760 = 892m/min
Surface speed (m/sec) = surface speed (m/min) / 60 = 892/60 = 14.87m/s

Wheel diameter 6 inches
Rotational speed 2840 RPM
Surface speed (ft/min) =
2840 x 3.14 x 6/12 = 53505.6/12 = 4458.8 = 4459 ft/min (or 4459/60 = 74.3ft/sec)

Matching abrasives to workpiece materials

The hardness of the material being ground is a key factor in selecting an abrasive, because grinding works best when used on hardened material. Mild steel, in its unhardened state, tends to clog a grinding wheel, so a soft grade of wheel is required to avoid this. Hardened steel, on the other hand, can be ground using a harder grade of abrasive. Not only will the finish tend to be better, but the abrasive wheel will not have the same tendency to clog as when grinding softer steel. The grit size is important too, with a coarser grit (smaller grit number) cutting faster but leaving deeper scores on the surface than a finer grit size (higher grit number). However; the grit size should be chosen bearing in mind the tendency for fine wheels to heat work more than coarse wheels, because a fine wheel will cut more slowly and the work will be in contact with the wheel for longer. Some jobs may require initial grinding using a relatively coarse wheel, followed by a finish grind using a finer wheel. On a tool and cutter grinder, grade 38 (or a smaller number) would be relatively coarse, while grade 60 or 100 would be a fine wheel. Finer grades would produce a finer and more polished finish on the work.

Table 4 lists abrasives and the workpiece materials for which they are best suited.

Abrasive	**Workpiece material**
Arkansas stone, water stone, India stone, Coticules, Belgian blue whetstone, ceramic stone, sandstone, oilstone, emery, rotten stone (Tripoli)	Mild steel, carbon steel, high speed steel. Usually used in the form of flat stones, for honing, or sharpening, rather than initial shaping. The harder the steel, the slower the process.
Aluminium oxide (corundum)	Mild steel, carbon steel, high speed steel. Softer steels have a tendency to clog the wheel more quickly than harder steels.
Silicon carbide (carborundum, Crystolon)	Tungsten carbide.
Diamond	Tungsten carbide. Non-ferrous metals. Hard non-metallic material (e.g. stone).
cBN (Borazon)	Hard steels.

Table 4: Abrasives used to grind common materials.

Grinding wheel shapes and grit codes

The range of wheel shapes, types, and grit sizes is wide, so International standards define several aspects of the codes used to categorize wheels. Other aspects are coded by manufacturers using their own proprietary codes.

International standards define the dimensions e.g. (BSI: BS ISO 603-6:1999 Bonded abrasive products- Dimensions- Part 6: Grinding wheels for tool and toolroom grinding), (BS ISO 525:2013 Bonded Abrasive Products. General Requirements), (ANSI: B74.13-1990: Markings for Identifying Grinding Wheels and Other Bonded Abrasives).

Fig. 29 shows how to interpret a "specification mark" according to BS ISO 525:2013. Note that the meanings of Optional codes (termed 'specification marks') in positions highlighted in green must be found by consulting a manufacturer's literature, as these vary from one manufacturer to another. The example code 32A46-JVBE translates to aluminium oxide, grain size 46 (coarse), hardness J (soft), vitreous bond, with manufacturer's optional codes 32 (mixture of abrasive types) and BE (special code).

In the USA, ANSI B74.13-1990 (Revised 2007) codes are almost identical to those of British Standard ISO 525:2013, although the 'Mixture of abrasive types' is termed 'Prefix', and the 'Manufacturer's special code' is termed the 'Manufacturer's Record' in the ANSI code.

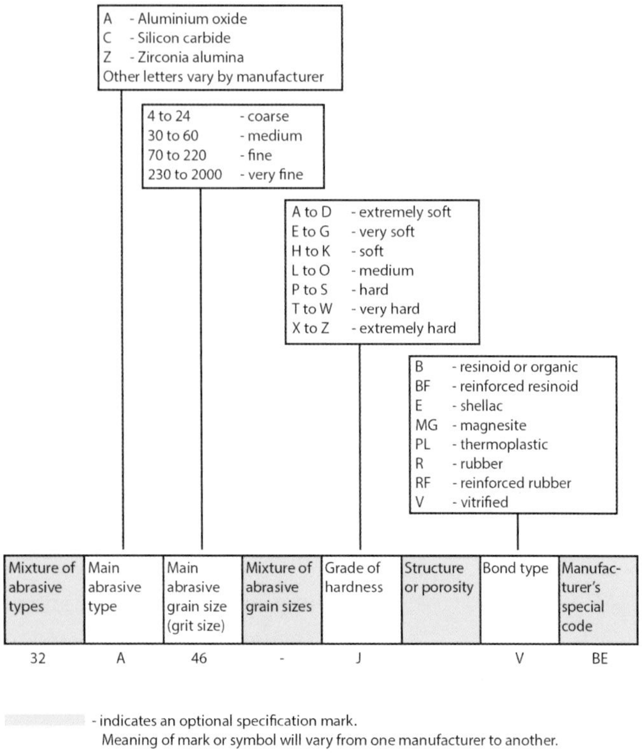

Fig. 29: Interpreting British Standard wheel markings.

Mounting a wheel

To mount a grinding wheel on an arbor (shaft) the hole through the centre of the wheel should match the diameter of the shaft. It is not unusual to find that the hole is much larger than the shaft, but that can be remedied by fitting a reducing sleeve to the hole in the wheel (Fig. 30). Sleeves are often made of plastic and are readily obtained at very low cost. In many cases, the reducing bushes come free with the wheels if the shaft diameter is specified at the time of pur-

Fig. 30: Wheel centre hole sizes may be reduced by using adaptor bushes.

chase. The wheel should be held between steel flanges, and Table 5 gives guidance on flange sizes, based on recommendations in BS 4581-2: 1984, which also specifies flange shapes and minimum flange thicknesses. Smaller low-cost offhand grinders often use two thin loose flanges, but toolroom grinders normally have one flange keyed to the shaft, to provide positive drive. A keyed flange may also have a hole in its periphery which allows a rod to be inserted so that the flange can be held stationary. This holds the shaft stationary, and helps when tightening the nuts at each end of the grinder shaft. Flanges should be relieved in the centre, so that contact between wheel and flange occurs only on a band near the outside diameter (Fig. 31). Loose flanges have the advantage that the small amount of friction drive may allow the wheel to slip more readily if it jams, but does limit the torque which can be applied to the wheel and the work. Blotters must be fitted between wheel and flange, on each side of the wheel (Fig. 31). These should be made of soft paper or card, and are intended to accommodate the difference in surface textures between the wheel and the flanges, preventing undue stress being created as a smooth, hard, flange crushes the points of the grains.

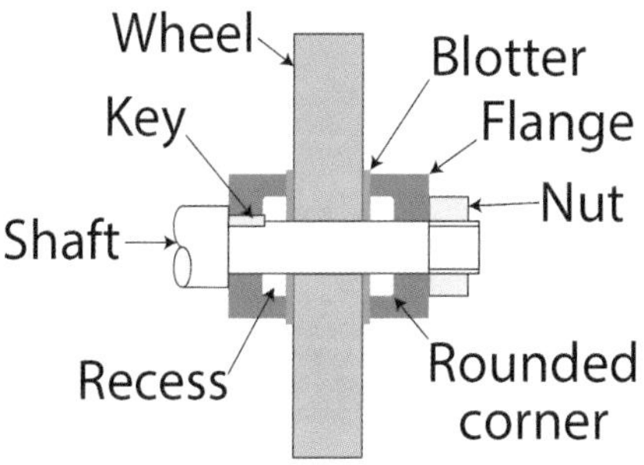

Fig. 31: Wheels are mounted between paper blotters and steel flanges.

Dressing a wheel

Before use, a grinding wheel needs to be dressed so that it rotates concentrically with the spindle, and its surface is in a fit state to grind work, with freshly exposed grains on its working face. After mounting a wheel in the grinder or grinding spindle, it is wise to dress it; even if the wheel is mounted permanently on its own arbor or boss. The purpose of dressing is:

- to shape the working face of the wheel by making it concentric with, or at right angles to, the axis of the spindle; or to give the operating face of the wheel a particular shape (such as giving the corner of a wheel a specific radius);
- to expose fresh grains ready for cutting work. This is particularly important if the wheel has become clogged with soft material (Fig. 32).

Fig. 32: A grinding wheel clogged by grinding soft mild steel, resulting in particles of steel sticking to the surface, reducing the effectiveness of the wheel.

Although the grit sizes in a wheel are determined during manufacture, different dressing techniques may result in a relatively fast-cutting wheel which does not heat the work much, or a wheel which produces a much finer finish but more heat in the tool.

Using a star wheel dresser

A tool with a group of hardened disc wheels and star-shaped wheels (Fig. 33) can be manually pressed against the surface of a wheel and will knock grains from the wheel. This is a messy operation compared to other methods, but it is quick and leaves a relatively rough finish to the wheel surface. Typically, star wheel dressers are used on bench grinders not used for fine tool grinding.

Most star dressers have two protruding legs which can be placed on the top surface

Fig. 33: A star wheel dresser contains hardened disc wheels and star-shaped wheels.

Grinding wheel flange diameters

Wheel diameter	Wheel type	Wheel bore (mm)	Flange outer diameter (mm)
100mm / 4 inch	1,6,11,12	12.7–31.75	35–34
125mm / 5 inch	1	12.7	80–64
	1,6	32	88–54
	11		80–54
	12		60–54
150mm / 6 inch	1	12.7	64–50
		19.05–32	88–60
180mm / 7.25 inch	1,5	12.7–32	100–60
200mm / 8 inch	1,5	15.88–32	100–67

Table 5: Guidelines for grinding wheel flange diameters. Summary based on information contained within BS 4581-2: 1984 and relates to wheels with bore diameters less than 76.2mm.

Fig. 34: The legs of the dresser can be used to steady the dresser on the rest, before sliding it into contact with the wheel.

Fig. 35: The star wheel dresser can be held on the rest with its legs hooked over the front edge of the rest, and tilted against the face of the wheel while traversing from one side to the other.

of the tool rest (Fig. 34), or hooked over the front edge of the grinding rest and used to guide the dresser as it is traversed across the surface of the wheel (Fig. 35). Set the dresser and rest so that the star wheel is close to, but not touching, the grinding wheel. Tilt the dresser by lifting the handle, to make contact. Then traverse the dresser across the surface of the wheel.

Some people recommend that this kind of dressing should take place after the grinder has been switched off and the wheel is coasting to a stop, but small grinders tend to have less momentum and the wheel is comparatively easily stopped, so that the grinder has to be repeatedly started and stopped. As a result, dressers are most commonly used while the grinder is under power. The star wheel dresser can be used to take a heavier cut than some other methods of dressing, although deep ridges or scores already in the wheel need to be dressed out in several stages. Ideally, the tool rest should be broad enough (side-to-side) that the dresser can sit securely clear of the wheel on either side, to give a secure start and finish during the whole of the traversing movement. A round bar can be clamped across the rest, to locate the legs of the dresser (Fig. 36), which is useful if the tool rest does not have a straight,

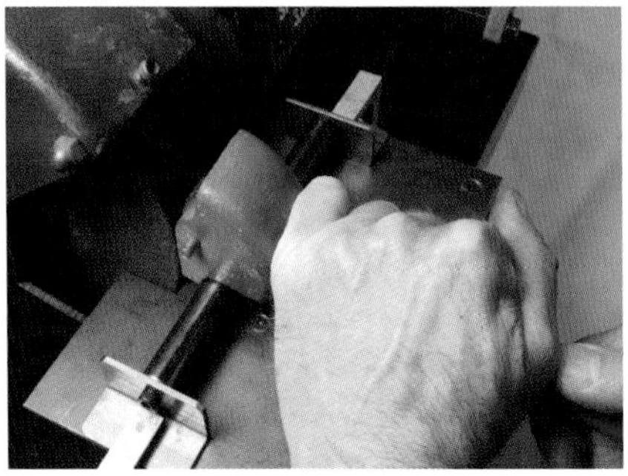

Fig. 36: Hooking the dresser over a bar clamped to the rest allows smoother control of the depth of cut by tilting the dresser.

uninterrupted, front edge. A round bar allows a smoother action and finer control of depth of cut by tilting the dresser, raising the rear handle to pivot the head downwards, to increase the cut. The bar shown in Fig. 36 is mounted clear of the rest, to allow room for the dresser feet to swing downwards to bring the star wheel into contact with the grinding wheel. The face of the wheel will be dressed parallel to the bar.

Using a dressing stick

A dressing stick is a rectangular stick of abrasive material which is pressed against the surface of the wheel in much the same way as a star wheel dresser (Fig. 37). The stick is made of a material similar to the wheel, or harder, and the bonding material is usually stronger than the wheel bond, so that the stick removes grains from the wheel. Sticks such as Norbide, made by Norton Saint-Gobain, are made from boron carbide which is one of the hardest man-made materials and is well suited to dressing most abrasive wheels except diamond.

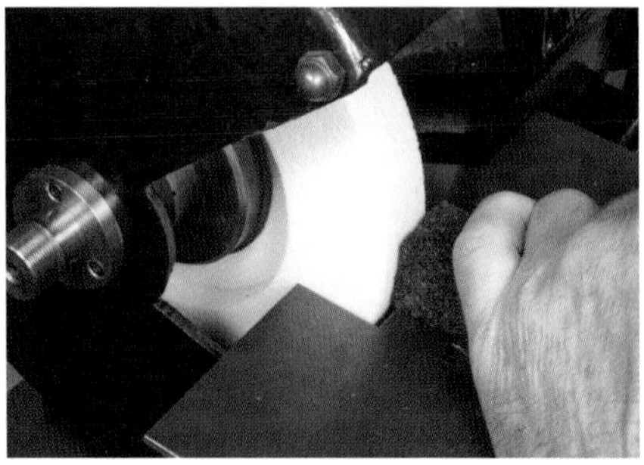

Fig. 37: A dressing stick is a rectangular stick of abrasive material capable of removing grains from the surface of the wheel.

Using a diamond dresser

Single-point diamond dressers consist of a single large industrial diamond mounted in a holder (usually a short length of cylindrical steel bar) as shown in Fig. 38.

Fig. 38: A single-point dresser consists of a diamond mounted in a steel bar.

Multi-point diamond dressers contain many diamonds embedded in the end face of a short length of bar (Fig. 39). The multi-point dresser is used in much the same way as a star wheel or stick dresser, traversing the dresser across the face of the wheel.

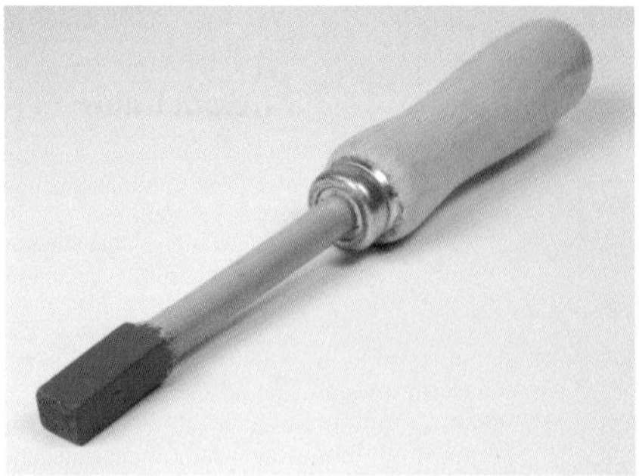

Fig. 39: A multi-point dresser contains many diamonds mounted in the end face of a small block.

The single-point dresser is traversed across the face of the wheel, but needs to be held so that the diamond trails the grains of the wheel. If the wheel is rotating downwards at the front, set the diamond at right angles to the wheel (or radial to the wheel, for the curved surface of a cylindrical wheel) then tilt it downwards by 10 to 15 degrees. The angle is best achieved by mounting the dresser in a holder which sets the angle (Fig. 40). On a bench grinder, this angle can be achieved by setting the rest below centre height (Fig. 41) at a height listed in Table 6.

Fig. 40: A single-point dresser in an adjustable holder which allows the depth of cut to be varied.

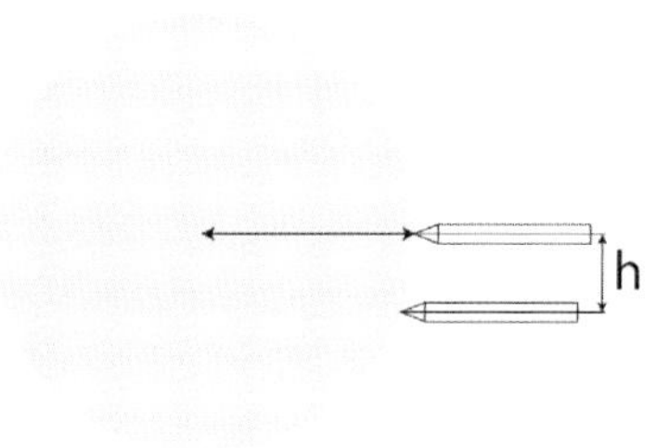

Fig. 41: The angle between dresser and wheel can be set by holding the dresser 'horizontal' a specific distance below centre height.

Height below centre for 'horizontal' single-point dresser	
Diameter of wheel (mm)	**Distance below centre height (mm)**
100	9 - 13
125	11 - 16
150	13 - 19
180	16 - 23
200	17 - 26

Table 6: Setting the dresser horizontal and at the given distance below centre produces an effective angle of 10 to 15 degrees.

Traversing time (seconds)					
Wheel speed	**Grit**	**Feed (mm/rev)**	**Wheel width (mm)**		
			12.5	**20**	**25**
1440 rpm					
	46	0.3	2	3	3
	60	0.2	3	4	5
	120	0.08	7	10	13
2880 rpm					
	46	0.3	1	1	2
	60	0.2	1	2	3
	120	0.08	3	5	7

Table 7: Traversing time across a selection of wheel widths, at a medium rate of traverse.

Recommended depths and feeds for dressing

When using a dresser which has a single diamond or a cluster of same-size diamonds, the diameter of the grinding wheel and the width of the face influence the optimum size of diamond needed to prevent excessive heat build-up. In practice, a diamond of 0.25kt, 0.33kt or 0.5kt will do the job perfectly well on wheels of diameter 150 or 200mm (6 or 8 inches).

The effect produced by diamond dressers, and to some extent by dressing sticks, depends on the depth of feed and the speed at which the dresser is traversed across the face of the wheel. Fine infeeds towards the wheel of 0.01 (fine grit) to 0.025mm (coarse grit) per pass should be enough, and that can be controlled by clamping the holder onto the table or rest then applying feed using the table feedscrew or by using a screw feed within the holder itself. The recommended depth of cut when dressing a wheel is the same for all types of dresser.

Relatively coarse feeds and a rapid traverse produce a more open finish to the grains on the wheel, resulting in a coarser finish on the work, but a relatively cool cutting process. Relatively fine feeds and a slow traverse will produce a smoother more closed finish to the wheel face, resulting in a finer finish on the work, but one which requires finer feeds and will cut more slowly, thereby generating more heat in the work. Although this is affected by the grade of the wheel, and cannot be used to make a very coarse-grained wheel behave like a very fine-grained wheel, it is a noticeable effect caused by the diamond cutting grains rather than ripping them from the surface of the wheel. Cut grains are less able to abrade the work and behave more like blunt grains, so this effect should be applied with care. For most applications, let the grade of the wheel determine the roughness, and use a medium rate of traverse, as suggested in Table 7, which gives an indication of the time to traverse across the faces of wheels of different thicknesses, on grinders with different spindle speeds. Traversing times are calculated based on linear movements in mm/rev to produce coarse (0.3mm/rev), medium (0.2mm/rev) and fine (0.08mm/rev) finishes on the wheel face.

$T = W/(LS \times RPM)$

where T is the Traversing time in seconds

W = wheel width (mm)

LS = linear speed (mm/min)

RPM = spindle speed in revolutions per minute

Flattening stones

Natural and synthetic stones wear as tools are rubbed along their surface (Fig. 42), in much the same way that grinding wheels wear. It is important that stones have uniformly flat surfaces, otherwise it becomes difficult to maintain a consistent angle between tool and stone. Just as a wheel is dressed to reform its working surface, so a stone should be flattened once it has worn. Flattening a stone also reveals fresh grains, restoring the cutting action of the stone. Two stones can be flattened by rubbing them together using a lubricant such as water or oil (Fig. 43), and a circular or figure-of-eight pattern is more effective than a simple back-and-forward motion. The high spots on each stone will be in contact and will wear, bringing lower spots into contact, until the whole of each surface is in contact, eventually. This process is most effective if the two stones are of the same material, so that they wear at the same rate, or if one stone is very flat and has a much harder more coarse-grained abrasive (Table 8). Two India stones of the same grade in contact with one another will flatten each other at a uniform rate, for example. Using two similar stones with different grades, such as waterstones of 1000 and 6000 grits will result in more rapid wear of the finer stone (6000 grit) but will eventually produce two flat stones. To save premature wear on the finer stones, a stone may be flattened by rubbing against an abrasive paper with a coating which is harder than the stone, such as aluminium oxide or silicon carbide 'wet or dry' paper. Place the paper on a flat surface, and rub the stone, working face down, against the paper (Fig. 44). Use a paper with a coarser grit than the stone, for faster results, and to expose fresh grains in the stone rather than simply blunting those grains and slowing the flattening process. At the other extreme, a DMT Dia-Flat lapping plate, which is very flat and covered in hard diamond grains, will flatten any other stone, grinding it to conform to the flat shape of the Dia-Flat plate (Fig. 45). Diamond is sufficiently hard to be able to cut any other abrasive material.

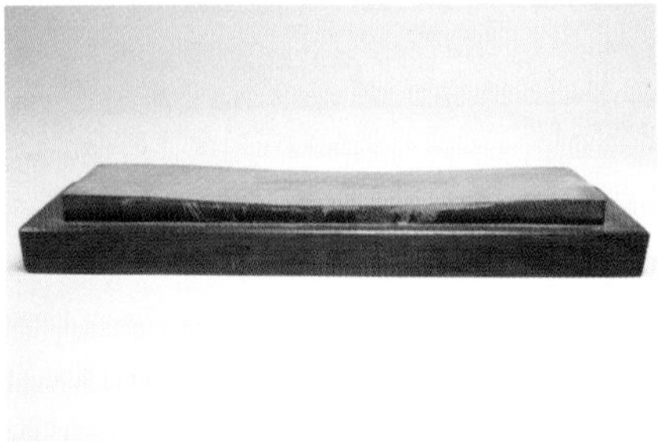

Fig. 42: A soft abrasive stone, worn concave by years of use sharpening pen knives.

Fig. 43: Two abrasive stones may be flattened by rubbing them together.

Fig. 44: Flattening a stone by rubbing against a harder abrasive paper.

Fig. 45: A DMT Dia-Flat Lapping Plate. Photo: DMT.

Forming or reforming curved faces

Flat stones can be made curved, and worn curved stones restored to their original curved shape by rubbing the stone against a suitably shaped coarser grade abrasive, in much the same way as when flattening a pair of flat stones.

For external (convex) curves, rub the stone with as much of the length of the face in contact with the other stone as possible. Hold a curved face parallel to the surface of a flat stone, and rock the curve against the flat surface (Fig. 46) while moving backwards and forwards. It is the sliding action between the faces that removes material. For internal (concave) curves, use either a smaller diameter cylindrical stone or abrasive paper wrapped around a cylinder of appropriate diameter. Rotate while sliding along and around.

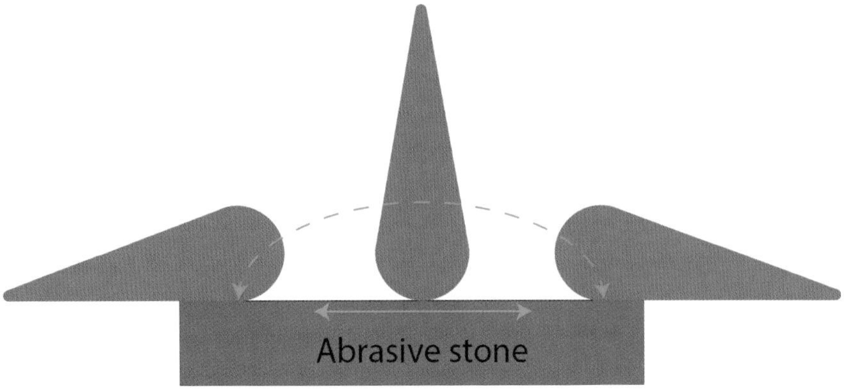

Fig. 46: Reform a cylindrical face by rocking while rubbing the face against a flat stone.

Diamond particle size (microns)	***Mesh size / Grit size***	***DMT product description***	***Stone grade***	***Wet & Dry 'P' grade (approx)***	***Description***
120	120	Extra Extra Coarse Diamond. Colour code: Silver		P120	Very very coarse. Use only on a severely damaged edge, if at all. Leaves deep scratches on the work. Removes material extremely quickly. Not recommended in most cases.
100				P150	
95	160	Hardcoat Diamond Grit			
90	140		Rapid metal removal.		Diamond paste, 90 to 25 microns.
80				P180	
60	220	Extra Coarse Diamond. Colour code: Black	Very coarse.	P240	Use only on a damaged edge. Rapid material removal, Not recommended in most cases.
45	325	Coarse Diamond. Colour code: Blue	Coarse.	P360	Use this as the coarsest grade, to re-shape a blunt or lightly damaged or nicked edge.
25	600	Fine Diamond. Colour code: Red	Coarse.	P800	Sharpens a blunt undamaged edge.
9	1200	Extra Fine Diamond. Colour code: Green	Medium.	P2500	DMT plate: produces a very sharp, polished edge. Diamond paste: used for lapping, prior to polishing.
7	2200	Ceramic Steel. Colour code: White	Medium.		DMT plate: a little more than razor sharp. Diamond paste: used for lapping, prior to polishing.
	3000		Between medium and fine.		Diamond paste: used for lapping, prior to polishing.
	5000		Between medium and fine.		Diamond paste: used for lapping, prior to polishing.
	6000		Finishing (fine).		Diamond paste: used for lapping, prior to polishing.
3	8000	Extra-Extra Fine Diamond. Colour code: Tan	Finishing (very fine).		DMT plate: ultimate sharp, highly polished edge. Diamond paste, used for final polishing.
0.25	60000		Final polishing.		Diamond paste.

Table 8: Approximately equivalent particle, mesh and grade values and descriptions for a range of abrasives.

2 Basic Movements

Tools have a wide range of shapes, and one of the challenges when sharpening a tool is deciding how best to position the tool and the abrasive surface so that the appropriate shape is produced. Ultimately, this is determined by the need to create a face or an edge in a specific position. Every tool will have a set of faces, and the edges, including the cutting edges, are produced between at least two faces. Those faces and edges must be created in a specific relationship to at least one reference face and at least one reference axis on the tool. The choice of reference face and axis depends on the geometry of the tool and the way it will be held, as well as the position of the face of the abrasive wheel or stone. There are also some simple ways of positioning a tool for grinding each face to sharpen the cutting edge.

A chisel, for example, has two primary (or main) faces, two secondary faces, and one cutting edge formed where the primary faces meet (Fig. 47). The faces and cutting edge are positioned in relation to the long axis of the chisel, because the chisel is held by its shaft. It makes sense, then, to take account of that axis, the planes representing the face of the wheel, and the surface on which the chisel will rest, when sharpening the chisel. The axis should be held at right angles to the abrasive surface (represented by the plane at right angles to the axis). The angle between the faces will be measured in relation to the plane running through the long axis, which may be approximately parallel to the lower and upper faces of the chisel (*but see page 66*).

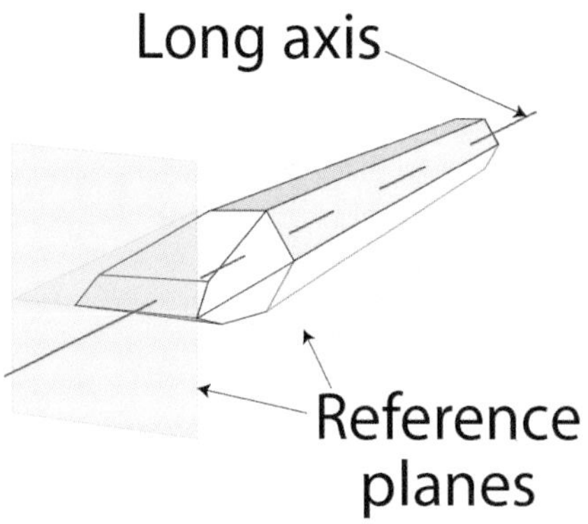

Fig. 47: An axis and two planes are used to define the initial position of the faces and cutting edge of the chisel, in relation to the surface of the wheel, and the rest or table of the grinder.

A lathe tool has more faces (Fig. 48) and is normally clamped in a holder with the bottom face of the tool in a fixed position. That face may then be treated as the base of the tool, and used as a reference plane. The work is cut by the end of the tool, or by a face at

Fig. 48: Faces of a lathe tool are positioned in relation to planes representing the bottom of the tool, and the face of the grinding wheel or abrasive stone.

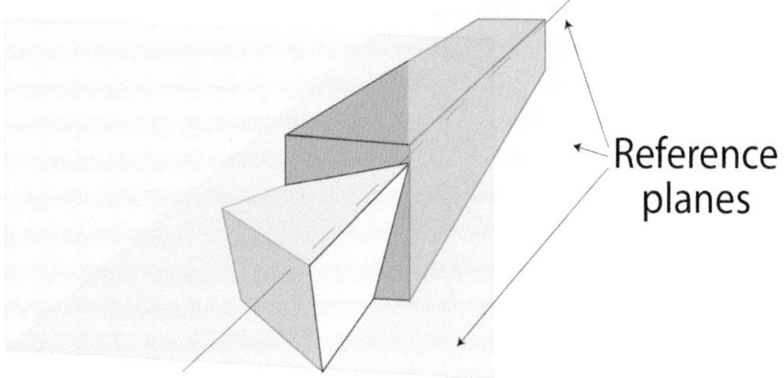

AXES AND PLANES

Axes and planes are imaginary geometric features which can act as useful references.

An axis is a line which acts as a reference. Every axis is infinitely long, but has no thickness, and exists in just one dimension.

An axis of rotation is a stationary line about which an object can rotate.

A plane is an imaginary flat surface which acts as a reference. A plane exists in two dimensions and is infinitely large.

Real objects exist in three dimensional space, but a two dimensional plane is useful when using a flat surface as a reference. Horizontal and vertical reference planes are also useful, as is the plane of the grinding surface of a flat-faced wheel, or the plane which is tangent to the line where a tool contacts a curved wheel.

The undersides of many tools are flat, so distances and angles can be measured from the plane of the underside. Grinder rests and tables are usually flat, and provide a useful plane of reference common to tool and rest.

the side, so it is useful to measure the angles in relation to three planes at right angles to one another; at the front, side and base of the tool. Each face will sit at an angle to the three planes, and those angles define the position of that face.

On a pointed punch (Fig. 49), a suitable reference axis might be the long axis through the point and the centre of the body of the punch. A reference plane at the pointed end, at right angles to the axis, represents the initial position of the face of the wheel.

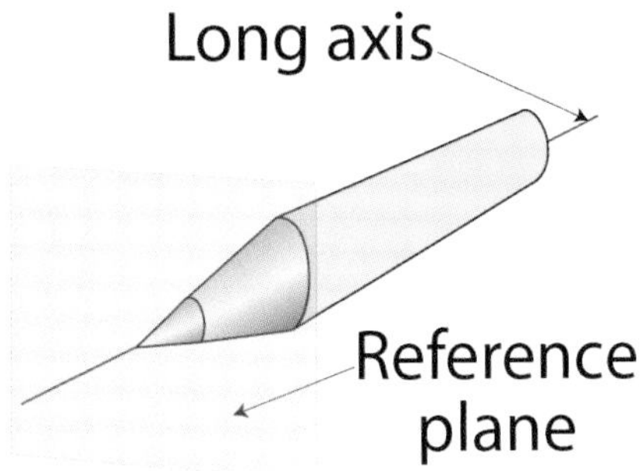

Fig. 49: On a punch, an axis through the point and body, and a plane at the tip, at right angles to the axis, can be used to define the conical point.

On this tool, the shape of the finished face is a cone, so the included angle of the cone, or the half-angle measured from the central axis to the surface of the cone will define the taper of the point.

BASIC POSITIONING MOVEMENTS

When shaping or sharpening a tool, there are three basic positioning movements used to set the orientation of the faces of the tool in relation to the abrasive surface of the flat stone or the face of the wheel. These are swing, tilt and rotate, and they allow a tool to be set up in an appropriate position so that when it has been ground the resulting faces or edges will lie at the correct angles to the related planes or axes.

Basic positioning moves are most easily understood using a lathe tool sitting on the tool rest of a grinder (Fig. 50). The reference planes are as shown in Fig. 48, and the base

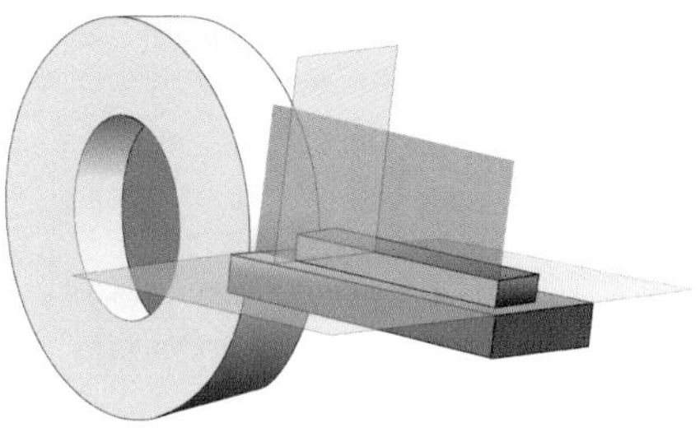

Fig. 50: The base of a lathe tool sitting on a grinding rest shares the same reference plane as the flat surface of the rest.

reference plane of the tool blank coincides with the plane of the flat surface of the grinder rest. The planes at the front and side of the tool will not necessarily coincide with the face or side of a grinding wheel. The reference plane of a wheel with a curved face is tangent to the curved face at the point where the tool contacts the wheel (Fig. 51).

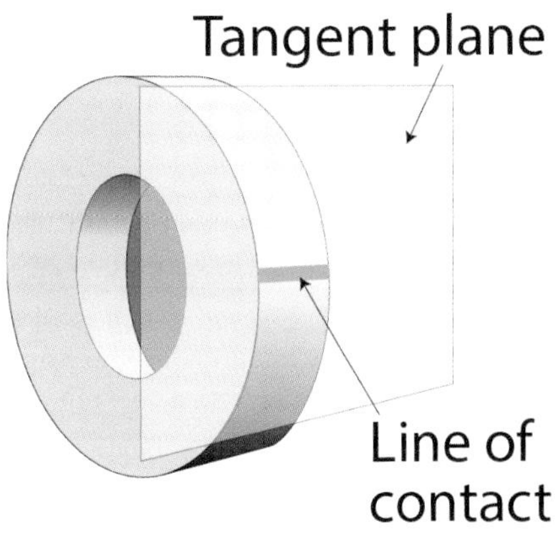

Fig. 51: On a wheel with a curved face, the plane at the front of the tool is tangent to the wheel where the tool touches the wheel.

Swing

During a swinging movement, the tail of the tool moves to one side, but the base of the tool and the base reference plane remain in contact with (or parallel to) the rest (Fig. 52). This is useful for creating a clearance angle at the front of the tool, or forming an angled face at the side of a lathe tool (Fig. 53).

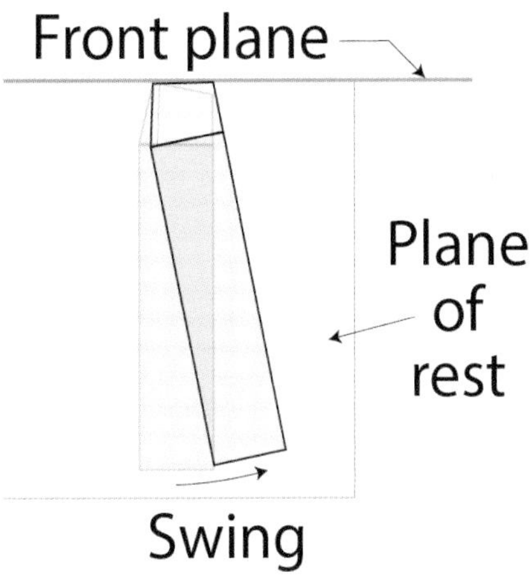

Fig. 52: Looking down from above, swinging a lathe tool on the rest aligns a cutting edge with the plane of the wheel face (the front plane), while keeping the base of the tool on the plane of the rest.

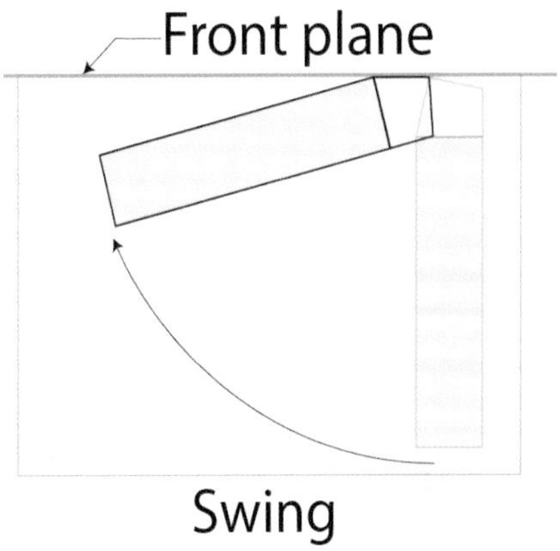

Fig. 53: Looking down from above, a tool can be swung in either direction, to suit the cutting edge to be ground.

Tilt

During a tilting movement, the tail of the tool is lifted or lowered (Fig. 54). Tilting is useful in preparation for grinding an angled face on a chisel, or a clearance angle on the front face of a lathe tool (Fig. 55). To maintain good support for the tool, the rest may be tilted along with the tool, or the tool may be held in a workhead which is then tilted. Tilting aligns the face of a tool with the plane of the face of the grinding wheel or stone.

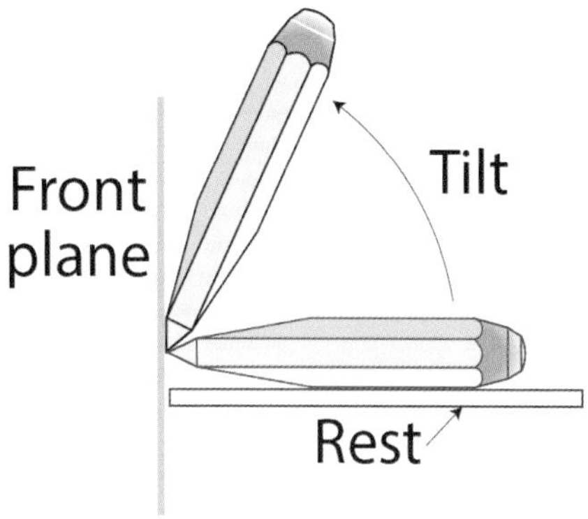

Fig. 54: Shown in a side view, tilting involves raising or lowering the tail of a tool.

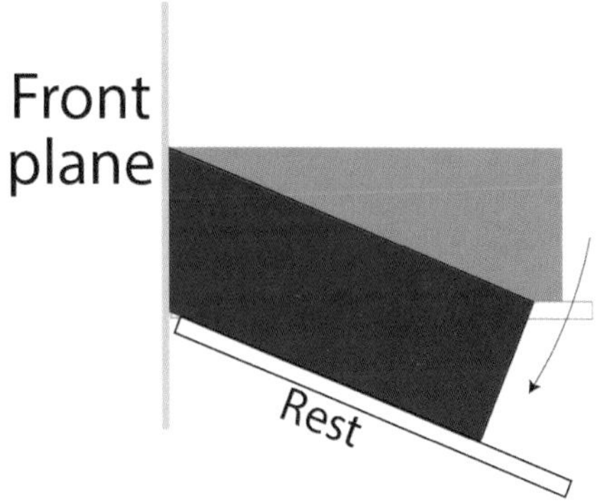

Fig. 55: The direction of tilt is chosen to bring a face of the tool onto the plane of the face of the grinding wheel. The rest, or workhead, may be tilted to provide support for the tool.

Rotate

During a rotation, the tool is turned around an axis (Fig. 56). This can be used to position a tool face, or to grind a curved face.

When the work is not in contact with the grinding wheel, a rotation can position the tool ready for a subsequent grinding operation. For example: a lathe tool held clear of the wheel might be rotated about its long axis in preparation for grinding a clearance angle on the side face (Fig. 56).

Rotation may also be used when the wheel is in contact with the work, when grinding a curved face. For example: the cylindrical end of a pin punch (Fig. 57) can be ground by rotating the punch about its long axis while in contact with the wheel.

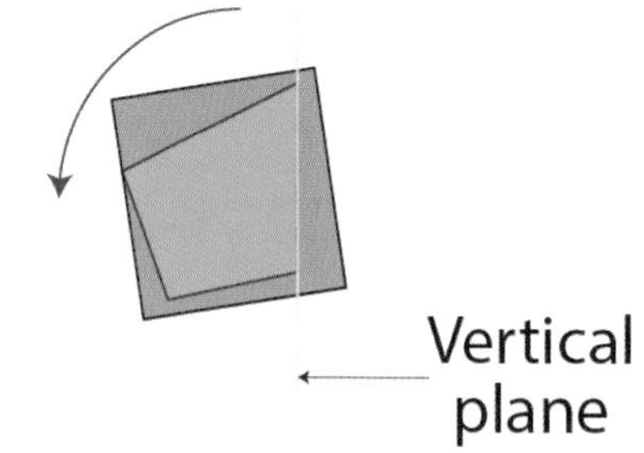

Fig. 56: Viewed from the front, rotating a lathe tool about its long axis positions the side face vertically to allow the side clearance to be ground.

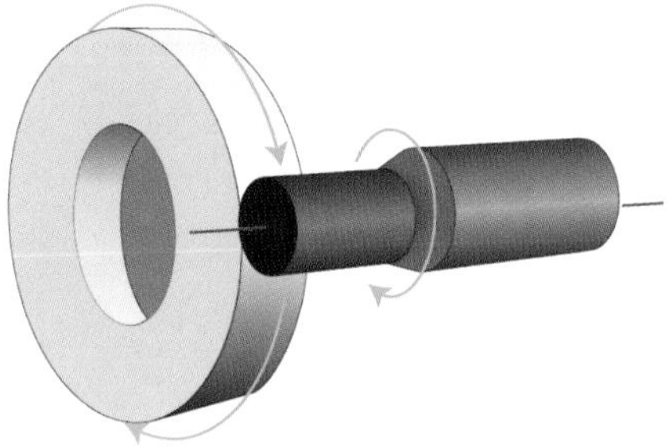

Fig. 57: The cylindrical end of a punch may be ground by rotating the punch about its long axis, while holding it against a grinding wheel.

If necessary, the tool can be rotated around any axis that will bring a particular part of the tool against the abrasive face. One face of a form tool, for example, may be given a radius by rotating the whole tool around a horizontal axis parallel to, but offset from, the tool's long axis, and one radius away from the wheel (Fig. 58).

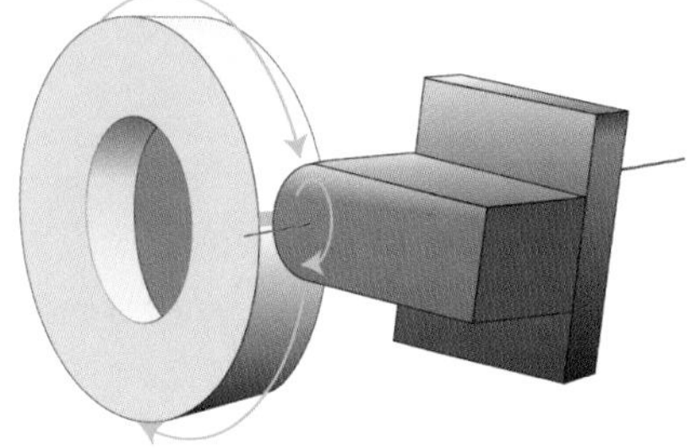

Fig. 58: Grinding the side face of a form tool may involve rotating the tool about an offset axis (shown here in red).

Combining movements

In many cases, more than one basic movement is required to position a tool for grinding. The face of a lathe tool, for example, is brought into position by swinging the tool (Figs 52, 53 and 59) to bring the cutting edge against the wheel; and the tool is then tilted backwards, *pivoting about that cutting edge*, to create the clearance angle, so that the whole face may be ground (Figs 54, 55 and 59). That is usually done by tilting the rest down at the rear (Figs 55 and 59).

Fig. 59: Swing (red), using a 'vertical' axis through the nose of the tool to bring the cutting edge parallel to the face of the wheel; then tilt (green) using an axis parallel to the rear edge of the grinding rest to create the clearance angle on the front flank.

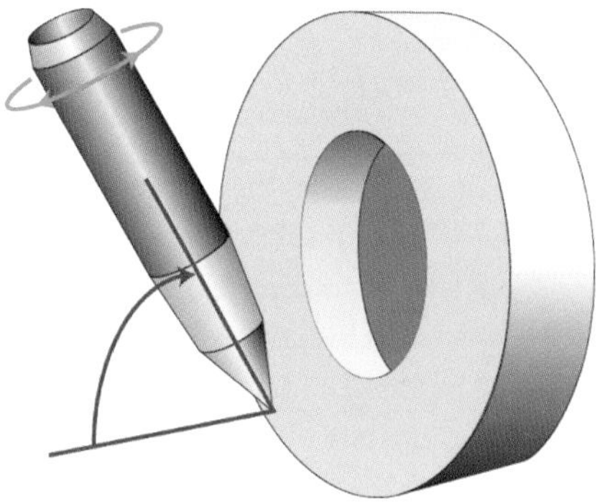

Fig. 60: Tilt (red); then rotate (blue) a punch about its long axis, to sharpen the conical tip.

A centre punch may be sharpened by tilting the punch to set the angle of the conical point then rotating the punch about its long axis as it is ground (Fig. 60).

The three basic movements are useful concepts which provide easy ways to visualize the movements required to position parts of a tool against a grinding wheel in order to grind faces at particular angles. This book uses the terms swing, tilt and rotate throughout; but you should feel free to use whichever terms and motions suit your own way of thinking. The end result should be the same: a tool correctly orientated to form or sharpen its edges and faces.

In most cases where a bench grinder is used to sharpen tools, swing takes place on the surface of a rest; tilt is a movement of the rest itself; and rotate most commonly involves turning a tool about its own axis. These three basic movements belong in the world of 3D geometry, and, depending on how the axes of the rest and any workholder are arranged, there may be an interaction between movements. In particular, the sequencing of movements is very important to ensure that what appears to be the correct angle of, say, the face of a lathe tool, is geometrically correct. Where angles are relatively small, errors are difficult to detect by sight, whereas larger angles tend to make any unexpected deviations from what is intended more obvious. This is particularly important with lathe tools (*see* Chapter 4: Tool type 7: Turning Tools).

This book gives guidance on a range of ways to apply swing, tilt and rotate to sharpen a wide range of tools, but getting some practical experience of using those basic movements when sharpening everyday tools on a bench grinder will help you understand how they are related. Practice often aids understanding of concepts.

BASIC MOVEMENTS ARE ALL ROTATIONS

The basic movements of swing, tilt and rotate can all be thought of as rotations which take place about different axes.

An axis of rotation is a straight line about which an object can rotate.

A swing is a rotation about an axis at right angles to the surface of the rest (Fig. 61).

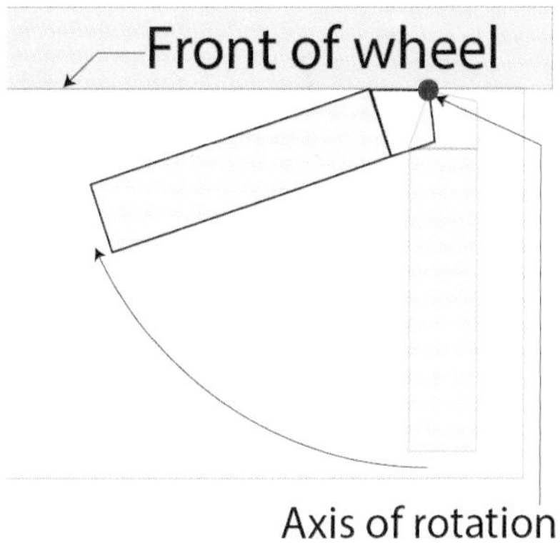

Fig. 61: Looking straight down onto the grinding rest, the axis of swing rotation appears as a point. The axis runs directly away, through the rest.

A tilt is a rotation about a 'horizontal' axis through the pivot of the rest (Fig. 62).

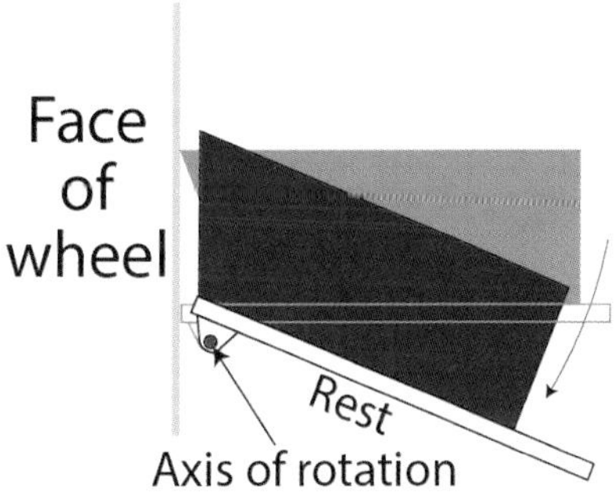

Fig. 62: Looking at the side of the grinding rest, the axis of tilt rotation appears as a point. The axis runs directly away, through the rest pivot.

Rotation of a tool takes place about an axis which is often the same as the long axis of the tool, or the axis of a tool holder.

TRAVERSING

A traversing movement is normally used to move the tool past the wheel or across a flat stone while the two are in contact (Fig. 63). This allows material to be removed from the tool, but a rapid movement prevents dwelling in one position, avoiding scoring and overheating of the tool. Traversing does not act in quite the same way as swinging, tilting or rotating, so is not normally considered as a basic positioning move. However; in deciding how to position work in a grinder, it is best to plan how to position the face to be ground so that it is traversed past the wheel by using the axis with the quickest movement, and avoid plunging the work into the wheel, if possible.

The axis of traverse

Although it is natural to think of the position of a tool face in relation to the face of the wheel, the relationship between the tool face and the axis of traverse is more important, in most cases. Fig. 63 shows that it does not matter if the face of the wheel is not quite parallel to the axis of traverse, because grinding takes place where the work meets the wheel. To prevent heat build-up, it is usual to either set the face of the wheel at a small angle to the axis of traverse, or dress the wheel to leave only a small flat area in contact with the work. Where the wheel is turned off-parallel, a large angle will result in the curved edge of the wheel grinding the face of the work concave. A small angle of up to 2 degrees is acceptable for most jobs. As a result, although common parlance typically refers to setting the tool face in rela-

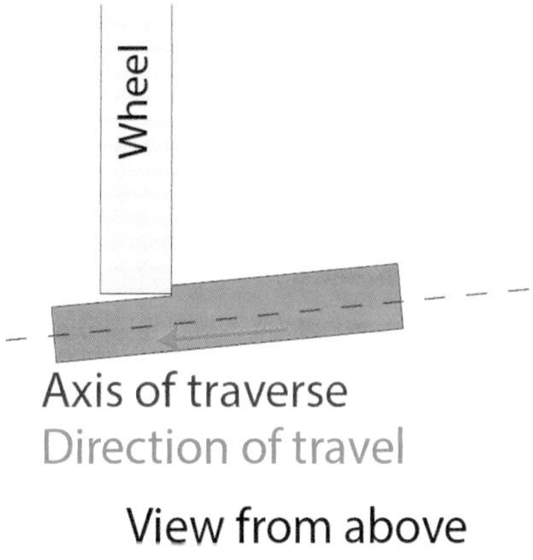

Fig. 63: The face of the wheel need not be exactly parallel to the (red) axis of traverse.

tion to the face of the wheel, the term more commonly used in this book is 'parallel to the axis of traverse'. An exception to this is where the face of the wheel is shaped and used to form grind the face of the tool, creating the inverse of the shape of the wheel face in the work (Fig. 64).

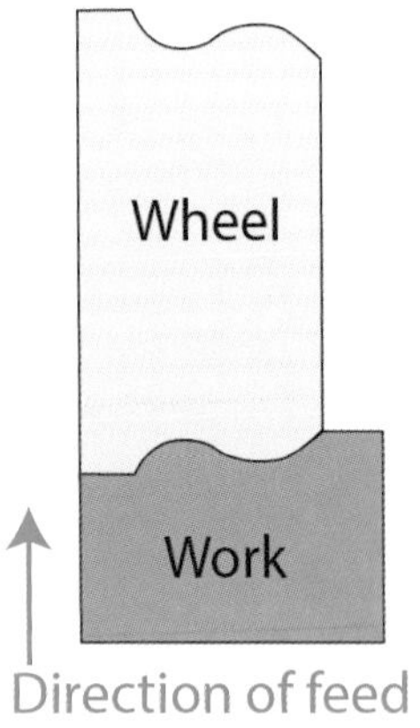

Fig. 64: Form grinding involves shaping the face of a wheel then feeding work into the wheel so that it is ground to the mirror image of the wheel profile.

INDEXING

'Dividing' is the process of splitting a circle into equal intervals. 'Indexing' is the process of moving from the start of one interval to the start of the next. Dividing and indexing are useful where a cutter has a number of equally spaced teeth. For example: to sharpen the Major cutting edges of a cutter with 4 teeth, dividing one revolution by 4 creates 4 equal intervals of 90 degrees. Positioning the first cutting edge at a zero position so that it can be sharpened, then indexing (rotating) the cutter through 90 degrees will position the second cutting edge ready for sharpening. Indexing again places the third cutting edge in position, and indexing again places the fourth edge ready for sharpening.

One common way of indexing is to position the first cutting edge ready for sharpening, then make this the zero position by locking the cutter holder, and attaching an indexing collar to the shaft of the holder. The collar will have a number of equally spaced holes around its circumference, and indexing takes place using a plunger or 'detent' carrying a pin which locates in any of the holes (Fig. 65). At its simplest, the collar would have the same number of holes around its circumference as teeth on the cutter. Indexing involves retracting the pin,

Fig. 65: Indexing can be carried out using a collar which has equally spaced holes, and a detent in the form of a pin which enters a hole, locking the collet shaft in position.

rotating the collar and shaft until the next hole is under the pin, and using the pin to lock the collar, shaft and cutter in that position. More holes in the collar allows division by the factors of the number of holes. So a collar with 12 holes allows indexing every hole to create 12 divisions; indexing every 2 holes to create 6 divisions; indexing every 3 holes (4 divisions), every 4 holes (3 divisions), or every 6 holes (2 divisions).

Fig. 66 shows a square indexing collar with a central hole bored to fit the shaft of

Fig. 66: A square-sided collar allows indexing in four positions by aligning one side vertically.

a workholder. Set the work in the zero position; use an engineer's square to set one side of the freely-rotating collar vertical; then lock the collar onto the shaft. Indexing involves rotating the workholder shaft until the next side of the square is vertical. A square allows indexing in four 90 degree quarter-turns, or two 180 degree half-turns.

GRINDING A RADIUS

In mathematics, a radius is a line from the centre of a circle to any point on its circumference (Fig. 67). In this book, the term 'grind-

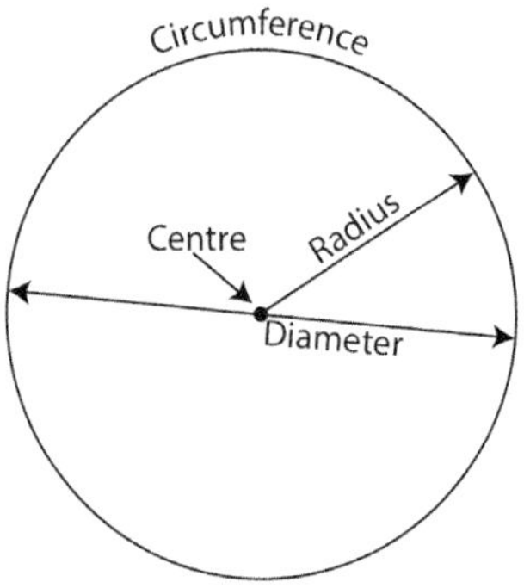

Fig. 67: The radius of a circle is the distance from the centre to any point on the circumference.

ing a radius' refers to grinding part of the circumference of a circle on a tool by swinging the tool around a centre point while the face of the grinding wheel is one radius away from the centre point (Fig. 68). The

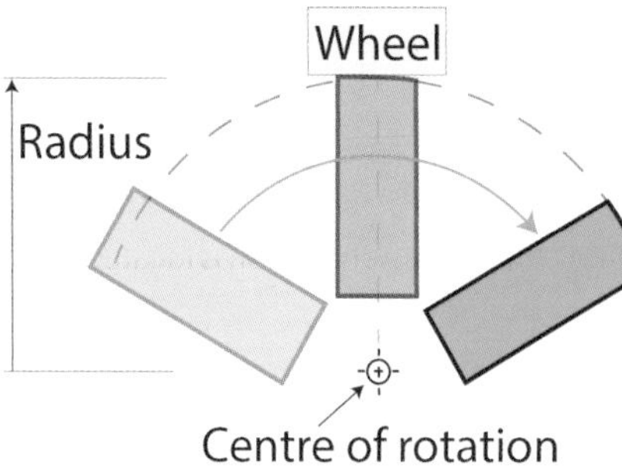

Fig. 68: Grind a circular curve on the end of a tool by choosing a centre point and setting a radius (the distance from the centre point to the wheel), then swinging the tool past the wheel.

basic setup uses a flat-faced grinding wheel, and a tool whose reference surface lies on a plane at right angles to the wheel. Fig. 69 shows a scraper with a curved end, held on a rotary table. The surface of the table is at right angles to the face of the wheel, and the radius is measured from the centre of rotation which lies on an axis at right angles to the surface of the rotary table and parallel to the face of the grinding wheel.

Fig. 69: Swinging the tool about the axis of rotation in the centre of the rotary table grinds a circular arc on the end of the tool. The nose radius is determined by the distance from the centre of rotation to the face of the wheel.

Fig. 70: A view from above shows the tool (blue), a reference edge (red), and a centre of rotation halfway across the tool. Swinging through a half-turn grinds a semi-circular curve.

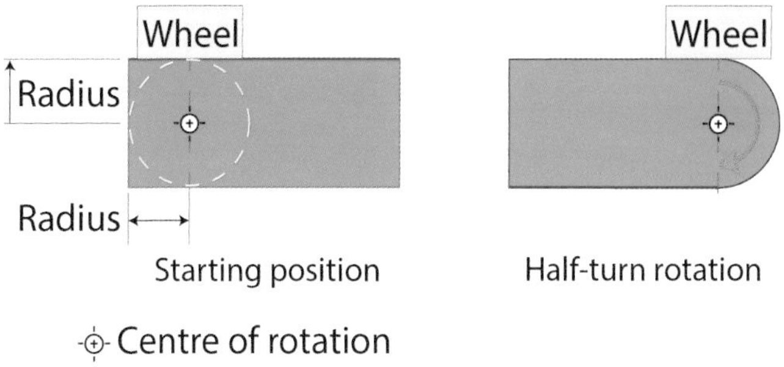

Fig. 71: A view from above shows that if the centre of rotation is positioned one radius away from the face of the wheel, a quarter-turn rotation will grind a quarter-circle on the corner of the tool .

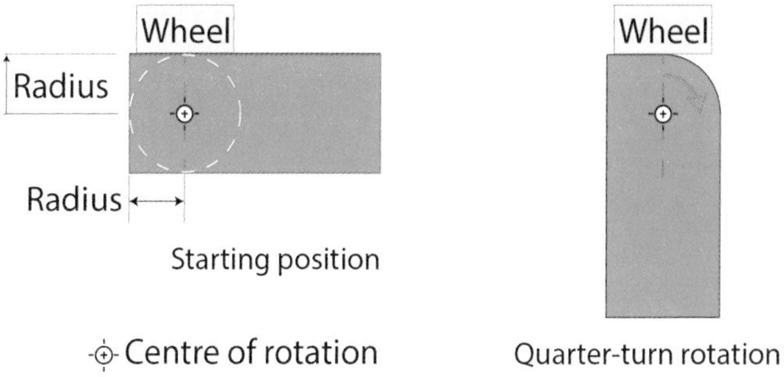

Fig. 72: Begin with the centre of rotation further away from the wheel than its final position. Repeatedly feed forward, and grind, until the centre is in its final position, one radius from the wheel.

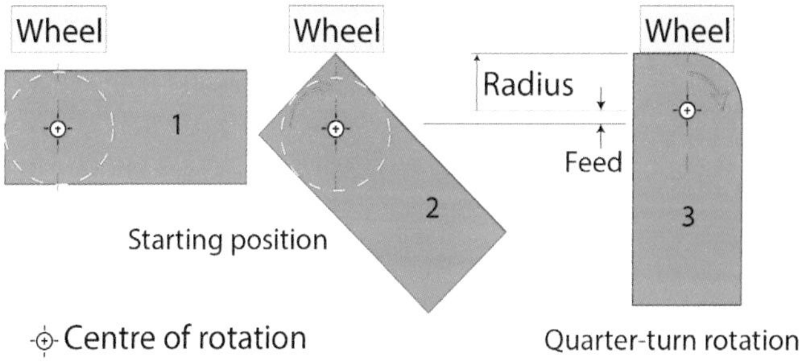

Fig. 73: A view from above shows that positioning the centre of rotation far enough from the front of the tool can create a radius which does not blend into the adjacent sides.

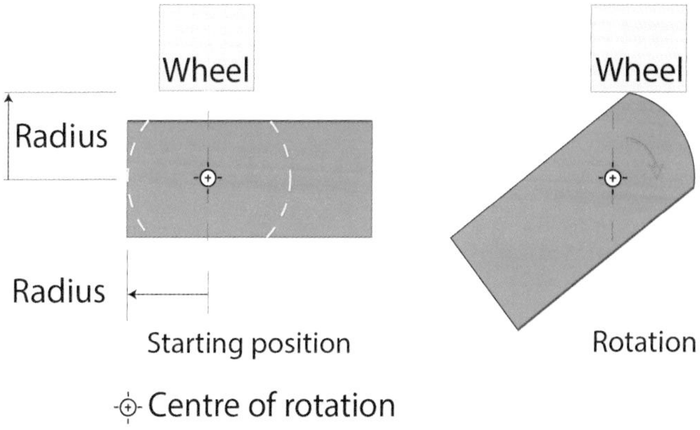

Fig. 70 shows the general arrangement for a rectangular lathe tool, with the yellow dashed line representing the circumference of the circle, and the red line being a visual reference for one edge of the tool.

Swinging the tool about the centre of rotation takes the end past the wheel, so that a half-turn produces a semi-circular end. Because the centre of rotation is located half way across the width of the tool, it is midway between the sides, so the end curve blends neatly into the sides. Fig. 71 shows the result of a quarter turn.

To avoid attempting to grind too much material from the tool all at once, begin with the tool further than one radius away from the wheel; swing the tool; then feed towards the wheel and repeat, until the centre point is one radius away (Fig. 72).

Changing the position of the axis of swing (the centre of the circle) and the radius produces a range of results. If the radius is greater than half the width of the tool, the resulting curve will not blend into the sides, but will produce a larger radius (Fig. 73). That is useful for form tools requiring a curve of a specific radius, or a curve which is deliberately designed to avoid having to blend into either of the adjacent sides (compared to Figs 70, 71 and 72, for example).

3 Bench Grinders

The so-called 'offhand' grinding machine goes by many names, but in its simplest form it is a bench or pedestal-mounted grinder which usually carries two narrow cylindrical flat-sided grinding wheels (Figs 74 and 75).

Fig. 74: A low-cost, low-power, bench grinder.

Fig. 75: A pedestal-mounted grinder fitted with a carborundum wheel and a silicon carbide wheel. Despite its size, this grinder is fitted with very small rectangular rests.

The term 'offhand' suggests that a tool being sharpened is held against the wheel and guided by hand during the grinding process (Fig. 75). This is 'offhand' or 'freehand' grinding, and it is not recommended because it is unsafe. For that reason, this book adopts the term 'bench' grinder, which is currently in more common use, despite the fact that almost any type of grinder could be mounted on a bench.

Small bench grinders are readily available, often at very low cost. The basic equipment supplied with the grinder is simply enough to comply with safety regulations, and normally consists of wheel guards, two tool rests, and eye shields to limit the spread of sparks and particles generated during the grinding process.

However; to achieve accurate results with this kind of grinder requires considerable skill and practice as well as a range of additional accessories, many of which are not available off the shelf. Roughly shaping tools as a preliminary operation can sometimes be done using nothing more than the basic tool rests (Fig. 76), but it is simply impossible to finish faces by hand at precise angles and create sharp edges on most of the tools used on a lathe or a milling machine unless some modifications are carried out to the grinder or its ancillary equipment. Tool rests, in particular, are often inadequate where work must be ground accurately at a specific angle.

Fig. 76: Removing the burr from the shaft of a chisel, using a rest to support the end of the shaft.

Despite the widespread availability of low cost grinders, the cost of a good sturdy bench grinder can be surprisingly high, and a robust and powerful machine with good quality ball bearings can cost over £500. Bench grinders are often supplied with two grinding wheels, one coarse and the other fine, or one designed to sharpen high speed steel and the other for tungsten carbide, but may also be supplied with one coarse wheel and a wheel-shaped wire brush, or with one or more polishing mops in place of a wheel. Brushes and mops suit a range of jobs which are commonly carried out in many workshops, especially where holding the work by hand, or partially supported by a simple rest, is more effective than having the work held firmly in a rigid workholder. Wire-brushing or polishing a curved surface such as a tube, the outside of a vase or the inside of a bowl would be all but impossible if the object was rigidly fixed. Human skill and hand-eye co-ordination are important for this type of job, but an awareness of safety issues is essential because even a low-powered grinder is quite capable of snatching work out of an operator's hands and throwing it straight back at them.

The power of an offhand grinder with 150–200mm wheels can vary from the low cost low-powered models using 100 watts, through the more capable 350 or 500 watt grinders, to more powerful 800 or 1400 watt machines. When used for initial shaping of a tool, removing a substantial quantity of material, 150 watts is likely to be the lowest power for effective use, while 350 – 500 watt models are much more effective. The larger 800 – 1500 watt models are intended for an industrial environment, running continuously for lengthy periods. When used for light sharpening, using small depths of cut to remove small quantities of material, the lower-powered models may be adequate.

Low cost is another matter, and lower cost is often associated with compromise in important features such as shaft run out (wobble) and the use of plain bearings instead of more substantial ball bearings. Motor efficiency is a factor affecting the amount of heat generated, and the ability of the insulation in the motor windings to withstand the heat generated during lengthy periods of heavy use.

The size of the grinding wheel on lower cost grinders is usually 150mm (6 inch) diameter and often 13mm (1/2 inch) thick, while larger and more powerful models feature 200mm (8 inch) wheels of up to 25mm thickness. Grinding should take place on the narrow curved periphery of the wheel, and grinding on the flat side of the wheel is not advisable, as that tends to weaken the wheel. Grinding wheels are designed to wear as they work, and it is easy enough to restore the worn surface of the curved periphery of a wheel by a 'dressing' operation, but the flat side of the wheel should not be thinned or flattened in the same way, because thinning the wheel makes it less strong and more liable to burst, especially where the wheel is already relatively thin.

Although there are many accessories available to allow grinding of tool faces on the flat side of a standard grinding wheel, that form of grinding is not recommended. A 13mm (1/2 inch) thick wheel is not strong when subject to sideways pressure, and a bursting grinding wheel behaves like an exploding grenade.

The diameter of the wheel affects the ability of a grinder to produce a flat surface, and Fig. 77 shows that the curved face of a small diameter wheel will produce a pronounced concave curve instead of a flat surface on the face of a tool. The larger the diameter of the wheel, the smaller the concavity and the nearer the tool face will be to a flat surface. On many tools, especially where they have a shallow face, a 150mm (6 inch) wheel will grind a shallow face sufficiently flat for most purposes, although that situation will deteriorate as the wheel wears and the diameter reduces.

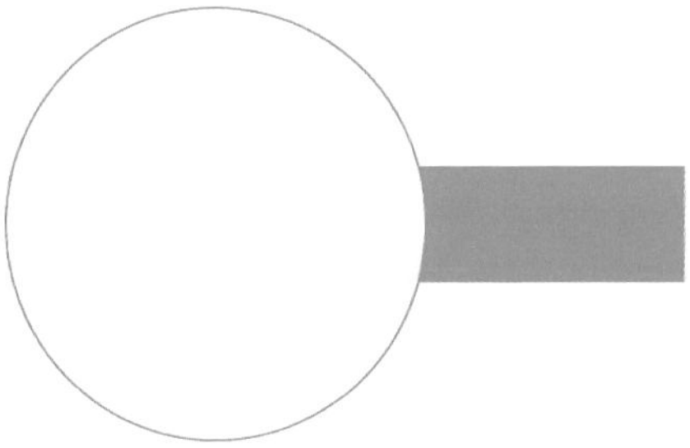

Fig. 77: The smaller the diameter of the wheel, the more pronounced the curvature ground on the work.

On higher cost grinders, a 200mm (8 inch) wheel is common, and that produces a flatter face on a tool. Fig. 78 shows that compared to a vertical front face, a 150mm diameter wheel grinds the face back at an angle of 4.952 degrees and that the total curvature amounts to 0.56mm on a tool 13mm thick. A 200mm diameter wheel (Fig. 79) grinds an angle of 3.727 degrees and a total curvature of 0.423mm.

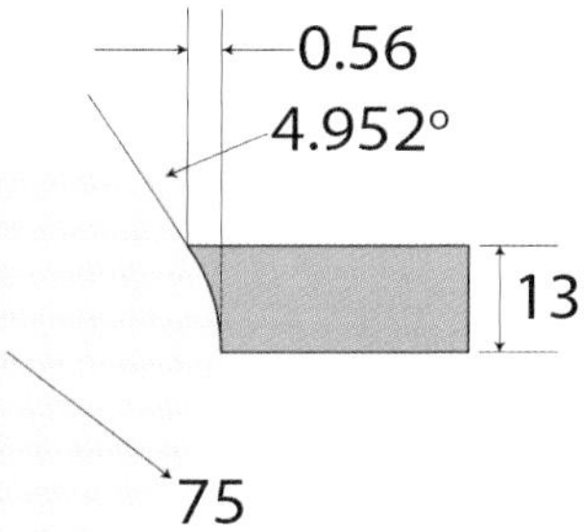

Fig. 78: A 150mm diameter wheel grinds a concave curve 0.56mm deep on a 13mm thick workpiece.

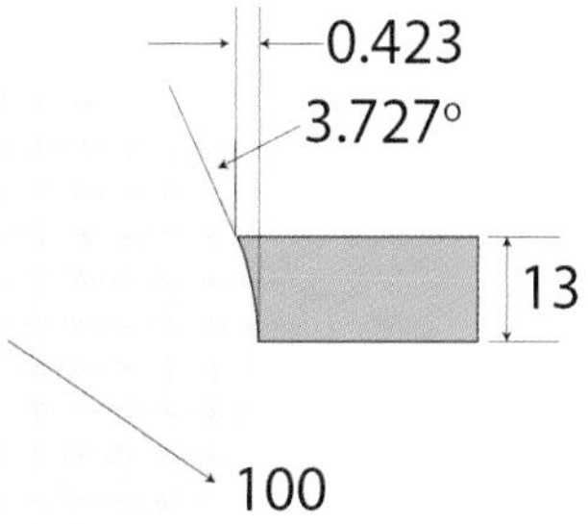

Fig. 79: A 200mm diameter wheel grinds a concave curve 0.432mm deep on a 13mm thick workpiece.

Fig. 80 shows a robust bench grinder fitted with substantial wheel guards and sturdy tool rests. This grinder has 200mm (8 inch) diameter wheels, 25mm (1 inch) thick.

Fig. 80: A robust bench grinder with 200mm diameter wheels, substantial guards and sturdy rests.

The peripheral speed of the wheel is limited, and 200mm grinding wheels are generally designed to turn at a lower speed (revs per minute) than 150mm wheels.

Bench grinders with wheels larger than 200mm diameter are less common in metal working shops, but are available for grinding woodworking tools. Some wheels for the Tormek T8 grinder (Fig. 81), for example, are 250mm diameter and 50mm thick; and some very old grinders use sandstone wheels of around 900mm diameter. These larger diameter wheels turn more slowly. The diameter of a grinding wheel must be

Fig. 81: The Tormek T8 grinder carries a wheel of 250mm diameter and 50mm thickness, as well as a leather honing wheel. Photo: TORMEK AB.

chosen so that it is rated at or above the maximum speed of the grinding machine (*see* Chapter 1). The wheel must also physically fit the grinder shaft and the safety guards.

Although the basic thin cylindrical type 1 wheel is not the most useful shape for tool grinding or sharpening, it is the shape most often supplied as standard with bench grinders, and it provides an initial starting point. Later sections of this book will deal with other, more useful, shapes of wheel for a bench grinder.

TOOL RESTS

Supporting tools only by hand while holding the tool against a grinding wheel is fraught with danger and is not recommended, so basic grinders are usually fitted with two simple tool rests to steady the tool (Fig. 82). These vary in quality and degree of robustness, and their usefulness is normally related to the cost of the grinder. The least helpful feature of the lower quality rests is their flexibility, because they tend to bend under pressure, changing the alignment of the tool in relation to the wheel, and upsetting the geometry of the tool faces. The rests are often rather small, limiting their usefulness when work has to be held at an angle to the front of the wheel. Some tool rests contain built-in grooves to help hold tools swung sideways at a particular angle (Fig. 83), and some incorporate an angled lip to help support work tilted upwards against the wheel (Fig. 84).

Fig. 82: Basic equipment supplied with most bench grinders includes two tool rests.

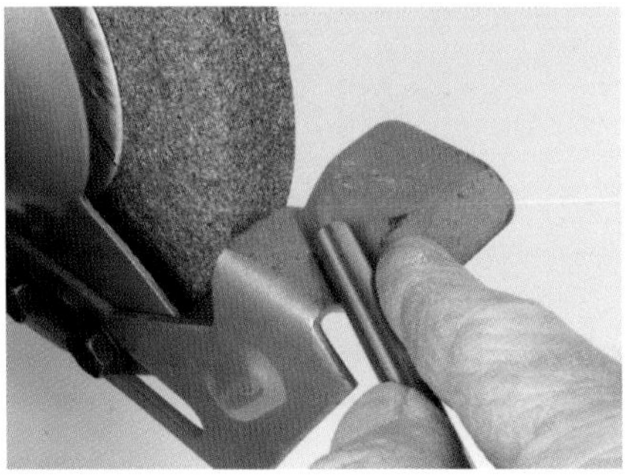

Fig. 83: Some tool rests have a built-in groove to hold work at a specific angle.

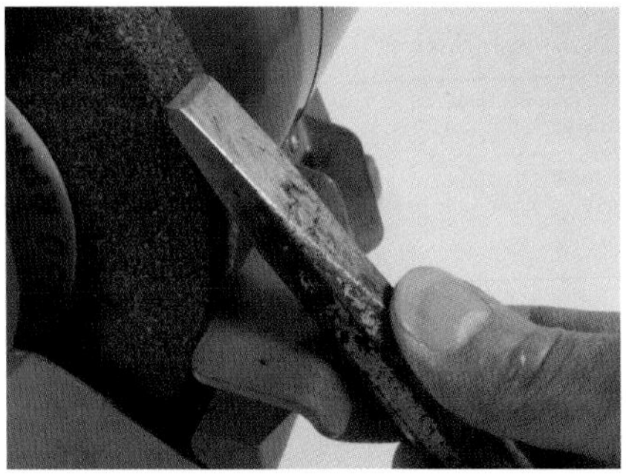

Fig. 84: Some tool rests have an angled lip to support work tilted upwards against the wheel.

Better quality grinders usually have sturdier rests (Fig. 85) which are not only less flexible, but often have some means of adjustment over a wider range. Methods of attachment are more robust, and Fig. 85 shows a 200mm (8 inch) grinder fitted with sliding bars which hold the rests. Each bar is attached to a sturdy and rigid wheel guard by two bolts which can slide in a horizontal slot cut in the inner wheel guard. This provides relatively coarse adjustment of the out-and-in position of the rests relative to the wheels. To adjust, the two securing bolts are slackened, and the bar is pulled out or pushed in, then the bolts are tightened again. There is no scale showing distance, so this kind of adjustment cannot provide a small precise movement during grinding, and is only intended for larger scale adjustments made when the grinder is switched off. Individual rests may be adjustable up and down, and may also be tilted backwards (Fig. 86) or sideways (Fig. 87), on some grinders.

Fig. 85: A rest can be attached to a sturdy wheel guard using an adjustable bar.

Fig. 86: Some rests may be tilted upwards.

Fig. 87 Some rests may be tilted sideways.

Rests are important, and fitting better rests, capable of a wider range of both coarse and fine adjustments, can transform the usefulness of a simple grinder, making it capable of the most common sharpening operations carried out by its more ambitious relative, the tool and cutter grinder.

A tool rest must be firmly secured in relation to the wheel. On bench grinders, the rests are usually bolted to the wheel safety guards, as those are fixed to the body of the grinder. Alternative tool rests can be secured in the same way, with fittings designed to suit the rests and the existing mounting arrangements, or they can be altered to a more convenient arrangement. If the grinder is fixed firmly to a bench or to a rigid base plate, rests can be mounted to that bench or plate if that is more convenient. That offers more scope for different designs of rest. Many alternative tool rests supplied by commercial companies are designed to be secured in that way, so that they can be fitted to a range of different makes of grinder. Provided the bench or base plate is sufficiently rigid, and both grinder and rest are firmly secured to the same surface, this method works well. Simple alternative approaches are useful (Fig. 88) but despite

Fig. 88: A simple rest, used with care, is better than none at all.

requiring great care in use, and some skill in judging the angle at which work should be presented to the wheel, using any support is safer than totally freehand grinding.

Although tools can be held on a rest, the shape of many tools leaves them less than fully supported, so tool holders or workholders which allow some means of securely holding different shapes of tools are often required (*see* Chapter 4: Sharpening in Practice).

Bar rests

Fig.89 shows an adjustable rest in the form of a T-shaped bar made of tube or solid round

Fig. 89: A rest in the form of a T-shaped bar, adjustable for height, and tiltable to adjust the distance between rest and wheel.

rod. The bar is clamped in an upright square tube by a screw, allowing the height of the bar to be adjusted relative to the wheel. The square tube is mounted on a pivot attached to the foot, allowing the foot to be fixed, but the rest to be tilted so that the bar can be swung closer to, or further from, the wheel. Pivoting a flat rest in that way would tilt the rest, but it has no effect on the angle of a round bar.

The challenge with this rest is in holding a tool at an appropriate angle to the wheel, and in maintaining that angle. With some tools, such as the chisel shown in Fig. 90

Fig. 90: Some tools have a narrow edge, and benefit from a steady.

feeding the tool towards the wheel causes the angle to vary because the shape of the section behind the cutting edge pushes the front of the chisel upwards. As a result, it is likely to be more convenient to estimate the angle at which a tool should be held; carry out a test grind; then change the angle at which the tool is held, until a satisfactory result is achieved. Where the tool is to be lightly sharpened, but the basic cutting angles are still present on the cutting edges, looking at the side of the wheel and sighting the contact between tool and wheel should give a good approximation of the angle required between tool and rest.

Where a tool has a narrow cutting edge, it may be enough to hold it in position on the rest, applying feed by sliding it upwards along its own axis. In the case of the plugging chisel shown in Fig. 90, there is only a narrow edge in contact with the rest, so a simple steady may help (Figs 90 and 91). To avoid a pattern of grooves on the tool and the wheel, and certainly when the cutting

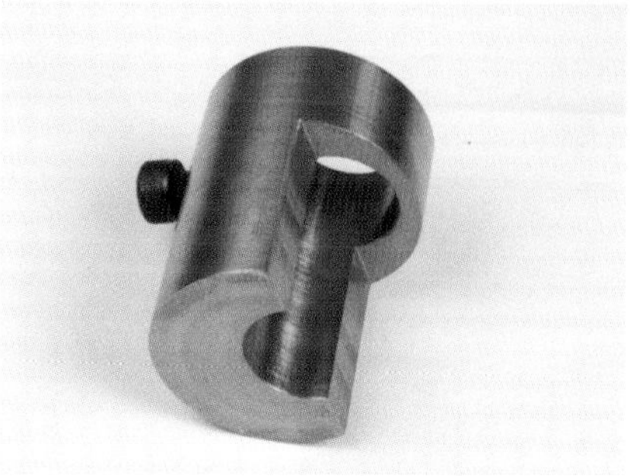

Fig. 91: A simple fixed steady. The cutaway allows the steady to be positioned close to the wheel.

edge is broader than the face of the wheel, the tool must be slid from side to side while being held in contact with the wheel. That movement requires co-ordination of the angle between wheel and work, the feed towards the wheel, and the sideways traversing movement. These complications mean it may be difficult to achieve accuracy of angles, and consistency of results when using the single-tube rest.

Adding a second tube or bar (Fig. 92) allows the angle of the tool to be fixed.

Fig. 92: Adding a second tube allows the rest to control the angle of the tool.

Adjust the height of the main tube, and hold the tool at an appropriate angle. Then swing the second bar into contact with the tool, and tighten the clamps. Provided the tool has a flat back at a constant angle to the cutting edge, the tool can now slide forwards to apply a cut, but the angle will not change. Grinding takes place by sliding the tool sideways, past the wheel. The tool can be steadied by using a guide which has two holes to guide it along the bars (Fig. 93), or a guide which slides on one bar and has a finger at 90 degrees to the bar (Fig. 94). A tool is held against the guide as it is traversed across the face of the wheel (Figs 95 and 96). Feed is applied by adjusting the tool in the clamp.

Fig. 93: A sliding plate can be used as a steady.

Fig. 94: A guide may slide on one bar but have a steadying finger which rests on the second bar.

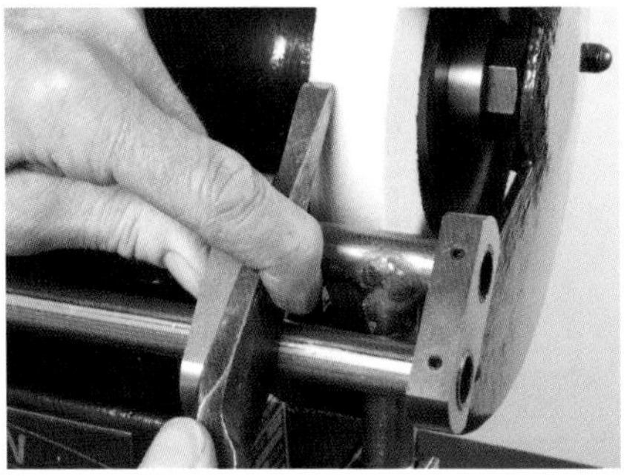

Fig. 95: Work can be held against a sliding steady as it traverses the wheel.

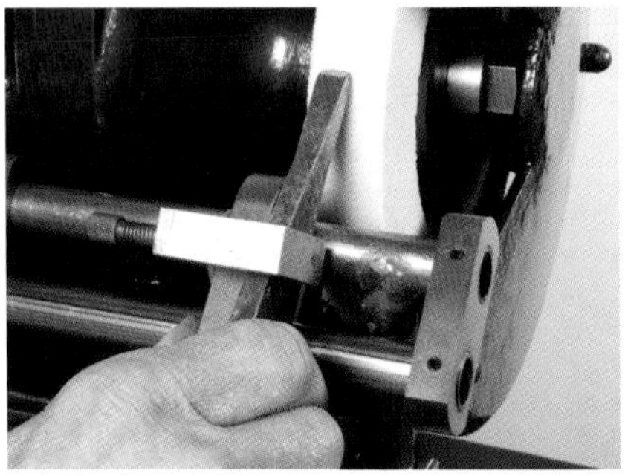

Fig. 96: Clamping the work against the steady provides more security.

The bar rest has its uses for lighter sharpening cuts on some shapes of tool, or for shaping cuts where the basic shape of a tool is formed, but no great accuracy is required. Its widest application is in sharpening woodworking tools, but it does not offer ease of use, angle setting or fine control of feed. So; for most metalworking tools we must look elsewhere, beginning with the flat rest.

Flat tool rests

Flat rests are the most useful shape, and they can be modified to extend the range of items which can be easily ground to shape. The rest alone is often not sufficient to ensure a tool is presented at an accurate angle to a grinding wheel, or moved consistently across the face of the wheel. In most cases, some additional means of work holding must be used in conjunction with a rest. The rest, however, provides the basic platform supporting tool and work holding devices. Improvements in the design of rests usually aim to improve the ease with which tools can be ground, and the accuracy of the results.

Extending the working area

One of the drawbacks of many tool rests is the small working area, but it is not difficult to create rests with a larger surface which can support tools safely at a range of angles to the face of the wheel.

Many tool rests have a straight front edge which is designed to sit clear of the wheel. In some cases, it is useful to have a small amount of additional support at the sides of a wheel to support a tool or tool holder

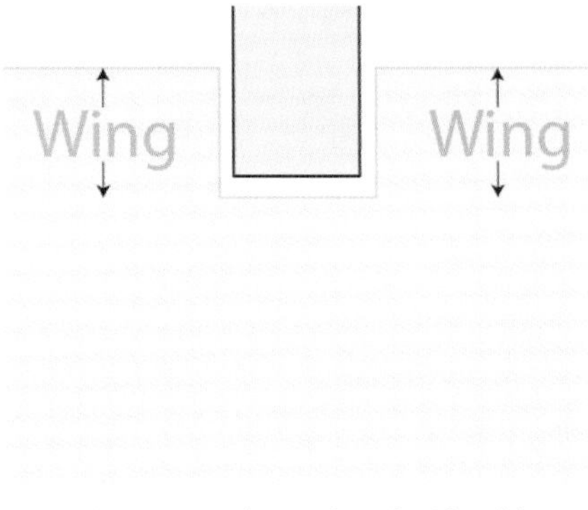

Fig. 97: 'Wings' extend a rest along the sides of the wheel.

which needs to be placed close to the side of the wheel (Figs 85, 86, 96, 98 and 99). These wings are not intended to support grinding on the side of the wheel. The disadvantage

Fig. 98: A larger than standard tool rest with a straight front edge.

Fig. 99: Side wings on a rest provide additional support for some tools or tool holders.

of side support 'wings' is that they may compromise any ability to tilt the rest sideways, and may foul the wheel guards when raised or lowered. Making the side extensions sit further from the wheel may reduce the support and create a dangerously wide gap between rest and wheel which allows small tools to become trapped between wheel and rest, causing damage to the wheel. Where a rest is designed to tilt sideways, a straight face with no side support 'wings' may be more practical. However; in most cases where grinding takes place on the curved front face of the wheel, a sideways-tilting rest is of little advantage.

Adjusting the height, tilt and gap

Because of the curved front face of a type 1 wheel, it is important to be able to adjust the height and tilt of a rest. As adjustments are made, the gap between the front edge of the rest and the face of the wheel may vary, requiring further adjustment to prevent this from becoming too large. In reality, all three adjustments are needed for most jobs involving tools with an angled front face, and although some tools will be mounted in workholders which sit on the rest, the rest itself is likely to require some additional adjustment, even if it is only to ensure it is level and at a known height in relation to the axis of the wheel.

There are many designs of adjustable rest available commercially, as well as many designs for rests which can be made in the workshop. On the grinder shown in Fig. 100 the vertical slot in the arm of the rest allows the height of the rest to be adjusted. The horizontal supporting arm can be slid out or in, to adjust the gap. The rest is designed to sharpen woodworking chisels and has a fixed angle between the platform and the

Fig. 100: A rest for sharpening woodworking chisels, with adjustments up or down, in or out.

square-section arm. Sliding the arm up or down, or in or out, causes the angle being ground on a tool to change, because of the curve of the wheel. Figs 101 and 102 show a commercially available rest which is capable of providing a range of inter-related adjustments for height, tilt and gap. The top surface of this rest incorporates a slot which allows accessories to be used to hold tools which can then be traversed across the face of the wheel. The slot in the arm of the rest provides adjustment of the height and gap, while the additional adjustment immediately beneath the rest allows the tilt to be varied. Together, these provide a wide range of adjustments. The object on the left of Fig. 101 is a multi-angle template which can be used to set the angle of the rest for sharpening chisels and plane irons.

Fig. 101: A rest with a wide range of adjustments, and a guide slot across its top surface, to control traverse. Photo: LEE VALLEY TOOLS LTD.

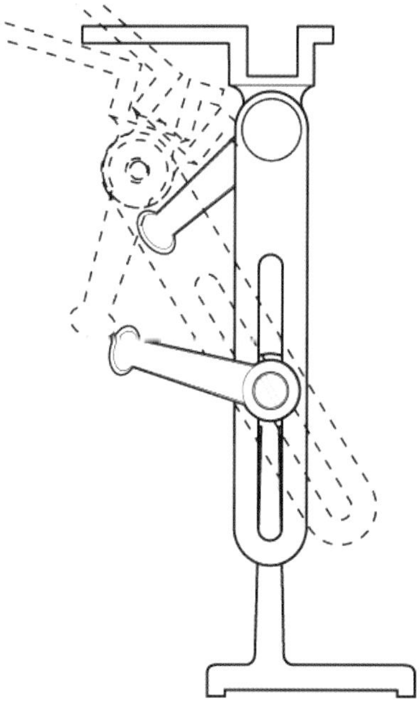

Fig. 102: The design of this rest provides a wide range of adjustments. Photo: LEE VALLEY TOOLS LTD.

Fig. 103 shows a rest on an articulated arm which can be adjusted to alter height, tilt and gap. This kind of rest can be simply made, and can provide a wide range of adjustment. It is also capable of holding a range of different platforms, each of which is secured to the top arm by screws located in a tapped block (Fig. 104). Some additional adjustment of the distance between rest and wheel is available using slots in the base of the rest, although this is not normally required unless the wheel is changed for one of a different diameter.

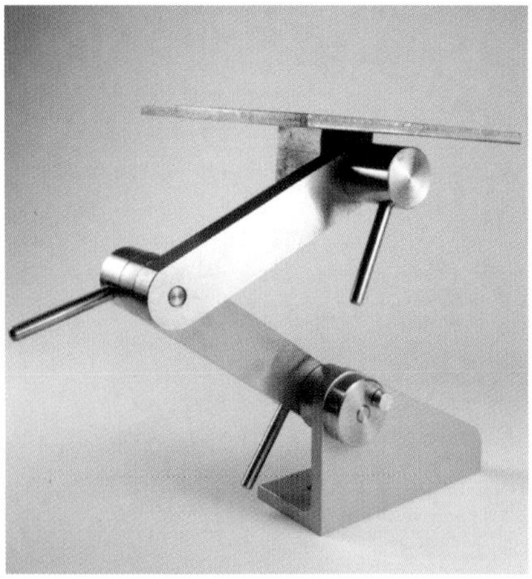

Fig. 103: A rest mounted on an adjustable articulated arm capable of altering height, tilt and gap.

Figs 105 and 106 show a rest in which a solid arm slides within a tube, providing adjustment of the height. The arm is held in place by a side-mounted screw. The platform tilts to adjust the angle; and the tube itself tilts to adjust the gap and the angle of the platform. The benefit of this design is that the additional clamp near the top of the tube grips the slotted plate at the side, providing a secure lock for the position of the tube. The foot is fixed, but although the gap may vary, the range of the tilt of the tube is sufficient to allow the gap to be adjusted as required.

There are many other designs of rests, and the choice depends on the job to be done, as well as being, to some extent, a matter of personal preference.

REST WITH ARTICULATED ARM

- Make the arms as short as possible. Each should be half of the total extended height.
- Use fine threads (e.g. M8 x 1).
- Arrange the threaded clamps so that they tend to tighten when the arms press downwards.
- Each clamp screw passes through a clearance hole in the arm nearest the clamp boss and handle.
- The L-shaped base bracket is milled or filed flat on both sides of the pivot hole, to provide a flat seat for the large washer which acts as a spacer and the washer with the tapped spigot.
- The large washer fits on the lower joint, between the arm and the L-shaped base bracket.
- The washer with the tapped spigot slides through the other side of the base bracket. The brass pin locks that washer.
- The angle of the lowest handle can be adjusted before drilling a hole through the washer with the tapped spigot, into the base bracket. The washer with the spigot is prevented from rotating by the steel pin with the brass head.

Fig. 104: Component parts of the rest, showing that the top platform is attached to the top block, and may be replaced by a platform of another design.

EXTENDABLE TILTING ARM

- Make the arm from solid bar and mill or file a flat along one corner.
- The centre of the arc of the locking slot is the pivot point near the bottom of the tilting tube.
- The locking slot plate is flush with the side of the tube nearest the tilting arm.

The pivot rod passes through a thick tube welded or brazed into the tilting tube, near the bottom, and another across the base foot tube.

- The washer at the pivot between the tubes adjusts the fit between the tilting tube and the locking plate.

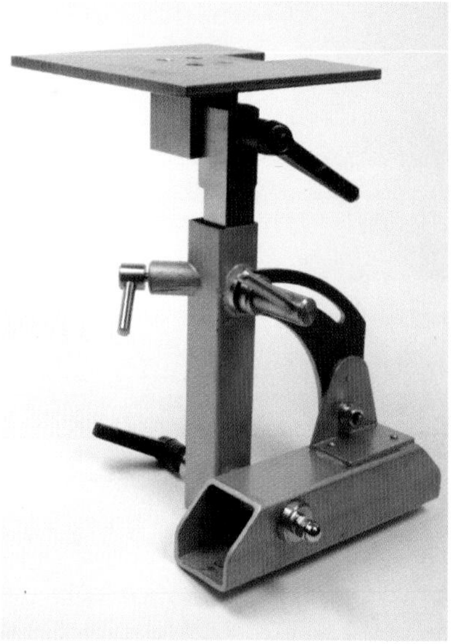

Fig.105: Tilting rest with height adjustment.

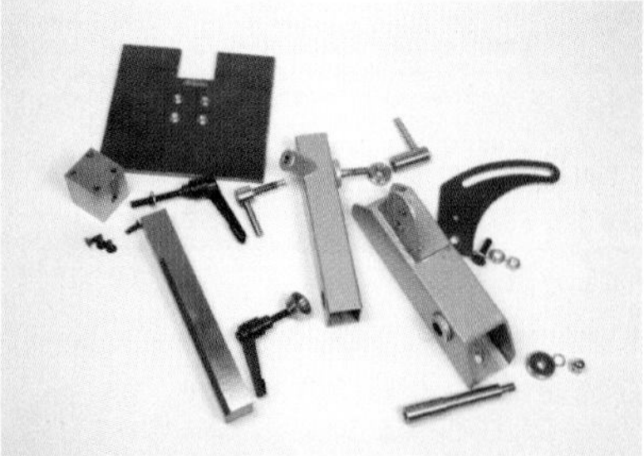

Fig. 106: Component parts of the rest, showing the base foot, the tiltable tube, the clamp screws, and the solid arm with top block and rest platform. Bristol handles make adjustment easy.

HOLDING THE TOOL AT AN ANGLE

A common requirement is for a tool to sit flat on the rest but be presented at a specific angle to the face of the wheel (Fig. 107).

Fig. 107: A lathe tool needs to be swung to the side, and tilted tail-down against the face of the wheel.

Judging an angle by eye is difficult enough, even with practice, but ensuring accuracy requires a method of setting and holding the tool at the required angle as grinding takes place. The three basic movements: swing, tilt and rotate (*see* pages 23 and 24) can all be accomplished in a variety of ways.

Swing

A swing is a pivoting movement and is usually carried out with the tool in contact with the rest or workholder. Pre-made angle guides (Fig. 108) may be clamped to the rest and provide a supporting edge along which the tool can slide. If the tool rest has a straight rear edge parallel to the face of the wheel, use that as a reference face for the angle guide (Fig. 109). The face of the wheel can be made parallel to the rear edge of the rest (the edge nearest the operator)

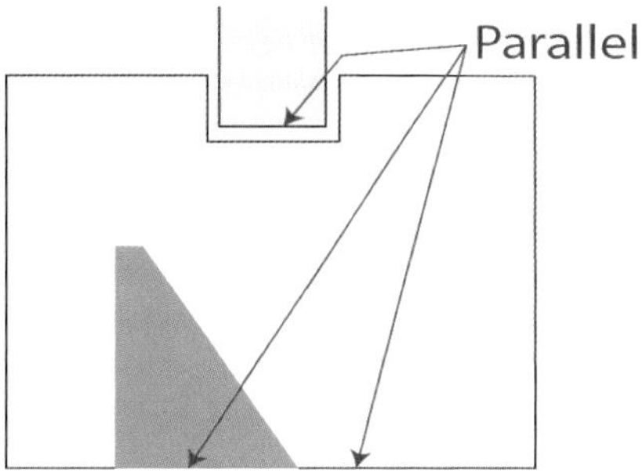

Fig. 109: Use the rear of the rest as a reference when placing the angle guide, provided the face of the wheel has been dressed parallel to that edge.

by using that rear edge as a reference when dressing the wheel. The angle guide should be thick enough to provide a secure location for the work, and should not be made of thin sheet metal, as the work may ride up and over the guide under sideways pressure. That suggests the guide should be at least 3mm thick, and may be much more. A small set of guides for commonly used angles such as 0, 5, 7, 10, 30 and 45 degrees covers most everyday requirements. Although a simple flat guide can be clamped to the rest, a more convenient method is to fix a solid bar or a length of steel angle underneath the rear edge of the angle guide, and use that to locate against the rear edge of the rest (Fig. 110). The guide can then be slid sideways without losing orientation. Once in position, the guide can be clamped or left free to slide sideways. Clamping the guide restricts the movement of the tool to sliding along the angled side of the guide. Allowing the guide to slide allows the tool to be positioned clear of the wheel where the feed can be set before holding or clamping tool and guide firmly together and traversing the pair across the face of the wheel. To avoid damage, the tip of the guide should not reach the grinding wheel. A slotted angle or plate fixed underneath the rest, flush with the rear edge (Fig. 111) makes clamping more convenient, and tee nuts (Fig. 112) sliding in the slot allow stops to be set to limit the travel of a sliding guide.

Fig. 111: A slotted angle fixed to the underside of the rest, flush with the rear (the right hand edge in the photo), provides a means of clamping guides, and of setting traverse limit stops.

Fig. 108: A pre-made triangular angle guide clamped to the rest, to set the angle when swinging the tool.

Fig. 110: The orientation of an angle guide can be maintained by a bar or angle fixed to the underside.

Fig. 112: Traverse limit stops can be set by using tee nuts tapped to take the stop bolts, and located at the back of the slot in the angle at the front of the rest.

Fig. 113: A plain bar can be set at an angle using a protractor referencing off the rear edge of the rest.

A plain bar can be set at an angle by using a protractor (Fig. 113), then clamped in position, or an adjustable angle guide mounted on a rear guide bar can be set to a specific angle by using a protractor (Fig. 114), then

Fig. 114: An angle guide equipped with a bar can be adjusted using a protractor, then traversed using the rear edge of the rest as a reference.

the guide and tool can be slid horizontally, across the face of the wheel, to grind the tool. The guide can be made just long enough so that it does not touch the wheel, provided the corners are rounded to clear the wheel as the guide swings around, or slotted so that it can be shortened or lengthened as the angle changes (Fig. 115), maintaining support for a tool near the face of the wheel.

Fig. 115: The protruding length of a slotted angle guide can be adjusted to maintain good support for the tool near the face of the wheel.

Fig. 116: A slot machined across the face of a Grind-R-Table rest provides a guide for traversing tool holders and accessories. Photo: GLENDO LLC.

A slot machined across the rest provides a guide for accessories as they are slid across the rest (Figs 101, 116 and 117). The face of the wheel should be dressed parallel to the slot, and it is essential that multiple slots are of the same width, as well as parallel to one another. A plain slot is limited to guidance, and a logical extension of this is to replace the rest with a tee-slotted table (Fig. 117) which offers the possibility of clamping tools, holders and accessories to the table. The slotted table shown in Fig. 117 is a good quality commercially available table from a small SEIG milling machine, with tee slots which are parallel and of uniform width. However; a heavy tee slotted table requires a robust support with secure clamping arrangements to hold it in position. A basic protractor can be slid along the rear of the rest, but a larger protractor with integral tool guide can be mounted on a bar and made to slide along a slot in the grinder rest (Fig. 118). The pivot point must be on the bar, but an integral clamping slot allows the angle to be locked once it has been set. This style of angle guide is often found on a circular saw table.

Fig. 117: A tee-slotted table from a milling machine may be used as a rest, and attachments may be mounted on a bar which can slide inside the slots.

STONING SLOTS

The slots in a milling machine table may require adjustment to ensure they are of equal width throughout their length, as well as having a good finish on their inner faces, to allow guides and accessories to have a smooth, shake-free, sliding action.

Better quality tables require little adjustment, and can be fine-tuned using a slip stone, while lower-priced tables may require re-machining before using a slip stone; but any re-machining techniques are outside the scope of this book.

Finishing slot sides using a stone involves these steps:

- Prepare two rectangular steel gauges: one of exactly the same size as a sliding guide, and one a little thinner. If the slots have been machined to a consistent size, one exact-size gauge will do.
- Choose a small carborundum stone of medium grit which fits inside the vertical faces of the slots.
- Use a lubricant such as a thin oil, paraffin or water.
- Using the thinnest gauge to test the fit, identify any places where the guide will not fit, and rub along these with the stone. Remove the stone, clean it, then test the fit of the gauge, at frequent intervals.
- When the gauge almost fits, or fits but does not slide smoothly, use sweeping strokes of the stone along the whole length of the slots, to provide a final smooth finish. Stop before the gauge becomes loose in the slots.
- Use the exact-size gauge to finally finish the slots to size. The sliding guide should slide freely but without side shake.

Fig. 118: A protractor with integral tool guide plate (known as a 'shoe') can be mounted on a bar and slid along a slot.

Fig. 120: A toolholder with a central upward-facing slot and front corners cut back at an angle so that when it is swung the corners do not foul the wheel.

Fig. 122: The tool holder can be removed from the plate; turned through 90 degrees; and relocated, allowing it to carry a side-pointing tool.

Using an angle guide which is sufficiently tall, the work can be clamped to the guide before traversing, but the clamps must be re-adjusted each time a cut is applied. Clamps may tend to obscure the view of the work but although smaller clamps give a clearer view, they need to be sufficiently large and strong enough to grip the work securely against the guide. Before traversing across the face of the wheel, make sure any protruding parts of the clamps will not foul

Fig. 119: A lathe toolpost used as a tool holder.

the wheel. Alternatives to simple clamps are dedicated workholders, like the lathe toolholder shown in Fig. 119. The toolholder can be held against the side of the angle guide, or could be attached by a clamp. When a broad rectangular holder is swung to allow the tool to be presented to the wheel at an angle, the corner of the holder is likely to foul the wheel unless stops are set so that the guide travels far enough to allow the whole tool face to be ground, but stops before the carrier hits the wheel. This usually means the face of the tool cannot be slid fully clear of the wheel. A remedy is to machine away the front corners of the holder, so that they are clear as far as, say, 45 degrees (Fig. 120), and mount this on a larger base to ensure that the toolholder does not tilt if the rear corner is unsupported while crossing a tee slot. The angled front relief is not enough for shapes such as threading tools, which have a more acute angle at the tip, but will allow many other tools to be traversed past the wheel. A small lathe toolholder may be pressed into service, and Fig. 121 shows the toolholder

Fig.121: A tool holder from a SEIG C0 lathe, mounted on a plate to raise the tools so that they do not foul the vertical side of the angle guide.

from a small SEIG C0 lathe which has been mounted on a base to give it a little more height, ensuring that the tool will clear the top of the angle guide. This tool holder can be removed, turned through 90 degrees,

Fig. 123: The tool holder can be fitted with a sheet metal shield, to protect the threads from abrasive dust.

then relocated on the plate, allowing it to carry a side-pointing tool (Fig. 122). It can also be fitted with a simple sheet metal cover to protect the threads of the clamping screws from abrasive dust (Fig. 123).

Fig. 124: The angle guide can be fitted with a shoe which provides a secure base for a tool.

Providing an angle guide with a shoe consisting of a plate covering the bottom of the guide as well as protruding to the side (Fig. 124) has two benefits. Firstly, a steel shoe will protect the protractor from the abrasive effects of embedded grit from the grinding process. This is particularly important if the guide is made of aluminium or one of the soft alloys often used for die casting. Secondly, the projecting plate provides a secure base for a tool, and less friction between the underside of the tool and the top of the grinding rest as the tool is traversed across the face of the wheel. The front corner of a projecting plate of this kind should be trimmed to prevent it fouling the grinding wheel at a typical maximum value of, say, a little over 30 degrees. Trimming the plate further than this risks removing support at the front of the tool at smaller angles.

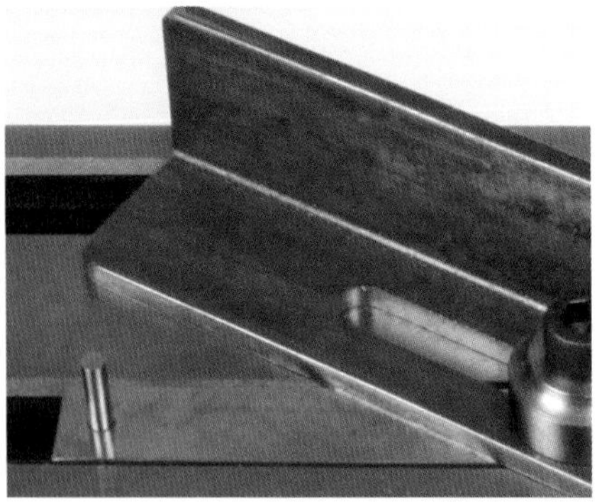

Fig. 125: The pin on the left side of the sliding bar of this angle guide can engage with a tee slot lock.

Fig. 126: A locking tee-nut engages with a pin on the sliding bar, locking the bar in position.

Fig. 127: The tee-nut used as a lock for the sliding bar.

Fig. 128: A sliding angle guide fitted with a shoe and a device for controlling initial positioning and depth of cut (feed).

Fig. 125 shows an adjustable sliding angle guide with a pin on the left which can be engaged with a separate lock, which uses a tee-nut to secure the bar at any position along the tee slot (Figs 126 and 127).

Fig. 128 shows a sliding angle guide which incorporates a shoe, as well as a rear-mounted adjustment device to control the depth of cut. That depthing device has facilities for a large adjustment (by sliding the clamp body along the left hand rod before clamping it in position with the right hand rod touching the work) and a fine feed of just a few millimetres, accessed by turning the thumbwheel on the right hand side of the body.

Angle guides of this type (Fig. 128) typically have one of two types of angular scale. Using a scale of the type shown in Fig. 129, the angle reads 0 degrees when the guide holds the tool at right angles to the face of the wheel, so when the guide is swung around, the scale indicates the deviation from that angle. Effectively, the front of a tool will be ground to the angle shown on the scale (Fig. 130).

Using a scale of the type shown in Fig. 131, the angle reads 90 degrees when the rest is set at right angles to the face of the wheel, so the angular scale indicates the included angle between the side of the tool and its front face (Fig. 132).

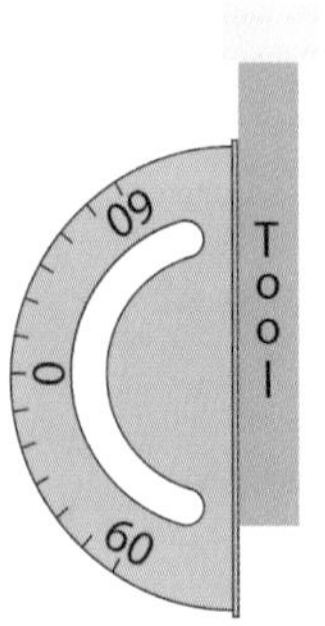

Fig. 129: An angular scale indicating 0 degrees when a tool is held at right angles to the face of the wheel.

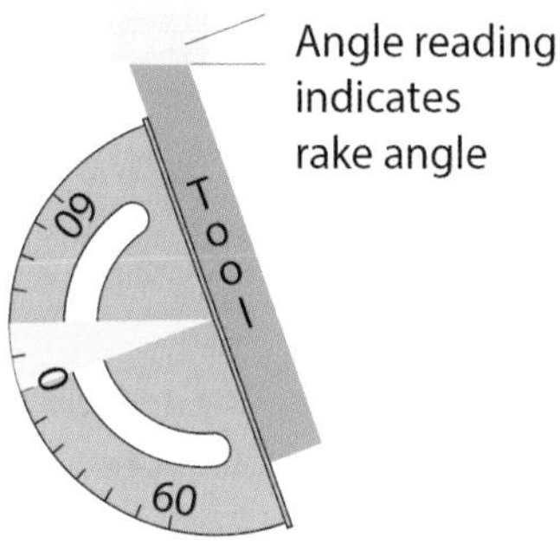

Fig. 130: The scale indicates the rake angle, which is the included angle of the material being removed.

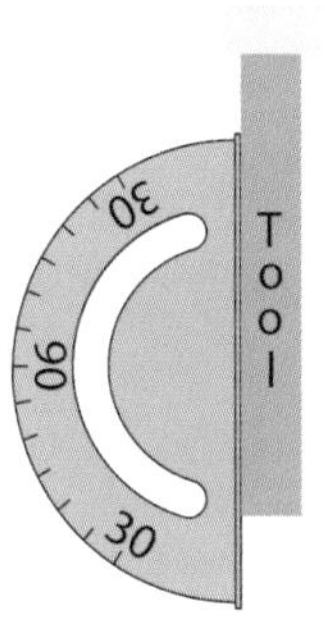

Fig. 131: An angular scale indicating 90 degrees when a tool is held at right angles to the face of the wheel.

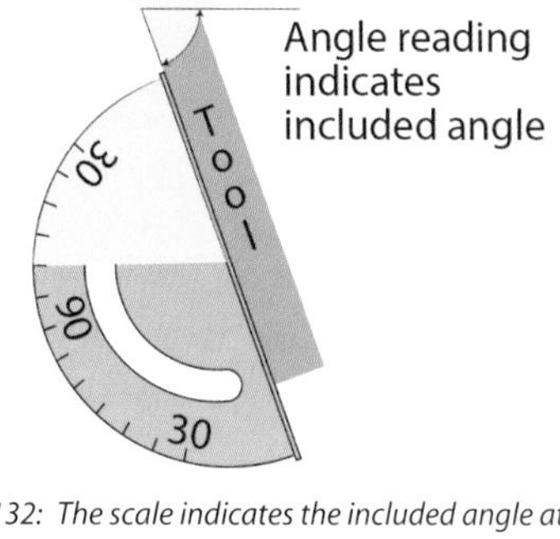

Fig. 132: The scale indicates the included angle at the tool tip.

Tilt

Basic tilting involves raising or lowering the tail of the tool. Fig. 133 shows an unground tool, with a horizontal plane representing the top of the tool, and a vertical plane the front. If the vertical plane

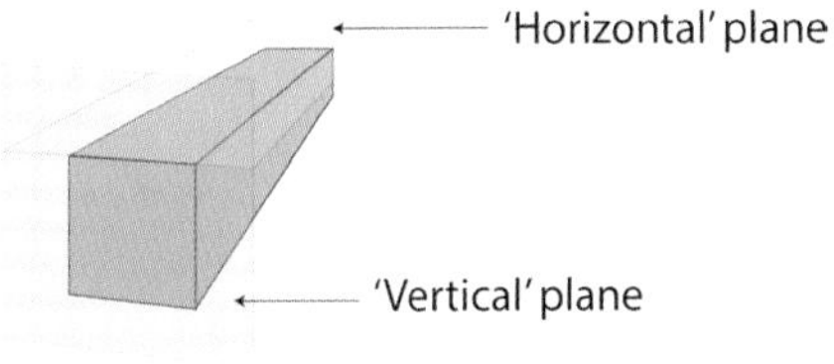

Fig. 133: A rectangular tool blank, with horizontal and vertical planes along top and front faces.

is the face of a flat grinding wheel, lowering the tail of the tool causes the heel of the front face to be ground off (Fig. 134).

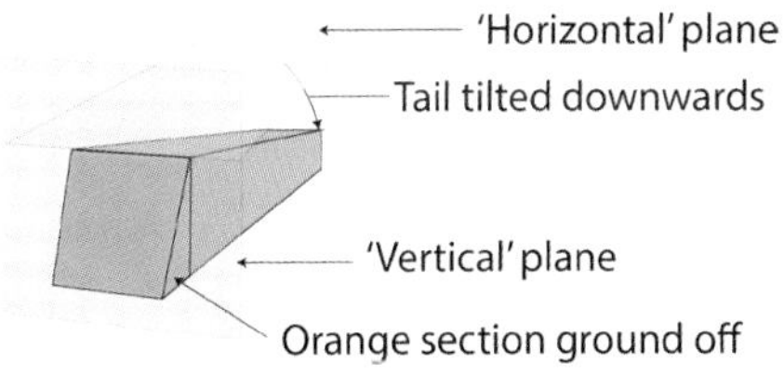

Fig. 134: Lowering the tail causes more to be ground from the heel of the front face.

Raising the tail of the tool causes the tip to be ground (Fig. 135). In practice, the tool sits on the rest, or in a holder which sits on the rest, so it is the rest which is tilted down, taking the tool with it, and creating the required angles.

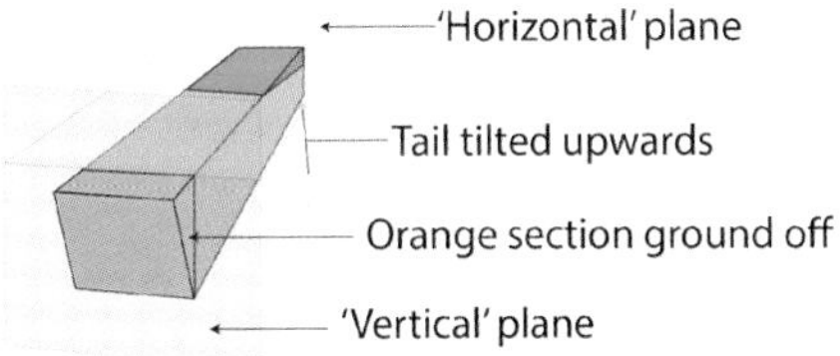

Fig. 135: Raising the tail causes more to be ground from the upper front face.

Setting an angle by tilting is quite straightforward if the face of the wheel is flat, but is potentially more complex when the face of the wheel is curved as on a type 1 wheel, because the angle ground on a tool depends on the height of the tool in relation to a radial line from the centre of the wheel (Fig. 136), the angle of the tool compared to that radial line, and the radius of the wheel.

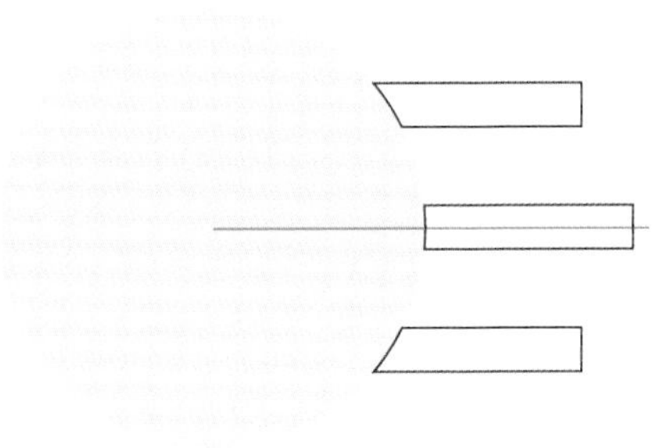

Fig. 136: The angle ground on the face of the tool depends on where it touches the face of the wheel.

The wheel will grind a concave shape onto the tool so the important angle is the included angle at the tip (Fig. 137), as that is the part of the tool that touches the workpiece.

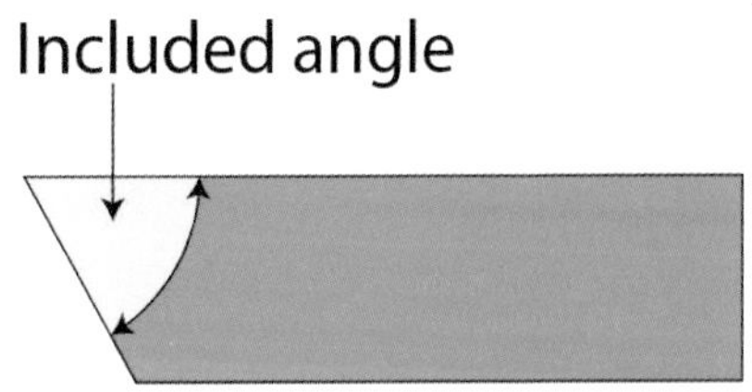

Fig. 137: A side view shows that for most lathe tools the important angle is the included angle at the tip.

Even when a tool is set on centre, a curved wheel will create a curve from the top of the tool face to the bottom. On, say, a lathe tool, that will not matter provided the diameter of the work being turned by the tool is smaller than the diameter of the grinding wheel (Fig. 138).

However; with an understanding of what is happening, and a few simple aids, the practical problems caused by the curved face can be minimized, and sometimes used to advantage.

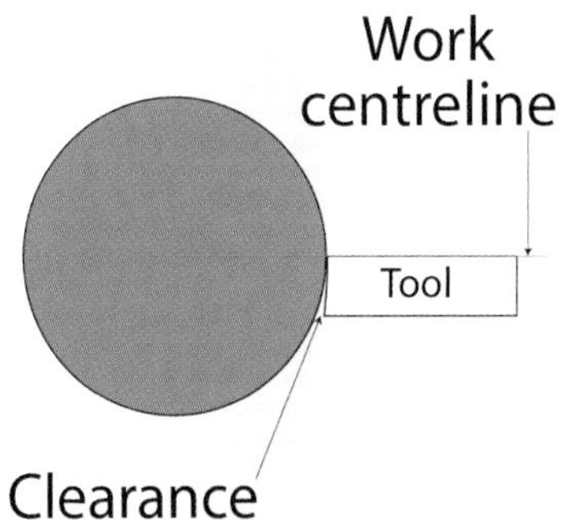

Fig. 138: With a lathe tool, the curved face of the tool will not affect work which has a smaller diameter than the grinding wheel.

Using a template to set the angle of the rest

Perhaps the simplest and quickest way to set the angle of the rest for a specific job is to use a template (Fig. 139). The angle

Fig. 139: An angle template provides an easy way of setting the rest at an angle.

required for the template should be the same as the angle of the face of the tool, measured from a plane through the cutting edge of the tool, parallel to the long axis of the tool (Fig. 140). For a chisel, it would be half the included angle of the tool (Fig. 140).

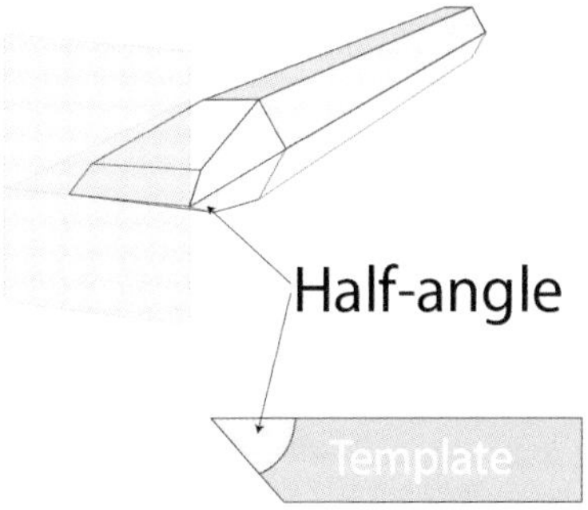

Fig. 140: For a chisel, the angle of a template should be the same as the half-angle at the cutting edge.

So, for a chisel with an included angle of 60 degrees at the cutting edge, make the template 30 degrees, measured from the horizontal top of the template. For a parting tool, the front clearance angle is usually known, so the required included angle would be 90 minus the front clearance angle (Fig. 141).

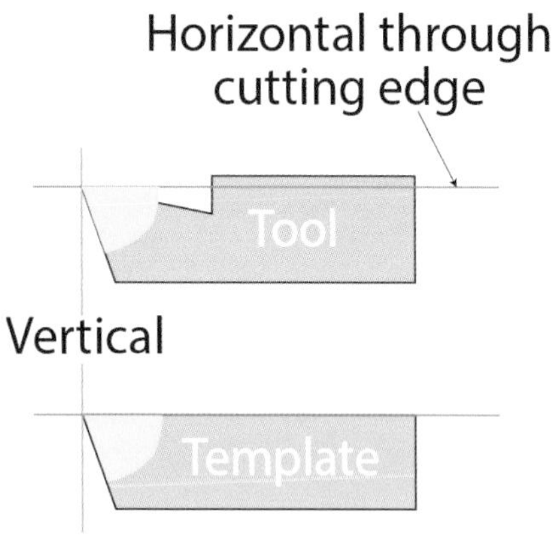

Fig. 141: An angle template provides an easy way of setting the rest at an angle.

For a parting tool intended to have a front clearance angle of 8 degrees, the template should have an included angle of 90 – 8 = 82 degrees. Note that the top rake of the tool plays no part in determining the template angle, because it is only the front face of the tool that is being ground in this operation. As a check, placing the template at the side of the tool, the lower angled face should sit parallel to the tool face below the cutting edge (Fig. 142). The height of the template should be a little greater than the height of the cutting edge of the tool when it is on the rest ready to be ground, with the tool in any required tool holder or sleeve, or sitting on

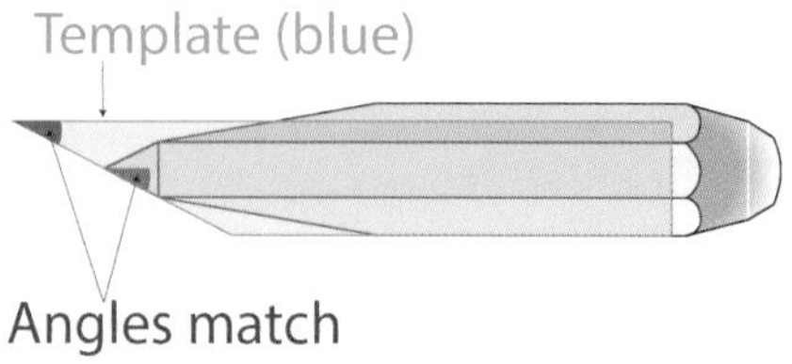

Fig. 142: An angle template should match the angle of the face being ground, at the cutting edge. On a chisel, this is the half-angle at the tip.

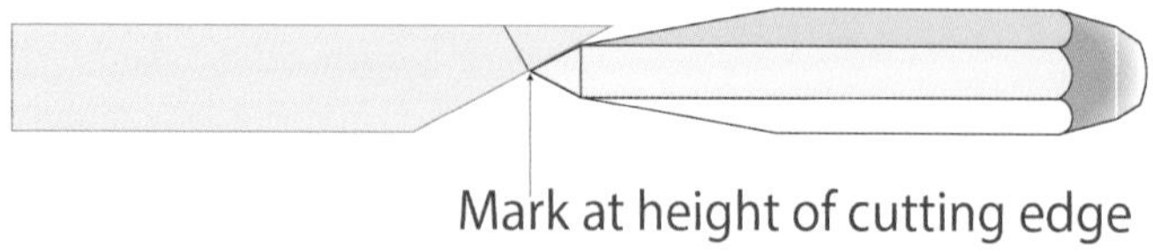

Fig. 143: Mark the template at the height of the cutting edge. Make the mark at 90 degrees to the edge of the template.

any vee block or other support that will be used to support it in the grinder.

- Sit the template and the tool (with any holder, sleeve, carrier, vee block, etc.) on the same surface, and mark the template at the height of the cutting edge (Fig. 143). Make the mark at 90 degrees to the edge of the template, because this makes the later task of alignment with the wheel easier.
- Sit the marked template on the rest, then slacken the locks on the rest and adjust its angle and height so that the line on the template touches the wheel (Fig. 144). This process is made easier if a magnifying glass is used to determine the touching point accurately. That touching point is the tangent point at which the tip of the tool should touch the wheel.

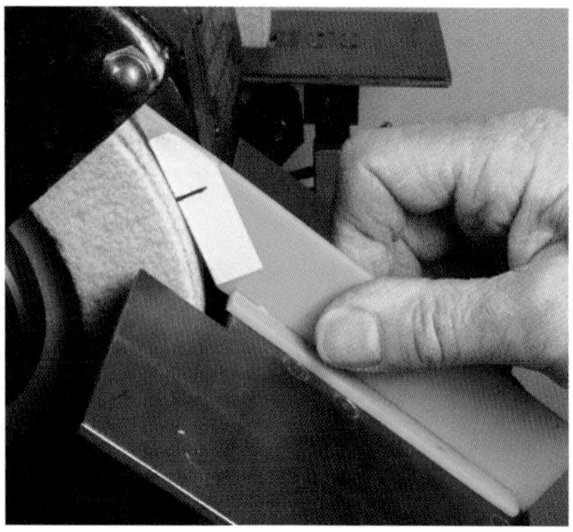

Fig. 144: With the template sitting on the rest, on the same surface as the tool, adjust the rest so that the template touches the wheel at the marked line.

- Lock the angle and height of the rest.

The tool may now be ground. If the template is to be used regularly, it is worth sticking a label onto its side, so that marks can be made easily and can be clearly seen. Labels can be renewed at intervals.

Setting on centre when using a wheel with a curved face

The basic tool rest 'on-centre' position has the upper face of the rest lying along a radial line pointing to the centre of the grinding wheel (Fig. 145). It may be convenient if the top surface of the rest is parallel to the horizontal surface on which the grinder sits, but Fig. 145 shows that the two are not related, and the rest does not need to be set truly horizontal. It is not enough to set the front edge of the rest in line with the end of a radial line; the whole top surface of the rest must lie along the line. At the instant the curved face of the wheel passes the end of the radial line, it is tangent to it (i.e. at 90 degrees to it), so setting the rest along a radial line means that the wheel will grind a surface at 90 degrees to the top surface of the rest. Although it may be at any angle to the real horizontal, the top surface of the rest effectively provides an artificial horizontal in that position, and the face of the wheel creates an artificial vertical.

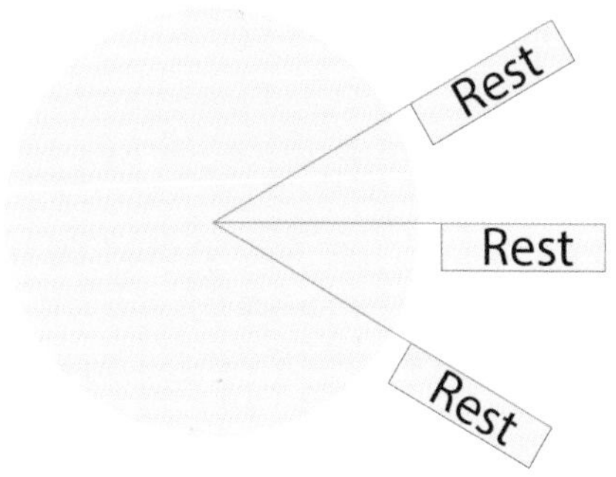

Fig. 145: In the basic position, the rest lies along a radial line from the centre of the wheel. That provides an artificial horizontal which may not coincide with horizontal from the viewpoint of a human operator.

It is not easy to set the top surface of the rest along a radial line by eye, so some aids are helpful. Figs 146 and 147 show a template with a curved edge corresponding to the curve of the grinding wheel. Placing the inner curve against the wheel positions the arm along a radial line from the axis of the wheel (Fig. 145). A wheel with a different radius will require a template with a matching inner curve.

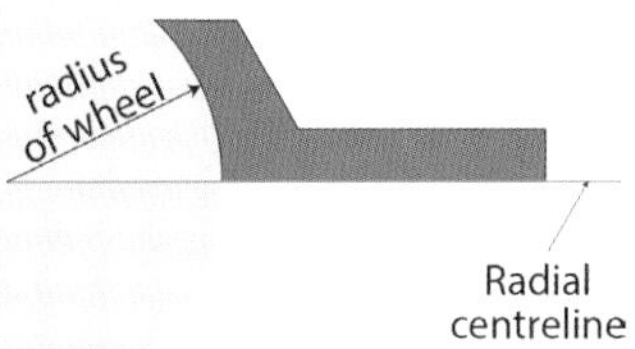

Fig. 146: A template with a curved edge can be drawn, and then cut out of wood, plastic or metal.

Fig. 147: Placing the template curve against the wheel and the rest against the underside of the arm aligns the rest along a radial centre line.

Fig. 148 shows a bar which can be mounted on a pivot aligned with the centre of the wheel and grinder shaft. The underside of the bar is aligned with a radial line from the centre of the wheel, and setting the rest against the underside of the bar sets the rest along a radial line. The bar does not need to be horizontal, because its underside always lies along a radial line, and always provides an artificial horizontal. The bar may be straight, or might incorporate a sideways bend to bring it closer to the wheel, and a slot to provide some adjustment of its length. A suitable length of slot may allow the same bar to be used on two grinders with different wheel diameters. The bar may pivot on an externally mounted shaft or on a shaft permanently mounted to the grinder, perhaps fixed to a sufficiently sturdy wheel guard (Fig. 149). In either case, the pivot must be aligned with the centre of the grinding wheel and shaft. Many grinders have a centre formed in the end of their shaft, and that provides a suitable reference point. If the pivot has a hole to provide a sliding fit for a rod with a 60 degree conical end, set the pivot so that the rod can be aligned with the centre of the grinder shaft, then remove the rod. The pivot shown in Fig. 149 was aligned in that way, before permanently fixing it in position.

Fig. 148: Set the rest 'horizontal' using a bar which pivots on the centre line of the grinder shaft, and whose lower edge is radial.

Fig. 149: A pivot fixed to the side of a sturdy wheel guard. The central hole is used for initial alignment of the axes of the pivot and the grinder shaft.

Normally, it is important to set the horizontal to coincide with the top surface of a tool rather than the rest, and the same technique can be used by holding the tool on the rest and setting the bar against the top surface of the tool (Fig. 150). However; in many cases, the top face of the tool is ground at an angle to the cutting edge, so there is no continuous surface against which to set the underside of the bar, and it is difficult to judge how the bar should be positioned. In that case, use a slip of material whose top surface will match the height of the tool cutting edge when it has been ground (Fig. 151). Often, a cylindrical tool bit will be ground on its top face, but will not be ground to half its diameter. Preparing a slip or a stack of material at the intended final height of the cutting edge allows the setting bar to be aligned correctly.

Fig. 150: To set the top of a flat-topped tool on centre, set the arm against the top surface of the tool.

Fig. 151: The bar can be set against a slip of material the same height as the cutting edge of the tool.

Offsetting above or below centre

Fig. 152 shows that the cylindrical face of a grinding wheel can create clearance angles if the work is set above centre height. The angle ground on the front of the work (orange line) will be tangent to the green radial line passing through the tool tip. The angle varies as the face of the wheel curves away below that point, but is at 90 degrees to the radial line which meets the tip of the

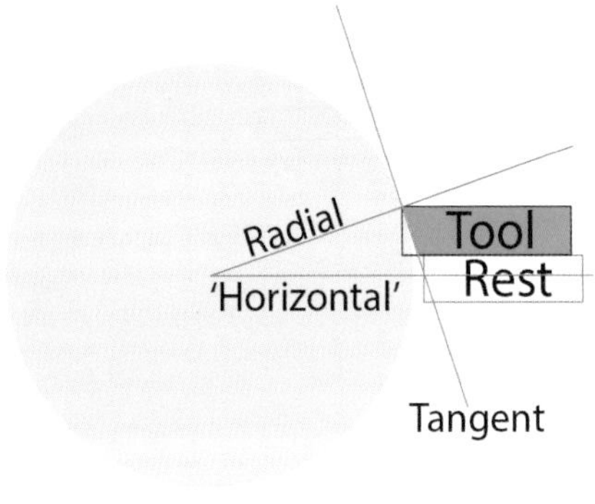

Fig. 152: Setting tool and rest parallel to a 'horizontal' radial centre line, then raising them 'vertically' will grind a clearance angle at the cutting edge.

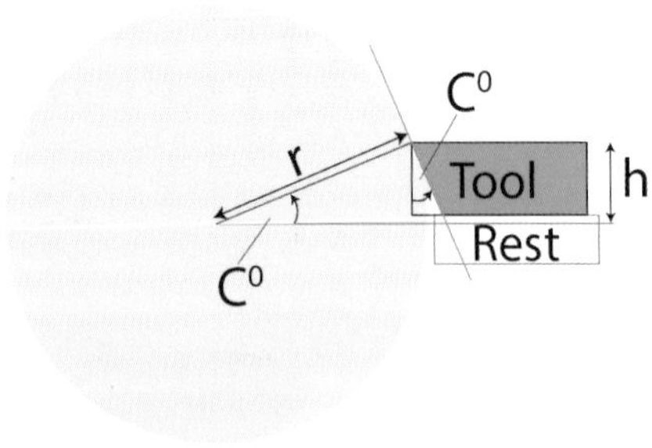

Fig. 153: The angle C is related to the height h above the radial centre line.

tool. Fig. 153 shows the relevant angles, and the height h can be calculated using the formula

h = r x SinC

where r is the radius of the wheel, and C is the additional angle (in degrees) to be ground at the tool tip. On a lathe tool, that is the clearance angle.
For example:
For a 200mm (8 inch) diameter wheel, and a tool clearance angle of 10 degrees,
r is 100mm (4 inches)
C will be 10 degrees.
h = 100 x Sin10 mm or 4 x Sin10 inches
h = 100 x 0.174 mm or 4 x 0.174 inches
h = 17.4mm or 0.696 inches

Table 9 lists values of h for common angles, both for 150mm (6 inch) and 200mm (8 inch) wheels.

For a tool such as a chisel, the reference is not the physical top of the tool, but the cutting edge, which is normally on the centre line through the shaft of the tool (Fig. 140). The additional angle will be 90 minus the half-angle:

For a 150mm diameter wheel, and an included angle of 90 degrees at the tip of a chisel (Fig. 153),
r is 75mm (3 inches) and C will be 90 - 90/2 = 45 degrees
h = 75 x Sin45 mm or 3 x Sin45 inches
h = 75 x 0.707 mm or 3 x 0.707 inches
h = 53mm or 2.121inches

In practice, it may be difficult to raise the centre line of the chisel 53mm above the horizontal because it may foul the wheel guard. One possible solution is to swing the rest down, and set it in the lower position shown in Fig. 145.

In theory, aligning the rest with a radial line, then raising or lowering the rest by the required amount will put it in the correct position. The challenge is to reliably move the rest up or down without tilting, because the surface of the rest must remain parallel to the radial line which was used as the 'horizontal' (Figs 145 and 152). It is easy enough to use a spacer between the setting arm and the rest, to lower the rest (Fig. 151), but many settings require the rest to be raised. However; the basic setting arm can be altered to include an adjustable plate as shown in Fig. 154 which has its reference edge in the zero position (radial to the centre line of the

Fig. 154: Setting arm with an adjustable plate which can be raised or lowered.

Heights to create clearance angles				
	Height (mm)		**Height (inches)**	
Wheel diameter	**150**	**200**	**6**	**8**
Clearance angle				
1	1.3	1.7	0.1	0.1
2	2.6	3.5	0.1	0.1
5	6.5	8.7	0.3	0.3
7	9.1	12.2	0.4	0.5
10	13.0	17.4	0.5	0.7
15	19.4	25.9	0.8	1.0

Table 9: Heights above centre to create additional (clearance) angles on different diameters of wheel.

grinder shaft) when the plate protrudes a set amount below the arm. For the plate shown in Fig. 154, this is 50mm. In that position, the underside of the arm is parallel to the radial 'horizontal'. From that zero position, slide the plate upwards by a calculated amount and lock it in position with its bottom edge parallel to the underside of the arm. Next, adjust the rest so that its surface is in continuous contact with the edge of the plate. So, if the rest is to be 10mm above the basic radial line, slide the plate upwards by 10mm so that it protrudes 50 – 10 = 40mm below the arm. It is essential that the lower edge of the plate remains parallel to the radial 'horizontal' as it slides up or down, and parallel lines engraved across the face of the plate can help. Set the rest against the reference edge, and lock it in position. This design of setting device can be used to set the rest to a specific height above the 'horizontal' by sliding the plate upwards, but it can also be adjusted to set the rest lower by sliding the plate downwards to extend it further below the arm. Setting the highest point of the cutting edge of a tool at a specific height above the horizontal is done by subtracting the height of the cutting edge above the base of the tool from the distance the plate is to be raised.

For example:

Using a 150mm diameter wheel, and a tool with its cutting edge 8mm above the base of the tool, intended to have a clearance angle of 10 degrees:

- Table 7 states the rest should be raised by 13mm.
- Subtracting the cutting edge height of 8mm leaves a rest height of 5mm.
- Set the bottom edge of the plate 5mm above its zero position.
- Align the surface of the rest along the edge of the plate, and lock the rest in position. Fig. 155 shows the result.

Grinding a face at a compound angle

A tool face can be ground at a compound angle (end relief and clearance, for a lathe tool) by swinging the tool, then tilting or raising or lowering the rest. Swing and tilt movements are independent of each other, so it is convenient to create the tilt first, then place the tool on the rest at the swing angle (Fig, 156). The end relief angle is set by the swing, and the curvature of the wheel creates the clearance. Traversing the tool across the tool rest grinds a single face with a compound angle comprising those swing and tilt angles. The front face will be curved from top to bottom, but the geometry will be correct at the tool tip. The larger the diameter of the grinding wheel, the less the curved effect, and the larger the front clearance angle, the less noticeable the effect.

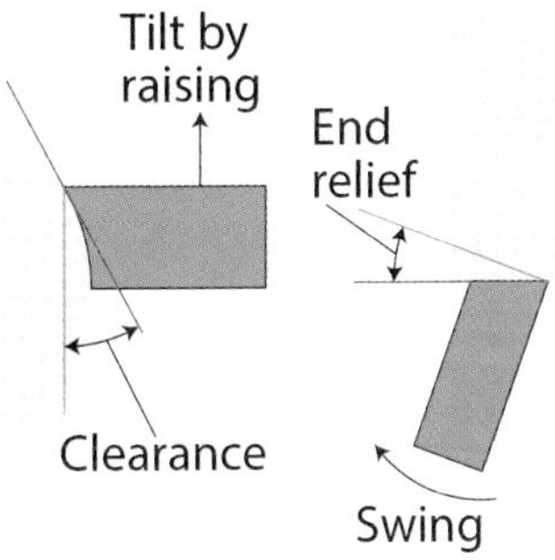

Fig. 156: Raise the tool to create a clearance angle, and swing the tool to create an end relief angle.

Fig. 155: Move the plate upwards by the amount given in Table 7, minus the distance from the cutting edge to the rest.

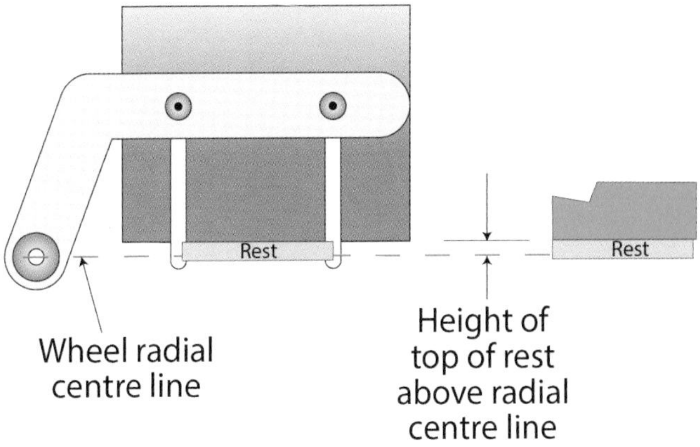

Moving the rest assembly

Moving the whole rest assembly alters the distance to the face of the wheel. Coarse movement can be by means of slots in the base of the rest to allow the base to be moved before tightening the securing bolts (Figs 104 and 157), or, less conveniently, a series of alternative mounting positions to allow the base to be positioned to suit the task (Fig. 158), with final positioning by adjusting the height and tilt of the rest itself.

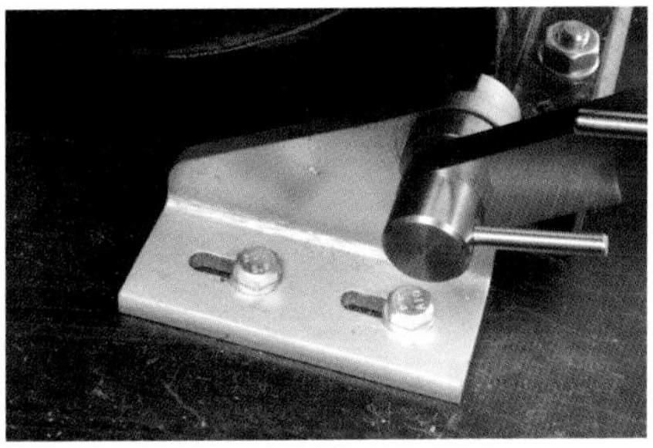

Fig. 157: Slots in the base of a rest assembly allow forward and backward adjustment of the rest.

Fig. 158: Alternative locations allow adjustment of the position of a rest assembly; in this case laterally.

Precise adjustment of the feed

While the rest remains stationary, forward and backward movements of the tool may be by hand, initially, to shape the tool. When grinding more precisely to final shape or size, finely controlled adjustments are needed, and these are best provided by screw adjustment of the workholder. Fig. 159 shows one approach, in which the tool, on its own or in a holder, is held in a guide by a clamp. The clamp is released, adjustment applied by screw, and the clamp retightened before making the next traversing pass. Fig. 160 shows a sliding plate with a workholder which can be pushed forwards by a screw. Once the workholder has been moved forwards, in preparation for the next

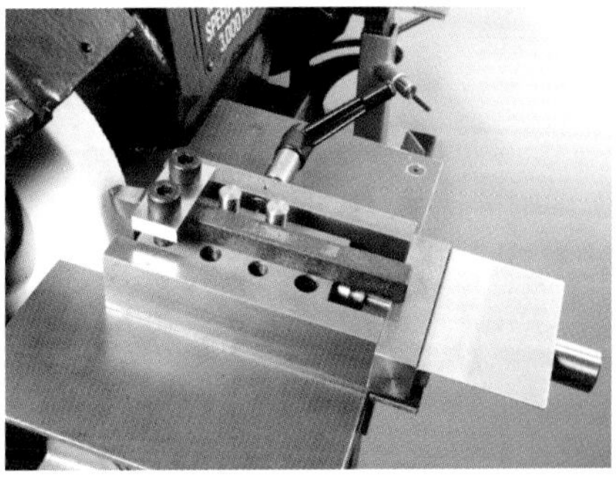

Fig. 159: In this tool holder, the tool is clamped to a carrier (a 20-30-50 block) and the carrier is clamped in the channel by a screw at the side. The screw at the rear, under the sheet metal shield, can be used to control the forward movement of the carrier, allowing fine control of the feed.

Fig. 160: In this arrangement, the sliding plate enables traverse, and the workholder sits on the plate, clamped by the vertical screw attached to the side of the plate. The screw and block assembly at the rear is clamped to the plate by grub screws on the underside, and provides fine adjustment of feed when the vertical clamp is slack. Once the workholder has been positioned, tightening the clamp ensures the workholder will not move on the plate during grinding.

cut, the workholder can be clamped to the plate by a vertical screw attached to the plate. Fig. 128 shows a device used to provide both coarse positioning and fine feed adjustments.

Parallel arm motion

A rather different approach to movement of the tool on a rest is taken by the Acute Sharpening System from Eccentric Engineering (Figs 161 and 162), which uses a pantograph system similar to that found on drafting machines and technical drawing boards. The pantograph ensures that the angle of the workhead on the rest (the swing angle) does not change as the workhead is moved over the surface of the rest. The pantograph arm is anchored to the table by a clamp which can be fastened at any convenient position on the edge of the rest to suit the length of the tool and the angle of the workhead. Once set at an angle to the face of the wheel, the workhead and tool can be moved across the face of the wheel to take a cut, but the swing angle will remain constant at all times. This means the rest does not need guides or slots to maintain the angle of the tool relative to the face of the wheel. The workhead can be fitted with tool holders which accept tools held in sleeves, and can incorporate a feed device to allow controlled forward movement of the tool holders, to take a cut. The Acute system incorporates angled shims or plates which tilt tools at angles commonly required for lathe tools and milling cutters, reducing the need to measure angles.

Fig. 161: The Acute Sharpening System uses a pantograph arm to guide the tool holder so that the angle between the tool and the face of the wheel (effectively the swing angle) remains constant in all positions of the arm. The swing angle can be set using a simple template lying on its side. The angle of tilt is set using a template held vertically against the face of the wheel and the rest.
Photo: ECCENTRICENGINEERING

Fig. 162: The pantograph arm can be clamped anywhere on the periphery of the rest, to suit the job. When sharpening an end mill, the depth of cut can be adjusted using a screw at the rear of the workholder.
Photo: ECCENTRICENGINEERING

DUST EXTRACTION

The dust shed by a grinding wheel is a hazard to health, and a good extraction system helps minimize the dangers. Fig, 163 shows two extraction pipes on the rear of the substantial wheel guards. They may be connected to an extractor unit or a vacuum cleaner using a flexible hose. Extraction from the rear requires powerful suction, as the dust must be sucked all the way from the point of generation at the front of the wheel to the rear of the guard. An alternative approach is to position a nozzle near the source of the dust (Fig. 164). Plastic pipe should be regarded as a consumable with a short life.

Fig. 163: Dust extraction pipes at the rear of the wheel guards on a bench grinder.

Fig. 164: An extraction system which draws from the front of the wheel, near the source of the dust.

USING AN ALTERNATIVE SHAPE OF WHEEL

The main disadvantage of the basic bench grinder is the shape of its wheel. The standard type 1, 5 or 7 plain cylindrical wheels all present a curved face to the work when the ideal for the everyday shaping and sharpening tasks is a flat face. Although a curved face allows clearance angles to be created by varying the height of the rest, a flat-faced wheel is more convenient for a wider range of sharpening tasks and simplifies many set-ups. Flat-faced wheels come in a range of shapes and sizes, including cup, saucer and dish wheels designed for tool and cutter grinders. A type 6 cup wheel or a type 11 taper cup wheel is easily mounted on most basic grinders (Fig. 165). However; it is likely

Fig. 165: Fitting alternative types of wheel usually means providing suitable wheel guards. As a general rule, cover as much of the circumference as possible for any given task. Slots in the guards allow lateral adjustment to cover thick wheels.

that the wheel guards will have to be altered to accommodate the new wheel shape, and these should provide shielding around as much of the circumference of the curved sides as possible, but allow access to at least one half of the front of the wheel. Provision for dust extraction is useful too (Figs 163 and 164).

Tool rests can be mounted next to the flat rim of the wheel, and the grinder can be turned through 90 degrees so that the flat face of the wheel faces the operator. The as-supplied tool rests will not be of any use with this arrangement.

Because the working face of the wheel is flat, there is now no need to set the rest or the tool with reference to a radial line through the centre of the shaft of the grinder. Nor is there any need to compensate for the height of the work above the radial centre line of the wheel. Where the wheel has a small diameter and the tool is tilted upwards, there may be a need to adjust the height of the rest or the grinder itself, to ensure that the tool does not overshoot the top of the wheel. One simple way to adjust the wheel height is to place spacers (termed 'risers' in this application) below the grinder body (Fig. 166). Although this is not as convenient as having a screw-operated height adjustment, it is a simple low-cost way of creating workable setups. A small selection of risers, together with suitable lengths of securing bolts or threaded rods, is capable of covering the typical working range of heights. The risers shown in Fig. 166 cover heights of 25, 40, 50 and 75mm. The small amount of time required to add suitable risers does not detract from the significant convenience of having a flat operating face on the wheel.

Fig. 166: A selection of risers which serve to increase the working height of the grinder and wheel. Pre-prepared matching lengths of screwed rod for securing grinder and risers are also shown. In the photo, the grinder is shown sitting on a pair of 40mm risers.

Fitting a flat-faced wheel to a bench grinder

Choose a grinding wheel which has a central hole of greater diameter than the existing grinder shaft. A good choice here would be a wheel with central hole of 31.75mm diameter (1.25 inch), as this allows a choice of wheels designed to be used on an industrial grinder or a surface grinder. Smaller wheels designed specifically for tool and cutter grinding may have smaller holes. Tool and cutter grinding wheels have a greater variety of shapes, and a range of central hole diameters. Bushes are available to reduce the bore of the wheel to suit the existing grinder shaft, provided large enough flanges are used to grip the wheel near the outer diameter of the label.

Fig. 167: A selection of hubs and flanges suitable for clamping alternative types of wheel. On the right are the original as-supplied flanges, for comparison.

A better approach is to make hubs with integral flanges which incorporate a central hole sized to be a close fit on the existing shaft, and have a hub diameter to suit the hole in the wheel (Fig. 167). Add plain flanges for the front of the wheel. These should have the same diameter as the integral flange which will grip the rear of the wheel. Recess both flanges to ensure they grip near their outer edge. When fitting hubs, it is preferable that the grinder shaft has low run out, although it may be possible to overcome any existing wobble by attaching a hub to the shaft, in a fixed position, and machining the hub in-situ. Where a hub is to be machined in-situ, it helps if the grinder shaft has an accurate centre at each end. Then, if the grinder is disassembled, it may be possible to fix hubs to the shaft using grub screws which grip in indentations in the shaft, or machine a keyway in the shaft and the hub. Mount the armature between centres in a lathe; carefully protect the windings from swarf; then machine the hubs to final size. Where the grinder shaft has no centres, or cannot conveniently be disassembled, hubs can be machined as independent items and slid onto the shaft. That will neither reduce nor eliminate run out, so any eccentricity must be dealt with by dressing the grinding wheels. Make the flanges to sizes which correspond as far as possible to the dimensions in Table 5 (*see* page 17).

Once the hubs and flanges have been machined, and the wheels mounted, it is usually more convenient to turn the body of the grinder so that the flat face of the wheel faces the operator (Fig. 168).

Using a baseboard

A grinder needs to be mounted securely, not just for safety, but to ensure accurate and controlled movement of the tool in relation to the wheel. A conventional grinder stand, as shown in Fig. 75, holds the grinder securely, but often does not allow for easy modification of the rests or their positions. A better arrangement is a stand with a steel top which allows some space at the sides and the front for mounting a rest, or a range of different rests (Fig. 164). An alternative is to mount the grinder on a sturdy workshop bench, leaving space at the sides and front for rests and accessories. A grinder may also be mounted on a worktop which allows it to be moved from one bench to another. If the worktop is solid, rigid and flat, a track system can be a useful way of attaching accessories while allowing their positions to be adjusted. Combining a track system with a few riser blocks (Fig. 168) gives considerable control over the relative positions of grinder, rests, tool holder and tool. Fig. 169 shows a section of T Track, one of several similar systems available, and Fig. 170 shows how this track can be recessed so that its top lies flush with, or just below, the surface of the baseboard. While not suitable for the traversing movement of a toolholder, this track allows easy positioning of a rest (Fig. 171) or adjustment of the distance between grinder and tool. Providing slots running left to right allows the tool rest to be slid left to right. Slots running from back to front allow initial

Fig. 168: Mounting the grinder so that the face of the wheel faces the operator is convenient, and makes the flat working face of the wheel much more accessible.

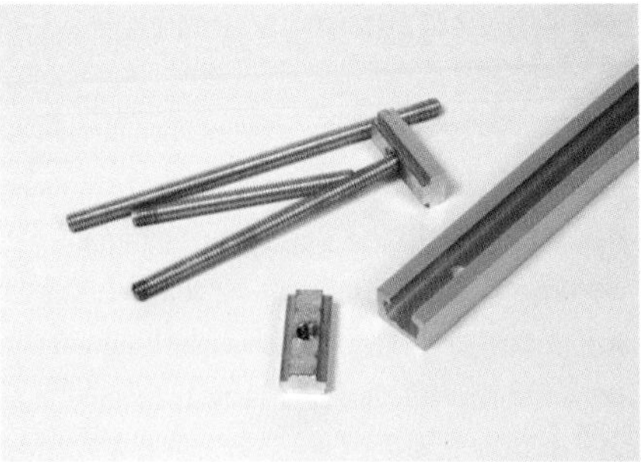

Fig. 169: T Track, or any similar T-slot system, may be used to hold a grinder and accessories on a baseboard. The track is designed to be recessed into the baseboard. The T-nuts shown here are home-made, but simpler nuts are available commercially.

Fig. 170: Recessing a track system into a baseboard provides secure attachment while allowing easy adjustment of a grinder and accessories such as rests. T-nuts locate in the tracks, and long bolts or threaded rods secure items to the track.

Fig. 171: T Track, or any similar T-slot system, allows easy positioning of a rest.

adjustment of the distance from the wheel to the rest. Smaller variations in distance can be made using the adjustments on the rest support. Setting an additional track into the board provides alternative positions which suit the grinder bolts when the grinder spindle is parallel to, or facing, the rest. It is important that in any new position the grinder and wheel should be squared-up carefully, and the wheel dressed before grinding begins.

Fig. 175: A modified cross-vice provides a lever to control traverse, and a feedscrew to provide accurate and fine control of cross-feed to create depth of cut. The black traverse lever sits horizontally on the right, at the front of the baseboard.

Adding a table top

If the baseboard has sufficient space, a table top may be added instead of a rest (Figs 117 and 172). This allows sliding accessories to be used in the T-slots of the table; and a suitable mounting arrangement allows the table top to be tilted (Fig. 173). This means swing takes place on the table, while rotation of the tool about its own axis must be provided by the tool holder, but tilt is created by tilting the whole table. Traverse is created by sliding the tool holder along a slot while the table remains stationary. Good quality table tops with T-slots of uniform width, and parallel to the sides of the table, are available as milling machine accessories, either as spare parts or as a way of converting an existing mill by giving it a longer table. These table tops tend to be heavy, and require a substantial support. This is particularly true of the table top shown in Figs 172 and 173, which is an SX1-105 long table conversion for a SEIG X1 mill, and weighs approximately 9kg. The traditional rest arms are usually too flimsy, and the clamps too weak to hold a T-slotted table of this weight securely.

Fig. 172: The T-slots in a table provide guidance when traversing a workhead or tool holder, as well as a secure way of mounting accessories.

Fig. 173: The T-slots provide accurate traverse, but the tool holder must provide rotation and swing. In the arrangement shown here, tilt is created by tilting the whole table.

Fig. 174: Mounting the grinder so that the face of the wheel faces the operator is convenient, and makes the flat working face of the wheel much more accessible.

Adding a cross-table

Taking this one step further by adding a small compound (X-Y or cross-table) table instead of a fixed table top (Fig. 174) provides control of the traverse, and fine control of the feed towards the wheel. A compound table requires a tool holder which provides rotation, swing and tilt. The table shown in Fig. 174 has been extensively modified and traverse takes place under hand control, as a fine pitch screw will not allow sufficiently fast traverse, and there is a danger of the work overheating during slow traverse. Nevertheless, adding a table like this can provide a convenient and accurate control of depth of cut.

Using a modified cross-vice

Fig. 175 shows a cross-vice which has been extensively modified to provide a lever and a linkage to control traverse. This gives rapid traverse left and right, preventing heat building up in the tool. The vice has fine control of feed towards the wheel, with a substantial graduated dial. As with a cross-table, the vice must carry an adjustable workhead providing rotate, swing and tilt movements.

4 Sharpening in Practice

In this section, you will find practical details of how to sharpen eight major tool types, chosen because they are commonly found in most workshops. Some are everyday objects, like knives, scissors and shears. Some are fundamental workshop tools like screwdrivers and chisels. Others are a little more specialized, and are more common in metalworking workshops. In addition, these tool types illustrate a wide range of sharpening techniques. Although it is possible to simply follow the instructions for each tool, there is more to be learned by treating each set of procedures as a useful addition to the range of sharpening techniques which can be applied to all sorts of common tools.

The first three tool types illustrate sharpening techniques using mainly abrasive stones, while the other tools make progressively more use of a bench grinder. Both are capable of accurate work, so the choice between the two is typically based on factors such as speed of metal removal, the quantity of material which needs to be ground away, and the range of accessories available to enable particular operations to be carried out. Sharpening a lightly used screwdriver requires much less metal removal than dressing a significant burr on a large chisel, for example. Similarly, sharpening a penknife requires less precise geometry than creating the top face of a lathe tool which must lie at a compound angle between two cutting edges.

OPPOSITE PAGE: *Fig. 176: A selection of holders and accessories for use with different tool types.*

There are many illustrations of accessories throughout this section. These are used to hold tools in particular ways or at specific angles. Many can be bought off the shelf, but others are not commercially available, so must be self-made. There are no specific drawings or instructions for their manufacture, but the photographs show their purpose and their major features. If you feel inclined, and have a decent workshop, you may find joy in making these items. If not, simply use something which performs a similar function; something of your own invention; or modify the procedures to suit the equipment you have at hand. An important purpose underlying this book is to enable you to think about what is required to achieve the geometry which will enable a tool to carry out its intended purpose. The procedures and techniques illustrated by the tool types are designed to demonstrate ways of achieving that geometry and to serve as a stimulus to provoke the questions at each stage of the sharpening process. Questions like: 'What are we trying to achieve here?'; 'What are the important features of this tool?'; and 'Why is this tool being sharpened in that way?'; should serve to develop an understanding of the geometry and the techniques shown here. There is usually more than one way to sharpen any given tool, and although space precludes an exhaustive explanation of all the alternatives, those included here are all practical methods which will produce the desired results for the chosen tool types, and may be extended to cope with other similar tools.

Many of the sharpening operations begin with details of how to create or significantly reform features of a tool. This may allow you to grind particular tools from a fresh tool steel blank. However; this is not primarily a book about designing and making tools, but about reforming the geometry of each tool. In an ideal world, tools would be lightly reground to sharpen them once they showed signs of any reduction in sharpness. That would simply involve recreating the geometry of the tool, with the various faces, flanks and edges as well as the angles between the various features of any given tool. In the real world, damage may extend beyond light wear and tear, so some indication of angles and the general design of tool types may be useful, and guidance is given for each tool type.

Sharpening, and, in particular, the time required to set up to sharpen some tool types, might be seen as a chore, but the time spent in sharpening is inevitably repaid many times over by the effectiveness of a sharp tool. Sharpening techniques, and some appreciation of the geometry required for a particular tool to work effectively, allows the performance of even new tools to be improved, sometimes significantly. So sharpening skills are a valuable addition to the practice of any workshop-based craft, and they may be developed and refined by practice as well as by applying the techniques to a wide range of tools. That way, you will experience the joy of working with sharp tools which add to the precision of all that you do in the workshop.

Tool type 1: Scissors, shears and knives

Knives, scissors and shears (Fig. 177) are in common use for all sorts of everyday cutting tasks, and there is a considerable range of sharpening aids available, varying from the simple, low-cost and relatively effective devices which can maintain a sharp-enough cutting edge, to more ambitious systems of jigs and abrasives which help maintain accurate cutting angles and razor-sharp edges. Some knives have straight cutting edges, and many knives, scissors and shears have curved cutting edges, but there are simple procedures for dealing with straight edges, and a number of different but straightforward techniques for sharpening curved edges. Most of these techniques rely on at least some manual manipulation, varying from the wholly manual technique of dragging a blade across an abrasive stone, to the semi-manual use of jigs which guide a stone across a blade at a fixed angle. With the exception of the straight cutting edges, few knives, scissors or shears lend themselves to the kinds of precise machine-based tool and cutter grinding devices required for milling cutters and lathe tools, but enthusiasts will be able to use grinding stones, offhand grinders and abrasive belt sanders to sharpen most blades. The easiest way to sharpen knives, scissors or shears is by rubbing the cutting edge against an abrasive stone, or the stone against the edge; and many knife blades will also benefit from final finishing by honing the edge. In many instances, jigs of varying design are of considerable use in setting and maintaining accurate angles at the cutting edges.

Fig. 177: Knives have a single blade which divides material; and scissors and shears have two blades which cut material as the blades slide past one another.

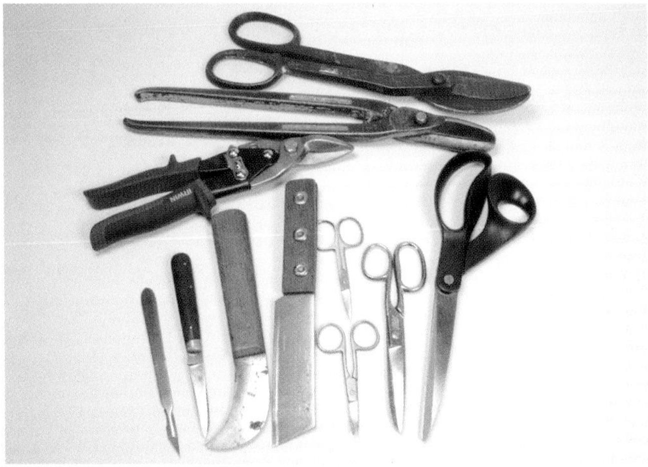

CUTTING EDGE GEOMETRY

Knives, scissors and shears all have cutting edges, and the angle of the cutting edge varies to provide a working compromise between the strength of the cutting edge and the characteristics of the material being cut. Knife blade angles are traditionally measured from the centre line of the blade, outwards (Fig. 178), while the reference for

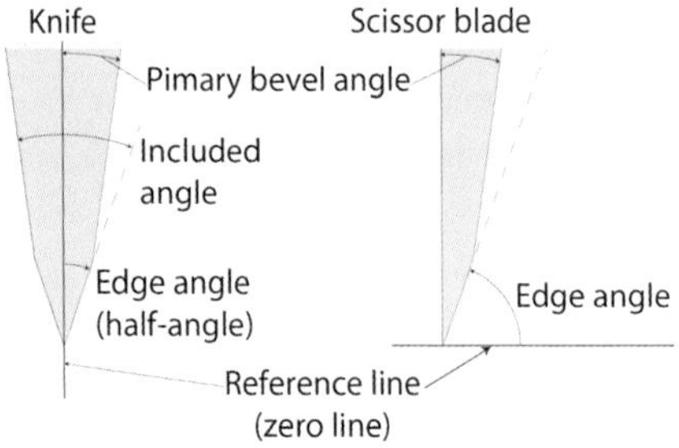

Fig. 178: The edge angles of knife and scissor blades are measured from different references.

SCISSORS, SHEARS OR SNIPS

The difference between scissors and shears is not always terribly clear, but two useful criteria are size, and duty.

Scissors are up to 150mm long, and have handles which accommodate one finger per blade. They are designed for lighter cutting tasks. The ends of the blades are normally pointed.

Shears have blades longer than 150mm, and have at least one handle which can accommodate more than one finger.

Shears are designed for heavier cutting tasks. The end of one blade may be pointed, but the end of the upper blade is more likely to be curved to prevent snagging when cutting cloth.

Snips are shears used to cut sheet metal.

From a sharpening point of view, the choice of names doesn't matter much; and it is only the angles of the cutting edges which are important.

blade angles of scissors and shears is at right angles to the inner side of the blade. The two different ways of measuring angles are influenced by the way in which different kinds of blade are shaped and sharpened. A knife blade may have a primary bevel angle, tapering from a thicker, blunt, back edge towards the cutting edge. The edge itself is normally formed by a shorter, steeper, secondary bevel (sometimes called a micro-bevel) with an edge angle. A single blade of a pair of scissors will normally have one 'flat' side designed to slide against the opposite blade, and an outer side with a primary bevel and a secondary bevel. The 'flat' side may be truly flat, but is more likely to be hollow ground so that the blades contact reliably at the cutting edges (Fig. 179).

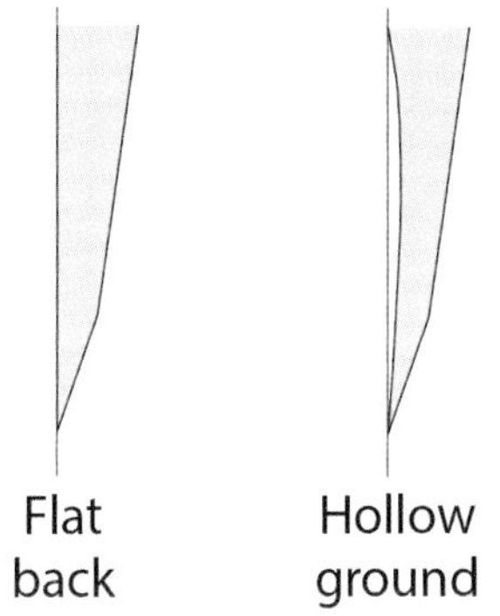

Fig. 179: The back of a scissor blade may be flat or hollow-ground.

Type of scissors or shears	***Typical use***	***Bevel angle (degrees)***
Safety scissors	Children's scissors for cutting paper and thin card.	0
Pinking shears	Woven cloth.	0–5
Paper scissors (cast iron)	Cutting paper and card.	5–15
Bandage scissors	Cutting cloth.	20
Garden trimmers	Grass and hedge.	25
Nail scissors, dressmaker's scissors	Finger nails, embroidery thread and fabric.	25–30
Tailor's shears	Fabric.	35–40
Gilbow snips	Sheet metal.	0–5
Irwin aircraft snips	Sheet metal.	25
Razor blade, scalpel	Very sharp edge for cutting paper, most thin materials, or flesh. Cutting edge is fragile.	17
Cutlery, cook's knife (e.g. fileting knife)	Cutting meat, fish and vegetables.	20
Hunting knife	Hunting and outdoor activities.	25
Heavy duty knife	Heavy cutting of carpet, card, plastic, wire. A strong edge, for heavy duty.	30

Table 10: Typical blade bevel angles for scissors, shears and knives.

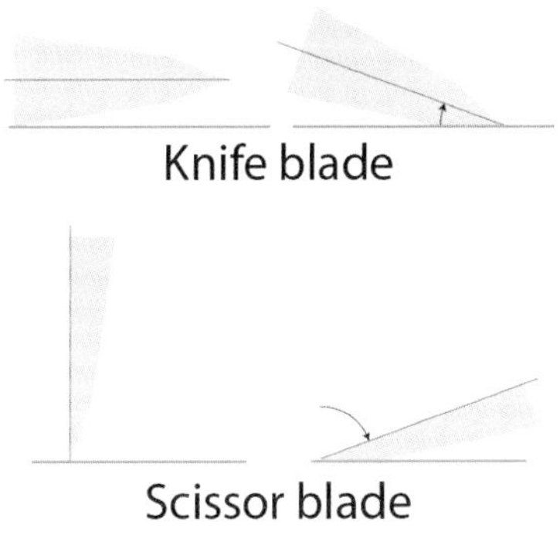

Fig. 180: Setting the angle for sharpening knife and scissor blades is done by measuring from the horizontal, for knives, and the vertical, for scissors.

Compared to scissor blades, knife edges are normally relatively thin and steeply tapered, and sharpening is most easily done by laying the blade flat against a stone or a belt then tilting it to create the correct edge angle (Fig. 180). Scissor blades, on the other hand, are more likely to be shaped and sharpened using machinery which holds the blade vertical then tilts either the blade or the abrasive wheel through the blade angle (Fig. 180). A steeply tapered cutting edge inevitably means a thin and relatively weak edge; fine for cutting soft materials, but not much good for harder materials which will cause considerable stress and may make the cutting edge crumble. A cutting edge with a greater included angle at the tip is stronger, but the angle of the edge is not well suited to cutting softer materials as it will tend to crush rather than penetrate the material. So the general rule is to use a compromise angle which allows the blade to cut while maintaining sufficient strength in the cutting edge. Table 10 lists recommended angles of scissor and shear blades for specific tasks, and typical knife blade angles.

USING A READY-MADE SHARPENER

Knife sharpeners

A typical knife sharpener consists of a plastic frame holding two or three pairs of abrasive wheels of different grit sizes. Fig. 181 shows a frame with three pairs of bevelled grinding stones with a slit located at an angle above each pair.

Fig. 181: A scissor sharpener consisting of a frame which holds three pairs of stones with coarse, medium and fine grits. Blades are guided by slots.

Sit the knife in the slit above the coarsest pair, and draw the knife firmly downwards and towards you, several times (Fig. 182).

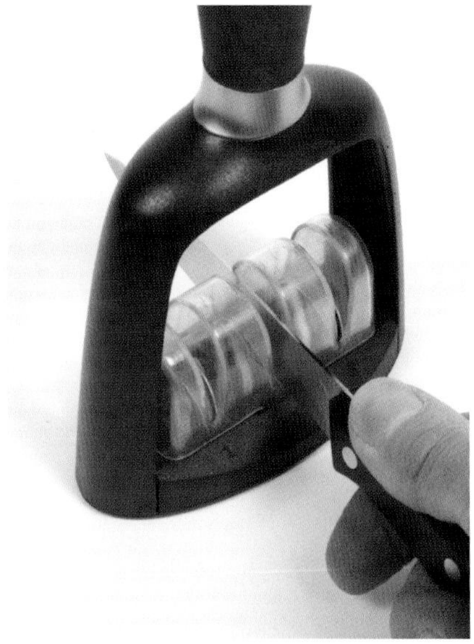

Fig. 182: Working through the three grades, in turn, from the coarse to the fine grit, insert the blade into the slot and draw it backwards through the stones.

Take care to control the blade as it exits the slot, as there is a tendency for the tip of the blade to move sharply downwards, cutting the surface on which the sharpener is sitting. Alternatively, start with just the tip between the stones, and push the knife through, up to the hilt. This is safer, but does tend to leave the tip unsharpened. Sharpening takes place because the blade drags across the angled surface of the wheels, abrading the surface and removing metal from each side of the blade. Taking care to protect your fingers, wipe the knife by drawing a cloth across the blade, at right angles to the sharpened edge, wiping from the blunt rear of the blade off the sharp edge (Fig. 183), to remove all grit and metal dust, then repeat the same sequence in the medium grade wheels, then the finest wheels. The blade can be touched up at intervals to maintain a keen edge, and may not need to be drawn across all three grades of wheel. It all depends on how blunt the blade has become. The angle at which the cutting edge is sharpened is preset by

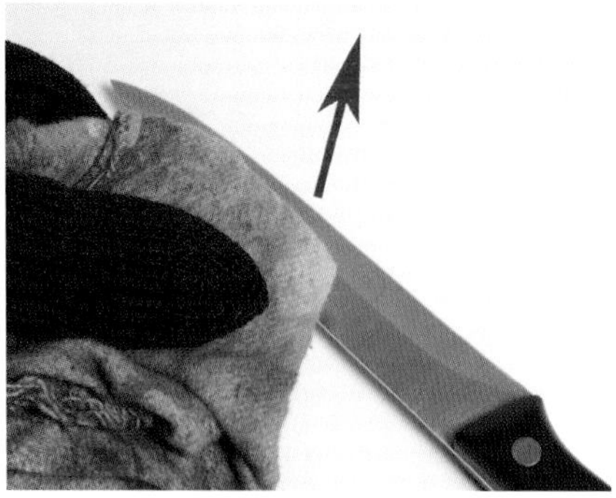

Fig. 183: Clean the blade between grits, by wiping from the blunt edge off the sharp edge of the blade.

the angle of the stones, and although this may be a reasonable compromise for kitchen or general purpose knifes, the angle cannot be changed.

Some single-stone sharpeners have no protective frame (Fig. 184) and there is a real

Fig. 184: A hand-held single-stone sharpener.

danger that the knife may slash your hand as the blade exits the wheel. Wear a cut-resistant glove woven with Kevlar or stainless steel thread. On this design of sharpener, use the vee grooves on each side of the central stone, one at a time, to sharpen each side of the blade. The grit of the abrasive provides a compromise between sharpening speed and finish, and may not provide a fine finish. The stone is set to grind at just one angle, which is not adjustable, and although the non-abrasive side of the slot is curved (Fig. 185), it would be very difficult to hold a blade at a constant depth to ensure the cutting edge was sharpened at a different angle.

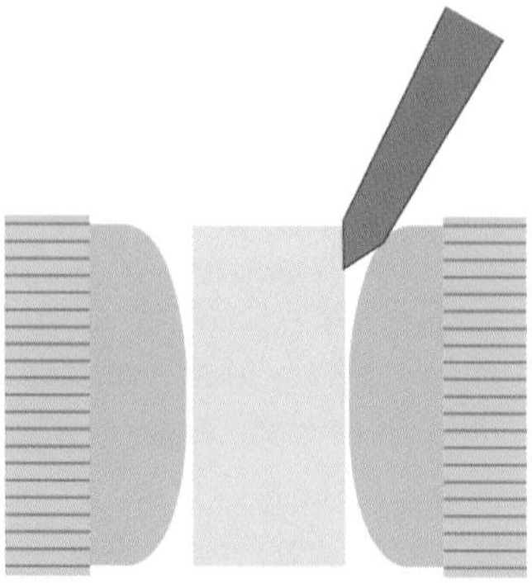

Fig. 185: This single-stone sharpener is designed to produce one fixed angle, and it is difficult hold a blade consistently at any other angle, because it must be steadied against a curved guide.

An electric sharpener uses a small motor to revolve an abrasive stone. Some of the popular low cost multi-function sharpening units incorporate angled slots to guide a knife blade across the revolving abrasive stone at a fixed angle (Fig. 186). On many of these machines, each side of the blade is sharpened separately. Draw the blade slowly through the slot to sharpen it. Holding the blade stationary at any stage causes uneven sharpening and will tend to overheat the blade, as shown by a change in colour, so keep the blade moving at a steady speed. If there are multiple slots, each presenting a different grit size of abrasive, remember to wipe the blade clean before drawing it through the next slot, to prevent cross-contamination of the abrasive stones, just as with a hand-held multi-stone sharpener.

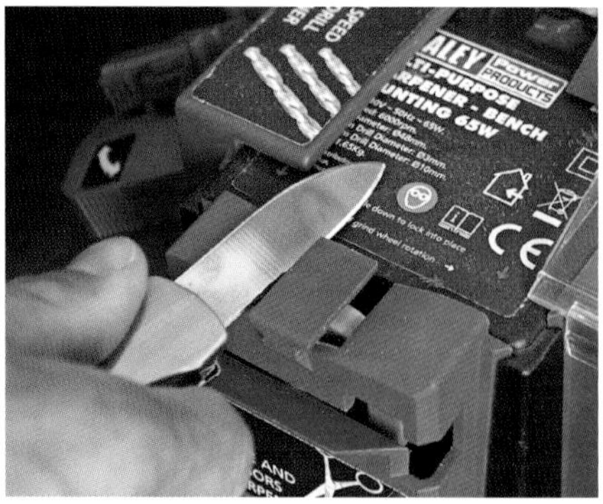

Fig. 186: Some electric sharpeners have a slot which guides a knife blade against a revolving stone. Photo: JACK SEALEY LTD..

Scissors sharpeners

Sharpeners for scissors are designed to create an edge with a specific cutting angle. Because of that, manufacturers sell sharpeners designed specifically for their own products (and sometimes only particular models within a range). Ideally, you should use the recommended sharpener.

A sharpener for scissors uses a stone held at an angle in a slotted frame (Fig. 187).

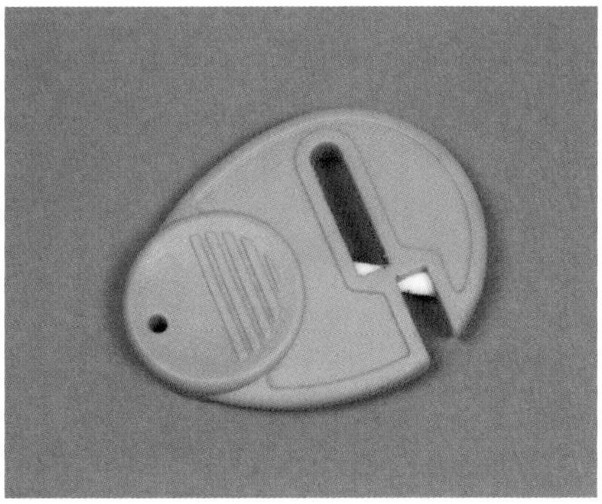

Fig. 187: A sharpener for scissors may consist of a stone held at an angle in a slotted frame. The model shown uses a ceramic rod as the abrasive.

Open and insert the legs of the scissors into the slots, then close the tips of the scissor blades on the stone (Fig. 188). Push the scissors into the slots while applying pressure. Pushing rather than pulling helps prevent the scissors dropping sharply out of the slot at the end of their travel, and causing injury. The stone is held at an angle to suit the bevelled side of each blade and sharpens that side of each blade. Repeat the action until the scissors are sharp. As an optional refinement, if you have a flat fine grit stone, place the flat back edge of a blade on the stone, in full contact, and pull it across the stone to remove any burr which has formed on the back of the cutting edge (Fig. 189). If the back of the blade has been hollow ground, the centre section will be dished and will not touch the stone, but that will not affect the deburring process. Repeat for the back of the other blade. Taking care to protect your fingers, clean the scissors under running water, then wipe each blade dry by drawing a cloth across the blade, at right angles to the sharpened edge, wiping from the blunt rear of the blade off the sharp edge (Fig. 183), to remove all grit and metal dust.

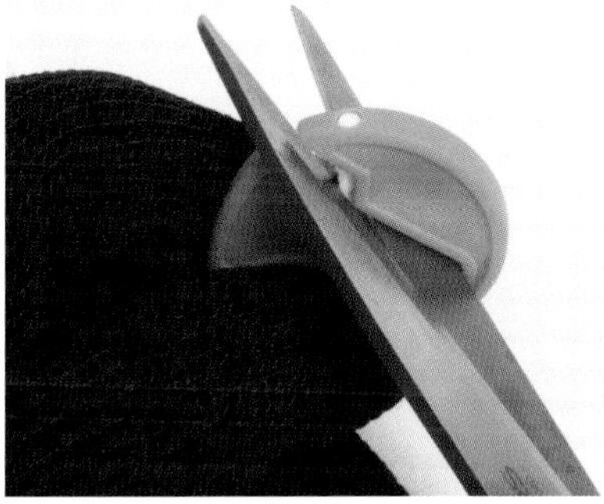

Fig. 188: Close the scissor tips on the stone, then push the scissor blades through the slots, to sharpen.

Fig. 189: After sharpening a blade, rub its flat back against a stone, to remove any burr.

HONING AND BURNISHING

Honing involves removing metal from a surface, using an abrasive stone. Honing sharpens, but slowly, using fine abrasives. Honing is normally used after basic sharpening, to produce a finer edge and a better finish on the bevel adjacent to the cutting edge.

Shaping differs from sharpening, in the degree of finish given to the work, so a tool might be shaped using a heavy grinding technique to remove the bulk of the metal to produce a close approximation of the shape of a tool and its cutting edge. The edge would be finished by sharpening, using a finer grade of abrasive.

Honing also differs from sharpening in the degree of finish given to the work. For many tasks, sharpening produces a sufficiently good edge. But honing continues the process, using much finer grades of abrasive, to produce a finer finish on the cutting edge and the area around that edge.

Burnishing is a non-abrasive process in which the work is rubbed, usually under pressure, to deform the surface and make it smoother and harder. Burnishing the area around a cutting edge produces a smoother finish, and a harder edge, both of which improve the performance of the cutting action and the finish on the object being cut. Technically, blunt grains in an abrasive surface will burnish rather than cut a surface. However; burnishing is normally understood as a separate process not involving abrasives.

Some multi-function powered sharpeners have angled slots to guide scissor blades across a revolving stone (Fig. 190). Draw the blade slowly through the slot(s) to sharpen it. Like powered knife sharpeners, these are designed for just one angle of cutting edge.

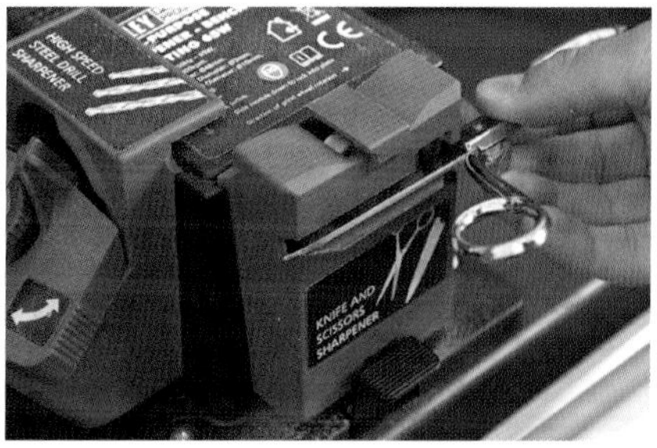

Fig. 190: On a powered sharpener, draw the blades of scissors through the slots, to sharpen them. Photo: JACK SEALEY LTD.

USING A FLAT STONE

Sharpening a knife

The grit of stone to use depends on the dullness of the blade, but a combination corundum stone with 400 and 1000 grit sides works well for most knives. The 400 grit brings a dull edge to shape very quickly, and the 1000 grit gives a good sharp edge, which is not surgically sharp but has a good combination of sharpness and shallow scratches on the edge which help the cutting process, providing sufficient sharpness for everyday use. A finer grit will give a keener edge, but the process will take longer.

Choose a stone of at least 180 x 65mm (7 x 2½ inch) and prepare the stone for use by soaking it in water or oil (*see* Chapter 1). The pores on the stone will tend to absorb the liquid. As the blade is drawn across the stone, the liquid acts as a lubricant and the particles of stone and metal shed in the process will combine with the liquid to form a slurry which helps sharpen the blade. If the stone is used dry it will smear as metal is removed from the blade but sticks on the surface of the stone, clogging it and inhibiting the sharpening process. Liquid also reduces the dust given off by the sharpening process. If using a stone dry, wear a dust mask.

Position the blade on one side of the stone, with the thicker blunt rear edge raised to form an edge angle of approximately 20 degrees, or whatever suits your own knife, between blade and stone (Fig. 191). Push the blade back and to the side, sliding the

Fig. 191: Holding a knife at its edge angle, push the blade diagonally towards the back of the stone while moving it across the stone.

cutting tip of the blade across the stone from heel to tip. Avoid letting the tip slide off the stone, as that may tend to round the point. Turn the blade over and repeat for the other side of the blade, using the same side of the stone. Continue this sequence until the blade has a continuous angled cutting edge which looks the same on both sides. If the blade is quite dull, quicker results can be achieved by making half a dozen strokes on one side of the blade, then half a dozen on the other side. Once the blade is sharp, take care to protect your fingers as you wipe the knife by drawing a cloth across the blade, at right angles to the sharpened edge, wiping from the blunt rear of the blade off the sharp edge (Fig. 83), to remove all grit, metal dust and slurry. Wash the blade under running water, then dry it carefully.

Turn the stone over to the finer grit, and repeat the process. This time, watch for a "wire edge" to form. This is a very fine thread-like sliver of metal which forms at the cutting edge (Fig. 192). Flip the blade over

Fig. 192: Watch for a 'wire edge' to form. In this photo, the fine wire-like sliver of metal is just breaking free from the edge of the blade.

and repeat the sharpening action until the wire just comes off. If no wire edge forms, just continue until the edge looks as sharp as you need. Clean the blade carefully; it's ready for use.

Angle guides can be used to set the angle at which the blade must be held against a stone, to create the bevel. The simplest might be a wedge with an included angle to match the angle of the bevel (Fig. 193). The blade can then be moved away from the wedge and sharpened freehand, but taping the wedge to the blade so that they move together will give the most accurate and consistent results. Double-sided tape may be useful for this. Simple plastic clips

Fig. 193: The edge angle of a knife blade may be set using a wedge, held in place using double-sided tape.

Fig. 194: A plastic clip may be used to position the blade approximately at the edge angle.

are available to hold a blade at an angle (Fig. 194), but most do not specify the angle, and, in any case, the angle will vary with the breadth and thickness of the blade. A broader blade will create a smaller included angle (Fig. 195) and a blade with a thicker rear edge will create a larger included angle.

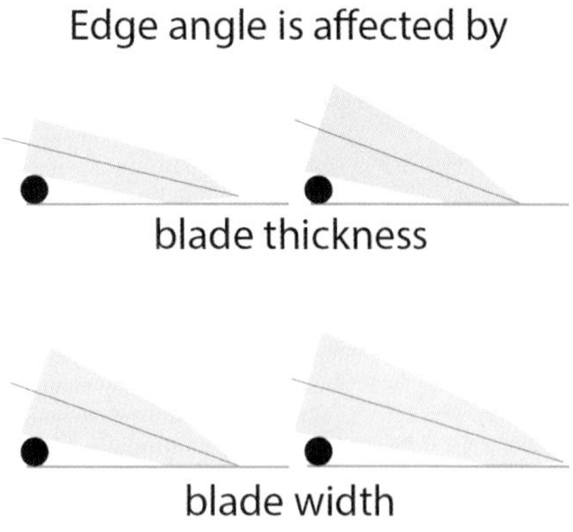

Fig. 195: When using a simple clip, the blade angle will depend on the blade's thickness and breadth.

Without a guide of some sort, it can be a little tricky to maintain the angle of tilt of a blade during sharpening, and the action can be made easier by tilting a stone or diamond plate (Fig. 196) to a near-vertical position. Hold the stone on a bench, with its

Fig. 196: Diamond-coated plates are available in a range of grades and dimensions.

working face vertical, then tilt it backwards by the half-angle of the blade (Fig. 197). Hold the blade vertically, with the cutting edge against the stone, and draw it down the stone. It is relatively easy to keep the blade vertical, and the initial tilt sets the grinding angle automatically. Perform five or six

Fig. 197: The blade may be held vertically, for sharpening, if the stone is tilted at the edge angle.

strokes on one side of the blade, then swing the stone around so that it is on the other side of the blade and repeat the process. Keep stroking and swapping until the blade is sharp. The Spyderco Tri-Angle sharpener (Fig. 198) takes this process a stage further,

Fig. 198: In the Spyderco Tri-Angle sharpener, pairs of stones are held upright, at the edge angle, and the knife is held vertically. Making alternate strokes down the two stones sharpens the blade. Photo: SPYDERCO.

providing pairs of stones of various grits mounted in a base unit and tilted at the edge angle. Between strokes the blade is moved across to the opposite stone, speeding the sharpening process.

A 'steel' (or 'honing steel') is a traditional tool used by butchers and chefs, and it consists of a length of steel, harder than the knife blade, which has ridges along the length of its surface (Fig. 199). It is used for burnishing rather than sharpening the cutting edge of a knife, but although it does not remove material, it will restore the sharpness of a slightly dulled cutting edge. A knife blade is held at an angle to the surface of the rod, so that the bevel behind the cutting edge is flat against the steel. The blade is then drawn down and across the side of the rod, ending with the tip of the blade coming off the rod near the bottom. Switch the blade to the other side of the rod; tilt to place the

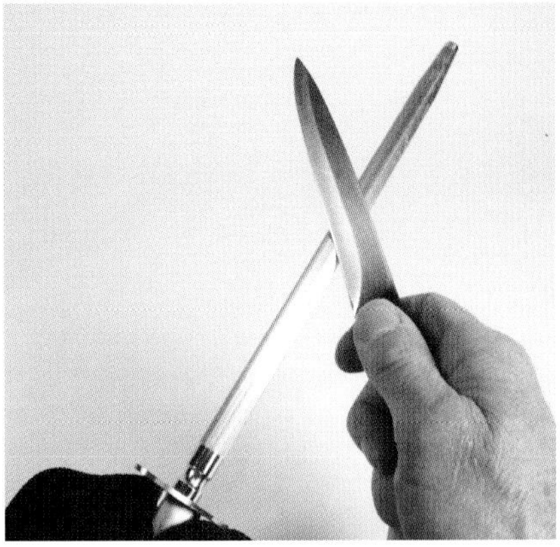

Fig. 199: The traditional 'honing steel' has ridges along its length. It may be made of hardened steel, ceramic abrasive, or diamond-coated steel. It is used for burnishing rather than sharpening blades.

bevel against the surface, and draw the blade down that side of the rod. The swiping-and-switching action can be repeated rapidly until the blade is sharp. Wear a cut-resistant glove throughout. Modern 'steels' may be made of steel or ceramic material, or coated with diamond particles. Ceramic and diamond particles are abrasives, so tend to sharpen rather than hone or burnish a cutting edge, but the action is faster.

Using a jig

A different approach is to hold the blade stationary and move a stone across the edge under mechanical guidance which maintains a controlled angle between stone and blade. Sharpening systems of this kind provide a holder for blades, a set of sharpening stones in different grits, and a rod system for fixing the angle at which the stone contacts the edge of the blade while allowing the rod to move in or out, and pivot up or down, at the hinge point. This provides a simple means of allowing the stone to swing across the blade while maintaining the angle (Fig. 200). The use of a jig allows the angle between stone and blade to be set initially, and maintained as sharpening takes place, because the stone cannot move further downwards than the

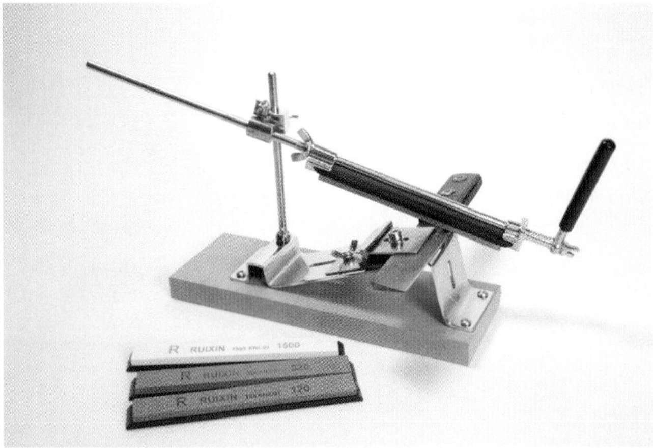

Fig. 200: Moving a stone under mechanical guidance allows the edge angle to remain constant along the length of the cutting edge.

edge of the blade. The sharpening action is a forward-and-sideways movement of the stone, releasing pressure or lifting off on the backward stroke. Work slowly along the length of the cutting edge. Long blades may be sharpened in stages, leaving the backstop in position. Critical features of these systems are: the rigidity of the jig; the effectiveness of the clamp (a common cause of problems); the grip between the base of the jig and the bench; and the effectiveness of the grip between holders and stones. Each make of system should be supplied with a chart giving details of the height at which to set the pivot to produce specific angles at the knife cutting edge. However; the best way to set the jig is to:

- clamp the knife blade so that the cutting edge butts against a setting stop (Fig. 201), then remove the stop;
- set the pivot in a low position and make a few back-and-forward swipes across the blade;
- use a magnifying glass to find where the stone is contacting the blade (checking for a bright line);
- adjust the height, and repeat the process of swiping and examining, until the stone contacts the whole of the bevel behind the cutting edge.

It is worth marking the gauge, or taking a note of the height of the pivot, for that blade. For a better finish on the cutting edge, repeat the process using finer stones.

Fig. 201: Position the cutting edge of a blade against a stop, then clamp the blade in that position. Remove the stop, to allow the stone to reach the cutting edge.

Sharpening serrations

Depending on the material being cut, serrations improve the cutting action of many knives. On some knives, there are serrations along one side of the cutting edge, but the opposite side is a plain flat face. In those cases, grinding the flat side may be enough to restore the sharp edge at the end of each serration, which saves a lot of work. Sharpening the blade in this way tends to shorten the serrations, so frequent sharpening will eventually change the shape of the serrations. Serrations lie below the surface of the cutting part of the blade, and if sharpening is required each serration needs to be treated separately. This requires a stone with a rounded edge, a cylindrical stone, a conical stone or a diamond file which is small enough to sit along the groove of the serration, although it does not have to be a perfect fit (Figs 202 and 203). Cylindrical stones to suit serrations are available for some sharpening systems, but an alternative is to use the standard stone tilted so that one corner lies in a serration (Fig. 204). Seat the stone in a single serration and rub it along the length of the groove (Fig. 204).

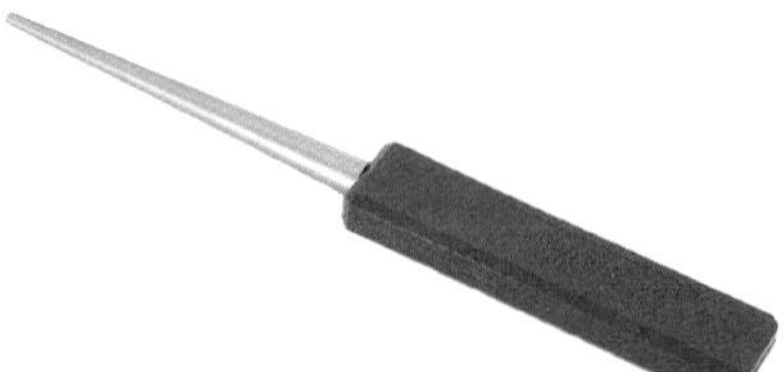

Fig. 202: A conical diamond file may be used to sharpen serrations on a knife. Photo: DMT.

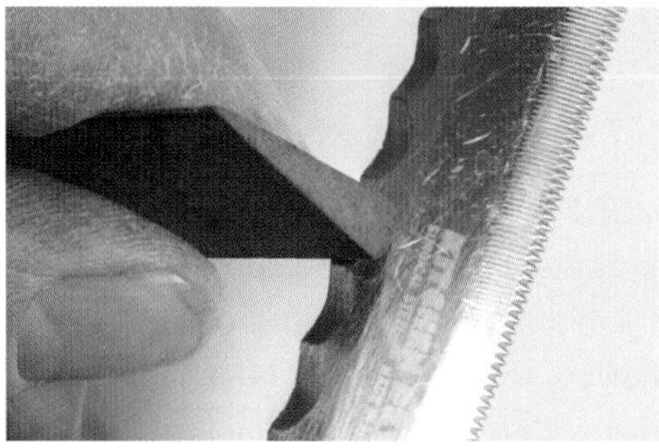

Fig. 203: Sharpen serrations using a stone with a rounded face.

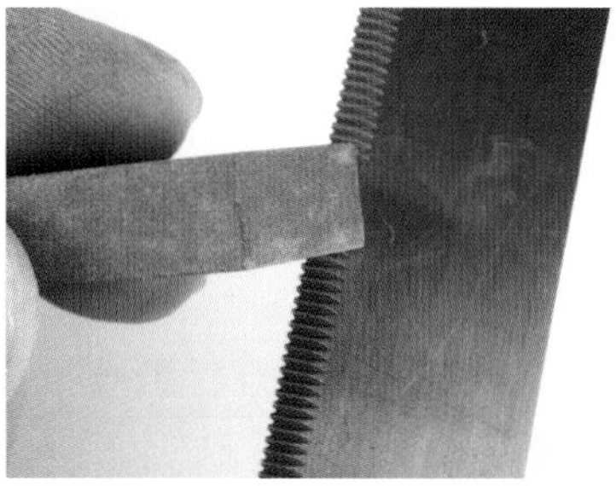

Fig. 204: Tilting a stone allows the corner to be used to sharpen a serration.

Where the serration is a broad scallop, roll the stone slightly from side to side, so that it sharpens the whole edge of that serration. Repeat for each serration. If the serrations are on both sides of the blade, repeat for the second side. If they are on one side only, turn the blade over and use the flat stone to gently remove any burr created by sharpening the serrations.

Dealing with curved blades

Blades which have an external curve can be sharpened on a flat stone, or in a jig (Fig. 205), in the same way as for straight-edged blades. The blade is swung along the curve as it is moved across the stone or the 'steel'. Using a jig, the stone naturally follows the curve of the blade. Blades which have an internal curve must be sharpened using an externally rounded stone (Fig. 206) or burnished against a 'steel' (Fig. 207), holding the blade at the edge angle throughout.

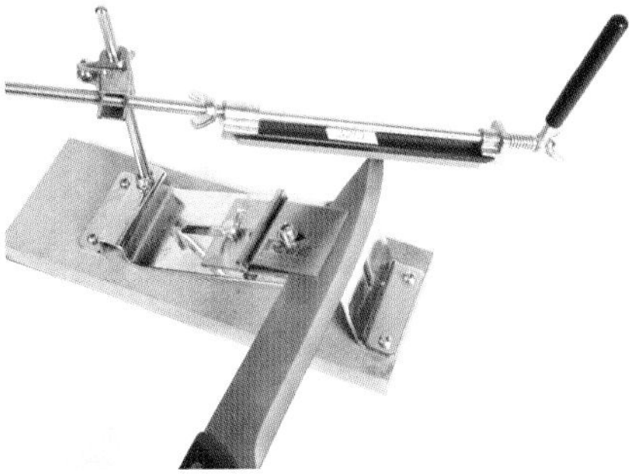

Fig. 205: An externally curved blade may be sharpened in the same jig as for straight blades.

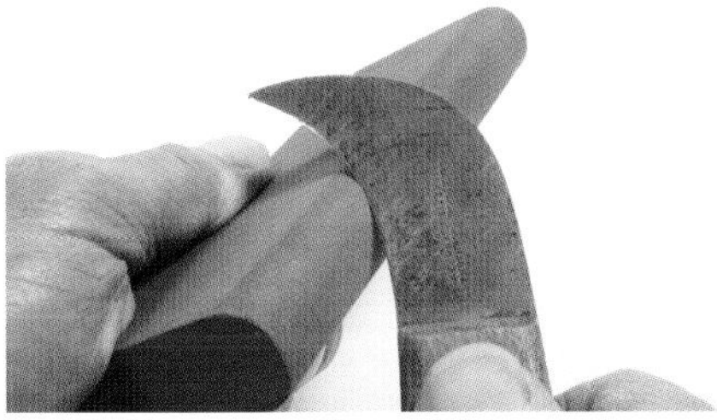

Fig. 206: Use an externally rounded stone to sharpen an internally curved cutting edge.

Fig. 207: Internally curved blades can be burnished against a 'steel' by holding the blade at the edge angle.

Sharpening scissors

Scissors which open more than 90 degrees can be sharpened on a stone. Scissors opening less than 90 degrees should be taken apart, if possible, to sharpen them on a stone. The cutting angle of scissors depends on their design and the task for which they are intended, so it is important to replicate the existing angle at the cutting edge. The flat back of a blade is never sharpened and although it may be rubbed while flat on a stone to remove a burr, it should never be held at an angle to the stone.

Freehand sharpening of scissors against a stone is not as easy as for a knife. Follow the process detailed earlier, for sharpening a knife blade against a stone, but take care to control the angle of tilt carefully and consistently; and control the other blade if the scissors are open, to prevent it contacting the stone or your fingers. It may help to place the stone at the edge of a bench, so that the free blade can hang in space. A template may provide a visual indication of the angle required, but gently rocking the blade while stationary may allow you to feel the bevel sitting against the stone. Alternatively, coat the bevel with marking-out blue, or a broad felt-tipped marking pen. The coating will be completely removed when the bevel is fully in contact with the stone as the blade is drawn across the stone. If the colour is only removed from the area nearest the cutting edge, hold the blade at a shallower angle. If the colour is only removed from the rear of the bevel, increase the angle of tilt. Fig. 208 suggests a different problem.

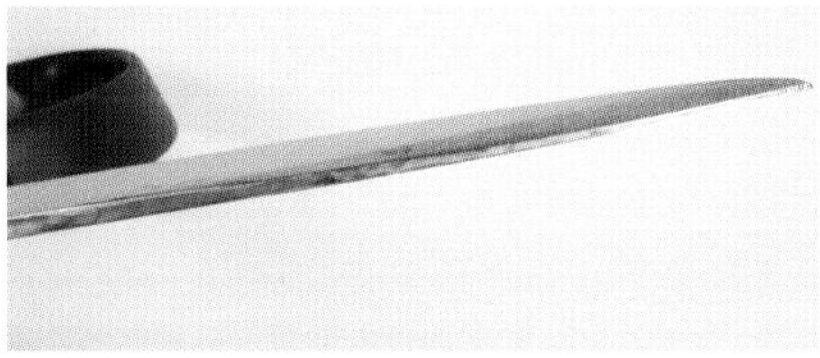

Fig. 208: The blue on this face indicates that the angle changes along the cutting edge, perhaps because the blade is not being held at a uniform angle, or because the initial grinding was inconsistent.

Fig. 209: Clamp scissor blades against the front face of a swinging-stone jig, to set the edge angle.

Scissors which can be disassembled may be sharpened using the same kind of jig, and the same technique, as for knife blades, but the blade is held against the vertical face of the base plate of the jig (Fig. 209) to accommodate the greater angle of the cutting edge.

Sharpening shears

Shears for cutting sheet metal are often called 'snips'. They tend to be heavier and have longer handles than scissors, and rather than moving the blade over a stationary stone it is sometimes easier to grip the shears in a vice and move a stone against the bevel (Fig. 210). The stone should be

Fig. 210: Shears may be held in a vice so that a stone can be moved over the bevel to sharpen the edge.

tilted to sit against the existing bevel, and should be drawn along and across the bevel to restore and sharpen the cutting edge. Gilbow fat-cheeked snips have an 85 degree angle at the cutting edge, while Irwin Aircraft Snips have a 25 degree angle, so it is important to inspect and measure the angle of the snips you intend to sharpen, perhaps by using an angle gauge or a Universal Bevel Protractor (Fig. 211), and try to replicate that angle accurately.

Fig. 211: An angle gauge or a Universal Bevel Protractor can be used to measure edge angles, especially when a good magnifier is also used.

As with a knife, use a coarse grade of stone to restore a blade which is very dull or which has minor damage such as nicks. Then use a fine grit to create a sharp edge. The angle of the cutting edge on shears is normally much more shallow than on scissors, because the cutting edge is under greater pressure, and needs more support.

The inside edges (the "back" of the blades) should be flat, with no bevel angle, and may be held against a stone for deburring.

Snips with curved blades (Fig. 212) are best sharpened by holding the blade stationary and using a hand-held stone with a curved face (Fig. 213).

Fig. 212: Snips (shears for cutting sheet metal) with curved blades can be used to cut curves.

Fig. 213: Snips with curved blades can be held in a vice and sharpened using a stone with a rounded face.

USING AN ABRASIVE BELT

A belt sander (Fig. 214) can be used *with care* to power-sharpen a knife or individual blades of scissors and snips, but not to sharpen assembled scissors or shears because there is too great a danger of the second blade catching on the belt or moving parts. Use a belt sander fitted with a 400 or 600 grit

Fig. 214: A belt sander, with the belt running horizontally or vertically can be used to sharpen a knife, or individual blades of scissors or shears. There are additional dangers when using a belt sander.

for initial sharpening, and 1200 grit for fine finishing. Use a cloth or mylar-backed resin-bonded aluminium oxide or silicon carbide belt. As an alternative, use the 400 or 600 grit belt until there is a wire edge or burr on the blade for finishing, then use a leather belt rubbed with a bar of honing compound to hone off the burr and finish the edge. When using a horizontal sander, the belt should be running away from you, and the back of the blade should be nearest you (Fig. 215). When using a vertical belt sander, the belt should be running downwards at the front, towards the rest, and the back of the blade should be uppermost (Fig. 216). If the rear tensioning plate is adjusted to keep the belt taut and flat against the plate, that helps present a

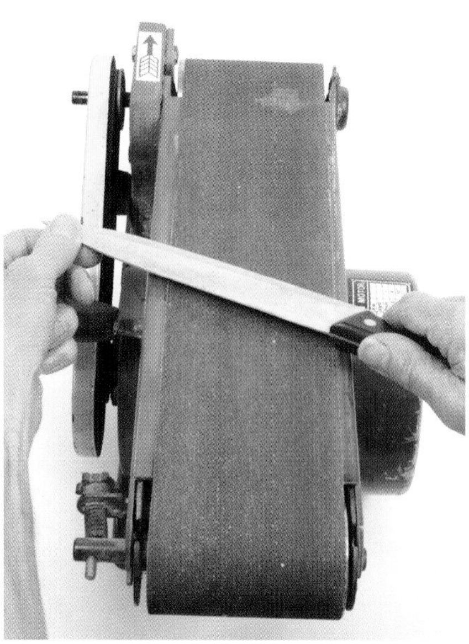

Fig. 215: When using a horizontal sander, the belt should be running away from you, and the rear of the blade should be facing you.

Fig. 216: When using a vertical sander, the belt should be running downwards, and the cutting edge of the blade should be facing downwards.

flat abrasive face to the blade, keeping the sharpened area well-defined. To produce a more rounded profile behind the cutting edge, adjust a vertical belt so that it is not kept taut by the rear tensioning plate, but move the plate backwards to allow some clearance between belt and plate (Fig. 217). The knife will press the blade backwards, creating a curve.

Note, however, that the rounded profile will not have the required angle right at the cutting edge, and these blades must be finally sharpened and/or honed by hand to create the correct angle.

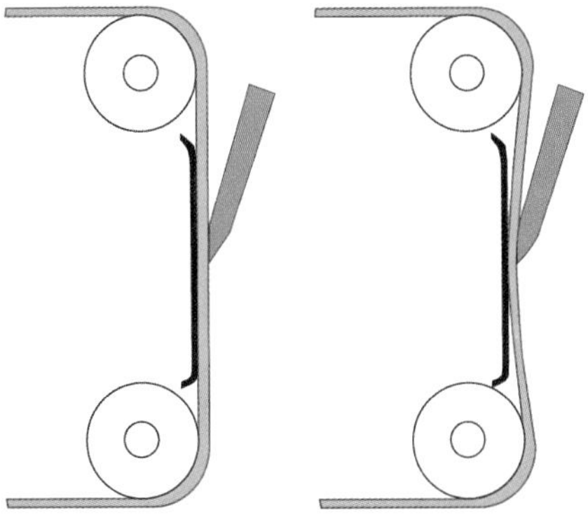

Fig. 217: Providing some clearance between belt and rear tensioning plate produces a more rounded profile behind the cutting edge.

Hold the blade as you would on a stone (Fig. 218), and move the blade slowly across the belt. Repeat for the opposite side of a knife blade or for the other blade of scissors or shears, sharpening the cutting edges equally. Take care not to apply uneven pressure or to sharpen for too long, as the rate of metal removal is much faster than with a stone. Use a light pressure and let the abrasive do the work.

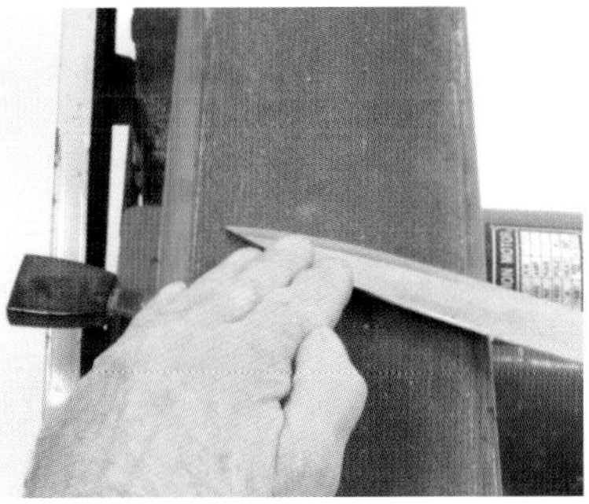

Fig. 218: Hold the blade as when sharpening on a stone, and move it slowly across the belt.

Once a blade has been sharpened on a belt, it will benefit from being honed using a very fine stone or a strop.

USING A STROP

A strop is a piece of material which is used to put a final razor-sharp edge on a sharpened blade. Strops are often made of leather, canvas, MDF or wood (Fig. 219), and they are used like an abrasive stone. A strop is used

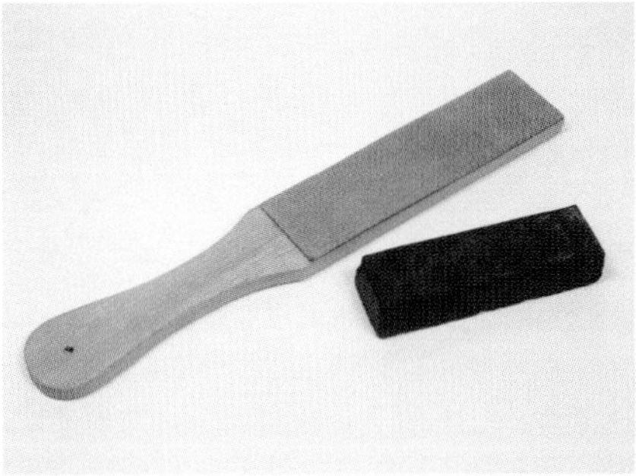

Fig. 219: A strop is made of material such as leather (shown here), MDF or wood which can be 'charged' (impregnated) with abrasive by rubbing it with a paste containing fine abrasive particles.

with an abrasive compound in the form of a paste which is rubbed onto the strop (Fig. 219). The paste contains fine grit particles which impregnate the strop, forming a fine abrasive surface capable of polishing the cutting edge. This kind of strop was common in older barbers' shops for putting a keen edge on an open cut-throat razor for shaving. The strop may be a strip of leather or canvas pulled tight by the operator. One end was sometimes fixed on a hook, and the other end pulled with one hand while the razor was moved quickly up and down the strop, held at the appropriate angle. More consistent cutting angles can be achieved if the leather or canvas is glued to a rigid strip of wood, so that the strop does not flex under the pressure of the blade and round the bevel at the cutting edge.

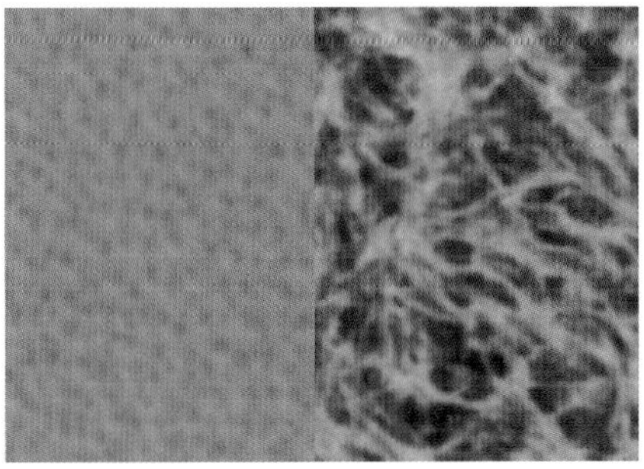

Fig. 220: A leather strop usually has two sides. The hair side (on the left) is smooth and is normally impregnated with abrasive paste. The flesh side (on the right) is sufficiently abrasive in its own right to be used as the final surface to give a very fine finish.

Rub the paste into the strop, then move the blade up and down the strop using the same action as when sharpening against a stone. Clean the blade under running water, and wipe it dry against a paper or cloth towel by dragging the blade back-first. Your hand should not touch the blade. When using different grades of abrasive, it is best to avoid cross-contamination by using a different strop for each grade, and keeping each strop for use exclusively with one grade of abrasive. Widely-held opinion suggests horse butt leather makes the best material for a strop, and two strops are a good idea. Leather has two sides (Fig. 220). The first is the hair side, which is the smooth side which faces out, on the animal. The second side is next to the flesh and is usually rough (although this side is used to make suede, if it is treated). Use the first strop hair side (smooth side) upwards. Impregnate with a fine abrasive paste (a proprietary paste bar, or 0.05 grit diamond paste), which can be diluted with baby oil to make it finer, if necessary. Hone the blade on this, then clean carefully (Fig. 183). Change to the second strop, which should have the flesh side facing up. Strop dry.

Treat the honed blade with respect; it is surgically sharp, so keep your hands and other body parts well clear, both when honing and when using the blade.

Tool type 2: Screwdrivers

Screws designed to be tightened using a screwdriver typically suit slotted, Phillips, or Pozidrive screwdrivers. Although it is possible to re-form the ends of Phillips or Pozidrive screwdrivers, this is often time-consuming and uneconomic. In many cases, Phillips and Pozidrive tips are coated with diamond dust to provide grip, and regrinding removes that coating, leaving the tips less useful. The humble flat-bladed screwdriver is designed to suit a screw with a slotted head, and sharpening this kind of screwdriver can be done quickly and economically.

Flat-bladed screwdrivers come in a wide range of shapes and sizes, ranging from the tiny watchmaker's sizes to the large two-handed jobs as long as a forearm. The geometry is similar, though, and the blades are ground in one of two patterns. The first is a tapered grind, where the faces of the blade have flat sides (Fig. 221); and the second is a hollow grind (Fig. 221), sometimes called 'gunsmith pattern'. The effectiveness of the two patterns differs, depending on the shape of the slot in the screw being tightened or loosened. Watchmakers often use a slotting file to create slots in screwheads. Those slots are likely to be tapered, so watchmakers' screwdrivers have a tapered grind to ensure they fit the slot snugly (Fig. 222). Modern machine-cut screw heads normally have a slot with parallel sides, but taper-ground blades only contact the top of a parallel-sided screw slot (Fig. 222), creating high pressure right at the top edge, which makes it more likely that the screwdriver blade will distort that edge. There is also a tendency for the edges of the slot to force the screwdriver blade upwards, out of the slot. Hollow ground blades sit nicely in a slot with parallel sides (Fig. 223), but cannot sit fully into a tapered slot, and tend to twist out of the slot. Choose the grind to suit the screw. One further factor is the direction of the striations on the working section of the blade tip. Rather than producing a finely honed mirror finish on the working faces, leaving scratches on the tip helps provide grip against the walls of the screw head slot. Opinions differ, though, as to whether the striations should run parallel to the screwdriver shank, or at right angles to the axis of the shank (Fig. 224), and in most cases the grinding method can be chosen to produce a particular orientation. Useful stones for sharpening screwdriver blades are: a medium grit India stone and, where a finer finish is required, either a fine India stone or a white Arkansas stone. A fine finish will reduce the depth of the striations, but reduce the grip.

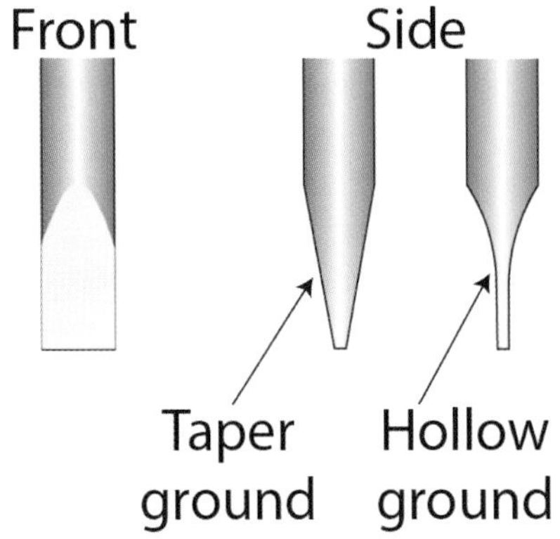

Fig. 221: Flat-bladed screwdrivers may be taper ground or hollow ground.

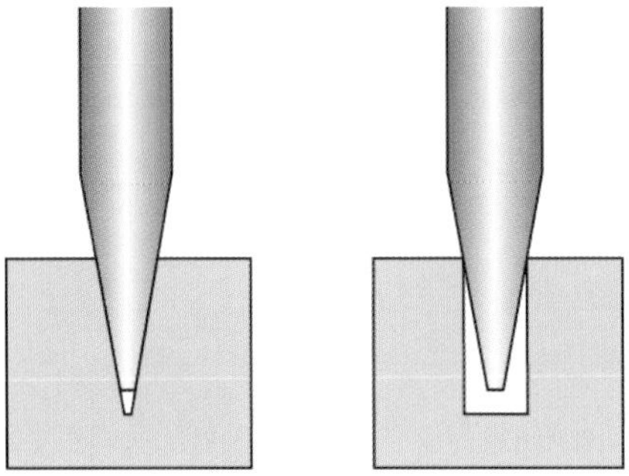

Fig. 222: Taper ground blades fit tapered screwhead slots, but stress the edges of parallel-sided slots.

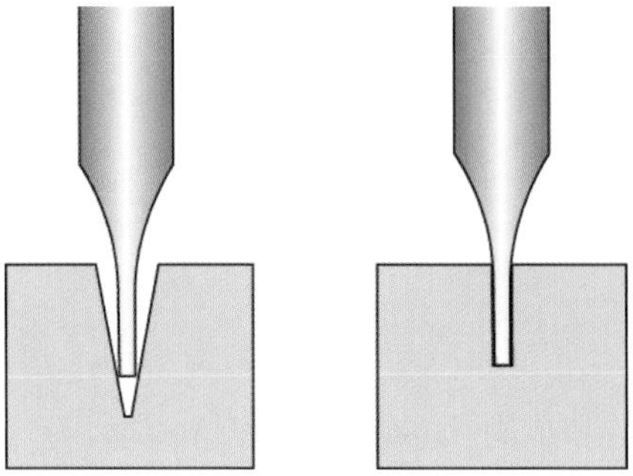

Fig. 223: Hollow ground blades fit snugly into a same-size parallel-sided slot, but not a tapered slot.

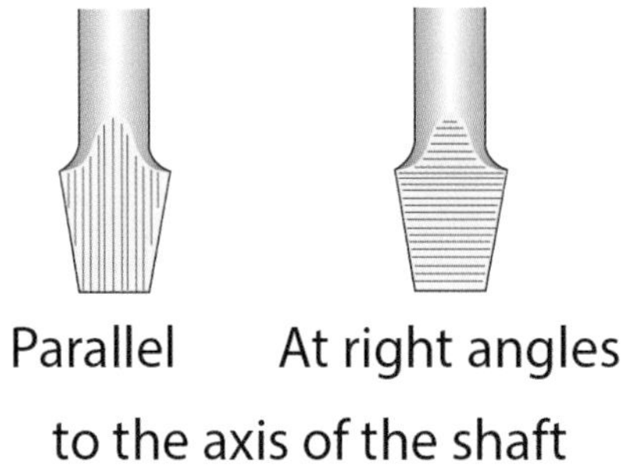

Fig. 224: The direction of the striations (scratches) is determined by the direction of the abrasive grains as they pass the blade.

BLADES AND HEADS

The operating end of a screwdriver, which sits in the recess in a screwhead and turns the screw, is a blade. The blade is at the end of the shaft, and has two faces. The blade end is sometimes called the 'head', or 'tip'.

'Flat-blade' describes the shape of the faces but also refers to a screwdriver designed to fit a screw with a slotted head.
These are sometimes called 'slot-head' screwdrivers.
'Slot-head' would be more appropriate for the screw, but it is the same kind of term as used to refer to a 'cross-head' screwdriver, meaning its tip fits a screw head with a cross-shaped recess.

Gunsmiths use the term 'turnscrew' to refer to a screwdriver intended for slotted screws.

Shanks often have a circular cross-section, but the 'London pattern' screwdriver has a flat shank, and some cabinet-makers' screwdrivers have a shaft which is flat near the handle, and has a circular section towards the blade.

Blades may be either straight (Fig. 221) or flared (Fig. 224).

Viewed from the front (Fig. 221), straight blades are the same width as the shaft, all the way down to the tip. This is often referred to as a 'cabinet'-style tip.

Flared blades have shoulders which are wider than the shaft, and taper down to a tip which is less broad than the shoulders (Fig. 224). This is sometimes referred to as a 'keystone' style tip.

TAPER-GROUND BLADES

The flat faces of small straight taper-ground blades can be sharpened by moving the tip of the blade along a bench stone while pressing the face against the stone to reproduce the existing angle of the face (Fig. 225). Uneven pressure on the front or rear will tend to grind the face at a different angle, and pressing more to one side than the other will tilt the blade to one side. Flip the face over (by rotating through half a turn) to grind the other face. However; any difference in side pressure makes it likely that the two faces will have a sideways taper towards

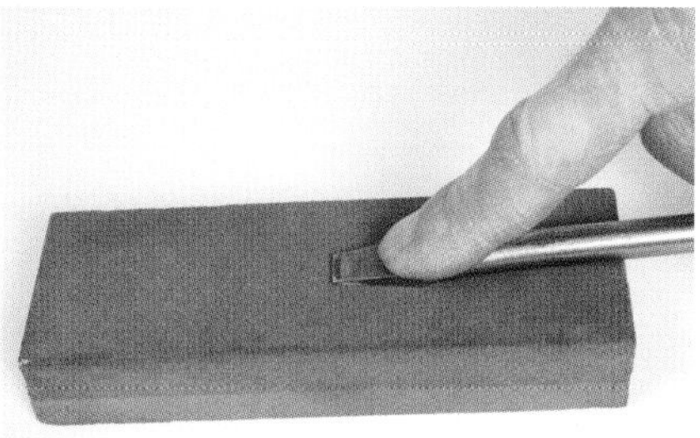

Fig. 225: Sharpening a taper ground blade by sliding it along a bench stone is possible but is likely to introduce errors if the tip is small and the blade tilts.

Fig. 226: A simple tool can be used to grip and guide a screwdriver blade as it is moved along the surface of an abrasive stone. The central hole opens as the wheels are squeezed towards one another.

one another. A more controllable method is to use a screwdriver sharpening tool (Fig. 226). Insert the screwdriver into the tool by squeezing the wheels towards one another to open the hole in the axle, and slip the screwdriver through (Fig. 227). The length of blade protruding determines the angle

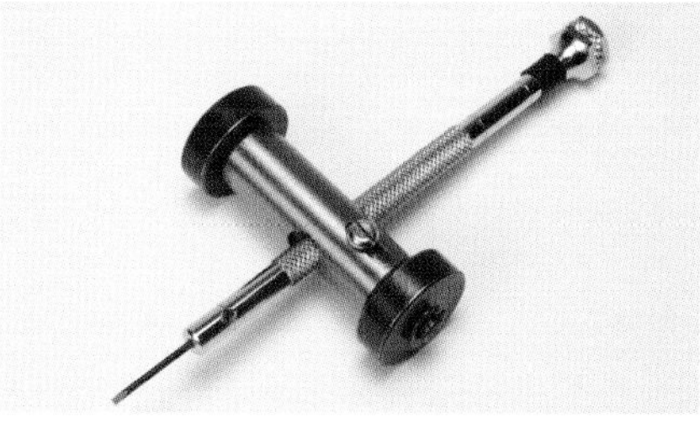

Fig. 227: The tool is spring-loaded and grips the screwdriver firmly.

of the face of the blade, and it is possible to adjust the projection while using a magnifying glass to examine the way the screwdriver sits against the stone, adjusting the protrusion until the face of the blade sits flat on the stone. Grind the face by moving the tool and screwdriver assembly backwards and forwards along the stone, using light pressure to keep the blade in contact with the stone (Fig. 228). For a more predictable

Fig. 228: Move the tool and screwdriver along the surface of an abrasive stone, applying just enough pressure to keep the blade in contact with the stone.

result, use an angle template, or set the protrusion of the blade from the tool by calculation and measurement. Fig. 229 shows that the angle of the face compared to the long axis of the blade (called the 'half-angle') can be calculated using the formula:

P = W / TanA

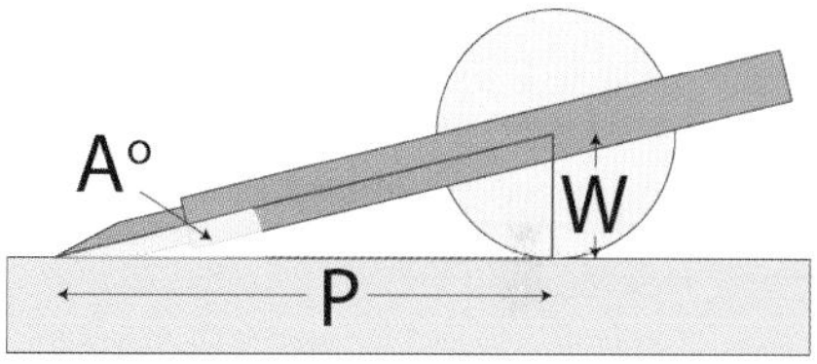

Fig. 229: The protrusion of the screwdriver determines the half-angle of the blade.

where P is protrusion; W is the distance from the stone to the centre line of the screwdriver, and A is the half-angle. The total included angle of a screwdriver blade is often stated as being 16 degrees (approximately), but the watchmaker's screwdriver shown in Fig. 229 has an included angle of 22 degrees so the half-angle is 11 degrees.

On the sharpener shown in Fig. 228 W is the radius of the wheel, which is 7.87mm, so:

P = W / TanA

P = 7.87 / Tan11 = 7.87 / 0.194

P = 40.6mm (41mm approximately)

Place a ruler at the side of the wheel and set the tip 41mm from the centre of the wheel, measured along the stone.

Where the stone is insufficiently broad to allow the sharpener to roll on its surface, the stone can be recessed into a wooden block (Fig. 230). Once the first face of the blade has

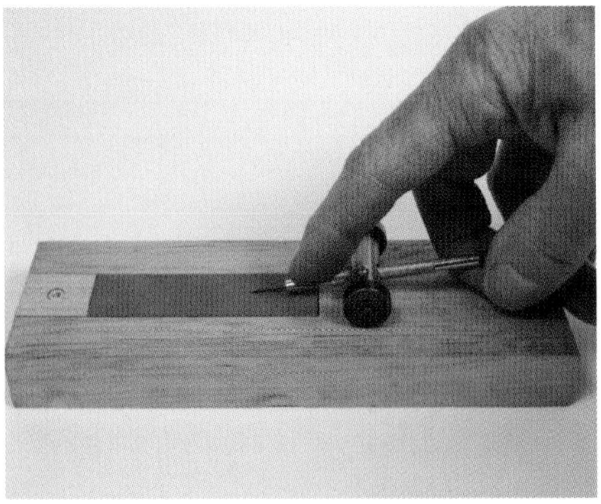

Fig. 230: A narrow stone can be recessed into a wooden or plastic block, with the top surfaces of stone and block at the same level.

been ground flat, leave the grip unchanged and flip the jig over, to ensure the second face will be ground parallel to the first. Once the second face has been ground flat, examine the positions of the points at which the faces meet the circular side of the shaft (Fig. 231). These points should be level, and opposite one another. If not, a few additional strokes on one side may help.

The sharpening tool shown in Fig. 227 produces striations parallel to the shank of the screwdriver, but in the VersaLab sharpener

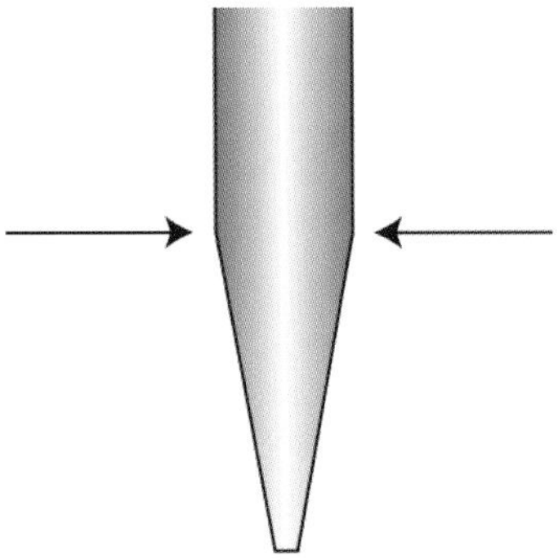

Fig. 231: When correctly sharpened, the points at which the faces meet the circular sides of the shaft should be opposite one another.

Fig. 232: In use, the VersaLab sharpener guides the screwdriver blade sideways across an abrasive stone, producing striations at right angles to the shaft. Photo: VERSALAB INC.

(Fig. 232) the screwdriver is moved sideways across a stone, producing striations running at right angles to the axis of the screwdriver. The angle of the stone is adjusted to suit the blade half-angle, using a template supplied with the tool, and the holder is guided along a steel bar positioned parallel to the stone. The holder is flipped over to grind the opposite face of the blade, ensuring both faces are parallel. Carry out the same check on the points at which the faces meet the cylindrical shaft, making a few extra strokes if necessary.

Once sharpened, the end of a screwdriver blade can be squared off by holding it vertically and drawing it backwards and forwards along a stone (Fig. 233). This is difficult to do freehand, but a screwdriver can

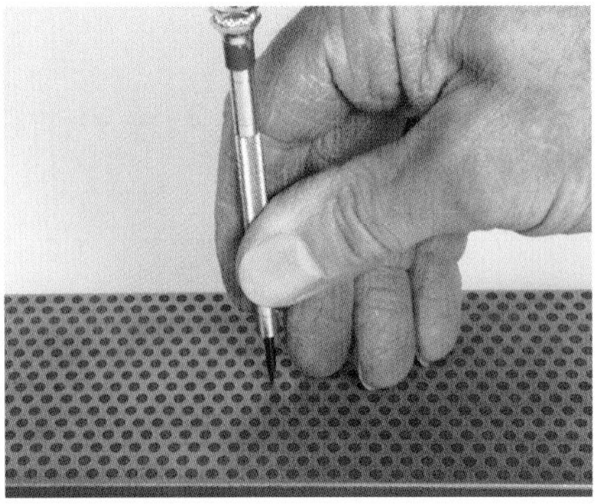

Fig. 233: It is difficult to hold a screwdriver vertical while moving it forwards and backwards along the stone, to square off the end face.

Fig. 234: To square the end of a blade, grip it in a sleeve in a two-roller sharpener, protruding so that one roller is held up in the air, then roll it along the stone until both rollers are in contact with the stone.

be held vertically in a sleeve in a two-roller graver sharpener (Fig. 234). Leave either the sleeve or the screwdriver loose, and allow the weight to push the screwdriver against the stone, assisted by light finger pressure if necessary. With the blade aligned approximately broadside to the direction of traverse, roll the sharpener backwards and forwards to square off the blade. Where a small screwdriver has a removable blade, it may be easier to mount the blade alone in the sleeve. Rather than pressing down on the screwdriver or blade, grip the blade in the collar, then set the end of the blade low enough so that one roller is held in the air by the thickness of a sheet of paper, then tighten the collar in the tool. Pushing the tool backwards and forwards over the stone removes material from the blade, and the sharpener descends until both rollers are in full contact with the stone. After that, no more will be ground from the blade, so this is a self-limiting process. To remove more material, set the blade a little lower, and repeat the grinding process. The Horotec sharpener (Fig. 235) holds the screwdriver vertically in a collet mounted in a plate and guided by horizontal bars. Although not visible in the photograph, there is a flat stone at the far side of the base, directly under the furthest collet hole, which can be used to square the end of a screwdriver blade.

Fig. 235: To square off the end of a blade in a Horotec sharpener, the blade is mounted in a collet above a flat stone (not visible in the photo, but on the far side of the front abrasive cylinders), and guided by rods. Photo: HOROTEC SA.

The faces of larger taper-ground screwdrivers may be ground against the flat face of a rotating medium or fine grit cup or tapered cup wheel. Fig. 236 shows a flat sliding guide plate fitted with a vee block and clamp which can hold circular-section shafts securely. The vee block assembly pivots in the square block, which has a lock to prevent unwanted rotation.

- Set the tip vertical by using an engineer's square before tightening the clamps.
- Mount a tee guide against the front of the rest, with the arm parallel to the face of the wheel. Swing the workhead to bring the face of the blade parallel to the axis of traverse (the face of the wheel).
- Apply a depth of cut by sliding the guide to the right, and clamp it or set a stop (Fig. 236), then traverse the blade forwards, across the face of the wheel. Fine, consistent, depth of cut can be achieved by releasing the stop; inserting a feeler blade between stop and sliding guide; resetting the stop against the feeler; then removing the feeler. Alternatively, use a screw-adjustable stop.
- Turn the screwdriver through half a turn and set the second side vertical. A cabinet-style screwdriver with a uniform circular-section shank and same-width tip can be gripped in a square-section sleeve seated in the vee block, to maintain alignment after a half-turn.

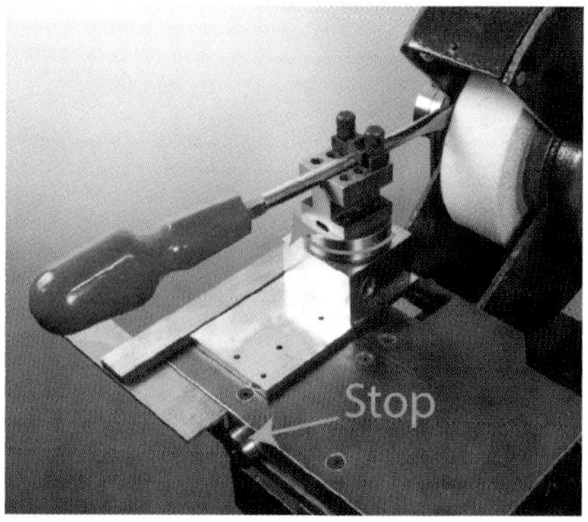

Fig. 236: Set a guide, and swing the workhead to bring the face of the screwdriver against the face of the wheel. A stop can be used to control depth of cut.

HOLLOW-GROUND BLADES

The tip of a hollow-ground screwdriver has parallel faces, and a blending curve where the tip meets the shank. Small hollow-ground blades, as found on watchmakers' screwdrivers, can be sharpened manually by traversing along between a pair of stationary cylindrical stones which sharpen both sides of the blade simultaneously, and shape the blending curves (Fig. 237). In the Horotec sharpener (Fig. 235) the curved surfaces of the two cylindrical stones shape the blending curve at the top of the blade, and the adjustable gap between the stones is set to the thickness of the tip of the blade.

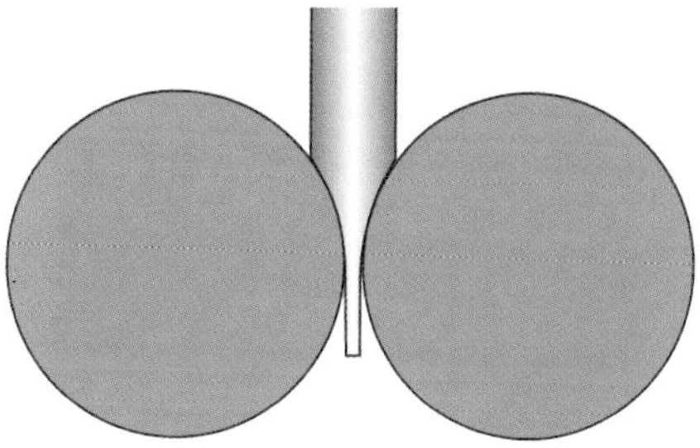

Fig. 237: Manually traversing a blade between two stationary cylindrical stones grinds the tip to the thickness of the gap, and blends the tip into the shaft.

The blade is held vertically in a collet during grinding, and the rails guide the movement of the tool holder backwards and forwards while gentle pressure is applied to the collet.

On larger screwdrivers, the blending curve can be ground against the curved face of an abrasive stone or a grinding wheel with a small enough diameter to match the curve of the top of the blade (Fig. 238). The working surface of the screwdriver is the tip of the blade, so an exact match for the top curve is not essential, but it does look neater if the curves blend or match closely.

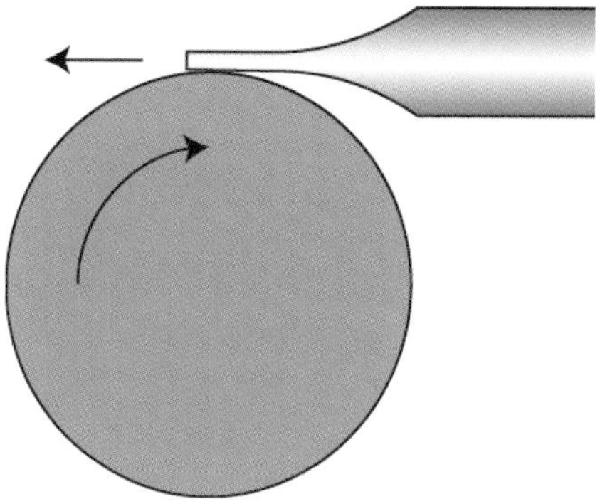

Fig. 238: A tip may be ground against a rotating wheel with a diameter to suit the blending curve.

The curve may also be ground against a rounded corner dressed on the edge of a type 1 wheel. (Fig. 239). Use a diamond dresser to shape the corner, finishing with a dressing stick.

Fig. 239: Set the blade vertical, then feed into the wheel, allowing the rounded corner to create the blending curve. Use a guide to control direction.

Tool type 3: Chisels

Chisels for metalworking are of two general types; cold chisels (Fig. 240), used for cutting metals which have not been heated to any great extent, and hot chisels, used for cutting metals which are in a hot softened state (typically red hot).

Most chisels in common use are cold chisels, but the same principles and tool shapes apply to hot chisels.

The included cutting angle of a cold chisel (Fig. 241) varies between 60 degrees and 90 degrees. Use 60 degrees for cutting relatively soft material such as aluminium, 70 degrees for cutting soft steel, and 90 degrees for cutting hard steel. A smaller angle allows the chisel to penetrate soft work relatively easily, but harder steels need more force, and a larger angle at the cutting edge makes the tip of the chisel stronger and better able to withstand the greater pressure before blunting or breaking. Chisels may also have a secondary relief angle to provide clearance for cut metal passing over the tip of the chisel.

Fig. 240: Four basic types of cold chisel. From the left: flat, round nose, cross-cut, and diamond point.

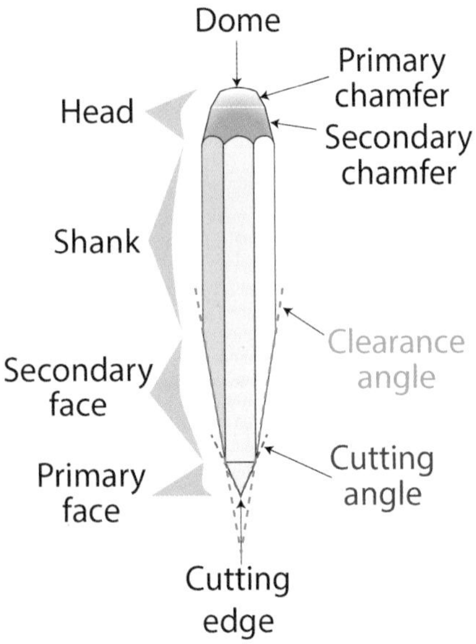

Fig. 241: The included angle of a cold chisel is the angle between the faces behind the cutting edge.

There are four principal shapes of cold chisel; flat, cross cut, round nose, and diamond point (Fig. 240); and there are other variations for more specialist jobs. Fig. 242 shows a bolster chisel (often used for splitting bricks, but also useful as a wide, thin, chisel on sheet steel) which has the same tip geometry as a flat chisel, but a longer cutting edge and a thinner secondary face (the blade).

Fig. 242: A bolster chisel.

REMOVING A BURR FROM THE HEAD

The head of a chisel is struck with a hammer, and because that end of the chisel is soft it will gradually deform. The shaft is strong enough to resist buckling under the force of the blow, so the metal at the end has nowhere else to go but outwards, forming a burr on the end of the chisel (Fig. 243). If the burr is not removed, it will spread sideways and split. Fragments may then break off and fly outwards with considerable speed, presenting a danger to the operator or anyone else in the vicinity. The head of the chisel is left soft because the face of the hammer striking the chisel is hardened, and

Fig. 243: Burrs form on the head of a chisel because of repeated hammer blows.

hitting one hardened surface with another is dangerous, as the surfaces may shatter. Although initially soft, the head of the chisel will work harden under repeated blows from the hammer, making it more likely that the burr will split and shatter, so the burr should be removed before it grows to any size, by grinding it off.

This is best done by pressing the burr against the face of a coarse grinding wheel, mounted on a bench grinder. Most of the burr can be removed by holding the chisel in one of the two positions shown in Figs 244 and 245. The end of the chisel may become hot, but should not be allowed to change

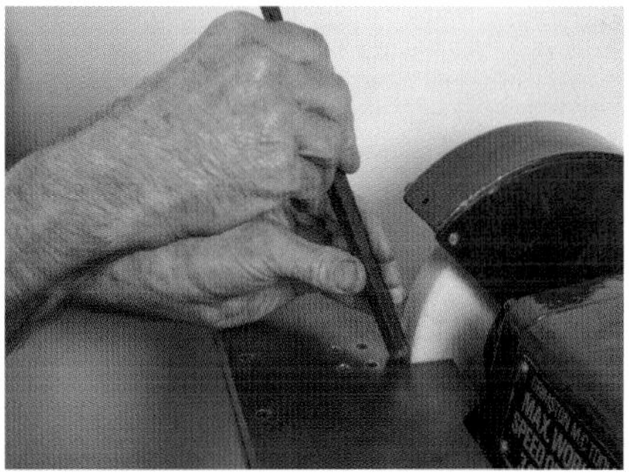

Fig. 244: A burr can be removed by holding the chisel nearly upright, supported by its dome, on the rest, while rotating it against the wheel.

colour (e.g. to blue). As the end becomes noticeably warm, allow it to cool naturally in air rather than quenching it in water, to minimize any structural change in the metal. If the chisel has changed colour, it is being heat treated, and quenching in water plays a part in that.

Fig. 245: A burr can be removed by holding the chisel almost flat on the rest while rotating the shank.

Once the burr has been removed, chamfer the head of the chisel by holding it at an angle to the wheel (Fig. 246) and rotating it. Chisels normally have a six or eight-sided

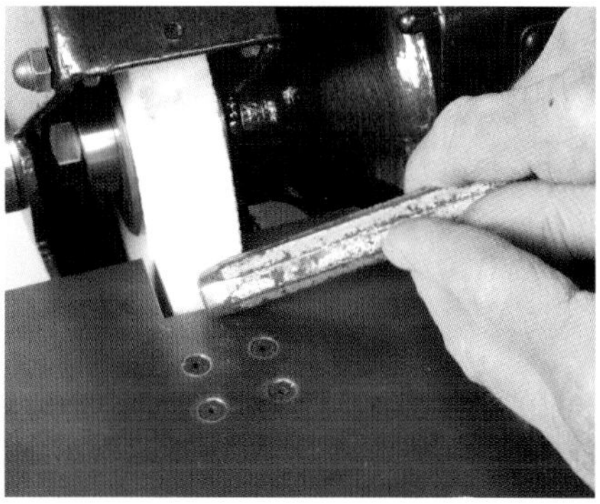

Fig. 246: To form a chamfer on the head, rotate the chisel while holding it at an angle to the wheel.

shank, which makes it difficult to rotate the chisel smoothly. The chisel can be held almost vertically, supported by its head in contact with the rest and tilted to create the angle of the chamfer. However; the length of metal in contact with the wheel will be relatively small, resulting in a rather small tapered area. Although forming this kind of chamfer on a chisel is not a precision operation, a simple jig can be used to give better results. Fig. 247 shows a chisel sitting in hole drilled in a short length of flat-faced steel bar which can be clamped to the rest. The internal diameter of the hole is slightly larger than the shank of the chisel, which allows the chisel to rotate smoothly. There is considerable leeway here, and the size of the hole is not critical. The fit should be

Fig. 247: A small chisel can be supported as it rotates in a hole in a steel block.

Fig. 248: Larger chisels can be supported inside a short length of steel pipe fixed to a plate.

loose, and one size of hole will serve for a small range of chisel shank diameters. Fig. 248 shows a pipe welded to a U-section channel and attached to a plate by screws. The assembly can be clamped on a grinder rest so that the chisel lies at a suitable angle to the wheel. Feed is by hand, feeding the chisel through the pipe as metal is removed to form the end. The chamfer angle is not critical, and might be approximately 20 degrees for a single primary chamfer (Fig. 249). The end may also carry a double chamfer, as shown in Fig. 249, to slow the growth of burrs even more. Using a single or double chamfer is a matter of personal preference.

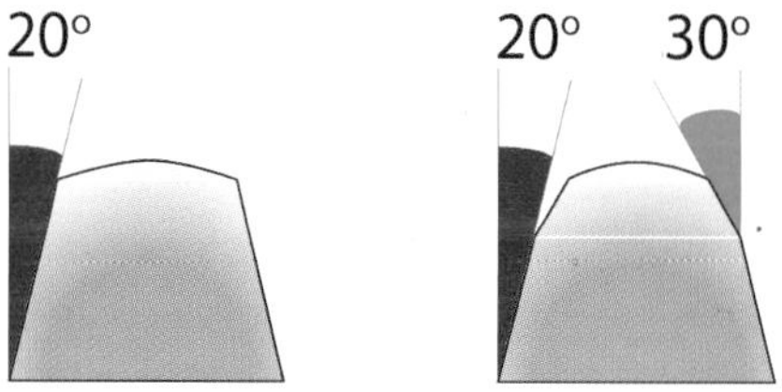

Fig. 249: Suggested angles for single and double head chamfers. These values are not critical.

A collection of pipes and bored blocks can be assembled to suit a range of chisels. Sleeves fitted with grub screws can be used to increase the diameter of smaller chisels, so that they can fit into the larger tubes (Fig. 250).

STRAIGHT OR CROSS CUT CHISELS

Fig. 250: Pipes and bored blocks with holes of various diameters can accommodate a range of chisels. Sleeves allow smaller chisels to be rotated in larger holes.

Using a bench grinder and the basic sliding feed plate

For speed, some people prefer to hand-hold a chisel against a wheel as shown in Fig. 251, resting the chisel on a single support. The theory is that with the wheel stationary, it might just be possible to feel for the angle of the cutting edge as the cutting face sits against the wheel. Holding the chisel at that angle, and moving it smartly across the rotating wheel freshens the face. Repeated

Fig. 251: It may be possible to rest a chisel against a single point of support, and 'feel' for the angle of the face against the wheel.

passes restore the cutting edge, and repeating the process on the other cutting face of the chisel completes the job. This is likely to result in varying cutting angles and a cutting edge which is not square to the axis of the chisel. It is also fraught with danger, so it is not a recommended method. The same basic method can be made much more precise by using some simple aids.

There is no guarantee that the cutting edge of the chisel will be parallel to any of the flats on the chisel shank, and viewing a selection of chisels from the cutting end, with one facet of the shank held flat against a reference surface, confirms that the flats cannot be used as a reliable reference surface (Fig. 252). This can be remedied

Fig. 252: Flats on a chisel shank may not be aligned with the cutting edge or the faces.

by using a sleeve with grub screws to grip the shank on one of its flats (Fig. 253). The grub screws will engage with a flat side of the chisel, but the circular-section sleeve allows the assembly to be rotated to orient the cutting edge with the tool rest and the wheel face. That effectively gives the chisel a circular shaft, allowing the assembly to be rotated until the face behind the cutting edge of the chisel is parallel to the face of the wheel. The sleeve can be clamped in a vee groove in a vee block (Fig. 253), a simple jig made from steel box section and angle (Fig. 254), or a bored block. Take up the slack on the external clamp but leave the sleeve free to rotate, for alignment. Sit the assembly on a flat surface, and arrange an upstanding edge parallel to the flat surface and a little

Fig. 253: A chisel in a sleeve can be clamped in a vee block.

Fig. 254: A chisel in a sleeve can be gripped in a simple holder made from steel box section and angle.

higher than the underside of the chisel (Fig. 255). The upstanding edge is set at right angles to the side of the external clamp, as that will be the surface used to guide the clamp towards the wheel. That way, the chisel cutting edge will be formed parallel to the upstanding edge, and at right angles to the side of the clamp. The assembly can be tilted upwards then lowered down against the upstanding edge to align the flat relief

Fig. 255: The chisel is aligned against an upstanding edge parallel to the flat surface on which everything sits, and at right angles to the side of the clamp. The chisel cutting edge will be at right angles to the shaft.

face of the chisel with the base of the holder. The clamp is then tightened, and the cutting edge will be parallel to the base of the vee block or jig.

The cutting edge must now be positioned parallel to the face of the wheel, and tilted upwards to create the primary cutting angle. The length of a typical chisel and the size of the cutting angle mean the chisel must be positioned high on the wheel, and the rest must be steeply tilted. There will be a spot which allows the cutting angle to be formed accurately, but although this might be calculated, it is much easier to use a template to set the rest. However; the height of the cutting edge above the rest must be taken into account. Whether the chisel shank is lying directly on the rest, or the chisel is held in a jig, the height of the cutting edge should be measured from the surface on which the template will sit; typically the rest or the slide which carries the chisel holder (*see* pages 40–43).

- Choose a template to match the angle of the cutting edge on the underside of the chisel. This will be half the included angle of the chisel cutting edge (30 degrees for a 60 degree included angle; 45 degrees for a 90 degree included angle).
- Sit both the template and the chisel in its holder on the same flat surface, and mark the template at the same height as the cutting edge of the chisel (Fig. 256). A small paper label, attached to the template, helps here. The template can be marked with a horizontal line, but judging the position of the template against the wheel (*see* the next step) may be easier if the line is drawn at 90 degrees to the edge of the template. If possible, position the template so that it faces the chisel.
- Place the template on the rest or the slide; free the height and angle adjustments of the tool rest; then position the rest so that the mark on the template touches the wheel at a position where the chisel will not foul the wheel guards (Fig. 257). Lock the rest in that position. The mark on the template indicates the tangent point, and this can be set more easily under good lighting, using a magnifying lens if necessary.
- Remove the template and put the chisel/jig assembly on the rest or the sliding feed plate (Fig. 258).
- Holding the jig against the side guide of the sliding feed plate, slide the jig forwards until it just touches the grinding wheel. Move the feed plate to the side; turn on the grinder; and take an initial pass. Apply a small amount of feed and repeat as often as necessary to form a straight unblemished cutting edge and a flat cutting face. For a chisel, the feed can be applied by hand, sliding the chisel forwards and holding it firmly against the side guide as it is traversed across the face of the wheel.

Fig. 256: Mark the template at the same height as the cutting edge.

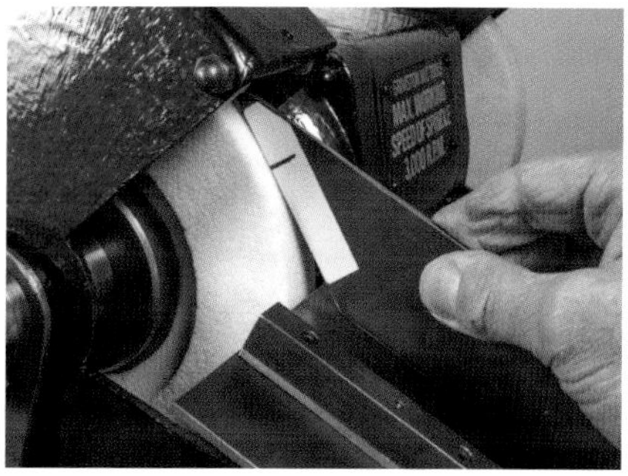

Fig. 257: Adjust the rest so that the mark on the template touches the wheel.

Fig. 258: Place the chisel/jig assembly on the rest or sliding plate.

To grind the other face, the chisel must be rotated through 180 degrees (a half-turn). One way to do this accurately is to use a longer sleeve and a square-sided collar. Keep the chisel/sleeve assembly clamped in the jig but loosely attach the collar to the sleeve, then set one side vertical (Fig. 259), and tighten it around the sleeve. Loosen the jig clamp, and rotate the chisel/collar/sleeve assembly half a turn, until the opposite side is vertical, then re-tighten the jig clamp. The previously ground face should now be uppermost, and the face on the underside is ready to be ground using the same method as for the first face.

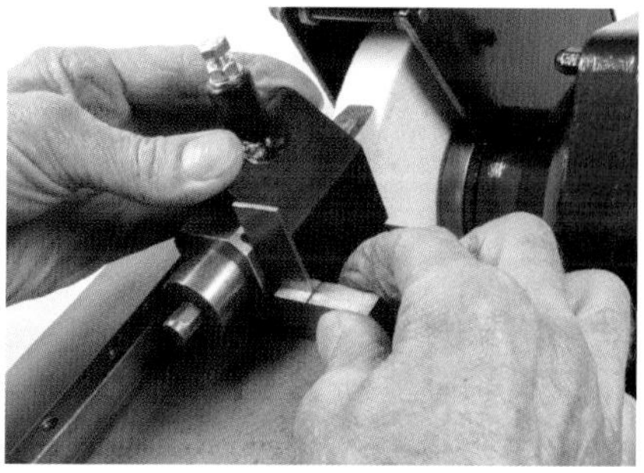

Fig. 259: Use a square collar as a simple indexing device to rotate the chisel through a half-turn.

As grinding proceeds, visually check where the cutting edge lies in relation to the centre line of the chisel. In most cases, the cutting edge should lie centrally, and although this is not particularly critical, a noticeable deviation may be corrected by grinding a little more from the smaller face.

For most chisels, the finish produced on the cutting edge and faces by a coarse grinding wheel is sufficient. In cases where a better finish is required, repeat the process using a finer grinding wheel.

The secondary (clearance) angle on a metalworking chisel is normally formed by forging the shank during manufacture, and in most cases will not require attention. Should that face be damaged it may be ground, but the challenge is often in producing a much longer face, because the contact between grinding wheel and tool is restricted to a narrow band, so that the chisel must be fed forwards a relatively large distance while the secondary face is held parallel to the face of the wheel. As a result, this is a job best tackled using a flat-faced wheel.

Using a flat-faced wheel to grind the secondary face

The secondary face is set at an angle to the long axis of the chisel, so the chisel must be swung to bring the secondary face parallel to the face of the wheel. Feed takes place parallel to the face of the wheel, so whatever arrangement is used to hold the chisel must cater for that offset angle.

- Mount a type 6 cup or type 11 taper cup wheel, and dress the flat face of the wheel. If there is a danger that the chisel might foul the grinder shaft, set the rest so that grinding takes place above or below centre, clear of the shaft and nut.
- Mount the chisel in a sleeve, using recessed grub screws to grip a flat face on the shank of the chisel. Sit the sleeve in a holder (Fig. 260), and use an engineer's square to align the secondary face vertical. *Optionally*, to ensure the primary and secondary faces are aligned, set the square against the primary face.
- Set a 90 degree guide on the rest (Figs 260 and 261) to ensure traverse takes place parallel to the face of the wheel. The holder shown in Figs 260 and 261 is fitted with two side screws which can be adjusted independently. Leaving the rear screw fully home, extend the front screw outwards, until the secondary face of the chisel is parallel to the face of the wheel while the holder is against the 90 degree guide (Fig. 260). A small increase in the swing will prevent the secondary face from becoming longer, and will help ensure enough of the secondary face can be ground before the holder meets the wheel. *Optionally*, add a lock nut to the front screw, and lock in position. This is not normally necessary for a single chisel.
- Fit an adjustable depth stop to control the depth of cut (Fig. 260).
- Apply a depth of cut, and traverse to grind, keeping the holder against the guide during traverse.
- Turn the chisel through a half-turn and grind the other secondary face.

Fig. 260: Position the long axis of the chisel parallel to the face of the wheel, with the cutting edge vertical.

Fig. 261: The angle can be created by adjusting the side screw nearest the front of the chisel.

FLAT-BLADED CHISELS

Bolster chisels may be sharpened using the same techniques as for straight or cross-cut chisels, holding the chisel in a sleeve inside a jig. The blade may project more than for a straight chisel, so sharpening cuts should be relatively fine, to prevent chatter. However; as there is no guarantee that the flats on the chisel shaft will be parallel to the cutting edge, a better method is to use a jig which uses the blade itself as the reference. In the two jigs shown in Figs 262 and 263 the blade of the chisel is clamped against the flat underside of a bar and held parallel to the base and the rest.

Fig. 262: A tool rest which has a slot to carry accessories and jigs; and a jig to hold a chisel located by its flat underside.
Photo: LEE VALLEY TOOLS LTD.

Fig. 263: A separate jig in which a flat-bladed chisel can be located against the flat underside of a steel bar.

On the Veritas jig, tilt is provided by the rest; feed is applied by slackening the clamp and sliding the chisel forwards, using the pin and the clamp screw on the left to keep the chisel at 90 degrees to the wheel. Traverse is guided by the slot in the rest and a locating bar attached to the underside of the jig.

For a plain rest, using the jig shown in Fig. 263, align a flat-bladed chisel with its cutting edge at right angles to the left side of the jig, as shown in Fig. 264. Slide the chisel

Fig. 264: Align the cutting edge at right angles to the left side of the jig.

forward to touch the front face of the angle plate, before fully tightening the clamp. An alternative would be to use a square to set the side of the jig at right angles to the front face of the angle plate or a block (as shown in Fig. 255). The jig sits on a sliding carrier plate (Fig. 265) which has a guide bar on the left, and a guide underneath, at the front, which locates against the edge of the rest. Tilt is provided by the rest; feed is applied by sliding the jig forwards while keeping the edge against the left hand guide. Traversing is carried out by moving the carrier plate. For

Fig. 265: The jig sits on a flat carrier plate, on the rest.

security, traverse from left to right, so that the jig is pushed against the left guide, but add a clamp (shown on the left of the sliding carrier plate in Fig. 266) to keep the jig in position. Feed can be controlled by adding a feedscrew (at bottom right, under the sheet metal cover, in Figs 265 and 266). Release

Fig. 266: A clamp, shown on the left of the sliding plate, keeps the jig in position while traversing.

the clamp; adjust the feed; the re-tighten the clamp.

Once the first cutting face has been sharpened, release the chisel from the jig. If the chisel has two cutting faces, turn it over and reset it in the jig, then sharpen the other face. As with a cold chisel, aim to have the cutting edge approximately central within the thickness of the blade.

Typical woodworking chisels, which are also useful for sheet metal work, (Fig. 267) do not have a uniform octagonal or round shaft, and the most convenient reference surface is their flat underside. The faces

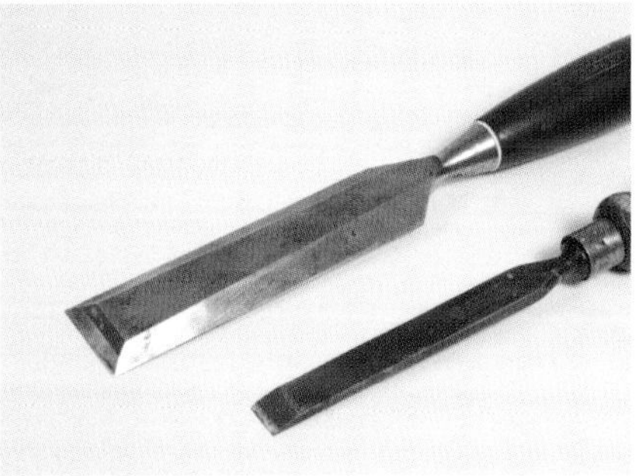

Fig. 267: Typical woodoworking chisels have a primary bevel at the front, followed by a less steep secondary clearance bevel.

behind the cutting edge are on one side of the chisel only, but there is a small primary bevel, and on many, but not all, chisels a longer secondary bevel (Fig. 268). If the cutting edge is blunt but undamaged, simply grinding the primary bevel will sharpen the cutting edge. If there is damage, such

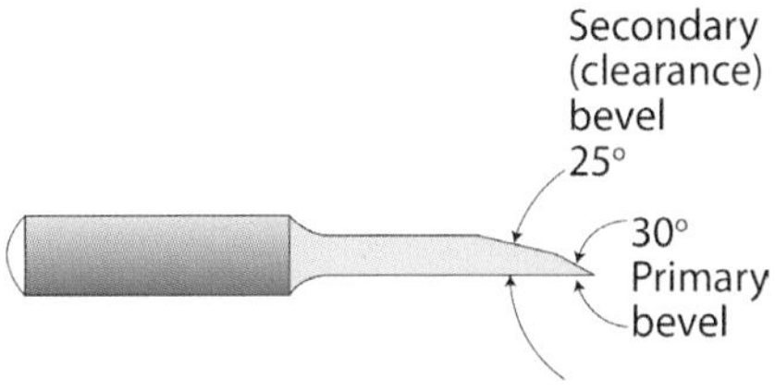

Fig. 268: Typical angles for the bevels of woodworking chisels.

as small nicks in the edge, grinding the primary bevel may remove so much material that the bevel becomes rather deep. In that case, grind the secondary bevel, then grind a small primary bevel.

A woodworking chisel may be sharpened on a bench grinder, in much the same way as for a flat-bladed chisel, using the same kind of jig to locate the blade from its flat underside (Figs 262, 263 and 269). On a bench grinder, use angle templates as necessary; one for the secondary angle and the other for the primary angle; or calculate the height the cutting edge must be above the rest to produce the required angles, and set the rest at the appropriate distance below a radial centre line (*see* pages 40–43). Sharpening should have removed all damage and

Fig. 269: A woodworking chisel may be located by its flat underside, using a suitable jig.

created a finished cutting edge, but may have left striations on the primary bevel and cutting edge. These will be reproduced in wood, so woodworking chisels should be honed to a very fine finish after grinding. Honing involves holding the chisel so that the cutting edge and primary clearance angle are maintained, by holding the primary face against a fine stone. Fig. 270 shows an Eclipse chisel honing jig which grips the chisel upside down, using shaped jaws to force its flat face against two flat strips on the underside of the side-mounted jaws. The projection of the chisel from the front of the

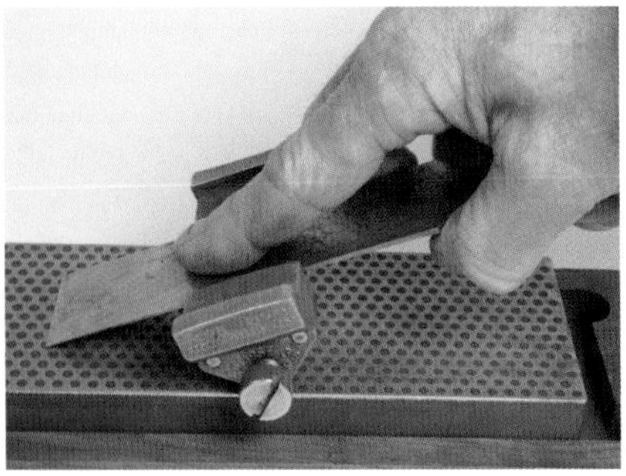

Fig. 270: During honing, a jig is used to keep the individual bevels at the correct angle against an abrasive stone.

jig determines the angle between the face of the chisel and the stone, and there is a legend on the jig giving dimensions for various angles. With the primary face against the stone, move the chisel backwards and forwards along the surface, using a lubricant. Begin with a 1200 grit diamond stone, and continue the movement until the primary face has a smooth finish. Use finer grades of stone for a finer finish, if necessary. The finer the finish on the face, the finer the finish on the work. If a wire-edge burr appears, turn the chisel over; place the flat face fully in contact with the stone, and rub that face on the stone, briefly, to remove the burr. It is not necessary to hone the secondary bevel, as that merely provides clearance, but a good finish on the flat face helps, as that face is in contact with the work over a very short distance.

GROOVING, SLOTTING, PLUGGING AND CAPE CHISELS

On a grooving, slotting or plugging chisel (sometimes also called a cape chisel), the secondary face and a substantial portion of the shank stand vertically (Fig. 271), to allow clearance at the sides of the narrow cutting edge while providing strength to the shaft. The remainder of the shank is normally octagonal, so these chisels may be held in a sleeve within a conventional jig

Fig. 271: A plugging chisel (on the left), and a small slotting chisel (on the right).

(Figs 250, 253, and 254). Although the projecting shank is stronger than, say, the blade of a bolster, the depth of grinding cuts should not be so heavy as to cause vibration and chatter. Grooving chisels are normally used to create grooves in metal or wood, while a plugging chisel is used to create grooves in brick or remove cement seams.

Large plugging or slotting chisels may be sharpened using a side steady, as shown in Figs 93 and 94. Smaller chisels may be fitted into a sleeve and aligned using a square referenced off the vertical side (Fig. 272). This does not guarantee that the cutting edge will be horizontal, although a first grind will rectify that. Alternatively, set the cutting edge horizontal by using a plastic panel engraved with vertical and horizontal reference lines (Fig. 273). They may then be set up on a grinder rest and sharpened as shown earlier (*see* Figs 256–259). Rotate the chisel half a turn before grinding the second face and check the cutting edge lies centrally.

Fig. 272: Set up a slotting chisel by using a square to set the side of the shaft vertical. That does not guarantee that the existing cutting edge will be horizontal, until after its first regrind.

Fig. 273: The cutting edge of a chisel may be set horizontal by comparison with lines engraved on a plastic rectangle. In this photograph, the 20-30-50 block is used simply as a means of temporarily raising the chisel to a convenient working height. It is then removed before proceeding to the next stage of sharpening.

Typical oil groove chisels (Fig. 274) have a cutting edge created by a rounded heel and an angled flat front face. Unless there is substantial damage to the heel, oil groove chisels should be sharpened by grinding the

Fig. 274: An oil groove chisel has a flat angled end face and a rounded heel.

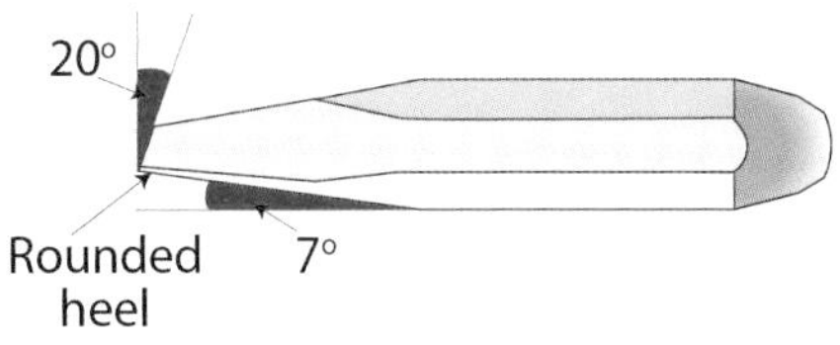

Fig. 275: Typical angles for the face and heel of an oil groove chisel.

flat front face at an angle of approximately 20 degrees (Fig. 275), leaving the rounded heel untouched. Damage to the heel can be rectified by honing against a fine bench stone or, to rectify heavier damage, grinding against a wheel first. Hold the heel parallel to the face of the wheel, and rotate gently, following the existing curve, while traversing (Fig. 276).

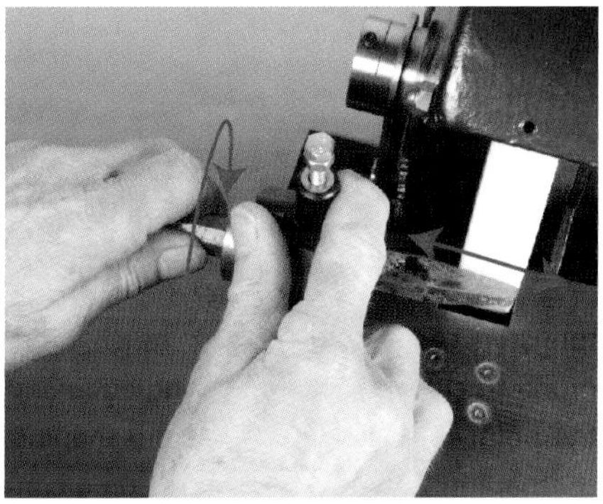

Fig. 276: Place the chisel in a holder and angle it so that the curved face lies along the face of the wheel. Rotate the chisel around the curved part of the heel as the chisel is traversed across the face of the wheel.

Finish against bench stones of increasingly finer grit. Hold the curved section against the stone, and rotate gently while moving the chisel backwards and forwards along the stone (Fig. 277). The heel is in contact with the work for a short distance, and should be reasonably well finished, but the finish on the section of heel beyond that is not as important. When an oil groove chisel is sharpened, the face will become wider. In some cases, this may create an unacceptably wide groove. If that happens, grind the sides to reduce the width of the face. Take care to preserve the angle of the taper on the sides.

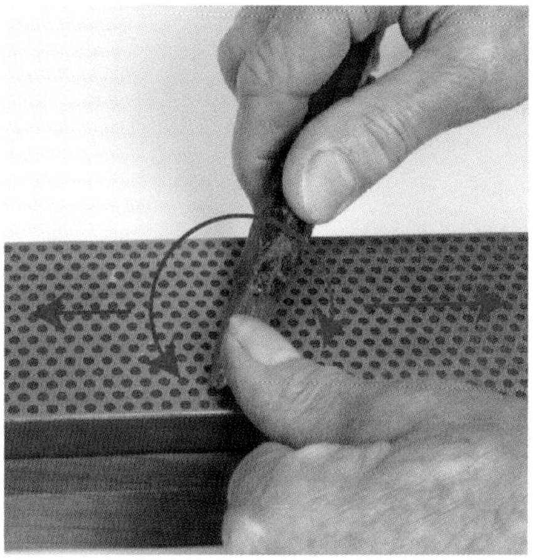

Fig. 277: To hone the heel, hold the curved section against the stone, and rotate gently through an arc while moving the chisel backwards and forwards along the stone.

SQUARE AND DIAMOND POINT CHISELS

Square and diamond-shaped points are created by arranging four flat faces to taper towards a common point, then grinding an end face at an angle (Fig. 278). The greater

Fig. 278: A square or diamond-shaped face at the front of a chisel is produced by four flat faces tapering towards the front of the chisel, and a vertical or angled front face.

the angle of the end face, the greater the distance between the top and bottom corners (Fig. 279). The lower cutting edges and the lower point do most of the cutting, and the lower faces should have a good finish. The tapered faces are forged then ground during manufacture, and most resharpening is confined to the angled front face, but, as with oil groove chisels, repeated grinding of

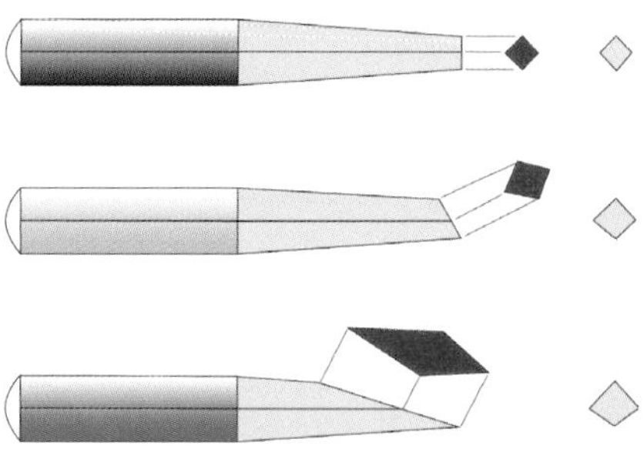

Fig. 279: The shape of the end face varies according to the angle of the face. The grey faces are viewed end-on; and the red faces are viewed at right angles to the face, to illustrate the differences more clearly.

the front face will widen the face, so it may be necessary to regrind the sides from time to time, to restore the overall width of the front face. These chisels are best sharpened against a flat-faced wheel, as that preserves the straight sides and cutting edges.

- Mount the chisel in a sleeve, in a work-head or holder, and rotate it so that *square-faced*: the top and bottom edges are both horizontal (Fig. 278). *diamond-faced*: the top and bottom corners are vertically above one another (although the top corner will be further back than the bottom corner).
- Tilt the chisel to bring the front face against the face of the wheel, then grind the face. Afterwards, finish the front face using a fine abrasive stone.

The sides lie at a small angle to the long axis of the chisel (typically 3 to 5 degrees, on a small chisel). To grind the sides:

- Orient the top and bottom edges, or corners, as when grinding the front face (*see* above). Set the long axis horizontal and parallel to the face of the wheel. *Diamond-faced only*: rotate to set one side face vertical.
- Swing to set the side parallel to the axis of traverse. Use the cross-feed to create a depth of cut, then traverse to grind the side.
- Rotate to bring the next side parallel to the axis of traverse, and grind that face. Repeat for each face.

Tool type 4: Gravers

Gravers are traditional hand-held tools used to cut or engrave metal, and clock and watchmakers often use a type of graver as a lathe turning tool, balancing the graver on a tool rest and using the tip to machine brass, mild steel and hardened steel (Figs 280 and 281). When using a graver for engraving by hand, the angles of the faces required for a graver depend on the kind of cut the engraver intends to make, as well as a degree of personal preference in how the graver is to be used. Although gravers used for hand engraving and for turning by hand in a lathe have different shapes and face angles, the general principles and methods of shaping, sharpening and honing graver faces are common to both types. Those techniques are explained in the context of the simpler hand turning gravers, which are more widely used in general metalworking, clock and watchmaking. Gravers used for traditional hand engraving of surfaces have more facets, but these can be formed by using the same general methods. Hand engraving is a skilful and specialised application of engraving, and the techniques are more fully explained in other books and demonstrated in videos solely devoted to engraving. This book focuses on creating and finishing graver faces, mainly for turning.

Fig. 280: A graver used for turning work in a lathe is a hand-held cutting tool. Skilled use allows a wide variety of work to be turned.

Fig. 281: When turning work, a graver is held by hand on a rest, and applied to the work.

GRAVERS FOR TURNING

Hand-held gravers used as turning tools are made of high-carbon steel, high speed steel or tungsten carbide. High-carbon steel was the material traditionally used before the development of high speed steel, and although it is easier to cut, form and sharpen high-carbon steel, the superior qualities of high speed steel have made this a much more common choice for gravers in modern times. Gravers made of tungsten carbide are a more recent innovation, providing a harder, sharper cutting edge, although at a much higher cost than high speed steel. Although they are ideal for turning hardened steel, tungsten carbide gravers are much more prone to chipping of the cutting edge and the point, which tends to make reshaping, sharpening and honing a more time-consuming process.

The cutting edge is formed on the tip of a graver by grinding the end face at an angle in relation to the long axis of the shaft. The angles are chosen to suit the cutting action required, and the shape of tip needed for a specific workpiece, but a graver intended for turning most commonly has a square, rectangular, lozenge (diamond or rhombus) or circular-section shaft (Fig. 282) and a front face which is normally ground to a diamond shape (Fig. 283).

Gravers and lathe turning tools share a common geometry, but the shape of a graver is normally simplified, because a graver is hand-held and can be tilted to create some of the angles required between work and tool, during turning. Top rake, for example, is the angle between a radial centre line and

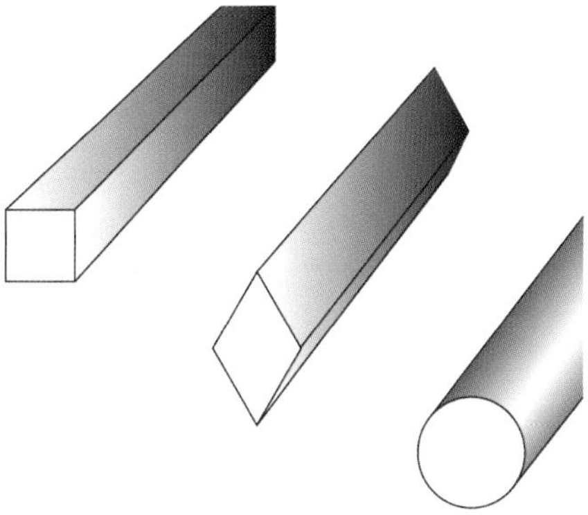

Fig. 282: Gravers may be created from tool blanks with square, lozenge or circular section.

Fig. 283: The diamond-shaped face of a graver used for turning. The small curve at the bottom is intentional. The face slopes backwards, into the photograph, from the upper corner to the lower, rounded, corner.

the top surface of the tool, and it can be set by tilting the graver in relation to the work (Fig. 284). That allows the same graver to be used for turning different materials, each of which would require a different top rake on the tool. Grinding the front face of a graver at a compound angle automatically creates angles on the front edges which help make the graver a versatile tool which will cut while contacting the work in a range of different ways (Fig. 285).

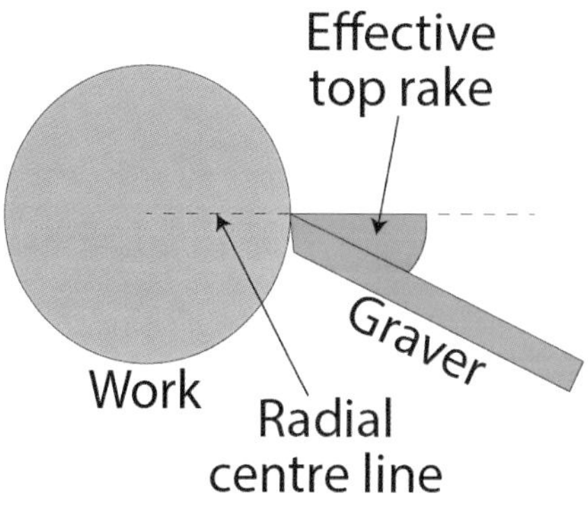

Fig. 284: Top rake depends on the angle at which the graver contacts the work, so tilting the graver handle downwards increases the top rake.

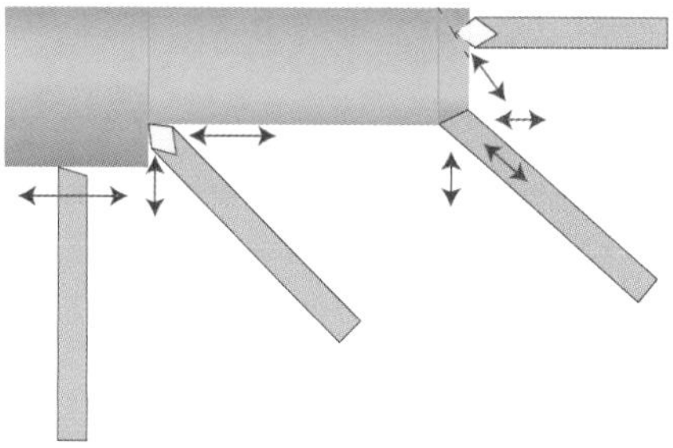

Fig. 285: A graver may be used to make a range of different kinds of cut, depending on how its faces are presented to the work.

Gravers for turning often have a 60 degree tip angle (Fig. 286) although that can be varied to make the face longer and the tip thinner (Fig. 287) to suit the shape of the work being turned, or to make the face shorter, giving the point a larger included angle and more support when cutting harder materials. For convenience, square- and lozenge-section graver blanks are often supplied with their end faces ground at a pre-formed angle, to reduce the amount of initial shaping required, but the point is easily and quite quickly shaped on a grinder.

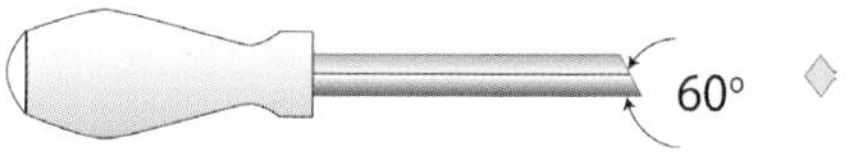

Fig. 286: Gravers for turning commonly have a 60 degree tip angle. The angle is measured between the bottom ridge and the face, with a side ridge facing outwards.

Compared to those with a square cross-section, circular-section gravers need much more preparation, as they require side and top faces to be ground flat, initially (Fig. 287), before forming the tip angle. Form side and top faces parallel to the long axis of the blank, leaving the cross-section as shown in Fig. 288. The underside can remain rounded,

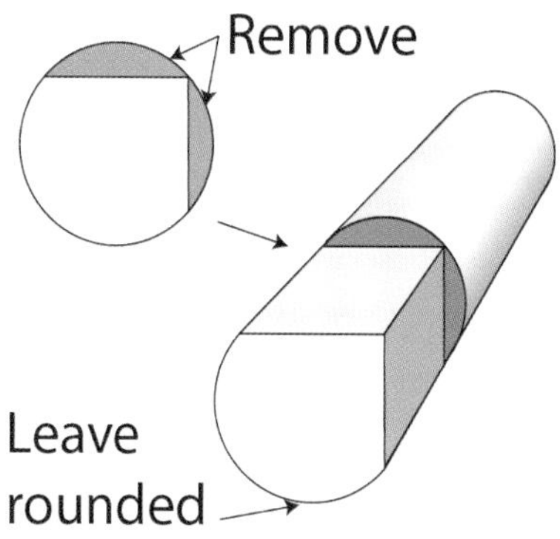

Fig. 287: Circular graver blanks require the top and side faces to be ground flat.

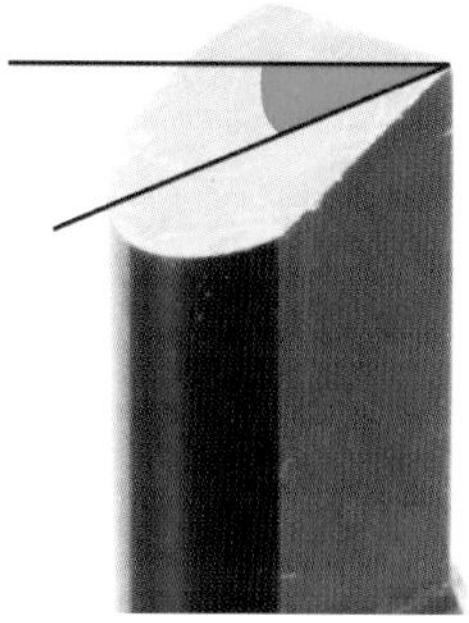

Fig. 288: The flat front face of a graver is ground at an angle running from the edge between two adjacent sides, and lying equidistant from the two edges. The angle shown in green is 90 degrees minus the included angle of the tip. On a circular blank, the curve opposite the cutting edge may be left curved.

as that curve contacts the rest and allows the graver to be rotated easily to suit the cut and the work. The front face may then be ground using broadly similar methods for both circular- and square-section gravers.

High speed steel gravers may be shaped using an aluminium oxide wheel of 100 grit or finer (higher grit number) followed by a cBN wheel of 600 mesh/25 microns. Tungsten carbide gravers are best sharpened by beginning with a 325 mesh cBN wheel followed by a 600 mesh diamond wheel. After initial shaping, both high speed steel and tungsten carbide gravers may be given a better finish by grinding with finer wheels, but a fine finish is normally achieved by honing the working faces of the graver (*see* later).

Creating top, side and front faces on a circular-section graver

To create the first flat side:

- Mount a type 6 cup wheel, and place a right angle guide on the rest to control the traverse forwards, with an adjustable stop to control the sideways feed (Fig. 289).
- Grip the circular-section tool blank in a suitable collet or sleeve in a square-sided holder. Place the side of the blank against the flat face of the grinding wheel (Fig. 289).
- Repeatedly apply a small cut by adjusting the stop, then traversing forwards across the flat face of the wheel. Stop before grinding away a quarter of the diameter. For a 6mm (1/4 inch) blank, grinding to a depth of 2.8 to 3mm (0.1 to 0.12 inches) creates the largest face. Smaller faces may be necessary when regrinding the sides during sharpening.

To create the second flat side:

- rotate the tool through 90 degrees, and repeat the grinding process to create another face. If the tool can be rotated within the holder, there is some advantage in increasing the angle of rotation by 2 to 6 degrees, to 92 - 96 degrees, to provide useful clearance on the side cutting edge.

To create the angled front face:

- Mount a type 1 wheel, then either place the holder in a vee block, or rotate the tool within the holder, to the 45 degree position, with the edge between the two ground faces pointing to one side.
- The angle of grind at the front of the tool is 90 minus the included angle of the tip. For a 60 degree included angle, that will be 90 - 60 = 30 degrees. Swing an angle guide to 30 degrees from the straight ahead position (Fig. 290).
- Grind the angled front face by feeding forwards manually, and traversing the face of the wheel. Repeat the sequence until the face is fully formed (Fig. 291).

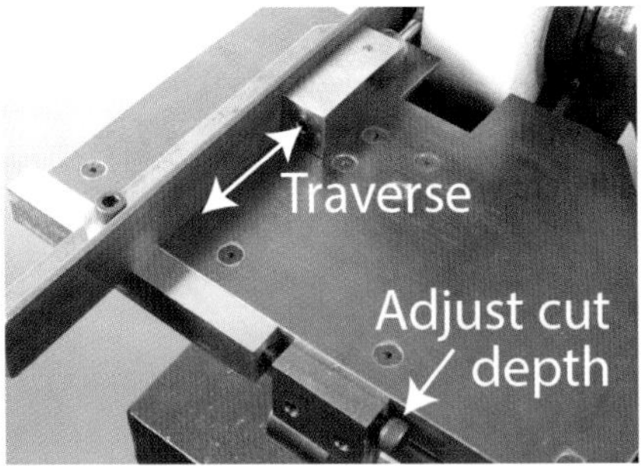

Fig. 289: Use a guide to set the side of the graver parallel to the flat face of a type 6 grinding wheel. Control the depth of cut using an adjustable stop.

Fig. 290: Set a guide at 30 degrees minus the included angle of the tip. Place the holder block in a vee block, or rotate the graver in its holder so that the ground faces form a horizontal vee.

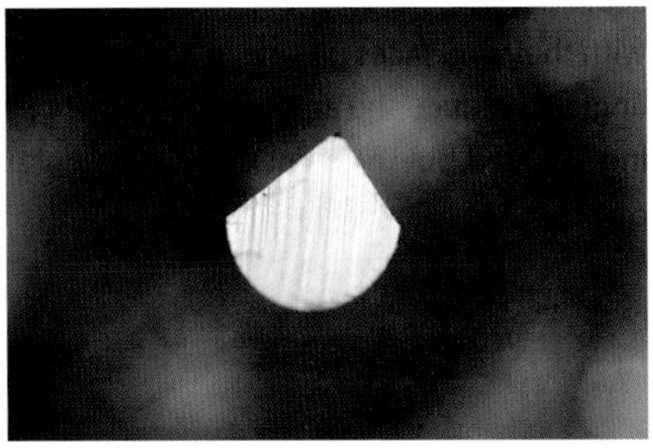

Fig. 291: Grind the whole of the front face.

Fig. 292: Set the graver with its tip uppermost and its long axis at right angles to the face of the wheel.

Creating the front face on a square-section graver

The front face can be hollow-ground using a type 1 wheel and a setup as shown in Fig. 292. A square-section graver is best gripped in a sleeve with a square hole, or clamped in a toolpost-style holder. The hollow will be corrected later, during honing. Where the graver has already been fitted with a handle, it may be more convenient to clamp it in a vee block. However; simply clamping the graver might be difficult if, as is often the case, the clamp will not reach far enough down the vee. In addition, the clearance groove at the bottom of the vee may be so large that the graver will not be securely located against the sides of the vee. Gripping the graver shaft in a sleeve with a square hole makes the assembly sufficiently large to locate fully and be clamped securely in a vee block. Because the outside of the sleeve is cylindrical it can rotate, so the graver is aligned with its tip uppermost, using an angle gauge set to 45 degrees (Fig. 293).

Fig. 293: A graver gripped in a sleeve with a square hole, clamped in a vee block and aligned using an angle gauge.

The angle of the face is determined by the height of the tip of the graver against the grinding wheel, so measure the height of the point of the front face above the base of the vee block, as shown in Fig. 294 (52mm in this case).

To set the rest using a template, sit the template on a spacer (52mm in this case) on the top surface of the carrier plate (the shoe attached to the angle guide, in Fig, 292).

Fig. 294: Measure the height of the tip of the graver above the base of the vee block (52mm in this setup).

To use a setting arm instead, measure the diameter of the grinding wheel (176mm in this case) and divide by two to find the radius (88mm). Using the formula on page 42, or by consulting Table 9, find the height the tip of the grinder must sit above the grinder rest. If the included angle of the tip should be 60 degrees, the angle between the tangent to the face of the wheel and the face of the graver should be 90 - 60 = 30 degrees. The formula gives:

H = r x Sin30 = 88 x Sin30

= 88 x 0.5 = 44mm

Use a setting arm to set the rest so that the tip of the graver will be 44mm above a radial centre line lying along the surface of the carrier plate on the rest. For the arm shown in Fig. 154 (page 42), the carrier plate on the rest will always be on a radial centre line when the edge of the setting plate is 50mm below the arm. Extend the plate downwards by the height of the graver tip above the base of the vee block (52mm) to lower the rest so that the tip of the graver will be on centre, then move the plate back up 44mm to lift the tip of the graver up the wheel to create the angle of the face. The gauge plate should be set at 50 + 52 - 44 = 58mm. Sit the carrier plate on the rest, then swing the gauge arm and adjust the height and angle of the rest so that the bottom edge of the plate sits snugly along the carrier plate. Lock the rest in that position (Fig. 292). Place the vee block on the carrier plate, with the graver at 90 degrees to the face of the wheel and set the graver with its long axis at right angles to the face of the wheel. (Fig. 292). Traverse to grind the face.

Rounding the bottom edge of a square-section graver

In use, gravers are supported on a rest, and a sharp lower edge will tend to prevent the graver from sliding easily along the rest. Avoid this by forming a small radius on the lower edge of square- and lozenge-section gravers. Hold the graver with its lower edge against a fine or medium grade stone (Fig. 295) and move it sideways while rocking it backwards and forwards to round the sharp edge. A small radius will do.

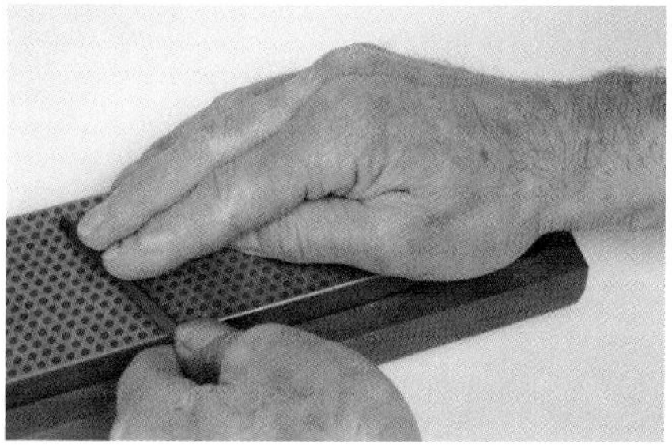

Fig. 295: Round the back edge of the graver by rocking it while moving the graver sideways along a medium or fine abrasive stone.

Deburring

Burrs are produced particularly during grinding of the front face, as the fine edges are created. Traversing tends to push material over the edges, leaving burrs which will impair the cutting action when the graver is subsequently used. Deburr by pressing each flat side against a fine India stone (Fig. 296) or a 600 mesh (25 micron) fine diamond stone,

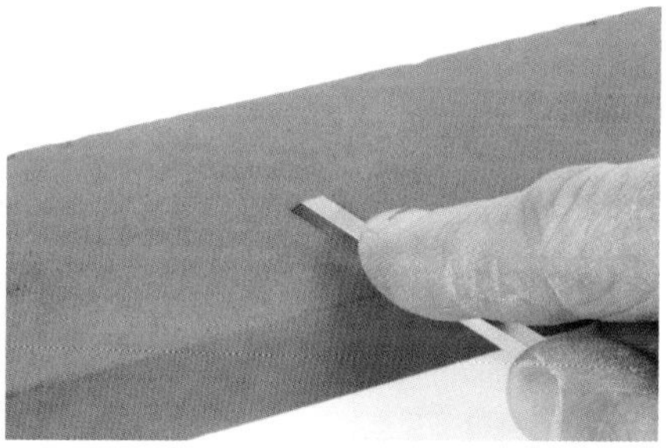

Fig. 296: Deburr the sides by holding them flat against a fine stone and moving them back and forth parallel to the long axis of the graver.

then moving the graver back and forth, parallel to the long axis of the graver, making approximately six strokes back and forth. The intention here is to remove or weaken the grip of any burrs, rather than to polish the sides (that comes later). It may be tempting to rub the front face against the stone to complete the operation, but that will create more work, later, as it requires a degree of precision not possible purely by hand. Wipe the sides and the front face perfectly clean, and move on to sharpening the front face. Any remaining burrs will disappear during that process.

Sharpening a graver

Once faces have been formed on a graver, it may be sharpened. All other factors being equal, the quality of the finish on turned work will reflect the quality of finish on the face and sides of the graver. Sharpening involves forming, or re-forming, then imparting a fine finish to the face of the tool. Honing is an extension of that process, giving a finer finish to the face and sides of the graver. It is a question of degree, but the process is carried out in the same way both for initial finishing and for any subsequent honing to a final finish.

Regularly sharpening a graver maintains the edges and avoids significant regrinding. Sharpening requires some precision, but is neither difficult nor time consuming. However; having carefully created the front face of the graver at a specific angle, it is advisable to use a mechanical aid to preserve that angle while giving the face a fine finish. It is also important that the keen cutting edges between the front face and the sides are maintained, so using a mechanical guide rather than sharpening by hand helps avoid rounding those sharp corners.

Honing uses finer abrasives than normally found on a bench grinder, and successive stages in honing use progressively finer grades. Honing can, but need not necessarily, produce a mirror finish on a tool.

For sharpening on a bench stone or plate, clamp the graver in a holder as shown in Fig. 297, rotate the graver to place the long edge at the front, then set the tip angle by altering the projection of the graver from the central axis of the plate. Rolling the holder along the stone will sharpen the face of the graver. As the graver is sharpened, the tip angle will change slightly because the graver tilts downwards as metal is removed from its face, but this is unlikely to affect the performance of the graver, as the angles are deliberately varied slightly during use on the lathe, to achieve the best results. There are four ways to find the appropriate distance:

Fig. 297: A holder which maintains the angle of the graver face during sharpening or honing.

- By feel and sight, adjusting the projection and the rotation until the existing face of the graver sits flat against the abrasive surface. This is a quick and easy method, but is suitable only for light sharpening or honing; and it will only reproduce the existing angles.
- By using a template (Fig. 298). Assemble the graver in the holder then, using a template, adjust the projection until the template fits against the shaft and the abrasive surface.
- By calculation. As shown in Fig. 299, P = B/TanA where:
  P is projection, measured along the top edge of the graver, from the front of the plate to the tip of the graver;
  B is the distance from the point at which the roller touches the stone to the top edge of the graver where it enters the body of the holder. Provided the diameter of the roller is small, this can be simplified by measuring along the centre of the side of the plate from the top of the graver to the bottom of the end curve of the plate. Any error will be small and can be ignored;
  A is the desired tip angle of the graver. For the common angles: tan60 is 1.73; tan55 is 1.43, and tan45 is 1. Other values can be found by looking up tables, or using a calculator.

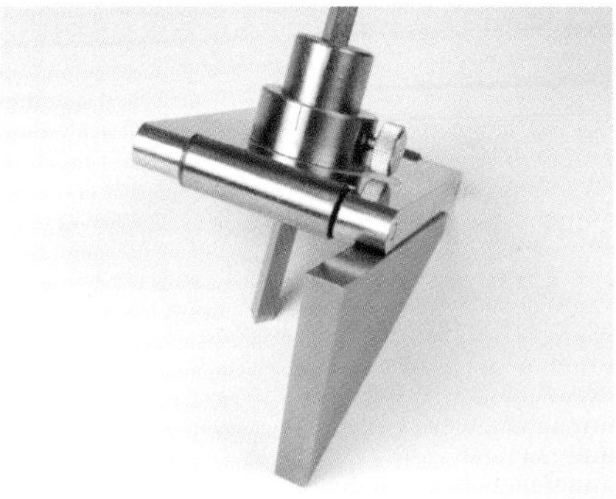

Fig. 298: Use a template to help set the projection of the graver from the front of the holder.

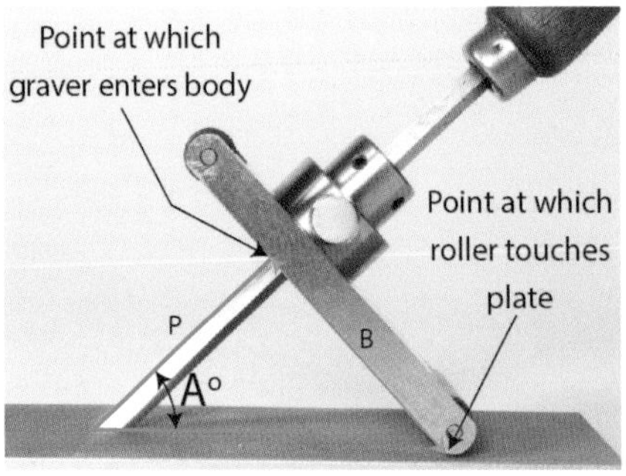

Fig. 299: The length B and the tip angle A can be used to calculate the projection P of the graver.

For example:

  As shown in Fig. 300, if the distance B from the stone to the top edge of the graver in the holder is 25mm, and the graver tip angle is 60 degrees:
  P = B/Tan60 = 25/1.73 = 14.45mm
  For a given graver in the same sleeve, the length B is always the same, and the angles are usually the same, so the projection will always be the same. Do the calculation once for a 60 degree face angle and again for a 55 degree angle and make a note of the answers.

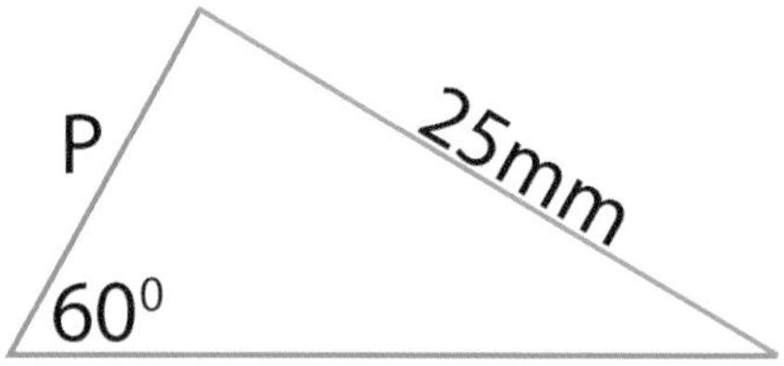

Fig. 300: Example dimensions used to calculate the projection, P.

- By slipping a predetermined length of tube over the end of the graver then adjusting the projection so that the tip of the graver is level with the end of the tube (Fig. 301). The length of the tube is found by calculation (*see* above). This is a quick and easy method which is used with commercial systems such as the Lindsay Engraving template system. Different angles require different projections and different lengths of tube.

Fig. 301: Use a pre-cut length of tube as a setting gauge. This graver must be retracted until the tip is level with the end of the tube.

Setting a traditional honing tool

Fig. 302 shows a traditional version of the tool shown in Fig. 297, and is designed to hold the graver at an appropriate angle. The roller at the rear of the tool is used to steady the graver and prevent it from rocking. The graver sits in a hole with a vee groove formed at the bottom and is gripped by a screw which is tightened down onto the

Fig. 302: With a traditional honing tool the projection determines the angle of the graver face. The tool is designed to hold the graver at a 45 degree angle of rotation (upper hole), or a 0 degree angle (lower hole), and uses wheels or a roller to guide the tool along an abrasive surface.

sharp top edge of the graver. To use the tool, slip the graver into the vee-shaped hole, and tighten the clamp lightly. Set the projection using any of the methods explained earlier, then tighten firmly.

With honing tools, the challenge lies in holding the graver at a constant angle and moving it without rocking so that the end face is ground flat rather than slightly curved. There are two important factors which may influence the effectiveness of the traditional tool. The first is that the clamping arrangements must hold the graver securely; and a screw bearing on the sharp corner of the graver shaft provides an insecure grip. The second is that the roller must be concentric with its shaft, to prevent the tool from wobbling as it rolls. A wobble will tilt the graver from side to side as the tool is moved across the stone, resulting in a curved face. This is not an uncommon fault.

Setting a versatile honing tool

In the graver honing tool shown in Figs 297 and 303 the graver is held in a sleeve. A sleeve with a square hole accommodates a square-section graver, and a sleeve with a circular hole accommodates a circular-section graver. Each sleeve has two or more recessed grub screws to grip the graver. The sleeve locates in a holding collar fixed in the plate, and can slide and rotate. The graduated collar acts both as a length stop for the sleeve, and as an indication of rotation. Using the projection calculated above, put the graver in the sleeve and set the required projection from the front face of the sleeve to the tip of the graver. Tighten the clamping screws. Then put the sleeve assembly in the holder, with the front face of the sleeve flush with the body. Attach the graduated collar, to prevent the sleeve from slipping forwards. Then rotate the holder to set the angle; normally 45 degrees for a square-section graver. Finally, tighten the clamp screw in the side of the sleeve holder, to secure the sleeve and graver in position.

Setting the angle by feel

In practice, when sharpening a lightly worn graver, the existing face can be used as a reference.

Using the traditional tool, slacken the clamp screw and hold the end face of the graver against the stone, letting the graver slip in the tool so that the tool and the sleeve move to accommodate the angle of the graver. Tighten the clamp screw.

Using the versatile tool, slip the shaft of the graver into the sleeve, with the grub screws nearest the handle end of the graver, and tighten the grub screws lightly, leaving the graver free to slide in the sleeve, then put the sleeve and graver into the holder, and hold the end face of the graver against the stone, letting the graver slip in the sleeve and the sleeve rotate in the holder so that the tool and the sleeve move to accommodate the angle of the graver. Hold the thumbnail of your other hand against the bottom end of the sleeve so that it is flush with the holder, then tighten the grub screws of the sleeve to grip the graver. Finally, tighten the external screw securing the sleeve in the holder. The sharpening tool is now ready to use.

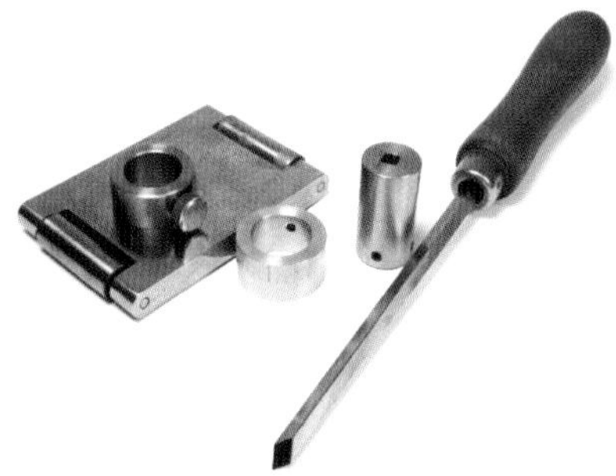

Fig. 303: Component parts of a versatile honing tool. The graver is gripped in a sleeve which is placed in a holder in the plate. The graduated collar allows the graver to be rotated, and the rollers guide the tool. The two ends cater for gravers of different lengths.

Using a powered hone

Although it does not take long to sharpen the face of a graver on a bench stone, frequent users may benefit from using a powered device like the GRS® Power Hone (Fig. 304). This has a horizontal abrasive disc which rotates under power, and holding a graver at a suitable angle to the surface finishes the face of the graver. Discs of various abrasive grades are available, and a ceramic disc may be used with diamond spray to create a superb finish. Fig. 305 shows a graver holder for use with the power hone.

Fig. 304: The GRS® Power Hone can be equipped with a range of horizontally rotating abrasive wheels or a ceramic wheel for use with diamond spray.
Photo: GLENDO LLC.

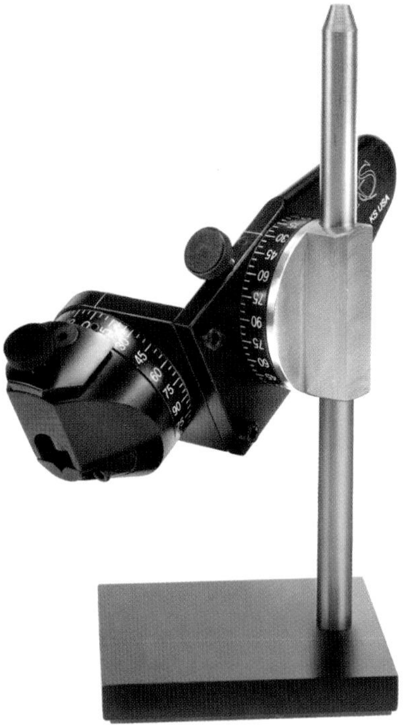

Fig. 305: Gravers may be held against the wheel of a power hone using an adjustable tool holder like this GRS® Dual Angle Sharpening Fixture.
Photo: GLENDO LLC

The honing action

Honing begins with a 600 mesh (25 micron) or 1200 mesh (9 micron) diamond stone, and uses increasingly finer grades of abrasive, until the finish is sufficiently fine and scratch-free for the intended purpose of the tool. If the graver has been sharpened using a 600 mesh diamond plate, one possible sequence of grades for honing would be: 1200, 2000, and 5000 mesh, finishing by using a ceramic lapping plate and diamond spray of 5 micron then 3 micron.

Lubricate an abrasive stone with water or thin oil, to suit the stone; but lubricate a diamond plate only with water – never with oil. With the stone or plate seated firmly on the bench, roll the honing tool forwards and backwards pressing just enough to keep the face of the graver against the stone. Inspect the face of the graver every dozen strokes, until the surface is flat and the finish on the face looks uniform. Then clean the face and the stone or plate thoroughly, and move to the next grade of abrasive.

Gravers sharpened against the curved face of a wheel on a bench grinder will be hollow-ground (Fig. 306), but these can be honed in exactly the same way, using the same jig. It is not essential that honing completely removes the hollow-ground section in the centre of the graver face, as that section will not touch the work. It is a little more work, but not at all difficult to sharpen or initially hone the graver face until it is completely flat, eliminating the hollow-ground centre section. At the very least, the point, heel and side edges should be honed to produce a narrow polished band adjacent to each edge (Fig. 307). Hollow-ground gravers were traditionally honed by hand using an India stone and the following technique:

- Sit the diamond-shaped face of the graver on the stone so that the tip and heel are in contact with the stone.
- Gently tilt the graver to one side until the side point comes into contact with the stone, giving three points of contact.
- Push or pull the graver across the stone, in the direction from tip to heel, perhaps a dozen strokes.
- Tilt the graver gently so that the other side point comes into contact with the stone, and repeat the honing strokes on that side.
- If necessary, repeat the honing operation equally on both sides, until the cutting edges are polished.
- Finish honing using a hard Arkansas or fine diamond stone.

Although this method will tend to result in the two side points being behind the line between tip and heel, this small difference will make no difference to the performance of the graver.

Honing a hollow-ground graver solely by hand is quick and easy, but is less accurate than using a jig, because there is a tendency to tip the graver slightly as it is moved along the stone, rounding the face, tip and heel.

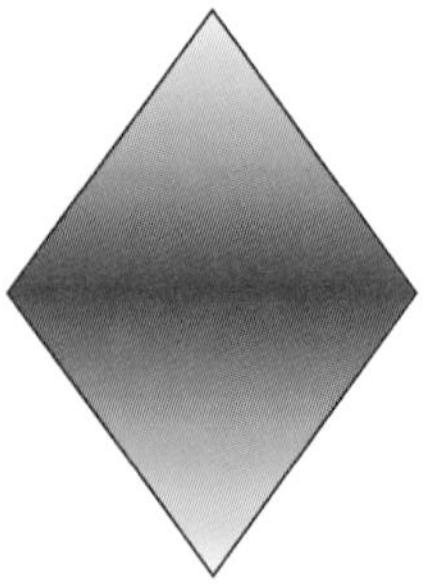

Fig. 306: The face of a graver shaped against a wheel with a curved face will be hollow-ground. The intensity of red denotes the depth of the hollow.

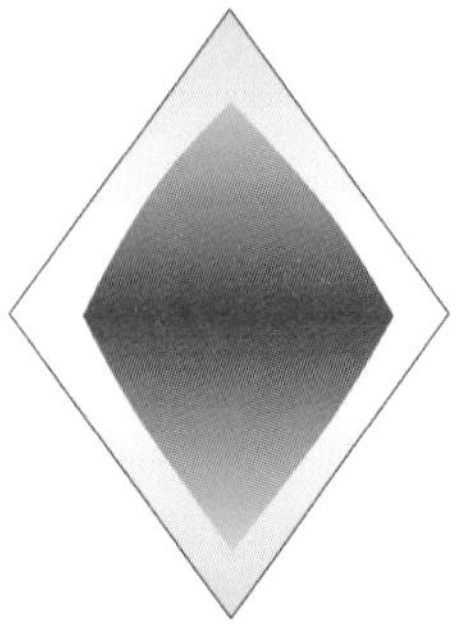

Fig. 307: On a hollow-ground graver face, the minimum requirement is that the area adjacent to each edge is given a polished finish.

Honing the sides of a graver

Just as the face of a graver should be polished by honing, so too the faces along the four sides of the graver should be polished, especially if the graver is being used for turning in the lathe, because depending on the orientation of the graver as it is used, the sides may contact the cut surfaces and contribute to the finish produced on the work. Hold each side in turn, on a fine India, Arkansas or diamond stone in the same way as for deburring (Fig. 296). Hone the sides by moving the graver backwards and forwards parallel to its long axis, using increasingly finer grades of abrasive stone, or spray on a plate, until all the scratch marks have been removed and the tool is polished.

During normal sharpening, the sides will not be ground, so, if they have already been polished, they will only need to be re-polished occasionally.

GRAVERS FOR ENGRAVING

Engravers traditionally use hand-held gravers, to score or remove metal (Fig. 308). In some cases, they are used to cut fine lines, but for thicker lines the graver acts as a kind of hand-operated chisel, creating broader or deeper grooves, and a 'scorper' (a broad-faced graver) can remove larger amounts of material. Gravers may also be used to good effect in powered devices such as the Lindsay AirGraver (Fig. 309). The cutting action

Fig. 309: Hand-held PalmControl air or CO2-powered AirGravers manufactured by Lindsay Engraving. Photo: STEVE LINDSAY www.airgraver.com

when engraving differs from that of a graver used in the lathe, and the position and angles of the cutting edges are quite different too. The preferred angles of the faces vary from one engraver to another, and from one type of job to another, but consistent angles will help produce consistent results.

Gravers should be held in a jig for sharpening, if possible, and the Lindsay Graver Sharpening System uses templates based on a similar principle to the sharpening tools for turning gravers, but each template has sides which are designed to produce specific face angles. Fig. 310 shows a template designed to produce the angles for the patented Lindsay Uniform Parallel Point, for hand engraving using the AirGraver or a traditional hand-held graver. The graver shaft is held in a collet, and the projection determines the angle of the graver face. The projection is set using a tubular length gauge. Gravers are sharpened against a diamond plate of 260 mesh, then honed using a sequence of 600, 1000 and, optionally,

Fig. 308: Gravers, burins and scorpers are used for hand engraving, which is capable of producing beautiful and unique patterns, such as lettering (right hand watch case), but machine assistance may be used when engraving more intricate and extensive patterns (left hand case).

Fig. 310: Lindsay Sharpening System with template. The protrusion of the graver point is set using a simple jig, making the angles repeatable. Photo: STEVE LINDSAY www.airgraver.com

2000 mesh. A slightly blunt graver can be resharpened by simply making a few strokes against a 2000 mesh stone. Coarser stones may be reserved for gravers which are damaged or more severely blunted, and finer grits may be used to produce a more polished finish, including the use of diamond pastes on a ceramic stone. For faster shaping, sharpening or honing, the GRS Power Hone and the Lindsay Engraving system can be used in conjunction with one another, to hold a graver at appropriate angles to create the various faces required for engraving. The same equipment may be used to hone the faces to a fine finish.

BURINS, GRAVERS AND SCORPERS

Burin

An ancient tool, originating in the Stone Age, and originally made from a thin slice split from the edge of a larger stone. Viewed from the end, a burin has a triangular shape, with an edge at the top which can be used as a cutting edge (left hand tool in Fig. 311). The burin is used as a small chisel and is normally pushed by hand rather than being struck with a hammer. Nowadays, burins are made of steel and are used as engraving tools. Burins have a small handle designed to fit into the palm of the hand. The cutting edges of steel burins may be straight, rounded like a gouge, or tapered to a vee point.

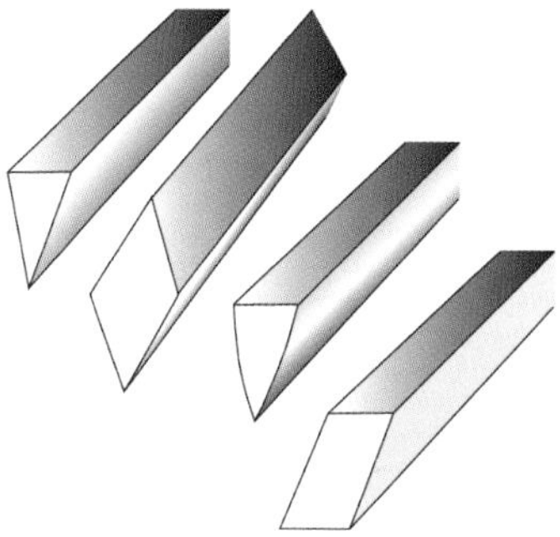

Fig. 311: A few of the shapes of faces of gravers, from a wide range of available styles.

Graver

The English name for a burin. However; although 'burin' and 'graver' may be used interchangeably, the term 'graver' would normally be used for a particular type of burin used in watch and clock making, where the shank of the graver is made from square, lozenge-shaped or round material and is designed to be used as a hand-held lathe turning tool. The end face of the graver is formed at an oblique angle to the shank, creating a point at the end (Fig. 311). The cutting edges are on either side of the point. Gravers used for turning normally have a more conventional file handle (Fig. 280) rather than the shorter and more full-bodied shape fitted to engravers' burins.

Scorper (Scauper)

A fine hand-held chisel-shaped burin or graver, designed to make a broad cut in wood or metal. The broad tip makes the scorper useful for quickly clearing larger areas when engraving or making wood blocks for intaglio printing. Like the burin, the scorper has a wooden handle to make the tool comfortable to use by hand.

Tool type 5: Punches

Flat-ended pin punches (Fig. 312) are designed to push pins or bolts out of their holes. They have a parallel, or nearly parallel, shank and a working face at one end square to the long axis of the punch. At the opposite end is a head which can be hit with a hammer, causing the punch to push anything which is against the working face. Pricker and centre punches have conical tips and are designed to make a small conical indentation to mark work or to serve as a starting position for a drill.

Fig. 312: From left to right: A hole punch, a transfer punch, two nail sets, a pin punch, a pricker punch, a centre punch, a half-centre punch, and two hollow clockmakers' punches.

Transfer punches (Fig. 312) are designed to transfer the location of a hole in a workpiece to another piece of material held below the hole. This is useful for when aligning hole positions on two parts, one of which already has holes, and the other which needs holes in matching positions. The ends of transfer punches are flat but have a small conical point in the centre. The outer diameter of the punch is designed to fit into a hole of a specific diameter, and the conical point acts as a centre punch, marking the centre of work under the hole.

Hole punches (Fig. 312) are designed to cut holes in thin sheet, such as paper, foil, cloth or wood. The cutting edge of a hole punch is around the circumference. Holding the punch against material and striking the end will force the cutting edge through the material, creating a hole by removing a disc-shaped piece of material.

The head of a punch deforms under repeated blows, and the working face may wear, perhaps by chipping at its edges, or simply by becoming blunt after repeated use. If uncorrected, the deformed head will tend to mushroom and the edges may fracture, rather like a chisel, causing sharp fragments to break off, creating a danger to all nearby. A blunt working end will make the punch more difficult to use, and may affect its accuracy.

One of the challenges in sharpening punches is in establishing reference surfaces and axes. In an accurately made punch, the body is likely to be more or less concentric with the head and shank, even if the body is knurled. The body can then be used as a reference. Sadly, that is not the case with lower quality punches, which will require much more complex set-ups, at least for initial shaping and sharpening. Some punches, like the hole punch shown in Fig. 312, do not have circular bodies, and are difficult to hold. However; once reference surfaces and axes have been properly established, future sharpening may be simplified by using those references.

DRESSING PUNCH HEADS

Punches usually have either a cylindrical or a square head (Fig. 313). When the head is struck, it will tend to spread outwards, eventually mushrooming and splitting. To help slow the spread, the top edge of a punch head is usually chamfered. A 15 degree chamfer is common, but the angle is not at all critical, and may vary up to 45 degrees.

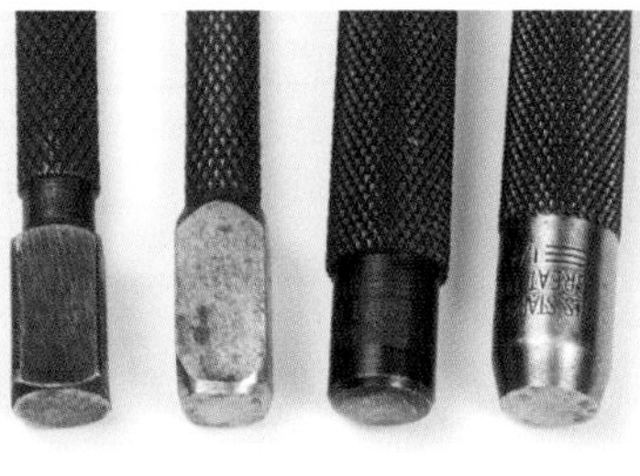

Fig. 313: Punches usually have either a cylindrical or a square head, with a chamfer around the top edge.

Dressing cylindrical punch heads

Cylindrical punch heads can be dressed using the same methods as for a chisel. The head should end up as a cylindrical shape, with a flat or slightly domed end, and a small chamfer of 15 degrees or more around the edge (Fig. 314).

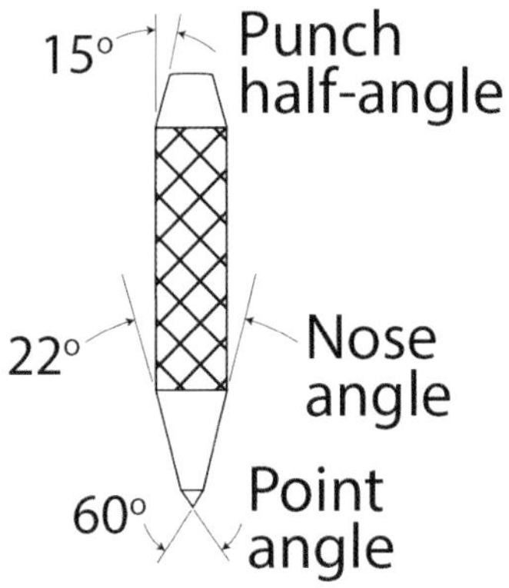

Fig. 314: Typical shape of a centre punch. The point angle may vary depending on the type of punch.

Using the punch body as a reference

Use a vee block to locate the punch by its body and allow it to be rotated about its long axis – but note that this technique is likely to cause scratches on the vee block. Set the punch at centre height with its axis at right angles to the face of the wheel, then grind the end of the head flat by advancing towards the wheel while rotating the punch about its axis.

- Set the axis of the punch on a radial centre line, then swing to an angle of 15 degrees from the face of the wheel (Fig. 315).
- Apply a cut by feeding towards the wheel while rotating the punch. Slowly increase the cut until all the burrs have been removed.

Fig. 315: Swing the punch so that its axis is 15 degrees from the face of the wheel.

Adding a collar to prevent the punch from moving forwards along the vee groove

Fig. 316: A collar limits the forward movement of the punch by acting as a stop against the vee block.

helps produce a more uniform chamfer (Fig. 316). In that case, the vee block and punch are moved forwards together. Traverse to the right or left will help prevent uneven wear on the wheel, but is difficult with a fixed guide, and very tricky to arrange even with a traversable guide without the vee block fouling the wheel.

A punch may also be mounted in a sleeve within a tilting workhead (Fig. 317). Tilt the sleeve to 15 degrees from vertical, then slide the workhead towards the wheel while rotating the sleeve.

Fig. 317: A small punch may be gripped in a tilting workhead. Set the lower end of the punch on centre.

Punches with non-cylindrical bodies

Punches with non-cylindrical bodies (e.g. square or hexagonal bodies) cannot be dressed by using the punch body as a reference, but they can be treated like chisels (*see* Tool type 3).

To help a non-circular shaft rotate reasonably smoothly, use a guide tube, or, in the absence of a tube of appropriate size, drill a clearance hole in a length of cylindrical or square-section steel. Set the punch on a radial centre line and swing the punch so that the angle between the axis of the punch and the face of the wheel is the same as the angle of the chamfer (Fig. 318). Rotate the punch while grinding to form the chamfer. Although not perfectly uniform all round, the chamfer should be perfectly usable.

Fig. 318: Use a guide tube or a clearance hole in a block of metal to help to smoothly rotate a punch with a non-cylindrical body.

Dressing the end face

To create the flat top to the punch head, set the punch on centre and with its axis at right angles to the face of the wheel, then grind the end of the head flat by advancing towards the wheel while rotating the punch about its axis. The punch can be supported on a vee block (Figs 315 and 316), or in a guide tube (Fig. 318), but because the axis of the block or guide tube is at right angles to the face of the wheel it is much easier to use a traversable guide to both support and guide the vee block and punch.

Dressing square punch heads

Dressing the end face

Using the same methods as for punches with cylindrical heads:

- Set the head of the punch on centre and at right angles to the face of the wheel.
- Feed forward while rotating the punch, to grind the end of the head flat. If possible, traverse while rotating.

Dressing the sides of the head

- Set the axis of the punch parallel to a flat-faced wheel.
- Rotate the punch to bring the side of the head parallel to the wheel. A parallel-sided block such as the stock of an engineer's square can be placed against a flat portion of the head so that the burr does not touch the wheel (Fig. 319). Clamp the head in that position.

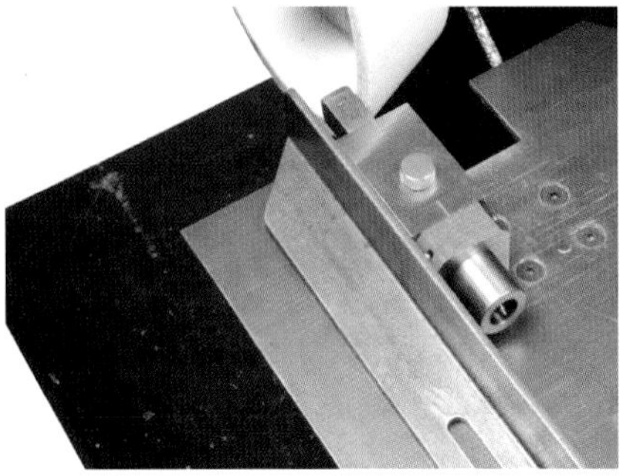

Fig. 319: The most practical way to flatten the sides of a square-headed punch is to use a flat-faced wheel.

- Apply a cut by feeding towards the wheel, and traverse to clean up one side, stopping before the body of the punch touches the wheel. Repeat for the other sides, rotating the punch through 90 degrees between sides.

The punch shown in Fig. 319 is gripped in a collet chuck. The shank of the chuck carries a collar with twelve holes around its circumference (Fig. 320) which allows simple indexing by 2, 3, 4, 6 or 12. The vertical detent (plunger) locates in a hole, preventing rota-

Fig. 320: An indexing collar on the rear of the spindle allows controlled rotation.

tion of the collar and the chuck. Initially, the collar is left loose, and the side of the punch head is set parallel to the face of the wheel. The collar is then tightened onto the shaft of the chuck.

Dressing the four edges

A punch with a square head should have a 45 degree chamfer between each side and the top of the head.

On a bench grinder, clamp a bar a short

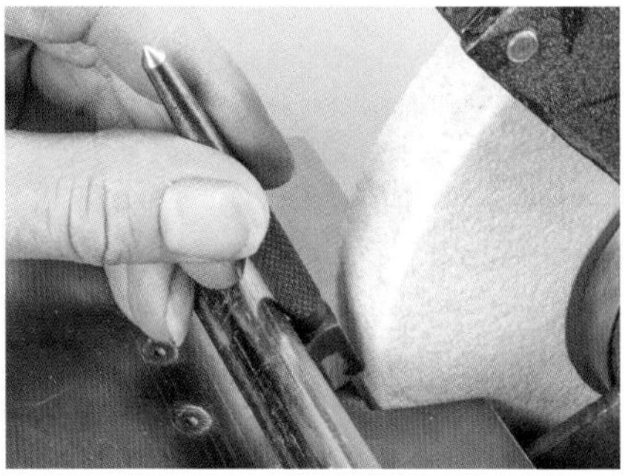

Fig. 321: One simple way to set the angle of the chamfer approximately is to use a bar on the rest as a support and a fulcrum.

distance from the wheel, arranged so that if the punch is tilted backwards at 45 degrees the front corner of a face will be against the wheel when the opposite (rear) face is supported on the top corner of the bar (Fig. 321). Repeat the action for all four sides.

Alternatively, use a punch holder or workhead (Fig. 322) capable of tilting at right angles to the face of the wheel and allowing rotation about its long axis. If the spindle can be locked in any position, the rotation

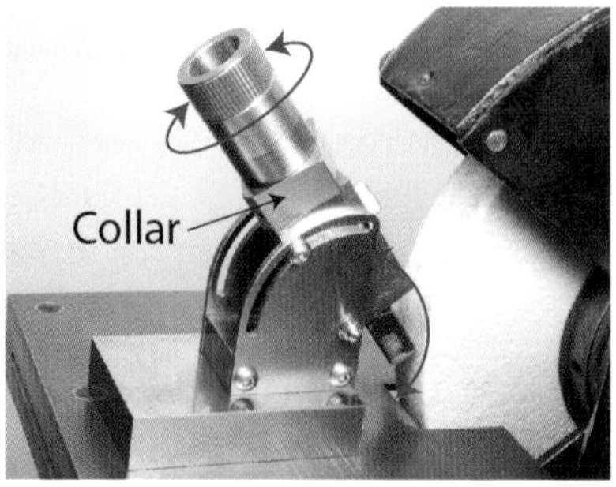

Fig. 322: A punch may be held in a tilting work head, and indexed using a square collar.

Fig. 323: Set one side face of the punch head vertical using an engineer's square.

can provide a simple indexing facility, to allow the four faces and edges at the top of the punch head to be ground. Indexing may be controlled using an engineer's square against the sides of the head of the punch, provided they are flat (Fig. 323) or by attaching a square-sided collar to the punch body and using that, in conjunction with an engineer's square, to set each side vertical in turn (Figs 323 and 324). In the tilted position, the angle makes it difficult to align the collar, so it may be easier to tilt the punch back to the zero position then align the col-

Fig. 324: Set one side of the collar vertical using an engineer's square, to position the corresponding side of the punch head.

lar using a square, before tilting back to 45 degrees to grind the next edge. As with the indexing collar shown in Fig. 320, leave the collar loose until the first side of the punch head has been set vertical. Then lock the collar with one of its sides vertical.

- Set the axis of the punch at right angles to the face of the wheel, then tilt the punch at an angle of 45 degrees to the face of the wheel (Fig. 322).
- Apply a cut towards the wheel, and traverse parallel to the face of the wheel.
- Index the punch head through 1/4 turn, and repeat the grind. Repeat for the other edges.

GRINDING PIN PUNCH SHAFTS

Pin punches have nominally parallel shafts and are typically used to knock pins out of holes. Pin punch shafts may be parallel or may have a small back taper (1–2 degrees included angle), so that the shaft has a smaller diameter nearest the handle end (Fig. 325). This provides a small amount of clearance as the punch enters a hole, and helps prevent the punch from seizing in the hole. It has the disadvantage that sharpening the punch by grinding the end face will result in a reduction in the diameter of the face. The steeper the taper, the greater the reduction. If diameter is important, leave the shaft parallel, or leave a short parallel section (perhaps 1–3mm long) before the taper. Normally, the working face of the punch is ground to sharpen or reform the end of the punch, because grinding the taper reduces the diameter of the punch. However; it is useful to be able to grind a taper when creating a new punch, or deliberately reducing the diameter of an existing punch.

To create the taper, the axis of the punch must be swung so that the side of the punch is parallel to the axis of traverse. That means the axis of the punch will not be parallel to the traverse, but will be swung through the half-angle of the taper (Fig. 326). That requires a workholder which can hold the punch at that angle compared to the traverse (Figs 327 and 328).

- Mount a wheel which has its working face at the side, at right angles to the grinder shaft. A type 11 taper cup wheel or a type 6 cup wheel both work well.
- Set a guide at 90 degrees to the axis of the wheel (Figs 327 and 328).

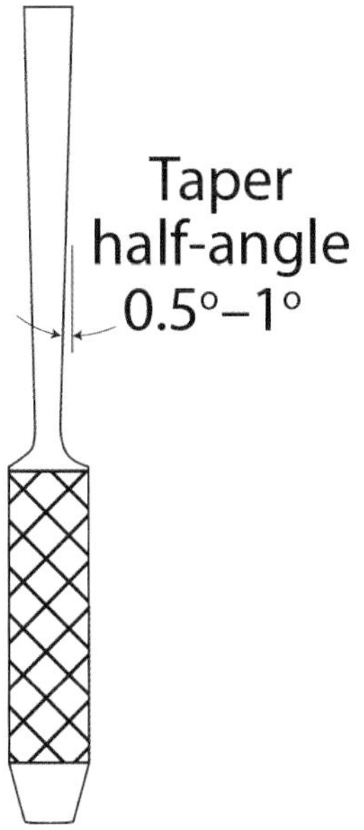

Fig. 325: The side of a tapered shaft lies at an angle to the long axis of the punch.

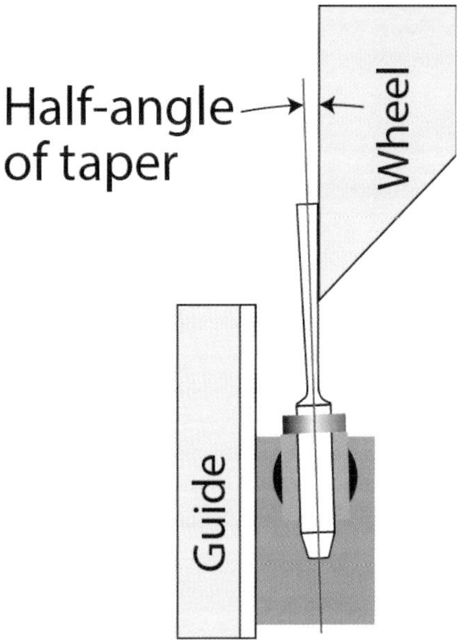

Fig. 326: Swing the tool while keeping the traverse guide at 90 degrees to the axis of the wheel spindle.

Fig. 327: A punch holder carrying two adjustable screws on the side next to the traverse guide. Adjusting one screw further outwards than the other sets the holder at an angle to the traverse, but traverse takes place along the side of the guide.

Fig. 328: A punch holder positioned with its axis at an angle to the traverse, making the side of the punch shaft parallel to the traverse and the face of the wheel. The angle is exaggerated in this photo, for clarity. Take care with this setup, because the workholder is heavy and the rest may require additional support.

- Set a workholder against the guide, so that traverse will take place along the guide. Use a workholder which is capable of remaining in contact with the guide while holding the punch at an angle (Figs 326 and 328). It is useful, but not essential, if the rest is adjusted so that the punch contacts the wheel at approximately centre height.
- With the punch in the workholder, and keeping the workholder against the guide, swing the punch holder through the half-angle of the taper (0.5–1 degree), taking the tip of the punch away from

the wheel. That is done by adjusting the screws shown in Figs 327 and 328. The side of the punch shaft should now be parallel to the axis of traverse, and the guide, but the shank will lie at an angle (Fig. 328).

- Move the guide and workholder sideways, towards the wheel, until the punch just touches the face of the wheel. Set an adjustable stop to control the feed (the sideways movement of the guide).
- The basic action is to slide the workholder along the guide, taking the punch shaft across the face of the wheel, then back, while rotating the punch continuously. If the direction of the wheel is downwards at the front, rotate the punch anti-clockwise (viewed from the rear) against the direction of travel of the abrasive particles in the wheel. Traverse-and-rotation is a two-handed job, and a lock is essential to prevent the guide from sliding away from the wheel. Feed is applied by moving the guide towards the face of the wheel, and an adjustable stop helps control the feed. Repeat the sequence: unlock the guide; feed to apply a cut; lock the guide; advance and retract while rotating the punch; until the punch has been reformed and has a sharp corner between the face and the shaft.

GRINDING PIN PUNCH WORKING FACES

Grinding the flat working face is often enough to restore a pin punch to working order. The basic method is to present the tip to the face of a wheel, and rotate the tip as it is traversed across the face.

- Mount a type 1 wheel.
- Grip the punch in a rotatable sleeve or collet, in a workholder which allows the face to be held vertically and parallel to the axis of the grinder, the face of the wheel, and the direction of traverse. Set the axis of the punch at wheel centre height (Fig. 329).

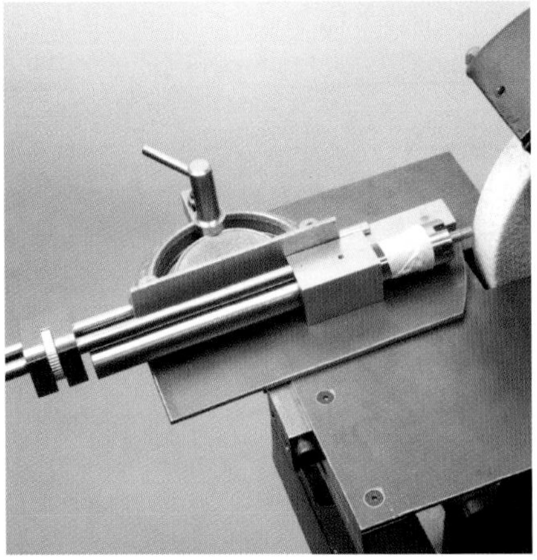

Fig. 329: This punch is gripped in a collet holder which has a long shaft. The holder can rotate in a bored block.

- With the punch clear of the wheel, apply a cut. Traverse until at least half the diameter of the punch face is in contact with the wheel; then rotate the punch. Continue to rotate while reversing the traverse, taking the punch clear of the wheel. Alternatively, rotate continuously while traversing across the face of the wheel, taking the punch clear on the other side.

Most flat-faced punches can be left with an as-ground finish, because the faces of these punches usually benefit from friction created by grinding marks to resist slipping in use.

SHARPENING CENTRE PUNCHES

Pointed punches such as centre, dot and pricker punches have a relatively simple geometry, with a long shallow nose angle of approximately 22 degrees, and a short conical point with an angle of between 30 and 90 degrees (Fig. 314). Although terminology varies, centre punches generally have a point angle of 90 degrees, dot punches 60 degrees, and pricker punches may have a point angle as fine as 30 degrees. The fine-pointed pricker punches are used to make a small initial mark, often at the intersection of two scribed lines. The dot or centre punch is then placed in that small indentation and struck more firmly to produce a depression large enough to provide a locating point for a drill. Centre punches need a 90 degree point angle to provide sufficient strength to prevent the point crumbling when the punch is struck. Finer points are less strong, but the dot and pricker punches are intended to be struck lightly to make smaller indentations.

Sharpening these punches involves holding the tip of the punch at an angle to the grinding wheel to form the required point angle. This is usually half the included angle of the punch point.

A sleeved punch holder

The relatively simple workholder shown in Figs 329 and 330, and the more sophisticated tilting holder shown in Fig. 322–324 both accept 16mm diameter sleeves which can be bored to suit smaller diameter punches, allowing these workholders to grip a good range of the punches in common use. The tilting workholder may be tilted from the vertical (0 degrees) position to the horizontal (90 degrees). Each sleeve has a groove which is engaged by a pin which can clamp the sleeve stationary or, if slightly slackened, can allow the sleeve to rotate without moving along the bore. Fig. 330 also shows a double-ended sleeve which can accept different sizes of punch at each end; a square collar for simple indexing; and a handle which can be attached to the rear of a sleeve, to allow better control of rotation within the workholder.

Fig. 330: A workholder based on a bored square-section block which holds 16mm diameter sleeves. The small screw locates in a groove in the sleeves.

Grinding the point

The punch may be held parallel to a flat rest, supported in a holder which allows rotation, with the point of the punch at the same height as the centre of the wheel (Fig. 331). Fit a collar to the rear of the punch shank, to prevent unwanted forward movement during grinding.

- Mount a type 1 wheel.
- Begin with the punch in its holder, lying parallel to the rest and with its long axis parallel to the face of the wheel. Swing the holder through the half-angle (Fig. 332).
- Apply a cut, then traverse across the face of the wheel while rotating the punch by hand.

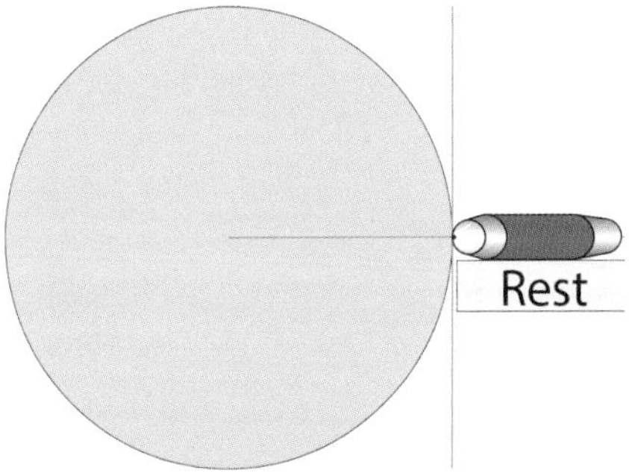

Fig. 331: Viewed from the side: the punch should be held with its point at centre height. For clarity, the holder is omitted from this view.

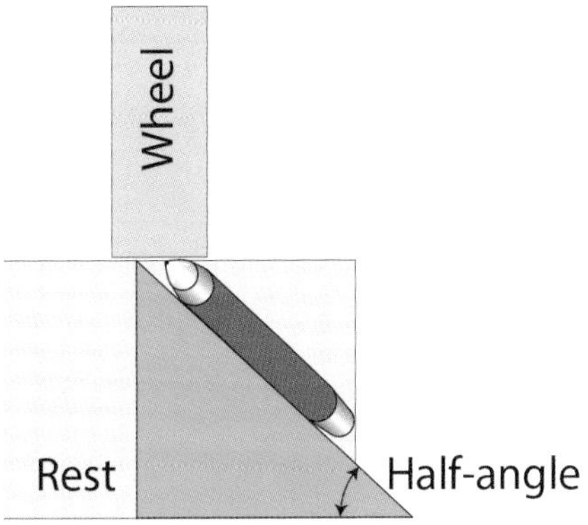

Fig. 332: Viewed from above: swing the holder and punch through the half-angle. of the point. For clarity, the holder is omitted from this view.

Although this general method is simple enough to produce a reasonably accurate result,there are better methods.

Ideally, the grinding marks on a punch should run from tip to body, rather than around the tip (Fig. 333). That makes the

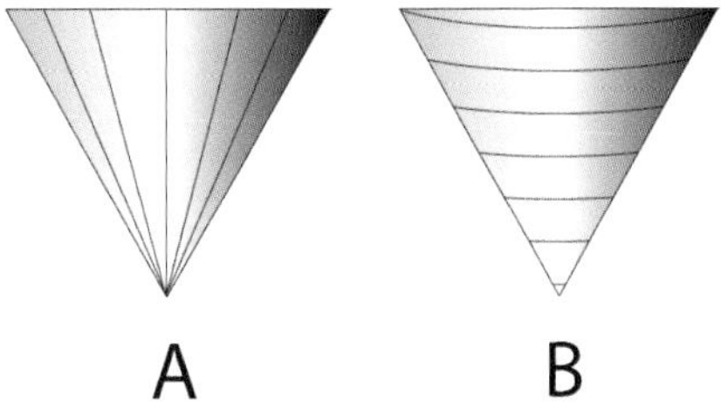

Fig. 333: Ideally, grinding marks on the tip of a punch should run as shown at A.

point of the punch stronger, and marginally improves the penetration of the point into the material being marked, because the displaced metal moves along microscopic grooves rather than jumping across ridges. That means the punch must be aligned with the direction of movement of the abrasive particles in the grinding wheel as shown in Fig. 334.

Traditionally, the punch is held as shown in Fig. 335, and although that is often done freehand, much better results can be achieved by using a workholder which grips the punch with the point downwards (Fig. 336). That avoids any tendency for the sharp point of the punch to catch and dig into the wheel.

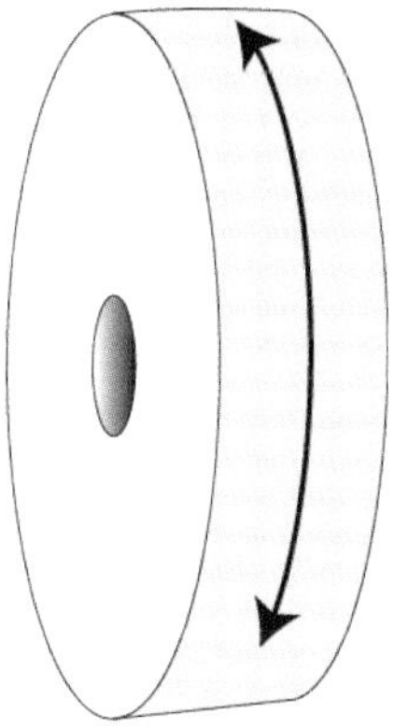

Fig. 334: For striations to run from tip to body, the axis of the punch must be aligned with the direction of travel of the grains on the face of the wheel.

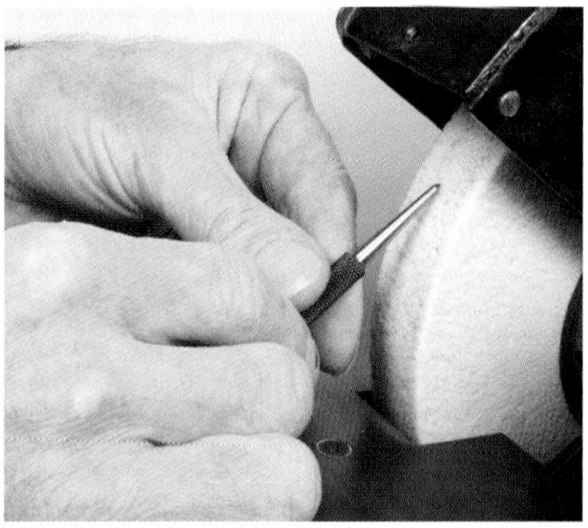

Fig. 335: Traditionally, the punch is balanced on the rest and held facing up the wheel.

Fig. 336: Tilt the workhead to the half-angle of the taper, and adjust the rest height to set the tip of the punch on centre height.

- Beginning with the punch in the workholder, pointing vertically downwards, tilt the holder backwards by the half-angle of the punch (22.5 degrees for a 45 degree tip, for example).
- Adjust the height and tilt of the rest so that the tip of the punch is on a radial centre line and the rest is parallel to that line (Fig. 337). Use a template or setting plate.
- Feed is applied by moving the workholder towards the wheel, and this is most easily controlled if the holder is located against a guide on the rest, set at 90 degrees to the face of the wheel. The shape produced is very slightly hollowed, but the effect is negligible over

the length of a short tip, and will not affect the performance of the punches.
- Rotate the punch to grind the tip.

Fig. 337: Set the tip of the punch on a radial centre line (red), with the rest parallel (green) to that line.

Grinding the long secondary taper

The long taper behind the point of the punch is normally formed before the tip is ground. As with the tapered shaft of a pin punch (page 83), the basic requirement is that, compared to the face of the wheel, the body or shank of the punch is held at half the included angle of the long taper, which is often 5 degrees included or 2.5 degrees half-angle. Traverse is carried out parallel to the face of the wheel, while rotating the punch. Feed is applied by moving punch and holder towards the wheel without altering the angle of the body of the punch in relation to the face of the wheel. Fig. 338 shows a suitable holder, similar to the holder used to grind tapered pin punches (Figs 327 and 328) but using sleeves instead of a collet holder. Punches which have non-circular bodies need to be securely located in a close-fitting cylindrical hole in a sleeve to allow them to be mounted in the holder (Fig. 339).

- Mount a type 11 wheel, and set the punch at approximately radial centre height.
- With the axis of the punch set parallel to the face of the wheel, swing the holder away from the wheel by the half-angle of the taper (typically 2.5 degrees for a 5 degree taper). On the holder shown in Fig. 338, this is arranged by adjusting the front side screw outwards.
- Move the guide to apply a cut towards the wheel, then traverse parallel to the face of the wheel while rotating the punch. Fine cuts are created using an adjustable stop against the guide.

Fig. 338: A holder which accommodates punches gripped in sleeves. Side adjustment screws swing the holder through the half-angle of the punch taper.

Fig. 339: Punches with non-circular bodies can be slipped into close-fitting cylindrical holes to allow them to be accommodated in the holder.

An alternative is to omit continuous rotation initially, and grind a series of small flats, turning the punch a few degrees between passes, without altering the feed. After a complete turn, blend the flats using continuous rotation.

When shaping a taper for the first time, monitor the heat generated as material is removed, and allow the punch to cool before it overheats.

SHARPENING TRANSFER PUNCHES

Transfer punches (Fig. 312) have flat ends which carry a small protruding centre point, rather like a flat-ended pin punch crossed with a centre punch. Designed to transfer the position of the centre of a hole from one workpiece to another, a transfer punch fits snugly in a hole of a particular size. The shank of the punch is parallel along its length, and is ground to a specific diameter. Striking the punch causes the centre point to make an indentation in work below. The centre point is small to allow the punch to be of use with short holes where a longer point would not allow the parallel shank to sit inside the hole.

Although most wear will take place on the point of the punch, it is often necessary to grind back the surrounding flat area to allow the conical section to continue to protrude a usable distance above the surface. Sharpening can take place in two stages, grinding the flat face then restoring the shape of the conical point. When grinding punches, it is useful if the workhead spindle is free to rotate.

Dressing the flat section of the face

- Mount a type 1 wheel, and dress the wheel face parallel to the axis of the grinder spindle, ensuring sharp corners between the front and sides of the wheel.
- Set the point of the punch on centre, with the axis of the punch aligned along a radial centre line.
- Set a traversing guide at right angles to the axis of the grinder spindle and the face of the wheel.
- With the punch set at 90 degrees to the face of the wheel, set a stop so that traverse ends just before the root of the central cone of the punch reaches the corner of the wheel (Figs 340 and 341).
- Beginning with the punch clear of the wheel, apply a cut by moving the punch

Fig. 340: Set the punch on centre and grind the flat area against the face of a type 1 wheel.

Fig. 341: Orientate the axis of the punch at 90 degrees to the axis of the wheel, and (optionally) set a stop to prevent the conical point from being ground. Note the tape protecting the threads of the collet holder.

holder forwards, then traverse while rotating the punch. Repeat as necessary to clean up the face of the punch. An alternative is to traverse to the stop; rotate the punch at least one full turn; then traverse clear while rotating.

- Set the punch at 45 degrees to the face of the wheel, and grind a very small chamfer around the outer edge of the flat face, to remove burrs and ensure an easy entry to any hole. To finish this chamfer off, put the punch in a lathe and use a fine Arkansas stone, a ruby burnisher or a similar fine abrasive to ensure the chamfer is burr-free. Shield the bed of the lathe against grinding dust.

Sharpening the conical point

It is possible to sharpen the conical centre point against the face of a type 1 wheel, but it is easier to support the punch when grinding against a type 11 wheel (Fig. 342).

- Mount a type 11 wheel, and dress the side face to form sharp corners between that face and the tapering front sides.
- Put the punch in a holder which allows the punch to rotate. Beginning with the axis of the punch parallel to the face of the wheel, swing through the half-angle of the conical point.
- Set a traverse guide at the half-angle (Fig. 343).

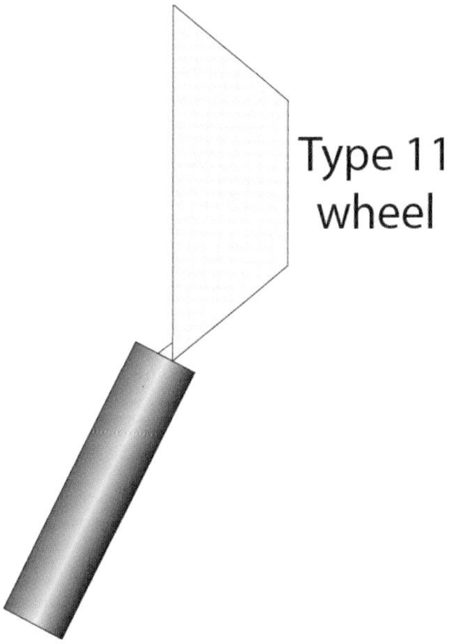

Fig. 342: Swing the punch to the half-angle and grind the conical centre against the face of a type 11 wheel.

- Set the height of the rest so that the central axis of the punch is horizontal and exactly on the centre line of the wheel. This ensures that for small depths of cut the curved edge of the wheel is less likely to foul the flat section of the face of the punch.
- Set a traverse stop so that the wheel remains clear of the face as the conical point is ground (Fig. 343).
- With the punch retracted clear of the wheel, apply a small cut by using an adjustable stop to control the movement of the guide. Slide the punch holder along the guide, to contact the wheel. Move the holder and punch further along the guide while rotating the punch, stopping before the wheel grinds the flat face of the punch. Retract; then repeat as required, until the cone is fully formed.

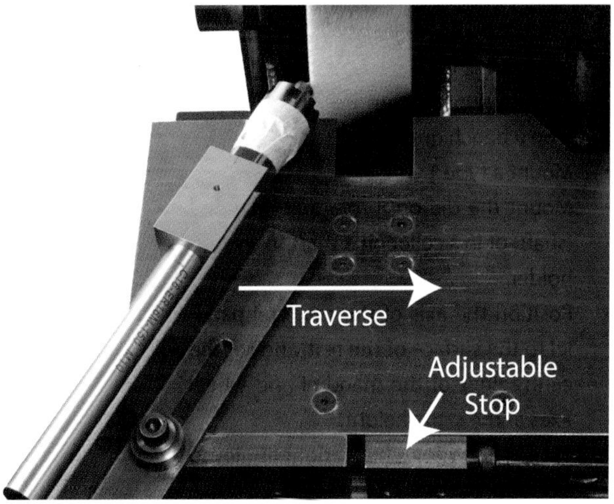

Fig. 343: Orientate the axis of the punch at 90 degrees to the axis of the wheel. Note the tape protecting the threads of the collet holder.

SHARPENING HOLE PUNCHES AND DIES

Hole punches work by pushing a male punch into a hole in a die. Any material between punch and die is pierced by the punch and a hole is produced (Fig. 344). The diameters of punch and die are fixed, so sharpening must not alter the outer diameter of the punch or the inner diameter of the die. On some flat-ended punches the end is at right angles to the axis of the punch and all the material around the edge is sheared simultaneously; but on others the end face is tilted to one side, so that the material is pierced at one point then sheared further round the edge as the punch penetrates more deeply (Fig. 344). That reduces the force required to shear the material. Other punches may initially pierce the work simultaneously at two or more points (Fig. 345). That can help balance the forces on the punch so that it does not tend to be pushed to one side. Punching forces can be high, and damage often occurs to both punch and die, so both may need to be sharpened.

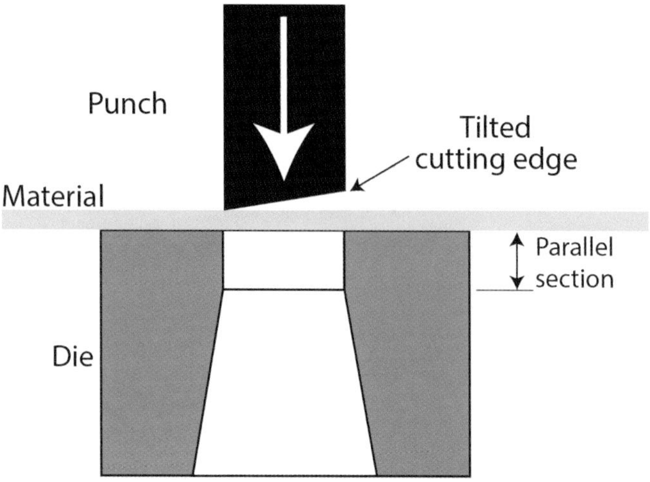

Fig. 344: A punch pierces the work and passes through into the die. The hole in the die determines the diameter of the hole in the work.

Flat-faced dies

The die is most likely to be damaged around its inner edge, so sharpening involves grinding the top face back to restore the edge. Dies often have a short parallel section at the top of the hole, so grinding the face lightly will not alter the size of the hole. Larger punches may need to be sharpened by grinding the top face in a surface grinder, but smaller punches can usually be sharpened on a bench grinder.

- Mount a type 1 wheel.
- Mount the die on a rotatable mandrel (shaft) or in a collet on a shaft, in a workholder.
- Position the axis of the mandrel parallel to the surface of the rest, and set the centre lines of the mandrel and wheel axes at the same height.
- Set a traversing guide at right angles to the axis of the wheel spindle (Fig. 346).
- With the die clear of the wheel, apply a cut by moving the workholder forwards.
- Rotating the die continuously, traverse across the face of the wheel until the wheel is grinding the width of the ring at one side of the central hole of the die. Continue to rotate as the traverse is reversed to take the die clear of the wheel. Where possible, arrange the direction of rotation of the wheel so that the frictional drag of the grinding action will tend to tighten the nut securing the die to its arbor. Viewed from the rear of the mandrel, a right hand thread is tightened when the left side of the die is in contact with a wheel rotating downwards.

Fig. 346: Position the face of the die vertical and parallel to the axis of traverse. Rotate the die continuously while traversing towards the wheel, as far as the width of the ring around the central hole, then reverse to take the punch clear.

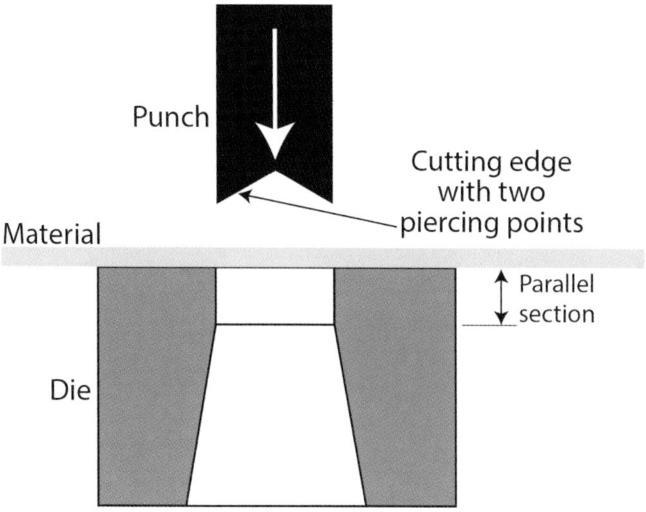

Fig. 345: A bifurcated punch initially pierces the work at two points, simultaneously.

Flat-ended hole punches

Flat ended hole punches which have their end at right angles to the axis of the punch are sharpened in the same way as for flat-faced dies and flat-ended pin punches (*see* pages 84 and 88). The punch should be gripped in a collet or a holder, or mounted on a mandrel which allows it to be rotated continuously.

Flat-ended punches with locating centre points

Some popular hand-held punch tools like the Whitney or the Sealey have flat-ended punches with little projecting pips in the centre, designed to locate in the dimple created by a centre punch (Fig. 347). These

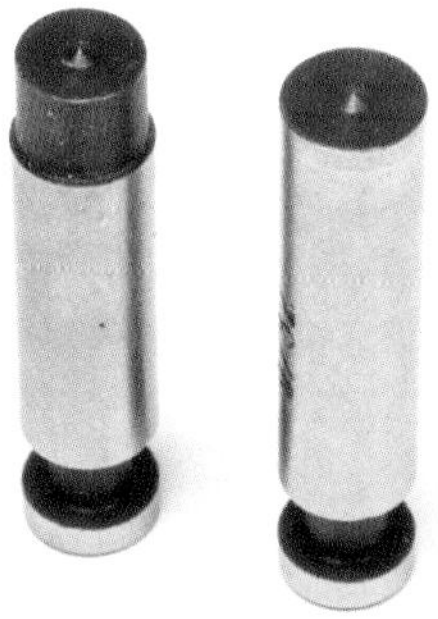

Fig. 347: Some hand-held sheet metal punches have central 'pips' which locate in a centre-punched dimple.

punches can be sharpened in the same way as for transfer punches (*see* earlier in this chapter). The central 'pip' may be quite small, so unless it is damaged, just grind the flat part of the end (*see* Figs 340 to 343).

Punches with flat bifurcated faces

Bifurcated punches have two flat facets arranged in a vee shape (Fig. 345). Depending on the angle of the vee, flat faces may be ground using one of three methods. Where a belt or grinding wheel is involved (methods 2 and 3), ensure a good grip by mounting the punch on a screwed arbor (shaft), or hold the punch in a collet or sleeve.

Method 1: Using an abrasive stone, if the vee is 90 degrees or more:

For each flat face in turn;

- hold the face against the surface of the stone, and traverse along the stone (Fig. 348).
- Check the sharpened points are at the same height.

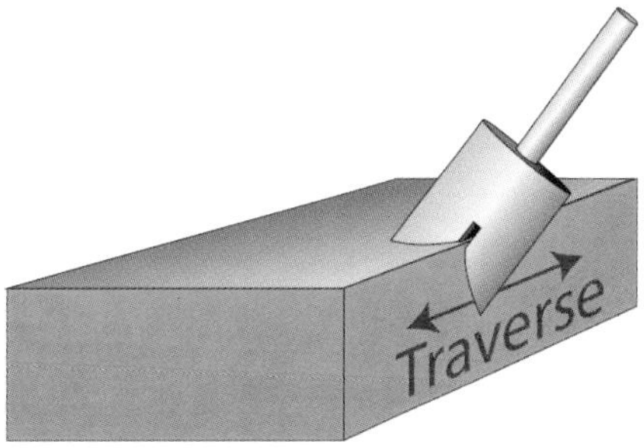

Fig. 348: If the angle between faces is 90 degrees or more, rub each face along an abrasive stone.

Method 2: Using a belt; if the vee is 90 degrees or more:

For each flat face in turn;

- hold the face against the surface of the belt (Fig. 349).
- Check the sharpened points are level.

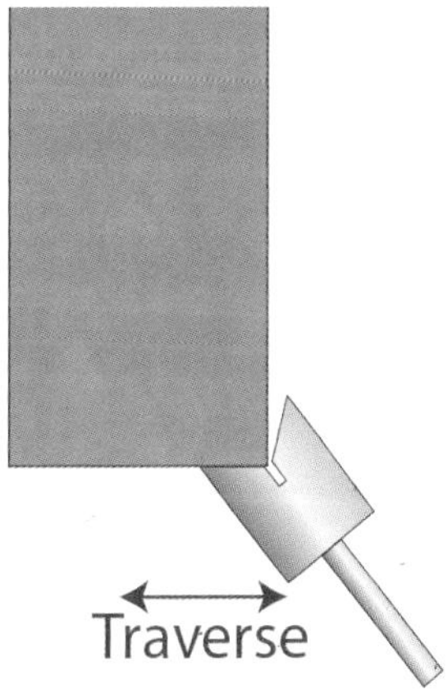

Fig. 349: Viewed from above: If the angle between the two faces of a bifurcated punch is 90 degrees or more, hold each face in turn against a belt.

Method 3: Using a grinder:

For each flat face in turn;

- mount a type 12 or 11 tapered cup wheel which can reach into the vee without grinding the other flat surface.
- Rotate the punch arbor and use a square to set one flat face vertical (Fig. 350).
- Set both the axis of the workhead spindle and the face of the wheel parallel to the axis of traverse.
- Swing the workhead, to set one flat face of the vee parallel to the axis of traverse (Fig. 351).
- Beginning with the face of the wheel aligned with the vertical flat, move the guide to apply a cut, and set a traverse stop to protect the other flat.
- Grind by traversing along the flat.
- Index and repeat for the second flat.

If the sharpened points are not level, grind more from the face with the extended point.

Fig. 350: Set one flat face vertical, using a square. The square collar at the front allows indexing.

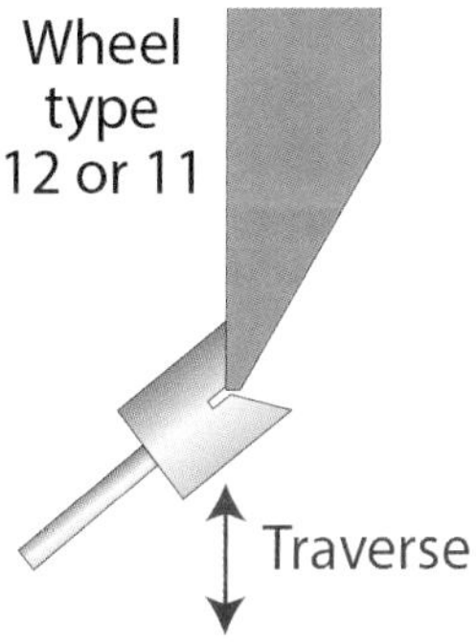

Fig. 351: Viewed from above: Swing the workhead, to set one face of the vee parallel to the axis of traverse.

Punches with an inner curved surface

Some punches, such as the popular Q-Max range, have curved bifurcated faces with four additional facets which create two points on the edges which pierce the work (Fig. 352). The extent of any damage will determine which parts of the punch must be reground: the curved face and the facets, or the facets alone.

Fig. 352: Q-Max punches use curved faces with additional facets to create two piercing points.

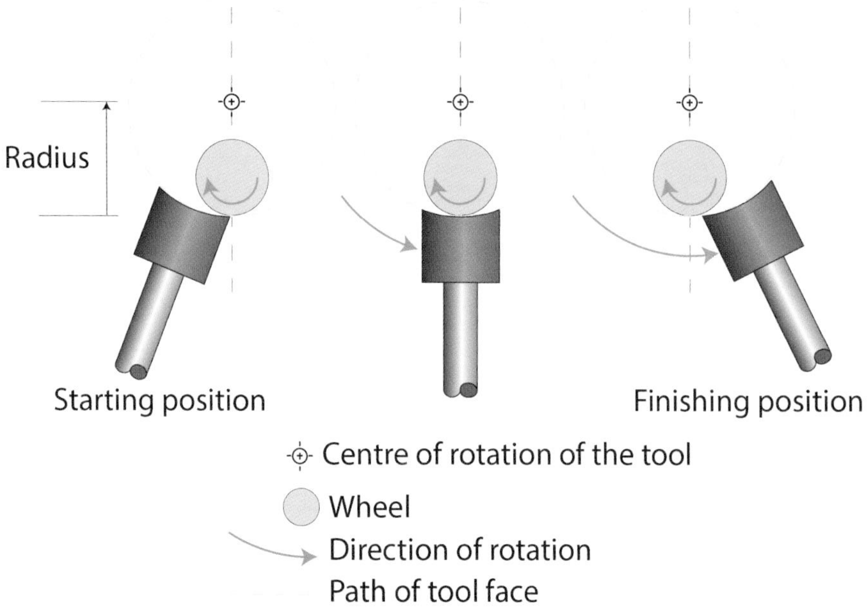

Fig. 353: The relationship between the work pivot point, the face of the wheel, and the face of the tool.

Grinding the inner curved surface

Grinding the inner surface of a punch with a curved face by using a wheel of similar radius will generate heat quickly because of the large contact area. A better method is to use the curved face of an internal grinding wheel or a cylindrical 'pin', which has a radius smaller than the punch face. The punch must be set up so that it traverses in an arc as it passes the face of the wheel (Fig. 353). The radius of the arc should be the radius of the curved punch face. Contact will be along a narrow line, so less heat will be generated. Fig. 354 illustrates the setup using a drilling machine as the spindle and a lathe topslide to hold the work and provide an axis of pivot as well as some adjustment of the cut. The topslide carries a plate, to which is attached a vee block (using screws underneath the plate). The topslide has a boss which pivots in a circular block attached to a bed plate, and the topslide has a drilled hole along the axis of pivot, to take an alignment pin. The vee block plate can be moved sideways a small distance. Fig. 355 shows the axes of the topslide pivot, the grinding wheel, and the mandrel which carries the punch to be ground. Those three axes must be in the same plane, so the axes of pivot and wheel must be parallel to the face of the punch, and pass through the long axis of the arbor. Alignment is most easily done in stages.

Fig. 354: A lathe topslide can be used to provide a pivot and a feed for the cut.

Fig. 355 The axes of the topslide pivot, the wheel, and the mandrel must lie in the same plane.

- To align the axis of the work with the axis of pivot, first loosen the vee block plate. With a setting pin in the topslide pivot, mount a cross-drilled bar in the vee block, so that the pin passes through the hole. Tighten the vee block plate onto the topslide (Fig. 356).

Fig. 356: Use a pin in the pivot, and a cross-drilled bar in the vee block to align the two associated axes.

- To align the axis of the wheel with the pivot axis, begin by swinging the topslide until it is approximately parallel to the side of the bed plate, and ensure the bed plate which carries the topslide assembly is free to move on the surface of the table. With a setting pin in the chuck, move the bedplate until the pin slides freely in the pivot pin hole (Fig. 357). Clamp a bar to the drilling machine table, lying along the side of the bedplate, to provide a reference. Remove the setting pin.

Fig. 357: Use a setting pin in the chuck, to align the axes of the pivot and the wheel.

- Mount, then dress, the wheel (Fig. 358). The topslide should be held stationary, cut applied by the topslide feedscrew, and traverse created by feeding the wheel down, past the diamond dresser.

Fig. 358: Mount, then dress the wheel.

- Slide the bed plate along the reference bar until the distance from the rear of the pivot pin to the front of the wheel is the required radius to be ground, plus half the diameter of the setting pin. Clamp the bed plate to the table.
- Mount the punch on its mandrel, and align the punch vertically by snuggling its face against the wheel (Fig. 359).
- Swing the topslide until the punch is in the starting position (Fig. 353) clear of the wheel.

Fig. 359: Align the punch vertically against the face of the wheel.

- Back off the topslide feed, to take the punch clear of the wheel, then set the wheel rotating, and swing the topslide assembly past the wheel then back to the starting position. Use the topslide feedscrew to apply a cut and repeat the swing. If the first grinding marks are at the tips, the radius may be too large; but if they are in the centre only, the radius may be too small. Adjust the radius by sliding the whole assembly along the reference bar, to change the distance between the pivot on the topslide and the face of the wheel. The topslide controls the depth of cut, but has no effect on the radius ground by the wheel.

Grinding side facets

The four side facets on a Q-Max punch create two points which initially pierce a sheet, and those points eventually wear. To sharpen these, use a wheel which is a reasonable match for the curve of the facets; smaller if necessary, but not larger in diameter.

- Mount the wheel in the drill chuck, lock the topslide pivot, and remove the side guide bar from the table.
- Set one piercing point vertically above the other, then slide the bedplate and topslide assembly freely until the curve of one facet sits against the face of the wheel (Figs 360 and 361). Clamp the bed plate.
- Mount a square-sided collar on the punch mandrel, against the vee block, and set one side vertical.
- Start the wheel rotating, and use the topslide feedscrew to feed straight into the facet. Aim to reduce but not remove half of the adjacent flat point. Note the final feedscrew reading.
- Rotate the punch through a half-turn and grind the second facet in the same way, stopping at the same feedscrew reading.
- Repeat the sequence for the other pair of facets.
- Use a centre height gauge to check that the points are centred across the diameter of the punch. Adjust, if necessary, by regrinding two diagonally opposite facets. Too fine a point will crumble under the stress of punching. Increase the width of the points by arranging the points vertically and as near as possible to the centre line of the wheel. Add a collar to the shaft, to act as a stop against the rear of the vee block. Apply a cut using the feedscrew, and rotate the punch about its horizontal axis through several full turns by rotating the mandrel. Repeat as necessary.

Fig. 360: Align one facet against the face of the wheel.

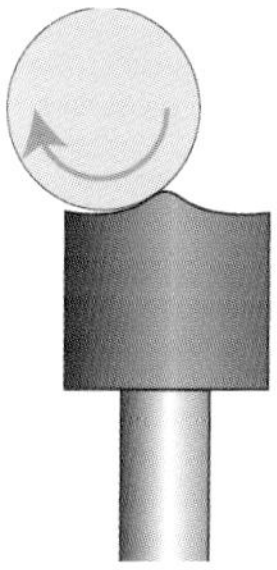

Fig. 361: Align the curve of one facet against the face of the wheel.

Tool type 6: Scrapers

A scraper is a hand-held tool used to remove tiny amounts of metal from a surface, to make the surface flat and create shallow oil pockets (Fig. 362). There are two useful types of scraper: the flat and the triangular. Traditionally, scrapers were made of hardened carbon steel, or HSS steel, but brazed-on or replaceable carbide tips are now popular. Scraping requires frequent sharpening of the tool, but in most cases this is confined to a light sharpening and honing, or honing alone. Scrapers can be sharpened on a bench grinder using a type 1 wheel, but it is often more convenient to use a flat-faced wheel (type 6 or type 11), with the grinder turned end-on and a rest placed opposite the flat face of the wheel. A useful addition is a series of inexpensive flat diamond or cBN wheels of 600, 1500 and 3000 grit, which allow final honing of the scraper faces (Fig. 363). However; these are thin discs and it is essential they are glued to, and backed by, a thicker disc of aluminium.

Fig. 362: From left to right: A flat carbon steel scraper with a hardened nose and curved cutting edges; a scraper with a steel shaft carrying a removable carbide insert at the tip; a three-sided scraper designed to be used inside bearings or holes.

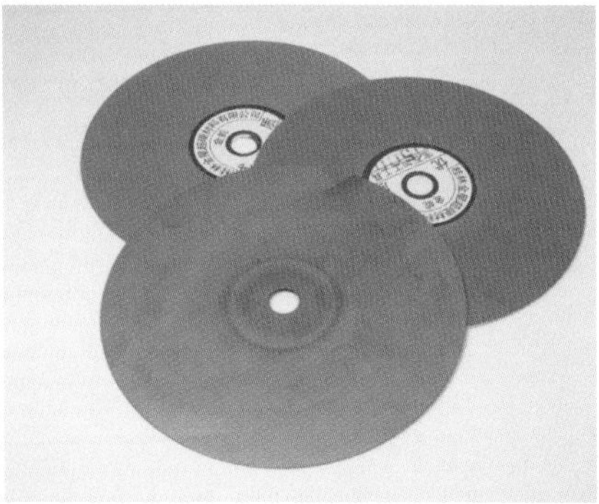

Fig. 363: Turning the grinder end-on then fitting a flat-faced wheel and a suitable rest makes sharpening easy and efficient.

FLAT SCRAPERS

A traditional flat scraper is a long thin piece of steel with a rectangular section and cutting edges at the front (Figs 362 and 364). Typically, a flat steel scraper will be approximately 5mm thick and 16mm wide. The last 40mm or so tapers down to approximately 1.5mm thick at a very hard tip. On each face of the blade there may be a single taper or a compound taper with primary (front) and secondary (rear) sections. On many scrapers, the tip is initially forged to produce a wider, flared, tip. The front face of a steel scraper is often ground at 90 degrees to the axis of the scraper, producing a single facet but two cutting edges (Figs 364 and 365).

More modern scrapers are likely to have a carbide tip, either brazed onto the end of a flat bar, like a traditional steel scraper, or

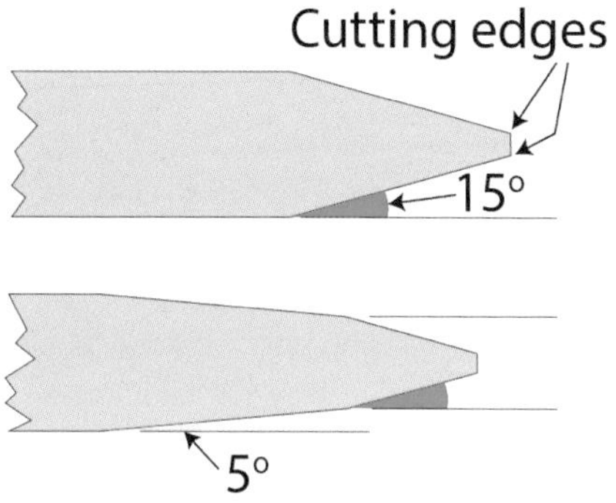

Fig. 364: A flat scraper with a rectangular blade tapers to two cutting edges at the front. The taper may have a single section (top diagram), or it may have a shallow secondary (rear) and a steeper primary (front) section (lower diagram).

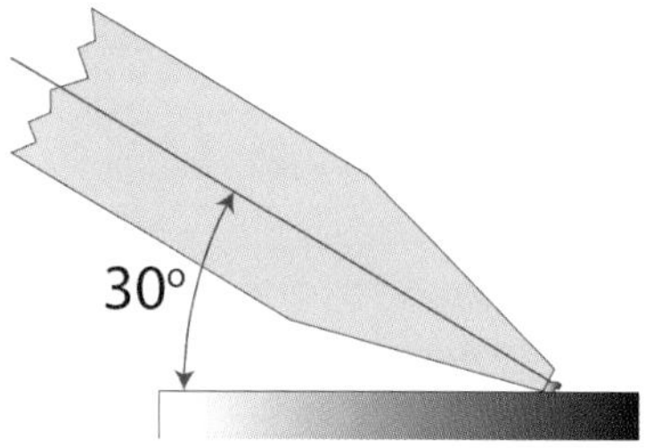

Fig. 365: In use, a scraper is typically held at an angle of approximately 30 degrees to the work.

fitted to a shank with a clamping system at the front (Fig. 362). A replaceable carbide insert is flat on top and bottom, but the front and rear both have two facets, each ground at 85 degrees, producing two cutting edges with a ridge between the facets (Fig. 366). A brazed-on carbide tip is ground

Fig. 366: The face of a replaceable carbide tip has two facets, each ground at 85 degrees. The facets meet on a non-cutting line in the centre.

like a replaceable tip, although its top and bottom surfaces may blend into the taper of the steel shank. On all three types, the cutting edges are at the intersections of the front face and the top and bottom faces (Fig. 364). In use, the scraper is held at an angle of approximately 30 degrees to the work (Fig. 365) although that angle varies with the material and with personal preference.

Shaping the tapers on a flat steel scraper

- With the grinder in the traditional orientation, mount a type 6, 11 or 12 flat-faced wheel.
- Set a guide parallel to the wheel face.
- Clamp the scraper onto a fixture plate, as shown in Figs 367 and 368. Then grip the fixture in a tool holder which can rotate around a vertical axis, independently of the guide (Fig. 368).
- Rotate the tool holder to set the long axis of the scraper at an angle to suit the taper (approximately 15 degrees to the face of the wheel for the primary taper, and 5 degrees for the secondary taper) as shown in Fig. 369.

Fig. 367: A fixture plate for holding a scraper in a lathe-style tool holder. One side of the plate has two pins to align the scraper, and a clamp bar. The other side has a square-section bar which can be gripped in the toolholder.

Fig. 368: A flat scraper held on a fixture plate which is gripped in a lathe-style toolholder for grinding the primary taper.

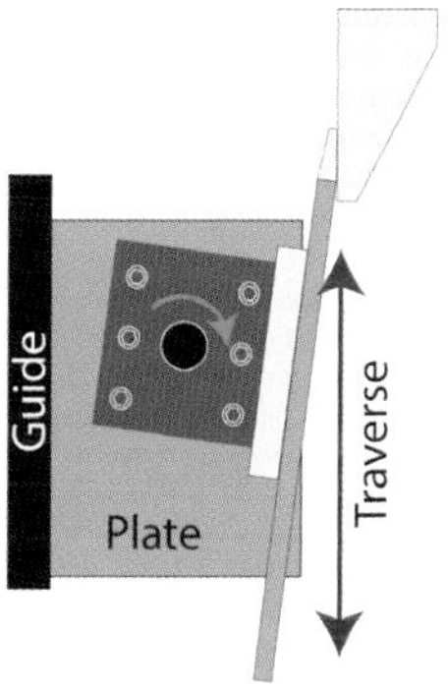

Fig. 369: Turn the toolholder to set the long axis of the scraper at the taper angle.

- Traverse forwards, parallel to the face of the wheel to grind the taper. When grinding the tapered face, use light cuts and rapid traversing movements, to minimize heat transfer. Steel scrapers have hardened tips, and heating to the extent that the colour of the steel changes will affect the temper of the scraper, making it less hard, and impairing its cutting performance. Take care to let the scraper cool frequently during grinding. Repeat the shaping operation on the opposite side, if necessary.
- Finish the tapered faces by using a fine flat-faced cBN or diamond wheel, or wait until the cutting edges have been sharpened, and hone all the faces to a fine finish. It is only the finish on the two or three millimetres of the primary taper behind the cutting edge that really matters.

Sharpening steel cutting edges

Normally, sharpening only involves lightly grinding the nose radius to produce sharp cutting edges. Having a radius on the tip is important, as it reduces the breadth of the cut, and helps prevent the corners of the scraper from catching and 'digging into' the work. The size of the radius is a matter of personal preference, and is not at all critical. It is possible to sharpen a scraper against the curved face of a type 1 wheel, but the most practical arrangement is to use the grinder end-on, with a flat-faced wheel and a rest facing the wheel (Fig. 369).

Sharpening by hand

Scrapers are often sharpened freehand, but it is useful to use a steel pin as a steady.

- Place a plate with a pin onto the rest, and clamp it securely in position (Fig. 370).

Type 1 wheel:

- With the grinder in the conventional position and fitted with a type 1 wheel, set the height of the rest so that the centre line of the scraper is on the horizontal centre line of the wheel when the scraper is sitting on the plate.

Fig. 370: The plate carries a post which is secured by a screw on the underside of the plate. The plate must be clamped securely to the rest.

Type 1 wheel, or type 6, 11 or 12 flat-faced wheel:

- Swing the scraper in an arc while in contact with the 'downhill' side of the revolving wheel so that the abrasive pushes the scraper down onto the table. Because of the tapers behind the tip, keep the untapered section of the blade in contact with the rest (Fig. 371).

Fig. 371: Holding the scraper against the post, and flat on the plate, move the handle end to the right to swing the scraper in an arc.

- Aim to produce a tip thickness of 1.5 to 2mm (0.060 to 0.080 inches). Finish against a fine diamond wheel, or move straight to honing.

Sharpening carbide tips and inserts

Carbide inserts can remain in the scraper, and only require the top and bottom front facets to be ground or honed. On a carbide insert or brazed-on tip, the radius is often very large, with a very shallow curve across the width of the tip.

- Mount a diamond wheel of 1500 to 3000 grit, and be prepared to use water as a lubricant.
- Adjust the tilt of the rest, to create the 5 degree back angle. An 85 degree template is useful for this operation.
- Where the radius is large it is difficult to use a pivot point on the rest, and a better arrangement is to grip the handle with one hand; steady that above one hip; and use that as a pivot point. The other hand can guide the front of the scraper with a sweeping motion (Fig. 372).

Fig. 372: Manually pivot a scraper to create a large radius on the nose. The rest is tilted downwards, five degrees at the front, to give an 85 degree included angle on the top face of the scraper insert.

- Turn the insert over in the scraper clamp, and repeat the sequence for the other facet. The bevel between facets should lie approximately in the centre of the thickness of the tip.

Honing the faces

Hone the end faces of the scraper to a fine finish using a fine diamond stone (Fig. 373). A steel scraper with a 90 degree end face can be supported at 90 degrees to the diamond face, but a carbide tip with an 85 degree angle requires a block with a taper running at 5 degrees downwards from the horizontal. Move the scraper backwards and forwards while following the nose curve to remove all scratches and produce a finely polished surface.

Fig. 373: Hone the nose against a fine diamond stone, by holding the stone vertical, supporting the scraper on a flat piece of wood, and swinging the nose across the stone.

When honing the flat primary tapered face of the shank of a steel scraper, precision is best achieved using a mechanical aid to steady the scraper and produce uniformly flat faces as well as consistent angles. Fig. 374 shows a scraper gripped in an Eclipse chisel honing jig designed to hold woodworking chisels at predictable angles. Although the jaws are shaped to hold chisels which taper at the sides, the inner sides of the jig are flat below the normal gripping area, so the scraper can be securely located against the horizontal pins which align the two halves of the body, and clamped using the normal clamping screw. The jig holds a tapered face of a scraper against a honing stone (Fig. 374), at an angle determined by the projection of the scraper from the front of the jig. Although it is possible to calculate the projection (*see* page 76), it is easy enough to hold one face flat against the stone, and

Fig. 374: The angle of the face against the stone depends on the distance the tip projects.

adjust the position of the jig to suit. Wrap a piece of tape around the blade of the scraper so that, when turning the scraper over and re-clamping to hone the taper on the opposite side of the scraper, the tape can be used to quickly establish the same position, and so create the same angle on the second side. Begin with a 600 mesh diamond stone; lubricate the stone; and hone until the face has a uniform finish. Further honing is not likely to be necessary, but can be carried out using finer grades of stone if required.

On a replaceable carbide tip, remove the tip from its clamp, and make one or two strokes with the flat sides against a fine stone.

TRIANGULAR SCRAPERS

Triangular scrapers (Fig. 362) have three faces, each set at 60 degrees to the adjacent faces. The tip is curved, and the faces meet at a point. The faces are normally hollow-ground, having been created by grinding as shown in Fig. 375. Although a hollow-ground face is not essential for the cutting action of the scraper, it is useful when sharpening the cutting edges, as it avoids having to fully grind or hone the whole surface of each face. These scrapers are used inside a hole (typically a bearing) by pushing sideways, at right angles to a cutting edge and using a short curling or flicking action to remove material without digging into the sides of the hole.

Shaping the faces

Faces may be shaped by grinding against the curved face of a type 1 wheel (Fig. 375), finishing by rubbing each face along a semi-circular stone (Fig. 376).

Setting the rest to an appropriate height will place the wheel as shown in Fig. 375, so that the curve will form the concave face of the scraper. A useful rule of thumb is that the surface of the rest should be set a distance of one quarter of the wheel diameter

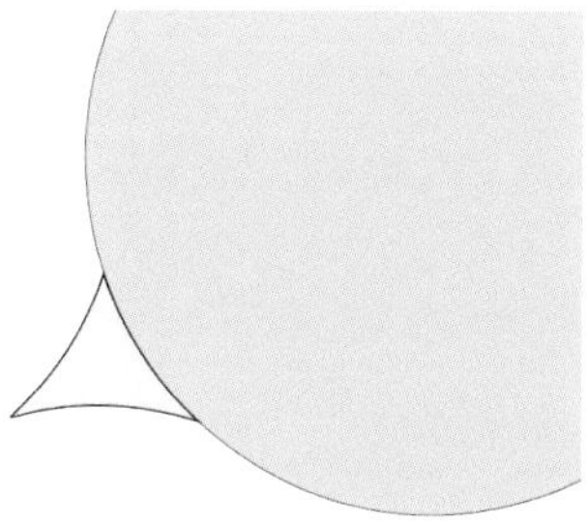

Fig. 375: A triangular scraper has three faces, each hollow-ground against a convex wheel.

Fig. 376: The faces of a triangular scraper can be given a hollow-ground finish by rubbing along a convex abrasive stone.

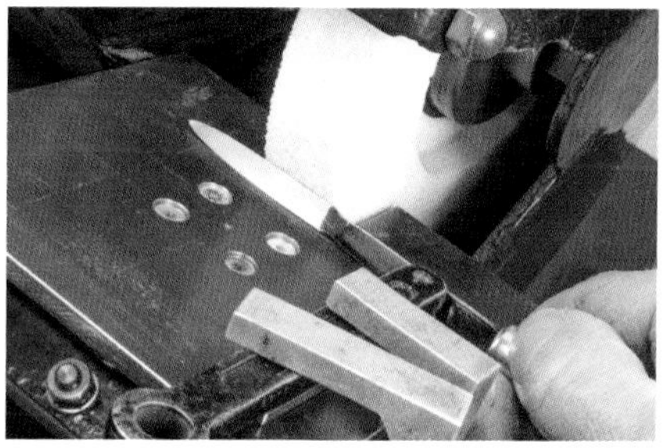

Fig. 377: The rounded end of a spanner shank may be used as a pivot when grinding scraper faces.

below radial centre height. Check that this will grind the curve, by sighting along the face of the scraper, adjusting as necessary. Adjust the rest so that the gap between the front of the rest and the face of the wheel is as small as possible. The cutting edge nearest the wheel will be supported by the rest on either side of the wheel, but it is sensible to ensure there is little opportunity for the cutting edge to slip into the gap. The scraper should be positioned with one face flat against the rest. It can then be pulled past the face of the wheel, following the curve of the tip towards the end.

Fig. 377 shows the shank of a spanner sitting on a slip of 3mm steel, and clamped to the rest. The end of the spanner is rounded and acts as a convenient pivot point and rear support for the scraper. The 3mm slip raises the spanner so that contact between the scraper and the rounded end takes place approximately half way up the face of the scraper, rather than on the wedge-shaped edge of the lower cutting edge. Individual preference comes into play, but it may be easier to begin with the tip of the scraper just touching the wheel near the right hand edge of the face, then push the scraper to the left. Stop when the whole face has been ground. The handle of the scraper will butt against the right hand edge of the rest, acting as a stop, so this is one situation in which it is an advantage to have a relatively narrow rest so that the whole face of the scraper can be ground.

Sharpening the cutting edges

Triangular scrapers are best sharpened by hand, rubbing the faces against a carborundum stone or a diamond plate just sufficiently coarse to remove any damage. Sharpen by hand, rubbing the edges of the scraper along their length, from the curved tip to the end of each edge. Keep pairs of edges against the stone, to preserve the angles of the edges (Fig. 378).

Fig. 378: Keep pairs of edges against a stone when sharpening. Rub lengthways along the scraper faces. Use a shaped wooden or plastic block to protect the fingers.

Tool type 7: Turning tools

As work rotates in a lathe, a tool (Fig. 379) can be forced under the top surface of the work, acting rather like a chisel and shearing material from the work (Fig. 380). That material may pass over the cutting edge of the tool like a ribbon (Fig. 381) or may take the form of short strips or flakes. Collectively, irrespective of their shape, these pieces of waste material are termed 'chips'. The tool creates stress in the material as it pushes it upwards, shearing the material from the work. Although this action is relatively complex, at the microscopic level, the effects are obvious to the naked eye. The quality of surface finish depends on a number of factors, but tool shape is critical. The tool has a cutting edge, and several adjacent faces. The angles formed by those faces relative to the surface of the work depend on the material being cut, as well as the direction in which the tool cuts, the surface finish required, and the efficiency of the cutting process.

British Standard BS1296-2: 1972 defines systems for naming faces, edges and angles of single-point lathe tools, and this book will use many of the definitions given in that documentation. Most are based on the 'tool-in-hand' reference system. Fig. 382 shows a lathe knife tool (a general purpose tool often used for turning), and names the main faces and edges required for sharpening.

The position of the cutting edge depends on the intended purpose of the tool, so that a knife tool may have its Major (or main) cut-

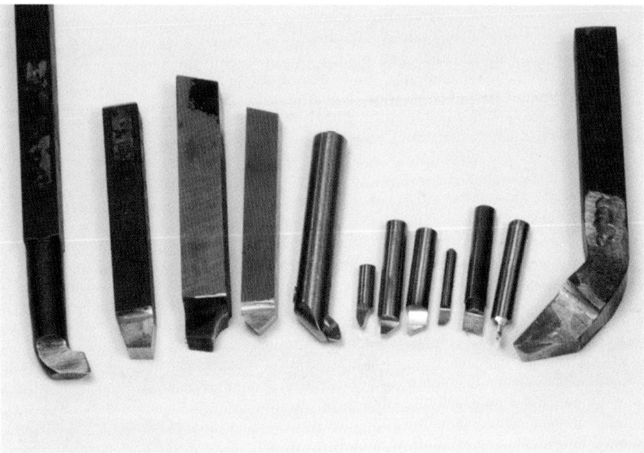

Fig. 379: Lathe turning tools are shaped to suit their function. Left to right: boring, roughing knife, form, vee, short boring bar with insert, six insert bits (screwcutting, two left-hand knife tools, internal curve form, external curve form, parting), cranked left-hand knife tool.

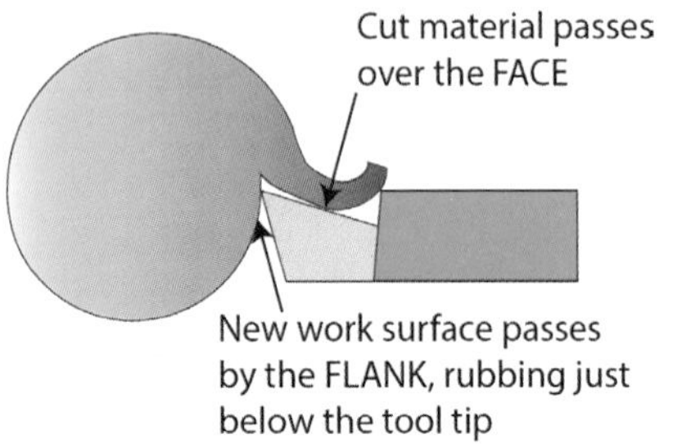

Fig. 380: A turning tool shears material from the work.

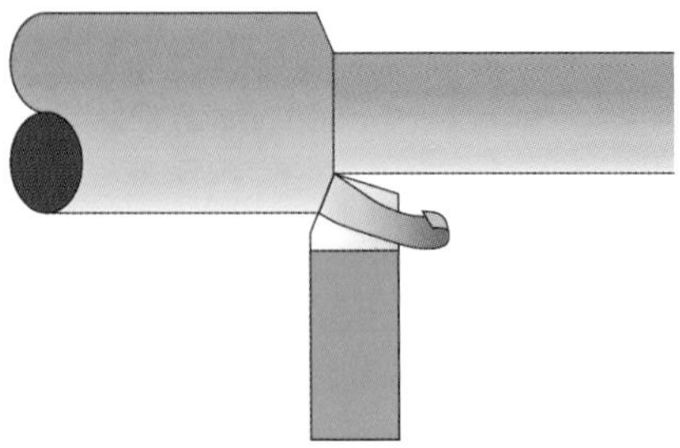

Fig. 381: Material being removed may pass over the cutting edge like a ribbon.

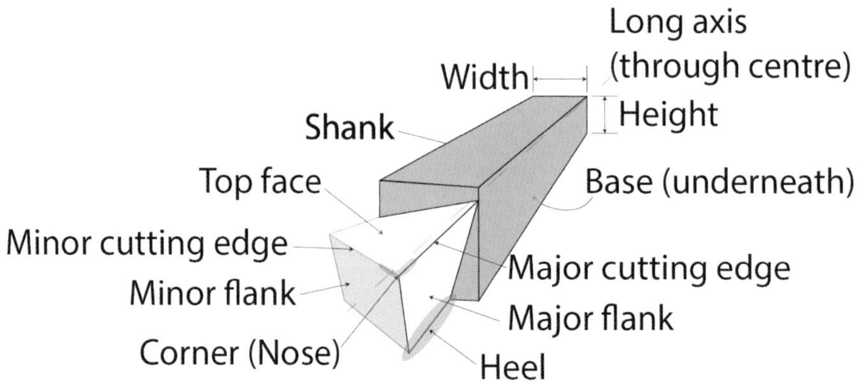

Fig. 382: The various parts of a knife tool, all of which have particular names defined in Standards documents. The nose will typically have a small radius or a flat.

ting edge at the side, to allow the diameter of a bar to be reduced as the tool moves sideways; while the parting tool will have its Major cutting edge at the front so that it can cut an increasingly deep groove as it moves straight forward, eventually cutting a slice off the workpiece. A cutting edge usually penetrates the work and acts to shear material from the workpiece.

The cutting edges are formed between flanks and faces of the tool. A face is a surface over which cut work flows. A flank is a surface over which the surface of the work passes. In other words, the chips flow over the face of the tool, and the material remaining on the work passes over the flanks of the tool, rubbing the flank for a short distance.

A corner sits at the junction between Major and Minor cutting edges, and may be sharp, rounded (radiused) or chamfered. The corner is sometimes referred to by the older term 'nose'. The heel of the tool is the edge between the flank and the base.

The cutting edges, flanks and faces lie at angles measured in relation to features of the tool, such as the base, sides or front, all of which represent planes at right angles to each other (Fig. 383). The three main planes are the 'working plane', the 'tool reference plane' and the 'tool back plane'. The working plane is at the front of the cutting part of the tool, and usually coincides with the workpiece (Fig. 384). The tool reference plane is the base of the tool (or parallel to it). The tool back plane is at right angles to both the tool reference plane and the working plane.

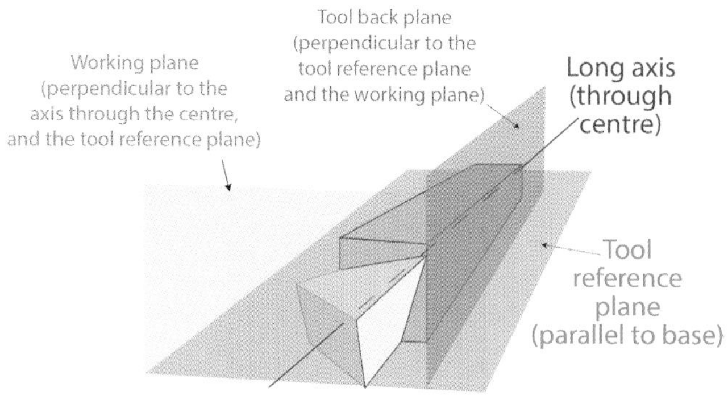

Fig. 383: Features of the tool are located in relation to three main planes: the working plane, the tool reference plane, and the tool back plane.

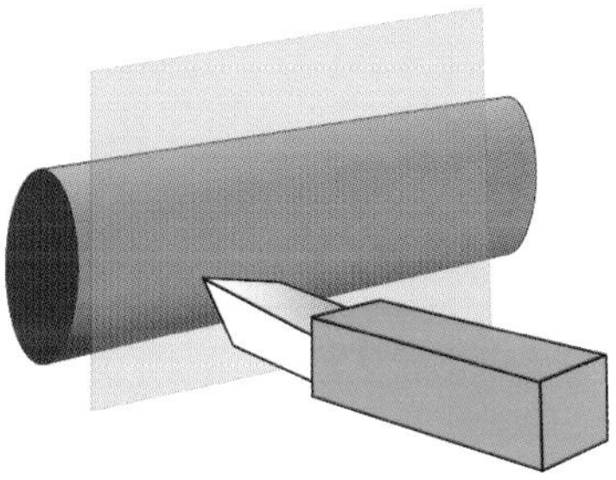

Fig. 384: In the case of a curved workpiece, the working plane will be tangent to the curved surface.

Perhaps surprisingly, the tool back plane is not at the back of the tool.

The cutting edge angle is measured from the working plane to the cutting edge (Fig. 385). The angle at which the cut material passes over the tool depends on the angles of the faces the chips flow over. The rake angle is the angle of the cutting face of the tool, relative to a reference plane parallel to the base (Fig. 386) which is a 'horizontal' plane which touches the tip of the tool. The rake angle is measured at right angles to the cutting edge (Fig. 387), and BS1296-2: 1972 calls this the 'normal' rake angle because it is measured in a plane at right angles to the cutting edge.

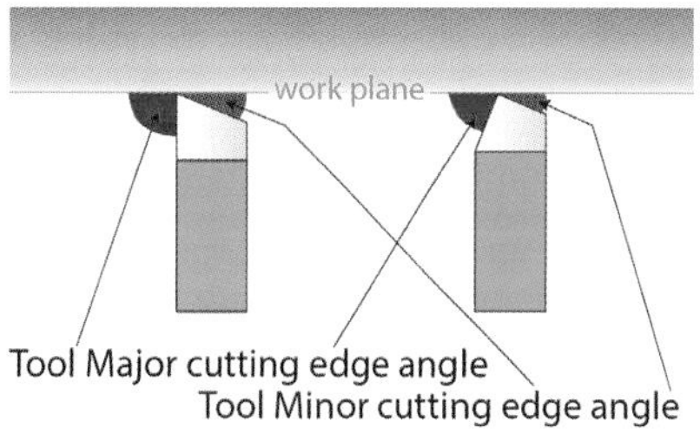

Fig. 385: The cutting edge angle is measured from the working plane to the cutting edge.

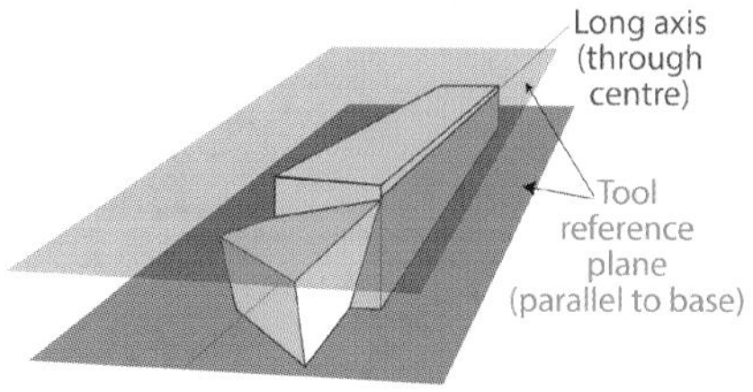

Fig. 386: For measuring rake, a useful reference plane is parallel to the base of the tool.

Fig. 387: A tool may have both side rake and back rake. The result is that the top face lies at a compound angle known as the 'true top rake'.

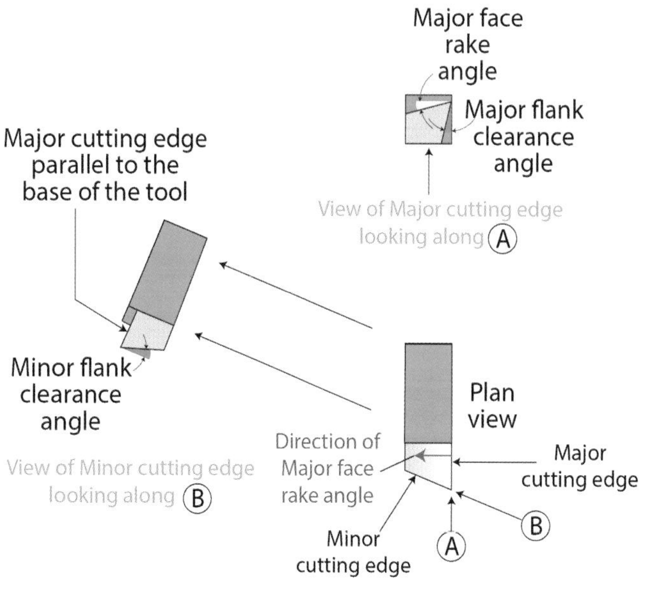

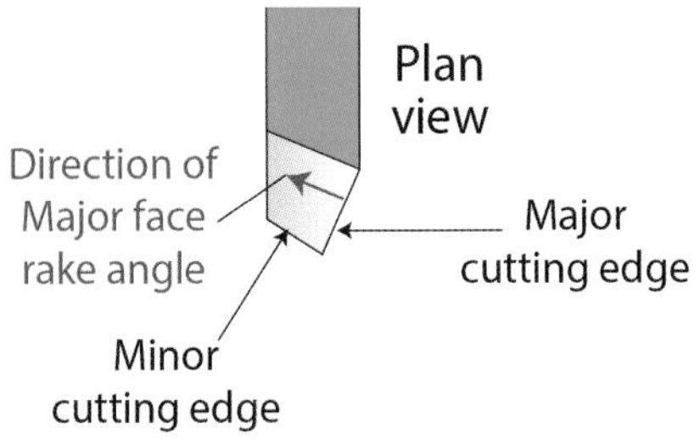

Fig. 388: Rake angle is measured at right angles to the associated cutting edge.

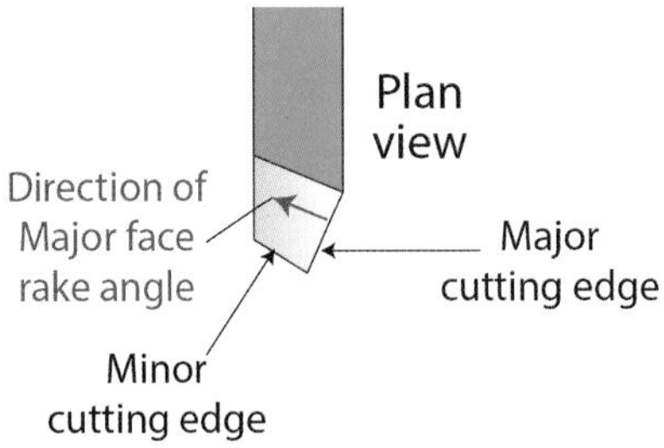

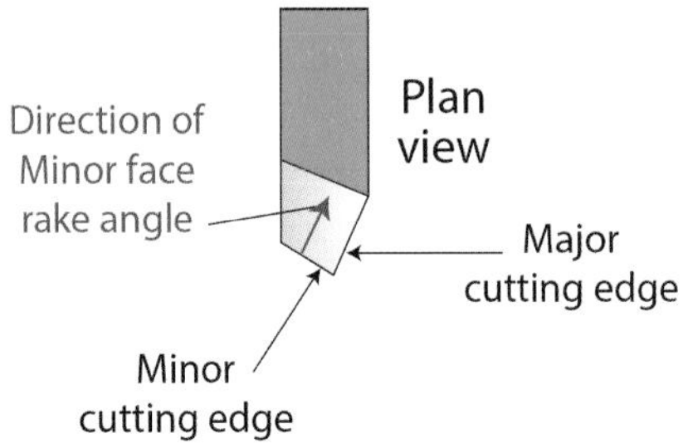

Fig. 390: Some tools have both Major and Minor face rake angles. Both views are of the same tool.

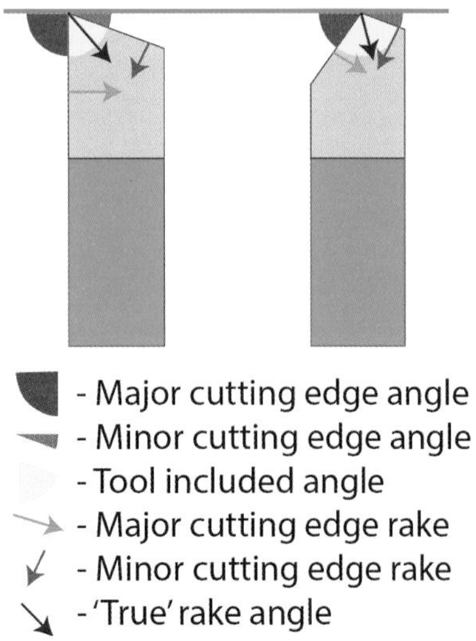

Fig. 391: The direction of chip flow is influenced by both Major and Minor face rake angles.

Fig. 388 shows the direction of the rake angle for a Major cutting edge set at an angle greater than 90 degrees. Fig. 389 shows the rake and clearance angles for a tool with its Major cutting edge at an angle of greater than 90 degrees. Fig. 390 shows two views of the same tool. The top face of the tool has a side rake (the Major face rake angle) and a back rake (the Minor face rake angle), because cutting takes place at both the Major (side) cutting edge and the Minor (front) cutting edge. On a tool with both Major and Minor face rake angles the 'true top rake' lies at a composite angle. As the chip slides down the Major (side) face rake, it also slides sideways along the Minor (back) face rake angle. The result is that the chip slides at an angle determined by both Major face rake and Minor face rake (Fig. 391).

Table 11 gives typical Major and Minor face rake angles for knife tools designed to cut a range of materials.

The finish produced on the work by the tool is affected by the sharpness of the cutting edges and by the finish on the faces and flanks of the tool immediately adjacent to the cutting edges. A small area next to the cutting edges rubs against the work, and marks on that part of the tool cause marks on the work. In general, the better the finish on the faces and flanks of the tool, the better will be the finish on the work.

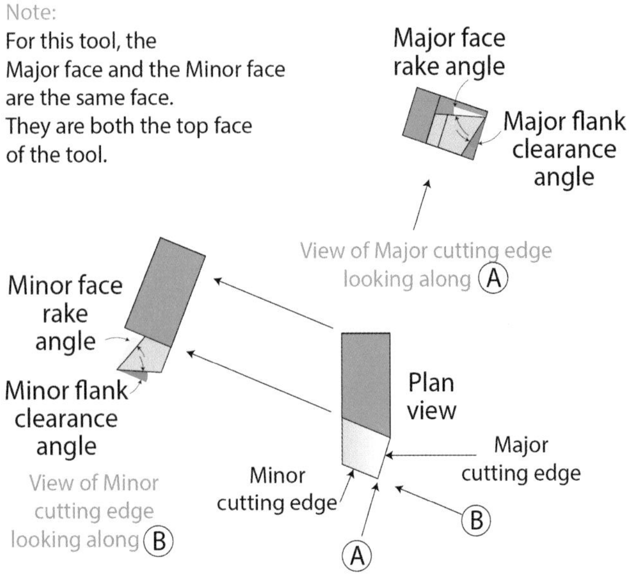

Fig. 389: Rake and clearance angles associated with a cutting edge angle of greater than 90 degrees.

Material	***Major and minor clearance angles***	***Major face (side) rake angle***	***Minor face (back) rake angle***
Mild steel	7 to 10	10 to 15	7 to 15
Carbon (tool) steel	10 to 12	15	5 to 10
Brass	10	5 to -5	0
Copper	10	20	15
Aluminium	10 to 12	15	35
Stainless steel (free machining)	10	8	5
Cast iron	10	10 to 15	5
Bronze	10	5 to -5	0

Table 11: Clearance and rake angles for Minor and Major faces, for a range of common materials.

HOLDING LATHE TOOLS

Most lathe tools are ground from square or circular-section blanks, so a wide range of workholding arrangements is possible.

Tools with flat bottom faces

Turning tools often have flat bottoms, and can be positioned directly on a grinding rest. This is not terribly convenient, though, when it comes to traversing the tool. The most versatile tool holding arrangements involve a carrier of some sort. For square-section tools, a tool holder from a lathe, mounted on a plate (Figs 120–123) or on a substantial angle bracket (Fig. 392), sleeves (Fig. 393), a 10-20-40 block with location pins and a clamp (Fig. 394), or a small vice (Fig. 395), can all be used.

Fig. 392: Square- or rectangular-section tools can be gripped in a lathe tool holder mounted on a bracket.

Fig. 393: Square-section tools can be gripped in a sleeve which has a square hole.

Fig.394: A lathe tool can be clamped to a 10-20-40 block, using pins for alignment.

Fig. 395: Square- or rectangular-section tools can be held in a small vice.

Inverting the tool

Sometimes when the cutting edge is against the wheel the holder may foul the body of the grinder. That might be avoided if the tool is mounted upside down in the holder, and ground with the cutting edge nearest the rest or the base of the grinder (Fig. 396). Angles are reversed, and movements may be reversed. Some concentration is required to ensure correct orientation of edges and faces.

Fig. 396: It may be more convenient to grip some tools upside down. This reverses the direction of tilt, and may avoid the wheel fouling the workholder.

Tools with circular-section shanks

Tools which have circular-section shanks can be gripped in a purpose-made collet (Fig. 397), a collet from a commercial system such as the 5C, 2MT, or ER series (Fig. 398), a sleeve with a closely-sized round hole to suit the shank (Fig. 399), or in a split sleeve designed to be held in a conventional tool-post (Fig. 400). Ideally, the collet or sleeve

Fig. 397: Circular-section tools can be gripped in a collet, mounted on a shaft to suit a tool holder block.

Fig. 398: A circular-section tool can be gripped using a commercial collet system such as ER, 5C or 2MT.

Fig. 399: A circular-section tool can be held in a close-fitting hole in a sleeve by using a grub screw. The sleeve may be gripped in a flat-sided holder.

Fig. 400: A circular-section tool can be gripped in a split sleeve which will be closed as it is clamped in a tool post or workholder.

Fig. 402: A lathe tool holder mounted on a plate with an additional security stop to prevent unwanted rotation.

Fig. 401: Collet holder blocks can grip circular-section tools with a range of diameters, and the faces of the bodies can be used to provide simple indexing.

Fig. 403: A tool holder with angled sides at the front provides more clearance, allowing a tool to be swung through a greater angle.

should be able to rotate so that the tool can be initially aligned in the holder (Fig. 400).

Fig. 401 shows a pair of collet holder blocks which can be positioned using the sides of the blocks as reference surfaces, providing a means of simple indexing. Note that the holder blocks shown have bodies smaller than the collet nuts, so the bodies must sit on a raising plate, or be held in a carrier to keep the nuts clear of the rest.

Fig. 402 shows a lathe toolpost mounted on a plate, and Fig. 403 shows a toolholder with angled sides at the front, which may be more useful for some tools as it allows two faces of a chamfering or threading tool to be ground without changing the grip between grinds. One central bolt is not enough to secure the toolholder, and Fig. 402 also shows an additional small plate which can be slid forward and turned at an angle if necessary, then secured with its own bolt to help prevent the toolholder rotating.

RIGHT-HAND KNIFE TOOL

The right-hand knife tool is the workhorse of lathework, in most workshops (Fig. 384). Although the Major (side) cutting edge angles may vary depending on the material being cut (Figs 385 and 391) all knife tools have a similar shape, with a Major and a Minor cutting edge. Knife tools are often used as a general purpose tool for removing material using the Major cutting edge when moving along the work, and for facing the end of a bar by removing material using the Minor cutting edge when moving forwards across the end of the bar. When end cutting, the cutting angles are a compromise, but the operation is possible, and commonly used for convenience. On a roughing knife tool the Major cutting edge is usually at an angle to the shank, so for facing the end of a bar the tool must be swung to create clearance on the side nearest the work.

Grinding the Major and Minor flanks is often enough to sharpen the Major and Minor cutting edges, but where there is wear or damage on the top face, that must be ground to complete the sharpening process. Some knife tools have no top rake at all. Tools for turning brass, for example, commonly have a flat top which is left unground, but polished by honing that face on a diamond bench stone. Knife tools designed to cut in one direction have top rake running only from the Major cutting edge. This simplifies any grinding operation on the top face. That makes the cutting action efficient, and simplifies sharpening. These tools are dealt with in the section on single-rake tools. Some knife tools have both Major face rake running back at right angles from the Major cutting edge, and Minor face rake running back at right angles from the Minor cutting edge, so the top face lies at a compound angle to both cutting edges – the 'true' rake angle of the top face (Fig. 391). These tools are dealt with in the section on dual-rake tools.

Grinding Major and Minor flanks

Both the Major and Minor flanks on a knife tool may be positioned in relation to the grinding surface by using the same sequence for each flank in turn.

- Mount a type 1 wheel, and dress the face parallel to the axis of the grinder shaft.

Grinding the Minor flank

Grind the Minor flank of the tool first, to remove any damage or wear:

- Set the height of the rest to create the clearance angle at the tip of the tool (the highest point on the cutting edge) by using a template or a setting plate (Fig. 404).
- Swing the tool on the rest to position the Minor cutting edge parallel to the axis of the grinder spindle (and the face of the wheel) (Figs 405 and 406).

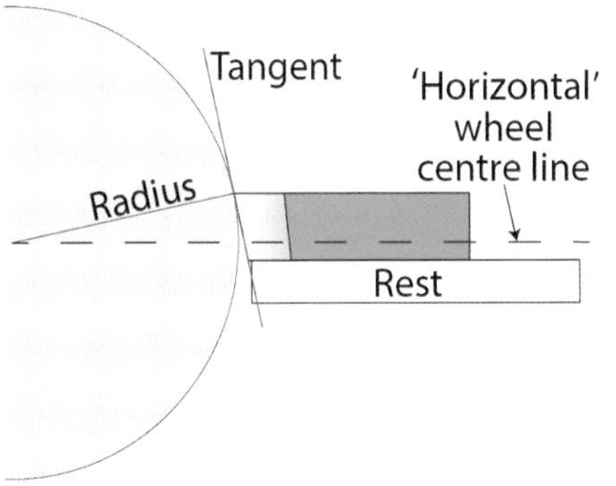

Fig. 404: Set the height of the rest, to create the clearance angle on the flank. The top of the rest should be parallel to a 'horizontal' line through the centre of the grinding wheel.

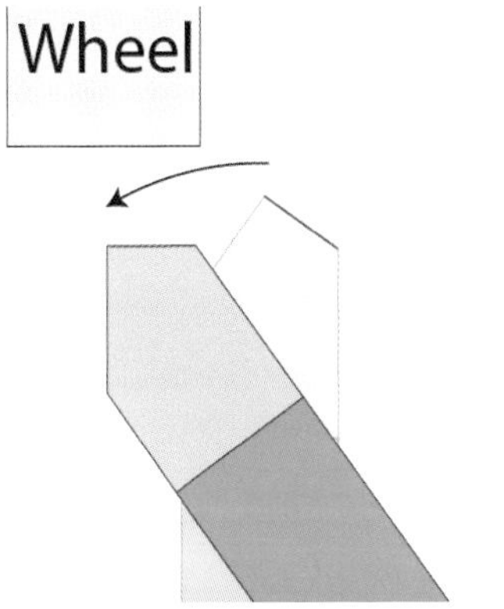

Fig. 405: Viewed from above, swing the tool to position the Minor cutting edge parallel to the face of the wheel.

Fig. 406: Swing the tool to position the Minor cutting edge parallel to the face of the wheel.

- Advance the tool to create a cut, then traverse to grind the flank. Repeat until any damage has been removed from the Minor flank.

Grinding the Major flank

Repeat the same steps as used to grind the Minor flank. That may require a different arrangement for holding the tool, but a similar setup procedure.

- Set the height of the rest to create the clearance angle.
- Swing the tool on the rest to position the Major cutting edge parallel to the axis of the grinder spindle (and the face of the wheel) (Figs 407 and 408).
- Advance, to create a depth of cut, then traverse to grind the Major flank.

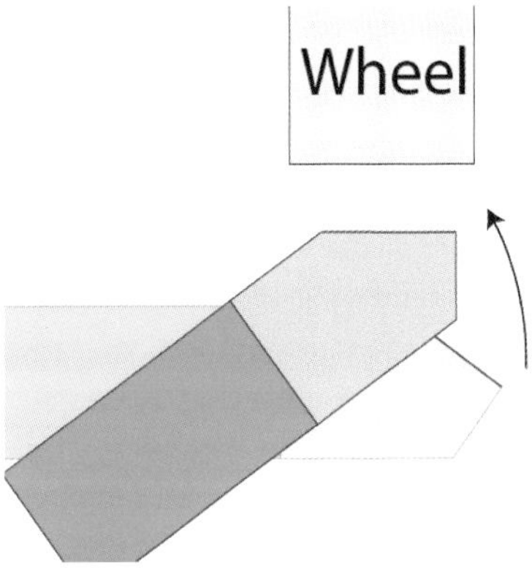

Fig. 407: Viewed from above, swing the tool to position the Major cutting edge parallel to the face of the wheel.

Fig. 408: Swing the tool, to position the Major cutting edge parallel to the face of the wheel.

- Repeat the grinding sequence as often as is required to remove all damage from the Major flank. That may be sufficient to sharpen the Major cutting edge.

Grinding a single-rake top face

Some knife tool top faces have a single rake angle running from only one cutting edge. This is a useful arrangement, as it makes sharpening straightforward.

- Mount the tool horizontally, on its side, with its Major cutting edge uppermost, and its top face towards the face of the wheel (Fig. 409). If necessary, rotate the toolholder about a horizontal axis to bring the Major cutting edge horizontal (Fig. 410). This requires a suitable mount for the toolholder. A steel angle mount

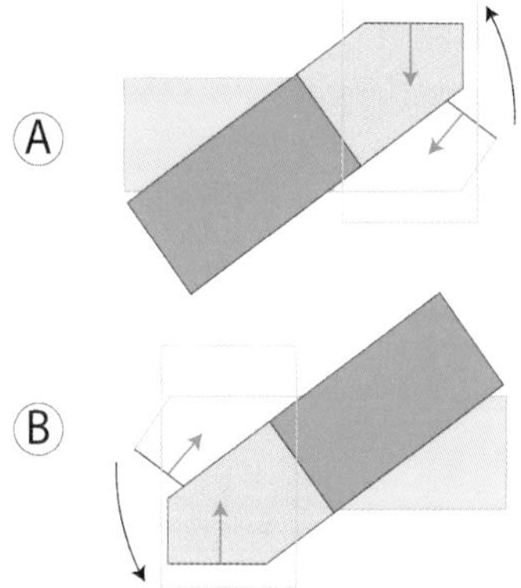

Fig. 409: Viewed from behind the grinder, looking through the wheel, position the tool as shown at A or B and swing to place the Major cutting edge horizontal.

Fig. 410: Hold the tool horizontal, then rotate about a horizontal axis to set the cutting edge horizontal.

(Fig. 410) is bolted to the plate shown in Figs 406 and 408. The tool points to the right (Fig. 318) to avoid the shank fouling the grinder casing.

- Set the height of the rest so that the curve of the wheel will create the Major face rake angle. Take account of the height of the cutting edge, and any tool carrier (*see* pages 40–43). As with the flanks, a template is useful for this operation.
- Keeping the cutting edge at the same angle, move the tool forwards to touch the wheel. Take the tool clear of one side of the wheel; apply a cut by moving forwards; then sweep the tool and cutting edge across the face of the wheel, stopping as the unground section of the shank reaches the corner of the wheel. A physical stop which limits the travel of the tool is useful here.
- Repeatedly apply a cut and grind, until the Major face is uniformly flat.

Fig. 411: The top face should be a flat surface incorporating the Major and Minor cutting edges. The yellow arrow lies at the true rake angle, which combines the (red) Major face rake angle and the (orange) Minor face rake angle.

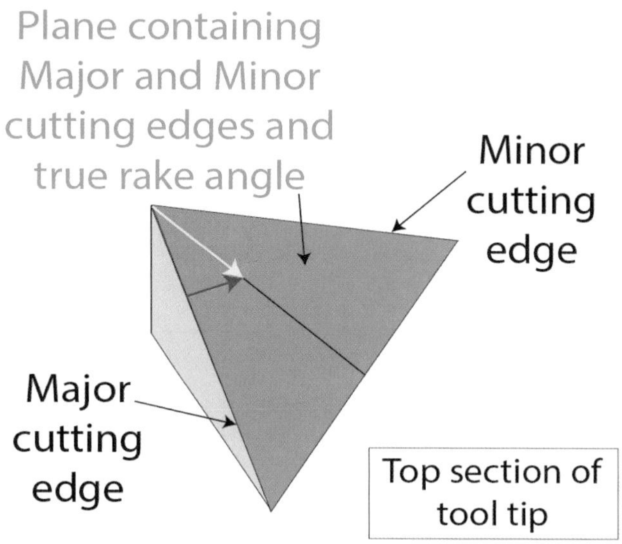

Grinding a dual-rake top face

The top face of a knife tool may have rake running back at right angles from the Major cutting edge, and rake running back at right angles from the Minor cutting edge, so the top face will be a single flat surface lying at a compound angle to both cutting edges – the 'true' rake angle of the top face (Figs 411 and 391). The disadvantage of this shape of tool is that neither cutting edge can be parallel to the base of the tool, because the Major cutting edge is angled downwards as a result of the Minor face angle, and the Minor cutting edge is angled downwards as a result of the Major face angle. The only point actually on centre will be the very tip of the tool, so regrinding always lowers the height of the tip above the base. One advantage is that the tool can cut in two directions; surfacing sideways along the work, and taking shallow facing cuts across the end of the work. The complication is that although the two rake angles should tilt back from each cutting edge at 90 degrees, the cutting edges themselves need to be at 90 degrees to each other, to allow a straightforward setup on a bench grinder. The greater the deviation from 90 degrees, the greater the error, although for minor deviations the error will be small. The general rule would be to set the Major cutting edge rake first, then set the Minor cutting edge rake as if the cutting edges were at 90 degrees. Errors will then affect the Minor rake, which is usually less important. There is a range of acceptable rake angles when cutting any material, and the Minor face rake is the least important of the top face angles, not least because the effect of the Major face rake is to take the Minor cutting edge progressively further below centre height and away from the work.

- Position the tool as though it has only a single rake angle running from the Major cutting edge, using the setup shown in (Figs 409 and 410), with the Major cutting edge horizontal, and the height of the rest adjusted so that the curve of the wheel creates the Major rake.
- Swing the tool and holder, taking the tail of the tool towards the face of the wheel, to create the rake angle behind the Minor cutting edge (Figs 412 and 413).
- Set traverse stops, then apply a cut towards the wheel and traverse the tool past the flat face of the wheel. Repeat until the whole top face has been ground.

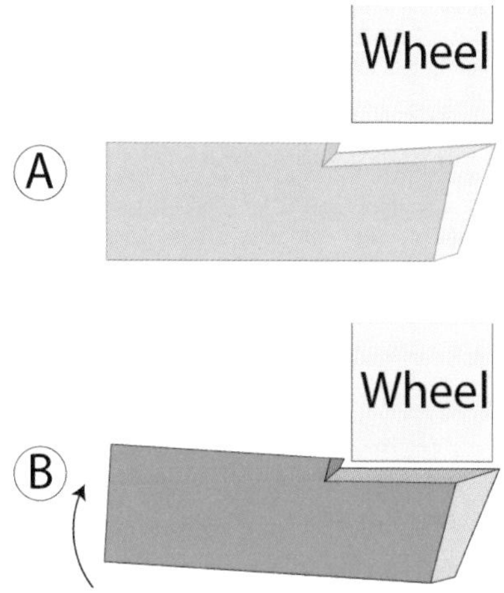

Fig. 412: Viewed from above: with the Major cutting edge parallel to the horizontal surface of the rest (A), swing the toolholder to bring that cutting edge parallel to the face of the wheel, then (B) tilt to bring the Major cutting edge parallel to the wheel face.

Fig. 413: Swing the toolholder assembly to create the rake angle behind the Minor cutting edge.

Finishing the nose

A knife tool can be ground until it has a sharp corner between the Major and Minor flanks, forming a sharply defined point. To give that point some additional strength, and to improve the finish the tool will leave on the work, it is often preferable to create a small flat, or to radius the corner to form a round nose. Ideally, a curve on the nose of a tool will blend into the adjacent flanks, and the neatest and most effective curve from tip to heel will result when the clearance angles on the Minor and Major flanks are the same. However; a small difference in those angles will not prevent the creation or restoration of a neat curve on the nose of the tool, because the clearances are designed so that the flanks are angled clear of the work, leaving only a small distance below the tip in contact with the work.

Grinding a flat nose

To leave a small flat:

- Swing to bring the Minor cutting edge against the wheel, then swing the tool clockwise through 90 degrees minus half the included angle between the Minor and Major cutting edges (Figs 414 and 415).

  For example:

  If the included angle is 70 degrees, the half-angle will be 35 degrees, so swing through 90 – 35 = 55 degrees.

  The exact angle is not critical. Tilt, or alter the height of the rest to create the front clearance.
- Grind to form a flat at the nose.

Fig. 416 shows a basic setup in which the toolholder is swung clockwise, leaving insufficient support for the sliding protractor guide on the rest, and the toolholder assembly at the front of the shoe. Fig. 417 shows a second method in which the tool is held upside down, with the protractor guide swung anti-clockwise, to allow good support on the rest and the shoe. Lowering the rest creates the clearance angle at the nose. Figs 418 and 419 show a setup with the tool on its side (bottom facing the guide), the nose horizontal, and the tool holder turned downwards 90 degrees minus the tool angle.

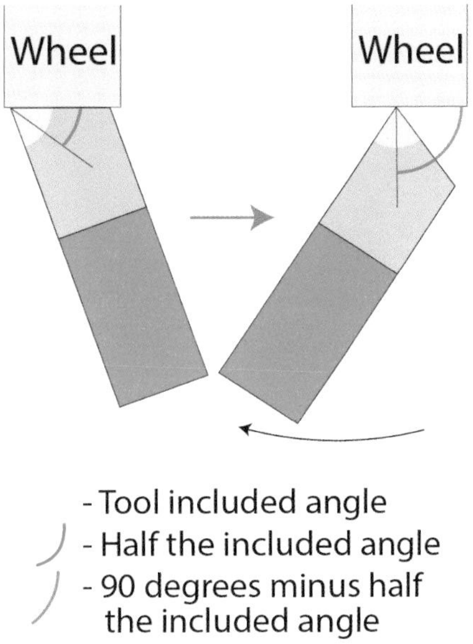

Fig. 414: Swing to set the Minor cutting edge parallel to the face of the wheel, then swing through 90 degrees minus half the included angle then grind a flat.

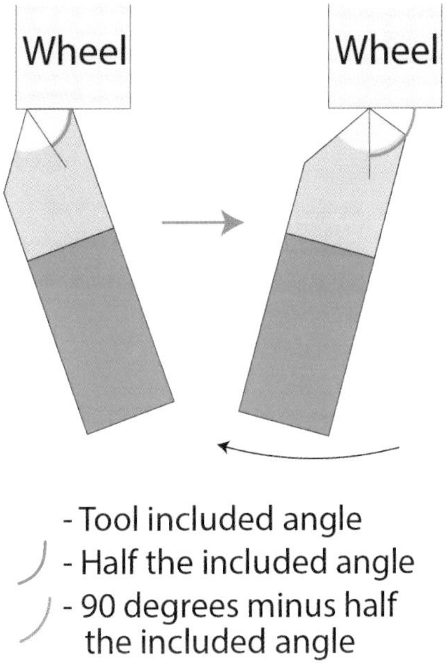

Fig. 415: A roughing tool is positioned in the same way before grinding a flat on the nose.

Fig. 416: Swing through 90 degrees minus the half-angle, to position the tool to grind a flat on the nose.

Fig. 417: When the tool is held upside down, swing anti-clockwise by 90 degrees minus the half-angle.

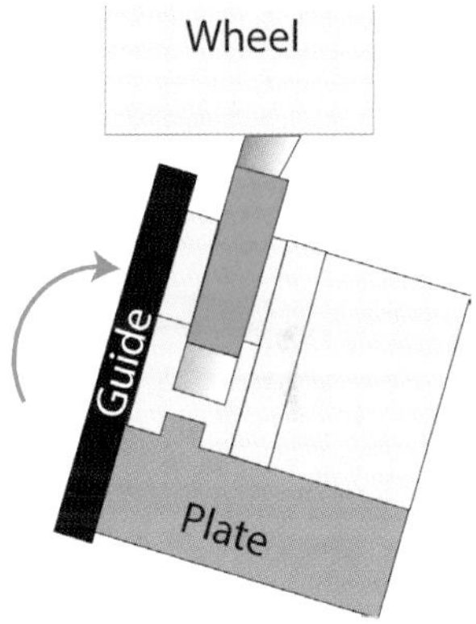

Fig. 418: With the bottom of the tool facing the guide, swing the guide to the nose clearance angle.

Fig. 419: Swing the protractor guide to the nose clearance angle, and face the tool downwards.

Fig. 420 shows a knife tool with a small flat ground at the nose. The taper from top to bottom appears as a result of the flank clearance angles which cause the vee to narrow towards the bottom of the tool.

Fig. 420: The nose of a left hand knife tool which has been ground flat using the method shown in Figs 418 and 419. The Minor flank is coloured, for clarity.

Rounding the nose

To form a small radius (as opposed to a specific radius on a form tool), do not form a flat on the nose, but remove the tool and create a curve using an abrasive stone, by hand. To use a stone, begin by holding the tool vertically, with its nose in contact with the stone, then tilt the tool so that the whole of the sharp corner between the flanks is in contact with the stone (Fig. 421). Move the tool along the stone while rocking from one flank to another to create a small radius (Fig. 422).

There is a compromise between a small radius which will produce a matching small internal corner on the work, and a large radius which may produce a better finish on the work but is likely to be more prone to chatter. The finish of the first one or two millimetres below the tip of the nose is important, as that is in contact with the work, but the shape and the finish below that is less important. One useful shape of nose is as shown in Fig. 423, where there is a small radius on the nose itself, blending into a Minor cutting edge which runs almost parallel to the work for at least a short distance.

Fig. 421: Position the tool so that the whole of the sharp corner at the nose is in contact with the abrasive stone. The line of light shows the bowed effect created by the curve of the wheel.

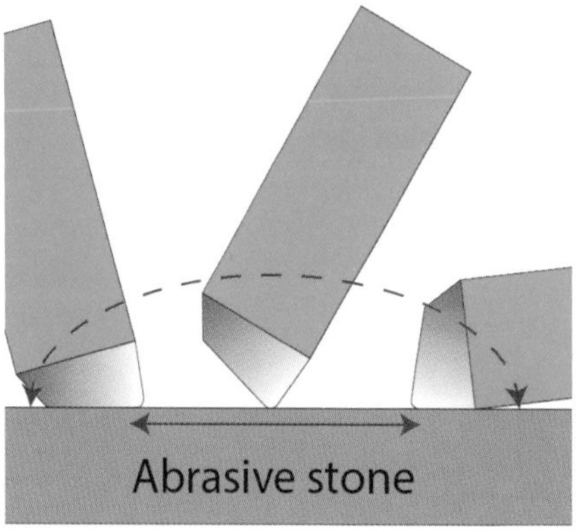

Fig. 422: Rock from one flank to the other, while moving the tool forwards and backwards along the stone. The precise radius of the curve is less important than a smooth transition between the flanks.

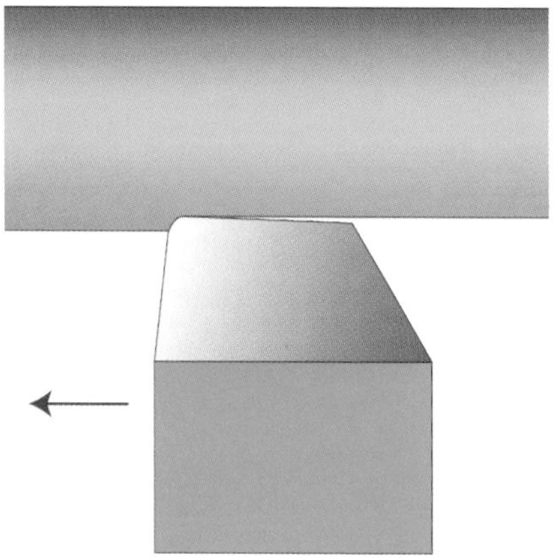

Fig. 423: A knife tool which has a small radius on the nose, blending into a Minor cutting edge which runs almost parallel to the work, can provide a good finish on a machined surface.

VEE CHAMFERING TOOL

A vee-shaped chamfering tool (Fig. 424) has a single Major cutting edge which is swept back around the point at the front of the tool to form a vee, but no Minor cutting edge. However; it is more useful to think of the tool as having two flanks, and two associated cutting edges, as these will be ground in two separate operations. One side of the cutting edge may be used at a time, or, occasionally, both sides may be used simultaneously when cutting shallow vee grooves.

Fig. 424: A vee chamfering tool has one continuous cutting edge but can be treated as though it has two distinct flanks, and two cutting edges.

The flanks are created by swinging the tool to the left or right. The angle of swing may be the same for both flanks, and typically 45 degrees, but other angles may be used, including different angles for the two sides (Fig. 424), to allow the tool to create chamfers or short tapers with different angles for specific jobs.

Creating a flank

- Mount a type 1 wheel and dress the face parallel to the front of the rest.
- With the base of the tool parallel to the surface of the rest, alter the height of the rest to create the clearance angle on one flank. Choose an appropriate reference surface, and set the height using a template, or a hinged setting plate.
- Swing the tool to create the angle of the cutting edge associated with that flank.

Fig. 425 shows a setup using a simple guide set at an angle of 45 degrees for a 90 degree vee tool, but better support is provided by using a toolpost mounted on a plate. Loosening the toolpost and swinging it to the angle allows the plate to remain against a guide at 90 degrees to the face of the wheel (Fig. 426).

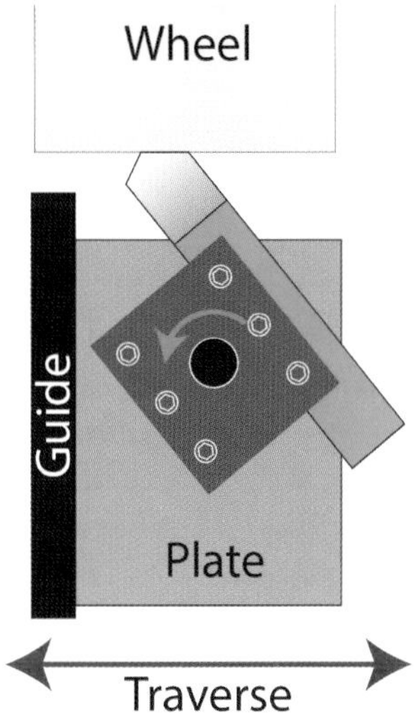

Fig. 425: The toolholder can be swung to bring the cutting edge parallel to the face of the wheel, while the plate remains against the guide.

Fig. 426: Swing the tool to the angle of the cutting edge. The height of the rest sets the flank clearance angle.

- Create a cut by moving the tool towards the face of the wheel; and traverse to grind the flank. Continue adding a cut and traversing until the flank has been fully formed and is free of all damage.
- Repeat the sequence for the other flank.

Creating the top face

The top face of the tool cannot have side rake, because one cutting edge would then be lower than the other. The tool can, however, have a small amount of top rake running from the point backwards towards the shank. Top rake has the effect of changing the angle of the chamfer cut on the work, but a small angle will have little practical effect. Grinding the top face can be done using a type 1 wheel, and setting the tip of the tool on the wheel centre line. Any small hollowing effect will be on the centre line of the tool, and will add to the rake angles.

- Grip the tool on its side, in a holder which can swing independently of a guide set at 90 degrees to the face of the wheel. This will allow the top face to be ground at an angle to the shank while traverse takes place parallel to the face of the wheel and the top face of the tool (Fig. 427). In this setup, feed (depth of cut) is created by sliding the plate, with the toolholder, along the guide, at right angles to the face of the wheel.
- Set a traverse guide parallel to the face of the wheel.
- Swing the tool holder so that the wheel will grind more from the rear of the top face than the front (Fig. 428).

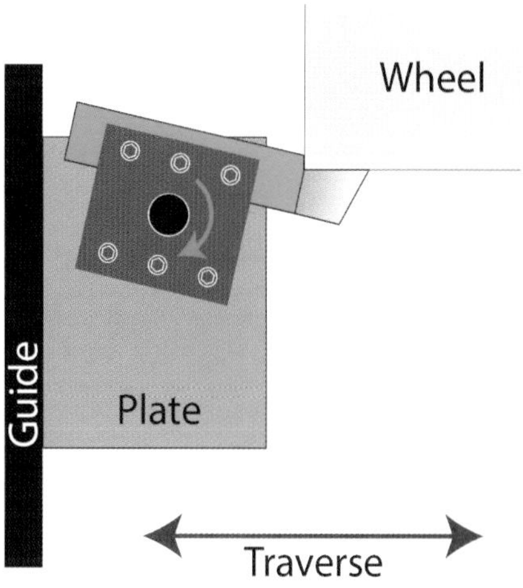

Fig. 427: Swing the toolholder independently of the plate, which remains against the guide. Traverse is parallel to the face of the wheel.

- Create a cut by moving the tool towards the face of the wheel; and traverse parallel to the face of the wheel, to grind. Continue adding a cut and traversing until the top face has been fully formed and free of all damage. Check that the cutting edges are sharp.

For a very fine finish, hone the faces of the tool using a diamond wheel, followed, if necessary, by holding each face in turn against a rotating disc with a fine abrasive surface, or a ceramic wheel and increasingly fine grades of diamond paste.

Fig. 428: Using a different setup from Fig. 427, to avoid the wheel colliding with the front corner of the plate, the tool is gripped on its side, pointing to the left. The toolpost is set square with the plate, and the guide is swung to create the top rake. Traverse is parallel to the face of the wheel.

SINGLE-POINT THREADING TOOL

Like the chamfering tool, a single-point threading tool has a vee shape. The included angle of the vee depends on the type of thread to be cut, as shown in Table 12.

Threadform	Included angle of vee
Metric	60
Unified	60
Whitworth	55
British Association (BA)	47.5

Table 12: Included angles for lathe screwcutting tools.

Threading tools often have no top rake. Top rake improves the cutting action of a tool, especially in steel or aluminium. But adding top rake will produce an incorrect threadform, with a vee which is too narrow. The sides of the tool will need some side clearance, so the effect of top rake is to intersect the tapering shape of the tool, and the greater the top rake angle, the narrower the vee at the lines of intersection (Fig. 429). The compensation needed involves calculating the reduction in the angle, using 3D geometry, or estimating the reduction using 3D CAD, and will mean the vee shape ground on the tool must have a larger included angle so that it ends up with the correct angle once top rake has been applied. This is unfortunate, but a simple way to avoid the problem is to leave the tool with no top rake. A better approach is to note that many threads involve a shallow depth of cut, so the error created by using a small amount of top rake (up to 5 degrees) will be small and will not prevent the thread from mating with a typical commercially produced nut. A third method is to judge the fit of the tool against a thread tool setting gauge, holding both parallel to the same flat surface and sighting directly down from above (Fig. 430).

Threading tools need side clearance, but that differs from the clearance on a plain turning tool such as a knife tool, because the groove which creates a thread is a helix which travels around the work at an angle (Fig. 431). That means the body of the threading tool must clear the helix, and the clearances must effectively lie at the helix angle, or at least be sufficiently large to avoid fouling the sides of the helix (Fig. 432). A large side clearance will weaken the tool and reduce support for the cutting edges, so it is better to create clearance which takes account of the helix angle. One result is that, depending on the method used to machine the thread, cutting a left hand thread will require a tool ground differently from a

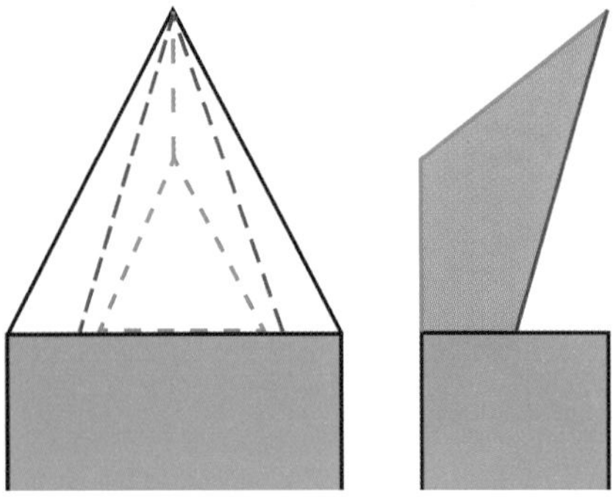

Fig. 429: Beginning with the full outline of the vee (plan view on the left: black lines), grinding a rake angle (side view on the right: red lines), reduces the width of the vee, and its included angle (red dashed line) because the flanks are angled inwards, from the black lines to the green dashed lines.

Fig. 430: Judge the angle between the sides of a threading tool by sighting vertically down onto the tool and a thread tool setting gauge. On this tool, the included angle is too small for a 60 degree metric threadform.

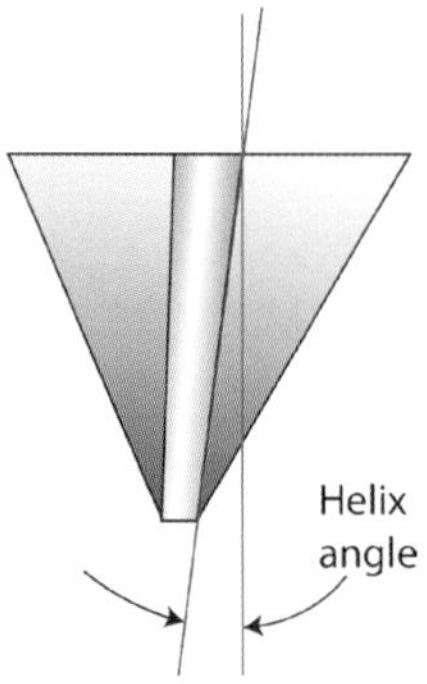

Fig. 432: The helix angle of the thread affects the angle of the nose of the tool and the clearance angles formed by the flanks.

Fig. 431: A thread is a helix, and the sides lie at an angle to the axis of the thread.

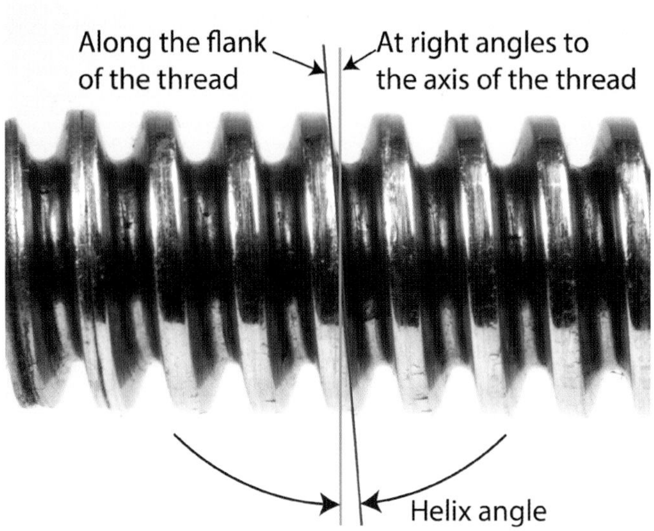

Thread diameter x pitch	Pitch diameter (mm or inch)	Helix angle (degrees)
Metric coarse	Millimetres	
M3 x 0.5	2.675	3.40
M4 x 0.7	3.545	3.60
M5 x 0.8	4.480	3.25
M6 x 1	5.351	3.40
M8 x 1.25	7.188	3.17
M10 x 1.5	9.026	3.03
M12 x 1.75	10.863	2.94
M14 x 2	12.701	2.87
Unified: UTC	Inches	
1/4 x 20	0.2175	4.19
5/16 x 18	0.2764	3.66
3/8 x 16	0.3344	3.40
7/16 x 14	0.3911	3.33
1/2 x 13	0.4500	3.11
5/8 x 11	0.5084	3.26
Whitworth	Inches	
3/16 x 24	0.1608	4.72
1/4 x 20	0.2180	4.18
5/16 x 18	0.2769	3.65
3/8 x 16	0.3350	3.40
7/16 x 14	0.3918	3.32
1/2 x 12	0.4466	3.40
5/8 x 11	0.5668	2.92
British Association (BA)	Millimetres	
0 x 1	5.4	3.37
2 x 0.81	4.215	3.50
4 x 0.66	3.205	3.75
6 x 0.53	2.48	3.89
7 x 0.48	2.21	3.95
8 x 0.43	1.94	4.04

Table 13: Helix angles for common threads.

right hand thread, because the helix angles tilt in opposite directions. When creating the clearances, one flank should have its clearance angle increased by the helix angle, and the other flank should have its clearance reduced by the helix angle (Fig. 432). This is done by adding the helix angle to the clearance on one side, and subtracting it from the other side. Find the helix angle by consulting thread tables or by using the formula:

Helix angle =
arcTan (Lead/pitch circumference)

where Lead = pitch, for a single-start thread, and Pitch circumference =
Pitch diameter x π

Pitch diameter is not the same as the outside diameter, and is normally read from thread tables, but using the nominal overall thread diameter will give a reasonable approximation. Table 13 lists some common pitch diameters and helix angles.

Add the helix angle to the flank clearance angle of one side, and subtract it from the flank clearance angle of the other side.

For example:

an M8 x 1.25 thread has a pitch of 1.25mm. Table 13 shows that its helix angle is 3.1683 degrees (or 3 degrees 10 minutes), approximately 3.2 degrees.

Assuming side clearance of 7 degrees, adding the helix angle to one side gives 7 + 3.2 degrees = 10.2 degrees clearance; subtracting from the other side gives 7 − 3.2 degrees = 3.8 degrees clearance.

To make angle setting easy, extra clearance will not go wrong, so these angles may be 10.5 or 11 degrees, and 4 degrees.

The tip of a threading tool has a specific shape to match the thread being cut. The shape of each threadform is defined by national and international standards. There is a basic, theoretical, shape for each threadform, and sets of tolerances for the features of each thread. So; for ISO metric threads, and UTS threads, the threadform has a 60 degree vee shape with a sharp point forming the vee. In practice, male threads are truncated to form a flat and avoid having to cut a perfectly sharp vee. To cope with the need for tolerance, and to allow a male and female thread to mate in the presence of dirt, both threads have an additional clearance at the roots of the threads, which has a rounded profile (Fig. 433), the size of which depends upon the pitch (P) of the thread, with a minimum of 0.125 x P and a maximum of 0.14434 x P for a male thread, and a value of 0.072168 x P for the nut (Fig. 433). Whitform threads (Whitworth, British Standard Fine, British Standard Pipe, Royal Microscopic Society

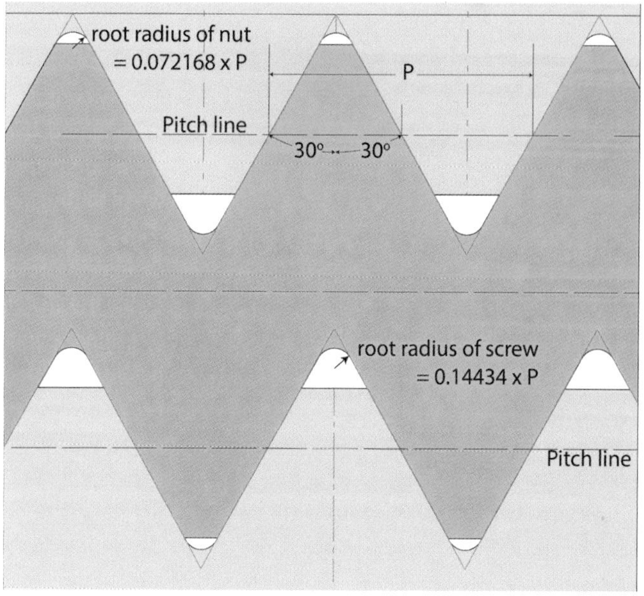

Fig. 433: Assembled male (orange) and female (grey) metric threads show the clearances at the roots of the threads.

microscope threads, and Model Engineering series threads) have a different shape and use rounded crests and roots. However; it is common to truncate the rounded crests on both male and female threads, giving them a flat-topped crest. This simplifies manufacture. It is important to know the dimensions of a thread, and its profile, before grinding a screwcutting tool to suit. The shape of the nose of the tool will also determine the depth of cut when screwcutting.

Rounded profiles on screwcutting tools are tricky to form accurately, but a close approximation is normally sufficient. For most roots, a smaller radius than the theoretical profile is normally good enough. That may provide a little extra clearance, but there is seldom any harm in that. It is important to match the shape of the cutting tool to the ideal profile of the threadform, so the top face of the tool should be compared to an accurate profile gauge (Fig. 434) or a profile etched on an optical inspection device such as an optical comparator, preferably under high magnification. Note that a thread profile gauge is not the same as a thread tool setting gauge which is used to set a lathe tool at 90 degrees to the axis of a workpiece, before thread cutting.

Although it is usual to create a radius running all the way down the front of a screwcutting tool, that is not essential, as long as the profile at the top few millimetres is correct and no part of the tool below that is in contact with the work. In practice, manually creating the radius is most easily done if the same radius runs all the way down the front of the tool. This will not be truly radial to the top of the tool, but the error will not affect the thread, as the radius simply creates clearance at the root of the thread.

Fig. 434: Compare the top face of the tool with an accurate thread profile gauge for the threadform and pitch corresponding to the thread the tool is intended to cut.

Screwcutting tools can easily be shaped and sharpened against a flat-faced wheel, but using a type 1 wheel will give good results, with the final finishing being carried out by honing against a flat abrasive stone. The nose radius, if any, is most easily created by hand, against a flat-faced stone.

Just as with vee chamfering tools, square-section tools can be held in a lathe-style tool holder, and circular-section tools can be held in a collet or sleeve which is held securely in a square or rectangular block.

Grinding the flanks

- Mount, then dress, a type 1 wheel with a curved face.
- Beginning with the tool axis parallel to the face of the wheel, swing the tool to the half-angle (30, 27.5 or 23.75 degrees for metric/UTS, Whitform, or BA threads respectively) to bring one cutting edge parallel to the face of the wheel (Fig. 435). Mounting the tool upside down, or swinging the toolholder instead of the guide helps provide better support when setting up to grind the other flank (Figs 436 and 437).
- Change the height or angle of the rest to create the clearance angle for that flank, by using a template or by calculating the height and using a setting plate.
- Feed towards the wheel; and traverse across the face of the wheel, to grind.
- Repeat the same sequence for the other flank, but alter the rest to suit the clearance angle for that flank, before grinding.

Fig. 435: Swing, to bring one cutting edge (highlighted in red) parallel to the face of the wheel and the direction of traverse.

Fig. 436: The tool can be inverted to sharpen the other cutting edge. Adjust the height of the rest to ensure the correct clearance angle.

Fig. 437: Swinging the guide to the other side can result in lack of support for the toolholder.

Dealing with the nose

Options for the nose are to create a tiny flat to give the nose some strength, or to form a small radius which should match, or be slightly smaller than, the radius on a thread gauge.

Creating a flat

On a type 1 wheel, contact between the work and the face of the wheel lies along a line (Fig. 51, page 23). If the tool lies on its side, with its nose towards the wheel, the nose will not be ground uniformly unless the tool is rotated to the helix angle (Fig. 438). Gripping the tool in a sleeve which can rotate in a toolholder allows the nose to be set horizontal, to match the line of contact. One way of doing this is to use a square-bodied sleeve holder, lying on its side, and sight against the vertical blade of an engineer's square (Fig. 438). Rotate to bring the tool nose vertical; lock the tool holder; then turn the tool holder through 90 degrees back onto its base. Finally, swing the toolholder through the nose clearance angle to set the nose parallel to the face of the wheel.

Fig. 438: With the tool holder on its side, sight along the vertical blade of an engineer's square and align the nose of the tool vertically. Then turn the tool holder back thorough 90 degrees, to sit on its base.

Creating a nose radius

Produce the nose radius by honing against a flat stone, and comparing the nose with an accurate gauge. Use the same technique as for a knife tool or a vee chamfering tool, rocking the tool smoothly over its nose while dragging the tool along the stone. Repeat as necessary to round the nose and give it a fine finish.

PARTING TOOL (LATHE TOOL STYLE)

A parting tool has its Major cutting edge at the front of a relatively thin blade which protrudes from the shank (Figs 439 and 440). Fig. 441 shows the most appropriate positions for the working plane and the tool back plane. The tool is designed to advance into the work, leaving the cut surface parallel to the direction of infeed. The Major cutting edge may be at right angles to the working plane, or it may be angled to one side, to ensure either the parted-off work or the remaining workpiece has a cleanly-finished face. There will normally be a Minor flank clearance angle on both sides, providing clearance from top to bottom of the blade. In addition the Minor cutting edges

Fig. 439: A typical parting tool ground from a solid tool blank, and a circular-section insert.

Fig. 440: A parting tool typically has Major and Minor flank clearances, and a top rake to suit the material being cut.

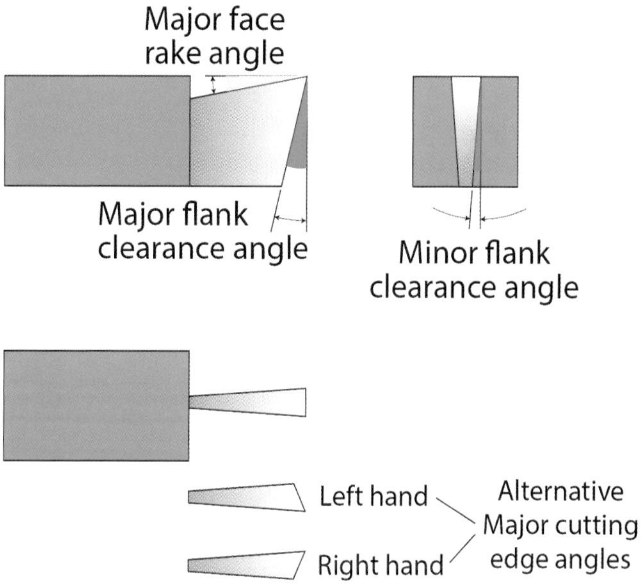

Fig. 441: Typical positions of the back plane and the working plane. The Major cutting edge may be angled to one side.

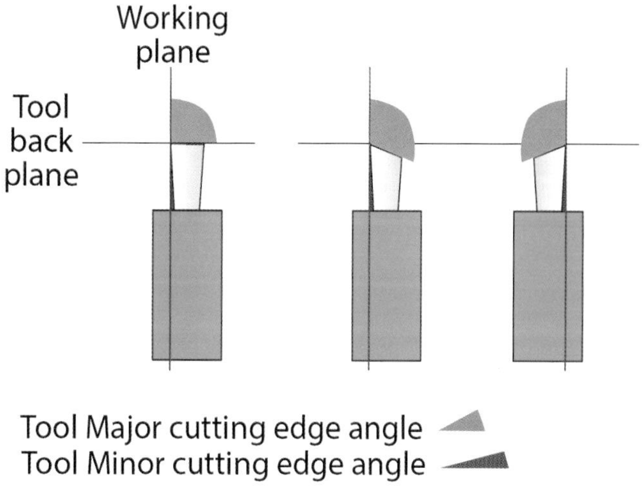

are normally angled inwards from the front of the blade, providing additional clearance as the blade enters more deeply into the work, and that makes the blade narrower as it runs towards the shank. When grinding a parting blade on the front of a rectangular shank, choose the base as the reference surface, so that the blade is formed at right angles to the base. Fig. 440 shows that there is a Major face rake angle, but a zero Minor face rake angle on the top face of the tool.

Shaping a parting tool

The first task is to decide where the blade should be positioned on the tool blank. Many parting tools have their blades positioned centrally, but some have their blades at the side next to the chuck, to allow parting off close to the chuck jaws (Fig. 442). Choose the best position for the job the

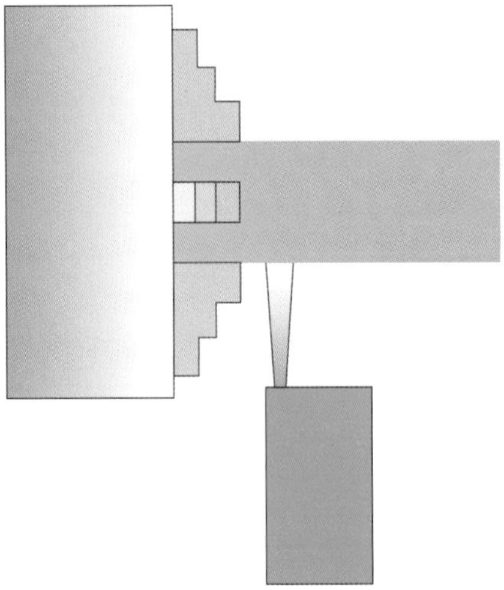

Fig. 442: A parting tool blade may be offset to one side.

tool must do. The basic method is to treat the parting tool as a turning tool, like a knife tool but with one Major (front) flank and two Minor (side) flanks. There may be a lot of material to be ground from a tool blank to produce a shaped parting tool, but let the grinding wheel do its job without applying undue pressure, which will only accelerate the creation of heat and dust.

Creating the Major (front) flank

There are two approaches to grinding the front flank.

Method 1:

- Set the tool in a reference position with the long axis of the shank at right angles to the face of the wheel and the front of the blade next to the wheel (Fig. 443).
- If necessary, swing to create an angled front to the Major cutting edge.
- Set the height of the rest to use the curve of the wheel to create the Major flank clearance angle.
- Grind the face, by repeatedly feeding forwards towards the wheel then traversing across the face of the wheel.

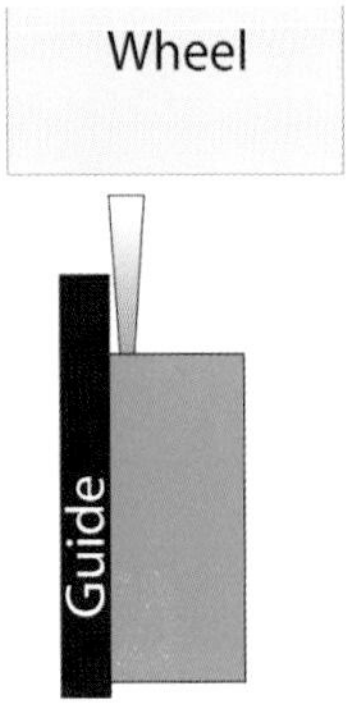

Fig. 443: Set the tool in a reference position, with the shank at right angles to the face of the wheel.

The disadvantage of this method is that the depth of the blade causes a noticeable curve on the face of the blade (Fig. 444). This weakens the tip of the blade.

Fig. 444: The curve of the wheel will create a corresponding curve on the Major flank.

Method 2:

- Lay the tool on its side, with the long axis of the shank at right angles to the face of the wheel and the front of the blade next to the wheel (Fig. 445). The horizontal centre line of the blade should be on centre.

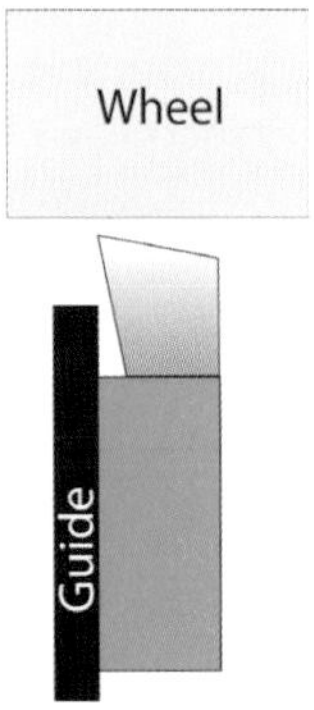

Fig. 445: Lay the tool on its side, with the long axis of the shank at right angles to the face of the wheel and the front of the blade next to the wheel.

- Swing to create the Major flank clearance angle (Fig. 446).

Fig. 446: Swing to create the Major flank clearance angle.

- If necessary, alter the height of the rest to create the flank front rake.
- Grind the face by repeatedly feeding forwards towards the wheel then traversing the tool across the face of the wheel.

The disadvantage of this method is that a fully formed blade will not be well supported during grinding, but that also applies to method 1, where traversing will cause a sideways force on the blade.

Creating the Minor (side) flanks

- Set the tool with its long axis parallel to the face of the wheel, with the Major (front) cutting edge to the right and what will be the left hand Minor cutting edge adjacent to, and parallel to, the face of the wheel (Fig. 447).

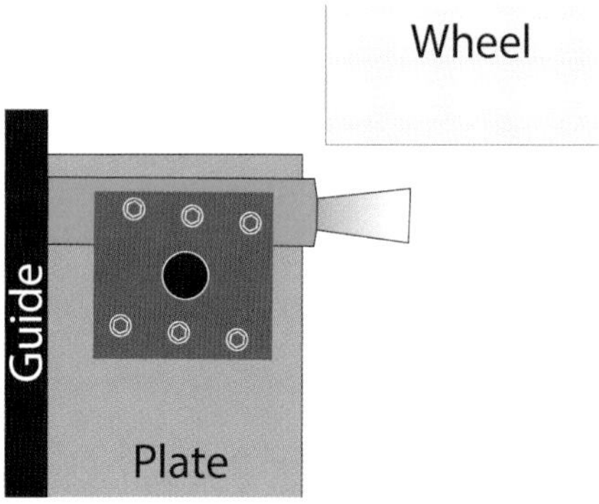

Fig. 447: Set the tool in a reference position, with the shank parallel to the face of the wheel.

- If the blade tapers from front to back (Fig. 448), swing the tool clockwise to form the side rake angle.

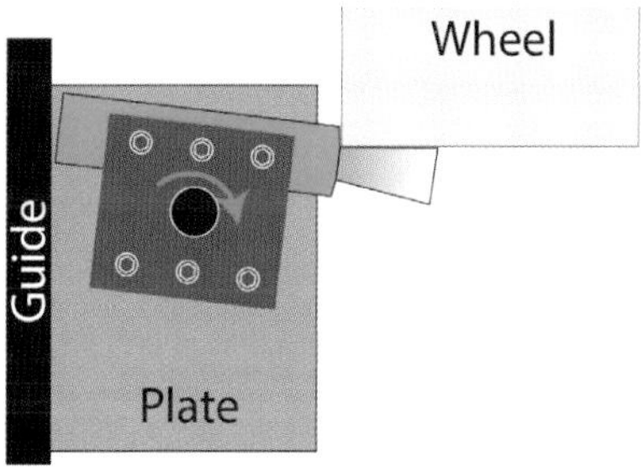

Set stops before traversing

Fig. 448: Swing clockwise, to form the side rake angle.

- Raise the rest, to create the Minor flank clearance angle. Set a stop to prevent the wheel from ginding the shank beyond the end of the Minor flank.
- Grind, by applying a cut towards the wheel then traverse the tool across the face of the wheel. Repeat the sequence as required.
- Repeat for the other side, beginning with the Major cutting edge facing left rather than right. If that causes the shank to foul the body of the grinder, set the tool with its long axis parallel to the face of the wheel, and with the Major cutting edge facing to the right, then turn the tool upside down and bring the second side into position. Set the height of the rest to create the side clearance angle. The rest will be lowered this time, because the angle runs outwards from the cutting edge to the 'bottom' edge which is now at the top of the shank.
- Grind as for the first Minor flank.

On a deep blade, the curved wheel creates a tangent angle at the cutting edge, but when the clearance angle is relatively small the clearance may reduce towards the bottom of the blade (Fig. 449). That can be eliminated by adjusting the height of the rest to create a second facet further down the face. The angle may be the same as the clearance angle already ground, or slightly less.

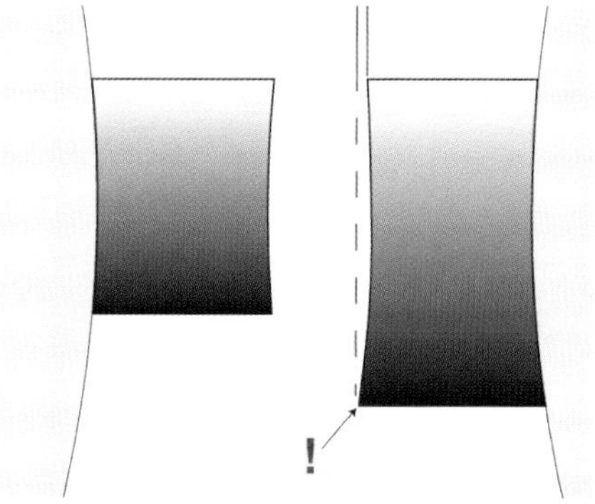

Fig. 449: On the deep blade on the right, the curve of the wheel has produced negative clearance from the centre towards the bottom of the blade.

Creating the top face

- Lay the tool on its side, with the long axis of the blade parallel to the traverse and the face of the wheel. If the tool has no side rake on the top face, adjust the rest so that it is parallel to a radial centre line passing through the centre of the Major cutting edge (Fig. 404). If there is to be side rake, adjust the height of the rest to create the rake angle.

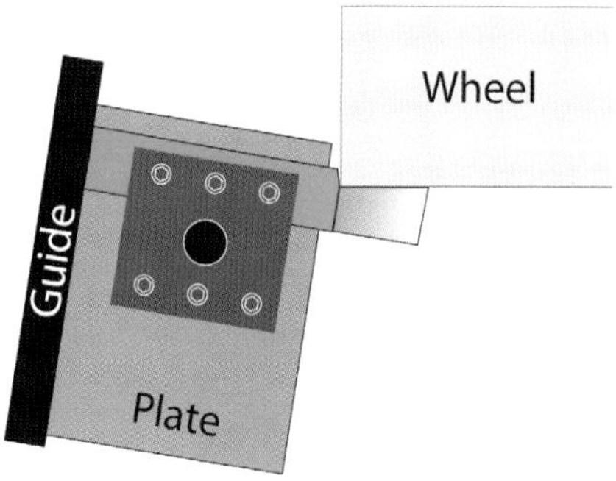

Fig. 450: Set up to grind the top face and cutting edges by first placing the tool in a reference position, then swinging to align the top face parallel to the face of the wheel.

- Swing the tool to create the Major (top) face rake angle (Fig. 450).
- Set a traverse stop, apply a cut and traverse the tool past the flat face of the wheel.

Finishing the faces

As with any other lathe tool, the faces and edges of a parting tool should be given a good finish. Use a fine grit wheel to finish the faces to size, repeating the setups used when shaping the tool. Afterwards, hone to a good finish using a stone, abrasive discs, or a ceramic disc and diamond paste or spray.

Sharpening a parting tool

A parting tool is sharpened by first grinding the Major (front) flank to restore the Major cutting edge. If necessary, grind the top face as well. Then hone to restore a fine finish and sharp edges. Depending on the wear or damage, the tool may be resharpened several times before it is necessary to reshape the tool. Note that where the blade tapers from front to back, each sharpening session reduces the width of the blade. Reshaping will involve removing the existing blade, to restore the full width of the Major cutting edge. That is the disadvantage of a backward-tapering blade on a parting tool ground from a solid blank.

PARTING TOOL (BLADE STYLE)

Some parting tools take the form of a flat blade (Fig. 451) which fits into a holder (Fig. 452). Other blades are ground on the end of a cylindrical blank and are used as inserts, in a sleeve in a holder. The blades are often supplied with pre-tapered sides to give Minor flank clearance as the tool cuts into the work. Parting tool blades may be kept in their tool holder and sharpened like a conventional all-in-one style tool (*see* previous section), but loose blades benefit from mounting the blade in a fixture which will provide better support and prevent flexing during sharpening (Figs 453–5). Some tool holders (Fig. 452) hold the whole blade upwards, so the holder tilt angle will create the top face angle. If the tool is kept in its holder and sharpened in the upright position, there will be no need to grind the top face. If a fixture in the style of Fig. 453 is used, it should be laid on its side (Fig. 454) with the blade set in the jig at the top rake angle, and the side of the jig at right angles to the direction of traverse and the face of the wheel. Swinging the jig creates the Major (front) flank clearance angle. To provide rigidity, keep the projection of the blade from the front of the fixture to a minimum. Raising the fixture to set the blade above or below wheel centre height creates side clearance.

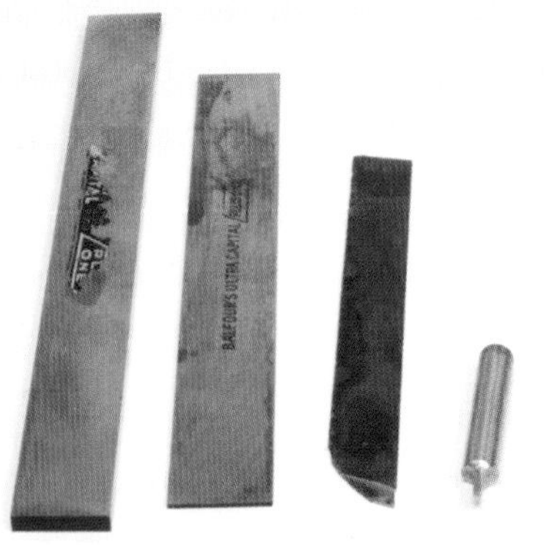

Fig. 451: Some parting tool blades are flat, with a rectangular or tapered section. Others may be ground on a cylindrical blank, then gripped in a sleeved holder.

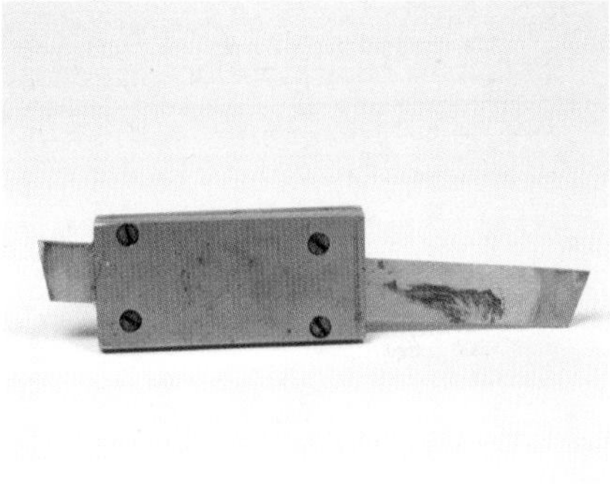

Fig. 452: Some holders grip the blade at an upward tilt to create a top rake angle. Keeping the blade in the holder during sharpening aids rigidity.

Fig. 453: Parting tool blades can be sharpened while clamped in a fixture.

Fig. 454: The fixture holds the blade at the same angle as the tool holder, and the protractor guide is set to the Major (front) flank clearance angle.

PARTING TOOL BLADE FIXTURE

- Two strap clamps hold the blade onto the fixture plate (Fig. 455). The bottom clamp has alternative hole positions for different widths of blade, and blades lying at different angles.
- The blade is aligned against two pins. Pins of equal diameter align the blade with the side of the fixture. Pins of different diameter hold the blade at an angle to the edge of the fixture, and can be used to help determine the front clearance angle when the blade will be mounted in a holder with a built-in upward tilt (Fig. 52).
- The required diameter of the large pin for a particular rake angle can be found using the formula:
  D = d + 2 x C x SinR
  where:
  d = diameter of the small pin
  C = distance between the centres of the pins, and
  R = rake angle, in degrees

  For example:
  If d = 5mm , C = 30mm , and R = 12^0
  D = 5 + 2 x 30 x Sin12
  D = 5 + 2 x 30 x 0.208
  D = 5 + 12.48
  D = 17.48mm

Fig. 455: A fixture for use when sharpening parting tool blades.

BORING TOOLS

Boring tools are designed to make an internal cut inside a hole in a workpiece, and they commonly have their Major cutting edges at the end of the tool (Fig. 456), or at the side (Fig. 457). It is not unusual to find that the same boring tool is used to increase the diameter of a hole and then to face the bottom (Figs 458 and 459).

Inside a hole, clearance is an issue. Unlike lathe tools which cut an external surface, which curves away from the tool below the cutting edge, the surface of a hole curves inwards, towards a boring tool, creating the danger that the wall of the hole will foul the heel of the tool (Fig. 460). That demands the tool be modified to take the heel clear (Fig. 461). Once the tool has been sharpened, an additional flat or curved facet may be ground at the heel, to ensure clearance in the bore.

Fig. 456: A boring bar with inserted bit and its major cutting edge at the end of the tool.

Fig. 457: A solid boring tool designed to cut a groove in the wall of a bore. Its cutting edge is at the side. This tool cuts the far wall, with the lathe running in reverse.

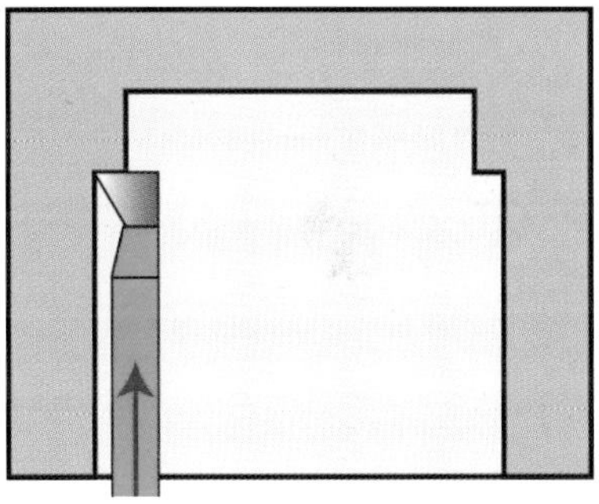

Fig. 458: A boring tool cutting the curved wall inside a hole.

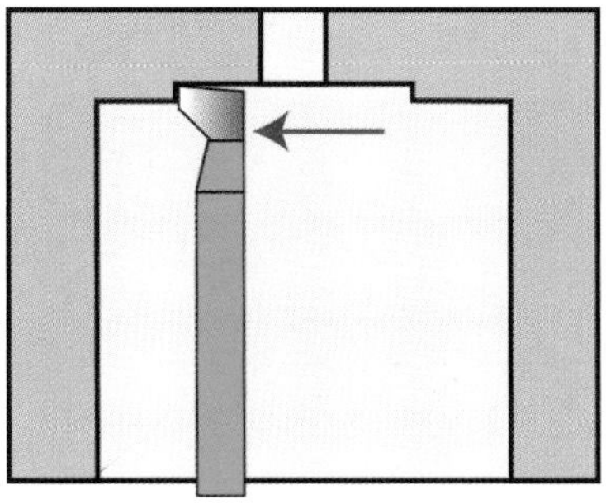

Fig. 459: A boring tool cutting a flat internal surface at the bottom of a hole.

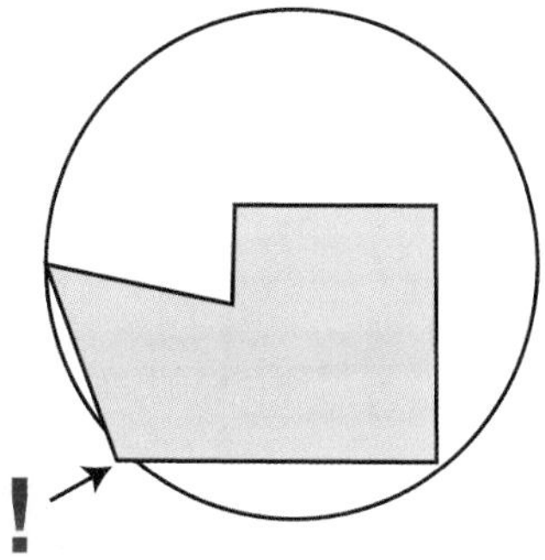

Fig. 460: Inside a hole, clearance for a boring tool can be a problem, especially at the heel.

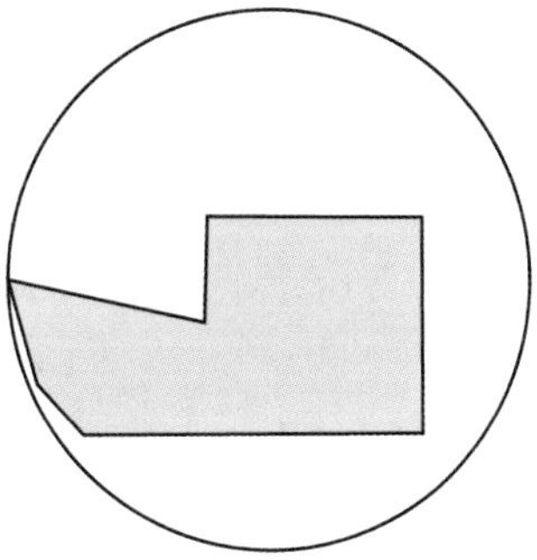

Fig. 461: An additional facet may be ground at the heel, to provide clearance.

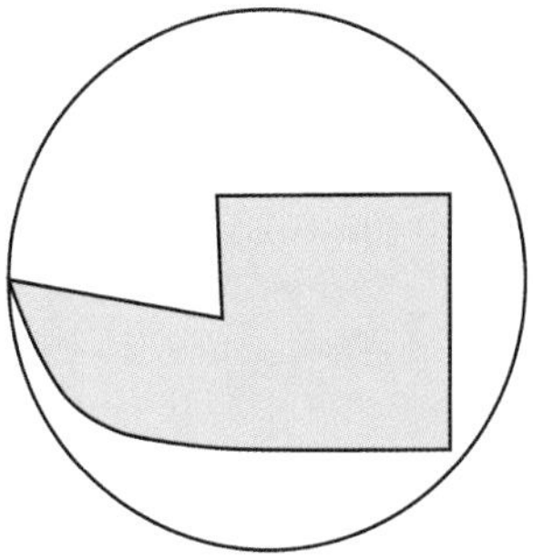

Fig. 462: A boring bar carries an inserted bit.

One common design of boring tool uses a bar as a shank, and carries an inserted cutting bit at, or near, the end (Fig. 456). This allows end cutting or side cutting, to suit the job in hand. Where possible, inserted bits should be removed and gripped in a collet or sleeve held in a tool block.

Boring tools with a shank, or insert bits held in a collet or sleeve

Boring tools are often end cutting, with their Major cutting edge orientated towards the bottom of the hole, so that they cut the wall of a hole as they move forwards, but some boring tools have their Major cutting edges towards the wall of the hole, and are designed to cut mainly across the bottom face of the bore, or into the wall, to create a groove or a recess. The methods used to sharpen the cutting edges by grinding the flanks and the top face of the tool, are the same; but the orientation of the toolholder may be different, to accommodate the position of the Major cutting edge relative to the shank. Focus on the position of the cutting edges in relation to the face of the wheel, and arrange the position of the toolholder to suit. Inserted bits should be held in a collet or sleeve, in a tool block. It is useful if the sleeve or collet can rotate in the block to set the initial orientation of the tool bit, but be held firm by a locking device before grinding commences. Depending on the design of the tool block, and the style of collet or sleeve, the lock may be a grub screw, a split clamp, or a collet nut.

Major flank

- Mount a type 1 wheel, and dress its face parallel to the direction of traverse.
- Swing the toolholder to bring the Major flank of the tool parallel to the face of the wheel (Figs 463–6). Add an indexing collar to the rear of the holder for an insert bit (Fig. 466).
- Adjust the height of the rest to create the Major cutting edge primary clearance.
- Apply a cut and traverse across the face of the wheel. Repeat as necessary.
- If the Major flank faces the curved wall of the hole, it may be necessary to grind additional clearance towards the bottom of that flank. If so, adjust the height of the rest to create a secondary facet, then apply a cut, and grind that facet. Repeat as necessary.

Minor flank

The Minor flank may have more than one facet, with a primary facet at the cutting edge, and a secondary facet providing additional clearance towards the bottom of the tool tip. The following method can be applied to each facet in turn:

- Mount a type 1 wheel, and dress its face parallel to the direction of traverse.
- Grip the shank of the tool in a holder mounted on a plate which will provide support if the tool is held beyond the face of the wheel (Figs 467 and 458). Because the sleeve holder for an insert bit must be swapped to the other slot on the tool holder, use the indexing collar to rotate the bit through a half-turn, to bring the top face uppermost.
- Swing the toolholder to bring the Minor cutting edge parallel to the face of the wheel (Figs 467–70). Make sure there is full support for the shank. Alter the height of the rest, to create the clearance.
- Apply a cut and traverse.

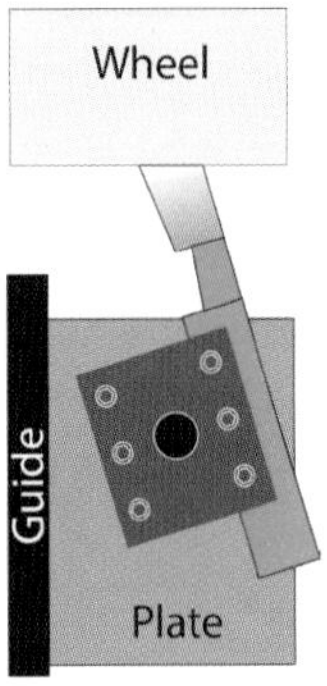

Fig. 463: The setup for the Major flank of a shanked boring tool.

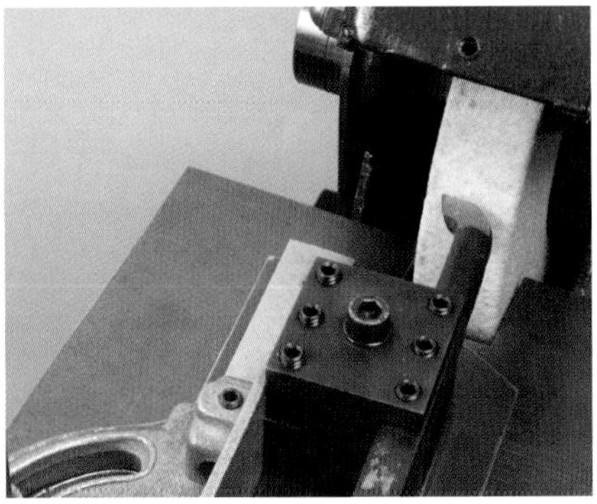

Fig. 464: Setup ready to grind the Major flank.

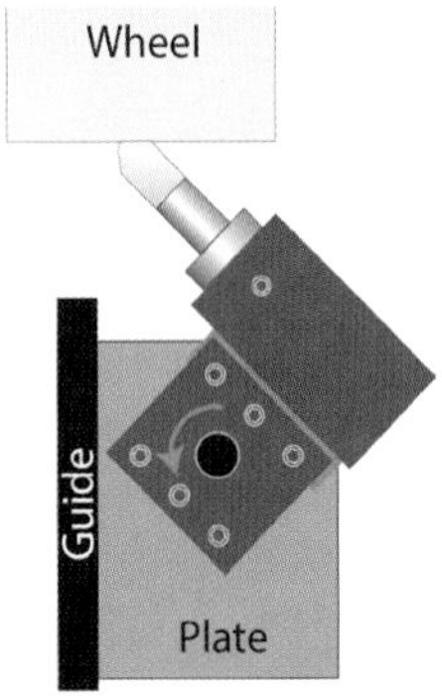

Fig. 465: The setup for an angled inserted bit.

Fig. 466: Preparing to grind an angled inserted bit.

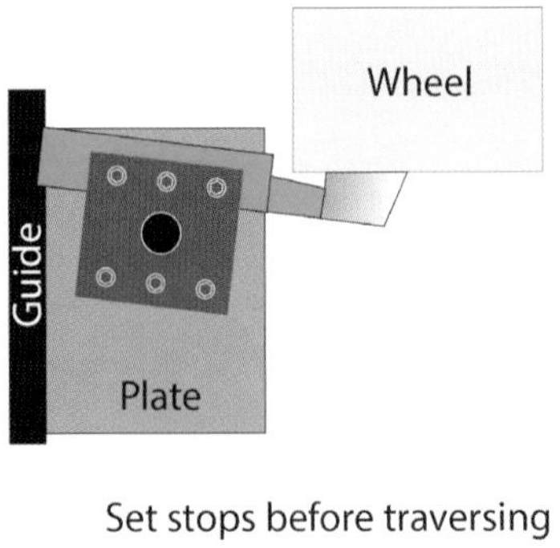

Fig. 467: The setup for the Minor flank of a shanked boring tool.

Fig. 468: Setup ready to grind the Minor flank.

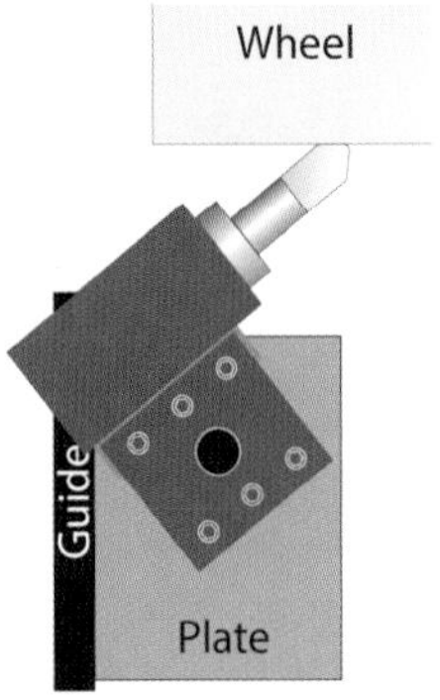

Fig. 469: The setup for the Minor flank.

Fig. 470: Preparing to grind an angled inserted bit.

Top face

The top face is simultaneously the Major face and the Minor face, and, as with a knife tool, it may have single- or dual-rake angles.

- Mount, and dress, a type 1 wheel.
- Use a rotatable tool holder with a horizontal axis. Turn the tool so that the 'top' (Major) face is nearest the face of the wheel, and rotate the holder to set the Major cutting edge vertical (Figs 471 and 472).

Fig. 471: Setup to grind a shanked boring tool.

Fig. 472: Setup to grind a boring tool bit.

- Swing the guide, to set the Major face rake angle (Figs 471 and 472).
- If necessary, adjust the height of the rest, to create the Minor face rake angle.
- Apply a cut and traverse. Repeat as often as required to form the top face.

Adding a heel facet

If necessary, grind an additional facet on the heel of the tool to provide clearance (Fig. 473). This can often be done by positioning the tool by hand.

INTERNAL SCREWCUTTING INSERT BITS

Internal screwcutting insert bits are sharpened in the same way as internal boring bits.

Top face

The top face will normally have either zero rake, or a single rake angle.

- Mount, and dress, a type 1 wheel.
- Rotate the tool, or turn it on its side, so that the 'top' (Major) face faces the wheel, with its point on the wheel centre line (Figs 474 and 475).
- Swing the tool holder or the guide, to set the Major face rake angle (Figs 474 and 475).
- Apply a cut and traverse. Repeat until the top face is flat and damage-free.

Fig. 476 shows an alternative setup which uses the front left corner of the wheel.

Flanks

For each flank in turn:

- Mount a type 1 wheel, and dress its face parallel to the direction of traverse.
- Set the 'top' face in its normal working position facing upwards. Swing the toolholder to bring the flank of the tool parallel to the face of the wheel.
- Set the height of the rest to create the Major cutting edge primary clearance.
- Apply a cut and traverse across the face of the wheel. Repeat as necessary.

If the tool has top rake, compare the angle between the flanks with a thread setting gauge, as for an external screwcutting tool (Fig. 434). Check the angle of the first flank before grinding, so that the vee is aligned at right angles to the shank. That simplifies mounting the tool in the lathe.

Finish the nose in the same way as for an external screwcutting tool, grinding a flat or, preferably, a radius to match the radius on a thread gauge, as for an external tool (Fig. 438). One radius can often be used when cutting a small range of thread pitches.

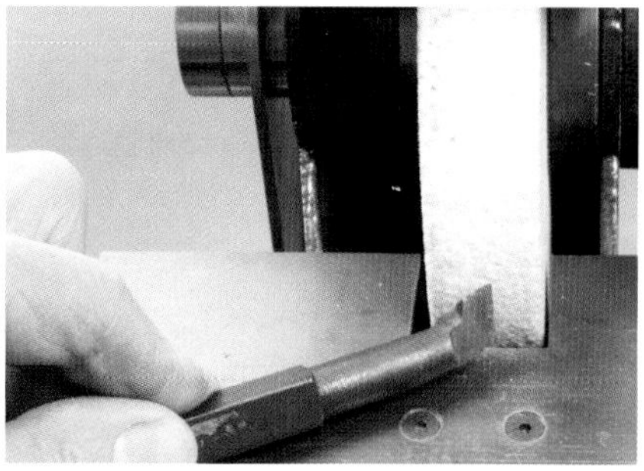

Fig. 473: If necessary, grind an additional clearance facet on the heel of a boring tool.

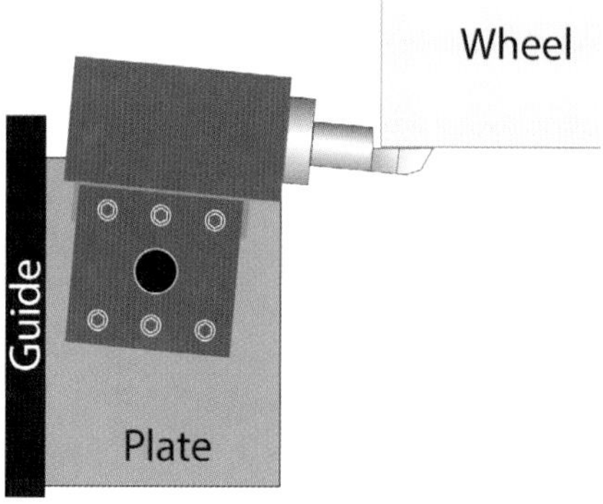

Fig. 474: Set the 'top' face towards the wheel, and swing to the rake angle.

Fig. 475: Swing the tool holder (shown) or the guide. Traverse left to right.

Fig. 476: Swing only the tool holder. Traverse forwards and backwards.

Tool type 8: Drills

Drill bits come in a range of sizes and types (Fig. 477), with each type intended to be suitable for a particular kind of job. In essence, a drill bit has cutting edges at the end, and turning the drill while pushing it into a piece of material causes the cutting edges to penetrate the material and create a hole. Early drills were rods with a cutting edge at the front, and a later addition was straight flutes (grooves) along the rod (Fig. 478). The flutes weaken the drill, but provide somewhere for the chips to go, to prevent the drill seizing in the hole. As chips are forced into the flutes,

Fig. 477: Drill bits come in a range of sizes and types.

Fig. 478: A small diameter spade drill has no flutes.

they tend to pack, and the pressure tends to force the chips upwards within the flutes. That action is improved if the flutes are made helical, as the twisting action of drilling tends to help force the chips upwards within the flutes. Whereas in a straight flute drill the rotation forces the chips against the straight side of the flute, a helical twist allows the chips to slide up and out of the hole more efficiently.

Most drills have two cutting edges at the tip, which provide a balanced cutting action. The geometry of the cutting edges provides the cutting action, and is affected by the material the drill is designed to cut. As with a more conventional lathe tool, the angle of the cutting edges and the adjacent tool faces is critical for good performance. Although these angles are obvious on a flat-faced tool such as a chisel, a lathe tool and flat-sided drill bits, the cylindrical shape of a twist drill obscures the true shape of its cutting edges and faces.

GRIPPING DRILLS FOR SHARPENING

Most drills have a cylindrical shank or shaft at the end furthest from the cutting edges; some have hexagonal or square shanks; and others use a proprietary shape such as on SDS drill bits. In use, drills are often gripped in a chuck or a collet, or a purpose-designed sleeve. During sharpening, the drill needs to be gripped or supported closer to the cutting edges. Although that is easily arranged with a plain shank, most of the commonly used 'twist' drills have helical flutes which run the length of the drill up to the shank, and gripping on the shank leaves too much of the drill unsupported during grinding. A 3-jaw drill chuck will not grip reliably on the edges of the flutes, but a 6-jaw chuck, or a multi-fingered collet such as the ER series will grip reliably. A vee block can be used to grip the body of the drill, but only where the upper clamp spans several contact points (Fig. 479), because the traditional single-

Fig. 479: A vee block and clamp, and an ER series collet which has multiple gripping 'fingers'.

Fig. 480: Some drill clamps have two sets of interleaved vee fingers capable of gripping reliably on the flutes of a twist drill.

Fig. 482: A simple jig allows the heights of the tips of the cutting edges to be compared, using a pointer or the front of the vee block as a reference. The end of the drill shank sits against a fixed stop, in this case a sheet metal tab attached to the vee block.

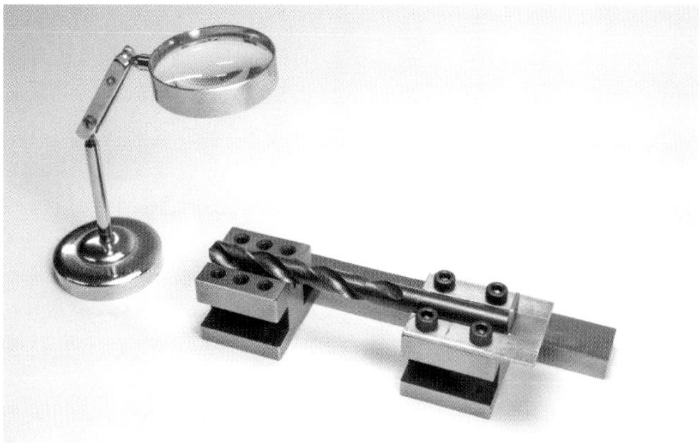

screw vee block clamp is not sufficiently secure. Some modern drill sharpeners use a two-part clamp with sets of interleaved fingers (Fig. 480) which provide an effective grip.

INSPECTION AIDS

Many sharpening devices produce variable results, so it is useful to have some means of inspecting a drill bit. A basic gauge can be used to inspect the angle of the cutting edges on a twist drill, and measure the lengths of the cutting edges (Fig. 481). This gauge is restricted to one tip angle (usually

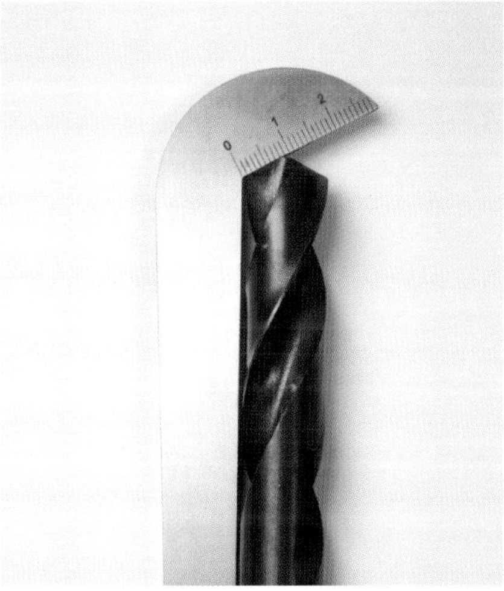

Fig. 481: A basic gauge can provide a check on the tip angle of a drill, as well as an approximate measurement of the length of each cutting edge.

118 degrees) and the accuracy with which the ruler-style scale can be read is limited. However; the gauge does indicate whether the cutting edges are of the same length. The cutting edges, the central chisel point and the outer corners of the cutting edges can be inspected using a jeweller's loupe, a microscope, or a USB camera/microscope.

The arrangement shown in Fig. 482 allows a comparison of the relative heights of the outer corners of the cutting edges. With the drill resting in the vee blocks, and the end of the shank resting against an end stop, turning the drill allows the position of the outer tip of each cutting edge to be compared against the front edges of the vee, the fiducial line engraved on the lens of a microscope, or a line or scale superimposed on the image from a webcam or USB microscope attached to a computer (Fig. 483).

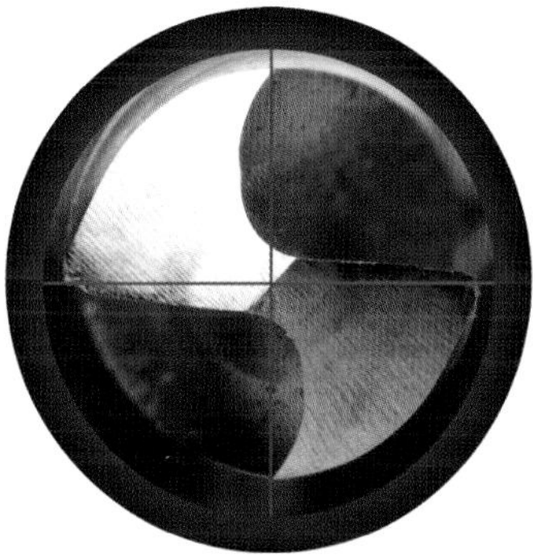

Fig. 483: The fiducial line on a microscope or a line superimposed on the image from a USB camera allows comparison of the positions of the corners of cutting edges.

A plain collar, sleeve or tube is also useful (Fig. 484). The internal diameter does not need to be exactly the same as the diameter of the drill, so a single collar can cover a range of diameters. Slipping the collar over the drill, and aligning it with the point at which one cutting edge meets the top of a flute allows a comparison with the corresponding point at the other side of the drill (Fig. 485). Unaided, the eye is easily

Fig. 484: A plain collar, sleeve or tube allows comparison of drill cutting edge height and clearance.

Fig. 485: Align the collar with the point at which one cutting edge meets the top of a flute.

deceived as it follows the clearance behind the cutting edge of a twist drill, but the top surface of a sleeve allows a visual reference surface. Following the curve from the tip of a cutting edge to the next flute gives an indication of the clearance behind the cutting edge. Clearance exists when the curve dips below the top of the sleeve. Make sure the axis of the collar and drill are parallel to one another, perhaps by using a vee block (Fig. 486). Collars of a specific thickness are useful for examining the results of machine sharpening (*see* later in this chapter).

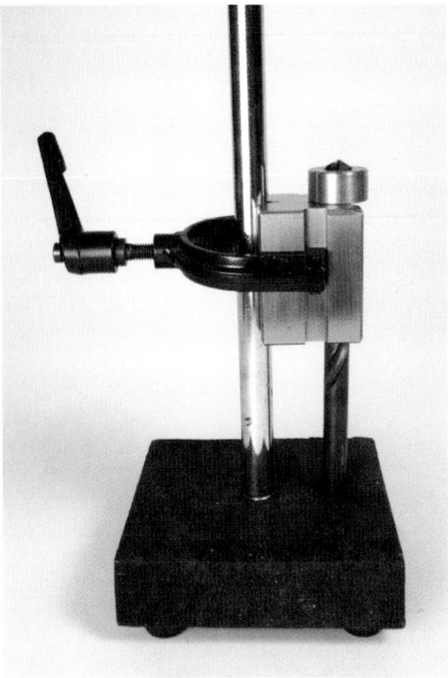

Fig. 486: Support the collar so that its axis is parallel to the axis of the drill.

On a properly sharpened drill, the faces behind the cutting edges meet in the centre. Depending on the method used to create those faces this may create a short edge, called a 'chisel edge' or a 'chisel point'; or some other feature (*see* later). The position of that edge or feature is critical, and should be inspected carefully. A useful aid is shown in Fig. 487 and consists of a vertical arm and a piece of clear acrylic sheet which has vertical and horizontal lines scribed on the side nearest the drill tip. The arm is attached to a height gauge, or a vertical rod, allowing easy vertical adjustment. Place a conical pointer on a vee block, and align the point with a vertical line engraved on transparent plastic. Replace the pointer with a drill. That vertical line acts as a reference for judging whether the chisel point (or other feature) is in the centre of the drill. Rotate the drill and check that the chisel edge can be aligned on the vertical line (Fig. 488). If the edge lies to one side, it is not central, in which case the drill has not been sharpened symmetrically, and will cut an over-sized hole.

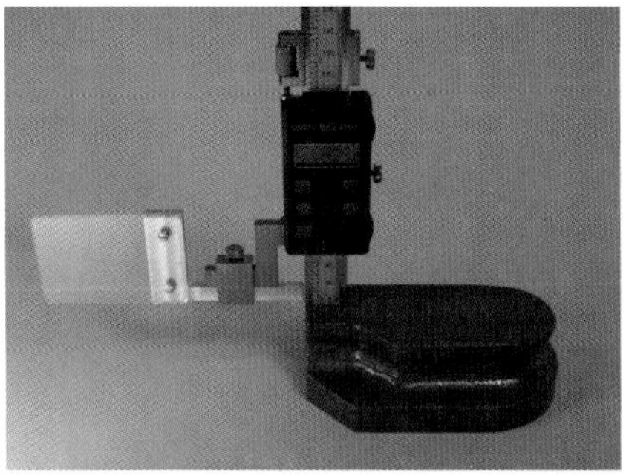

Fig.487: A height gauge carrying a clear acrylic plate engraved with horizontal and vertical lines.

Fig. 488: Comparing the position of a chisel edge with a centrally located vertical reference line reveals whether the edge lies centrally on the end of the drill.

It is often inconvenient to remove a drill from a workhead for inspection, so a pointer mounted on a workhead may be used to indicate the position of the outer corner of one cutting edge (Fig. 489). Rotating the drill through 180 degrees allows the position of the opposite corner to be compared with the pointer. If the two corners are in the same position relative to the pointer, the drill cutting edges are of equal length.

Fig. 489: A pointer allows the positions of opposite corners to be compared, to indicate whether the corresponding cutting edges are of equal length. The tip of the pointer provides a reference. The height of the pointer is micro-adjustable. The vee blocks provide loose support for the drill, but allow it to turn freely, enabling a comparison of the tips at each side.

ORIENTATING CUTTING EDGES

In most initial setups, drill cutting edges should be orientated parallel to, or at right angles to, the rest. Setting the cutting edges of a drill parallel to the rest can be done on a flat surface, away from the rest, for convenience, using the device shown in Fig. 487. Adjust the gauge vertically, until a horizontal line passes through the centre of the drill point (Fig. 490). Then rotate the drill until the cutting edges lie parallel to the line, and tighten the clamps securing the drill. A similar procedure, using the vertical line, can be used to set cutting edges vertical.

Fig. 490: To set drill cutting edges horizontally, align the edges with a scribed horizontal line.

Most drills are designed to rotate clockwise (viewed from the shank end) and when the drill is held horizontal, with the tip and

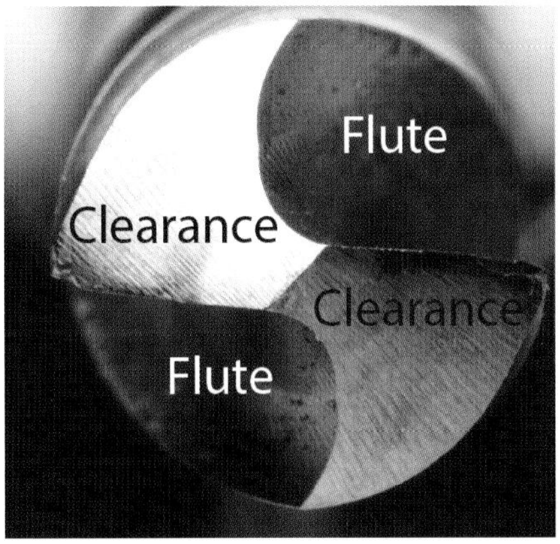

Fig. 491: With the cutting edges horizontal, the clearance is on the clockwise side and the flute is on the anti-clockwise side of each cutting edge.

cutting edges orientated as shown in Fig. 491, the clearance behind the right hand cutting edge is visible on the upper surface. The flute in front of left hand cutting edge is visible, and the clearance behind the left hand cutting edge is not visible.

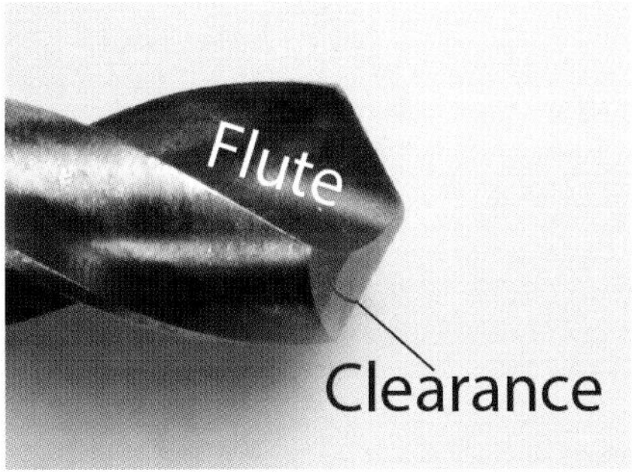

Fig. 492: With the cutting edges horizontal, the flute spirals backwards and the clearance increases towards the back, as it blends into the body of the drill.

If the drill is held horizontal and the cutting edges are horizontal, the visible flute spirals backwards away from the cutting edge, and the clearance behind the hidden cutting edge increases as it twists backwards, meeting the flute and blending into the body of the drill (Fig. 492).

FLAT-HEADED DRILLS

Flat-headed drills (Figs 477 and 493) have flat faces behind the cutting edges, and the

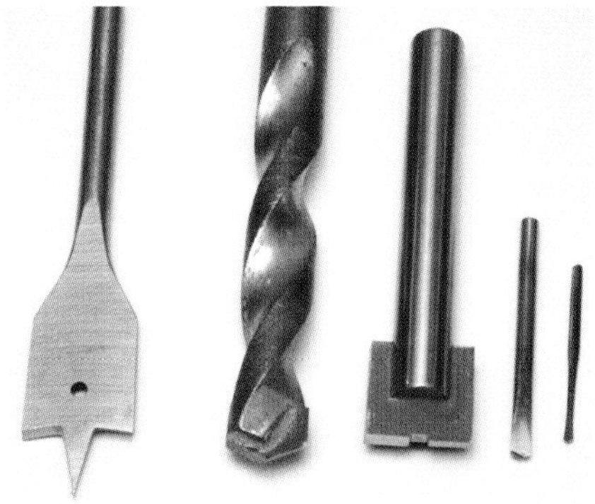

Fig. 493: A selection of flat-headed drills, including: a drill for wood, a carbide-tipped masonry drill, a spade drill, a small spade drill, and a spear-point drill.

shank is often a plain cylindrical shape with a diameter less than the width across the cutting edges. Flat-headed drills include flat drills used for woodworking, spade drills and spear-point drills used for cutting metal, and masonry drills used for drilling holes in concrete and brick. Masonry drills have a shank like a twist drill (*see* later), but the cutting edges are formed on an flat piece of carbide incorporated into the tip. Flat-headed drills all have a broadly similar cutting action, but the precise geometry depends on the material the drill is intended to cut. Some flat drills for woodworking are made from high - carbon steel, and are relatively soft, while spade drills are made from high speed steel or have ceramic inserts, and masonry drills have carbide tips which can be ground with a modified geometry to allow them to cut metal.

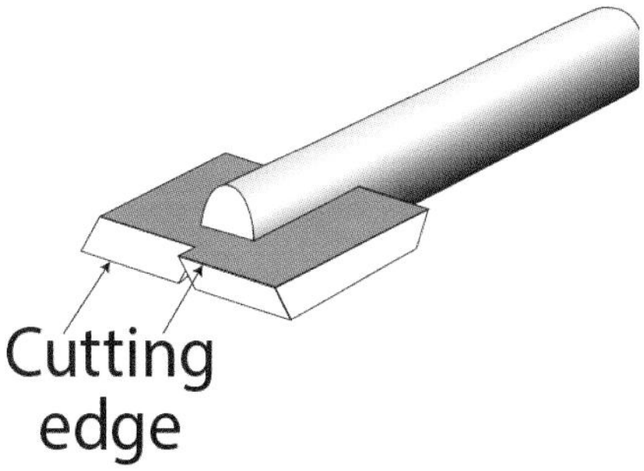

Fig. 494: On a flat-headed drill, the cutting edges meet and form a central ridge.

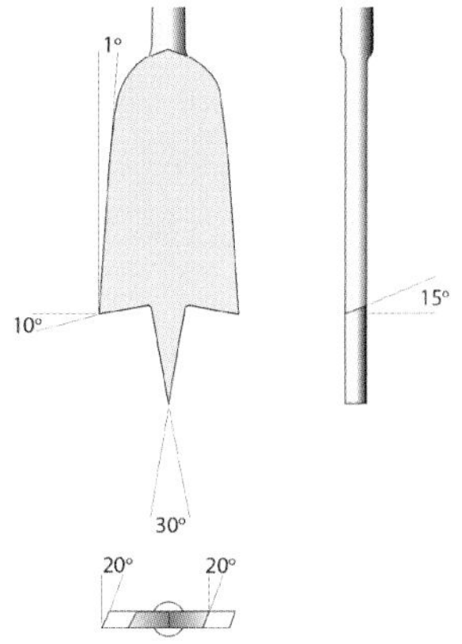

Fig. 495: On a flat-headed drill designed to cut wood, the central point is drawn out from the cutting edges, forming a tapered pilot section.

Flat-headed drills have two cutting edges which meet and form a central ridge (Fig. 494). On a drill designed to cut wood, this central ridge is drawn out from the main cutting edges (Fig. 495), forming an elongated point which penetrates the work first, cutting what is effectively a tapered pilot hole and steadying the drill as the main cutting edges engage with the material. Spade drills are normally intended to be preceded by a pilot drill, and are often started inside a short section of pre-bored hole, so there is no point on the tip. As a flat-headed drill creates a hole, the chips are able to move into the spaces between the flat faces and the edge of the cylindrical hole. In a shallow hole, the chips remove themselves quite easily because the spaces around the flat faces are relatively large, and the rotary movement of the drill swings the chips around at a sufficiently high speed that most vibrate out of the hole. In a deep hole, the drill must be retracted partly out of the hole, at intervals, to eject the chips. When creating a hole, it is important that the drill is never retracted so far that the outer tips of the main cutting faces come out of the hole, because attempting to replace the drill in the hole while it is rotating usually results in some misalignment, causing damage to the top edges of the hole as the outer tips catch on the surrounding material.

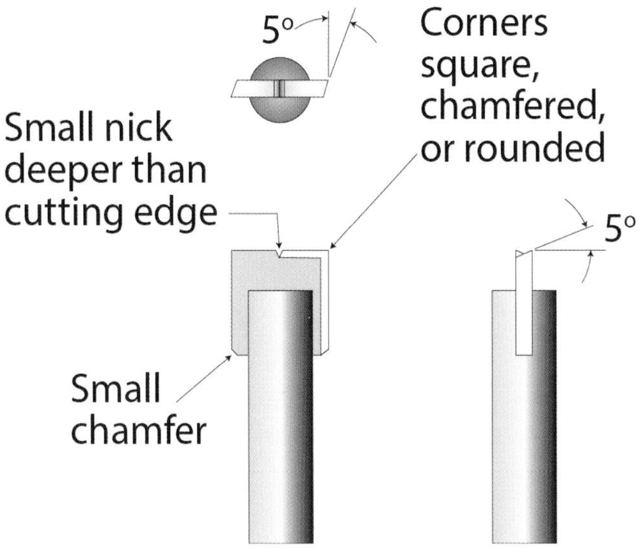

Fig. 496: Typical geometry found on a spade drill. The 'nick' removes the ridge between the cutting edges, but means the spade drill cannot cut at its centre, and must be preceded by a pilot drill.

The faces adjacent to the cutting edges are flat, so that the tool angles are similar to a lathe tool or a chisel except that there is no top rake (Fig. 496). In an ideal world, the two cutting edges would be diametrically opposite one another, so the two halves of the flat bit would have to be staggered (Fig. 497). This is inconvenient for manufacture, and in most cases the cutting edges are formed on the front edges of a single piece of flat material. One useful effect is that there is a stronger section at the centre, with less tendency to split where the two stepped halves meet. This arrangement is similar to the way the cutting edges meet on a twist drill (*see* later).

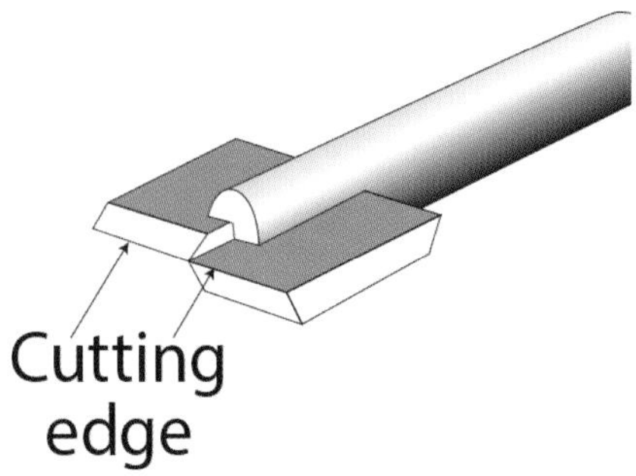

Fig. 497: Staggering the two halves of a flat bit would place the cutting edges diametrically opposite one another, but would complicate manufacture, making this design desirable but impractical.

Spade and masonry drills

Spade drills and masonry drills re-purposed for drilling metal share a similar geometry (Figs 496 and 498) and can be sharpened using the same methods. One difference is that the included angle between the cutting edges is 180 degrees on spade drills, but 130 to 140 degrees on masonry drills. The materials used for the cutting edges are different, too, and although the cutting tips of spade drills are often made of high speed steel and can be sharpened using aluminium oxide grinding wheels, the tips of masonry drills are usually carbide and must be sharpened using a grinder fitted with a wheel made of silicon carbide ('green grit'), or coated with cBN (cubic boron nitride) or diamond.

Figs 496 and 498 show the cutting edges and faces of modified spade and masonry drills, with typical angles. The Major cutting faces are flat, and the area immediately behind each cutting edge is ground at approximately 5 degrees, to create clearance. This geometry is not ideal, as there is no top rake. However; both types of drill are effective in cast iron, and the carbide masonry tips are capable of drilling hardened steel. Although a standard twist drill has an included point angle of 118 degrees (*see* later), the larger 140 degrees shown in Fig. 498 is suitable for drilling harder materials. An ER collet can grip a masonry drill effectively by the flutes, and the cutting edges can be set horizontal using a clear plastic sheet engraved with horizontal and vertical lines (Fig. 487).

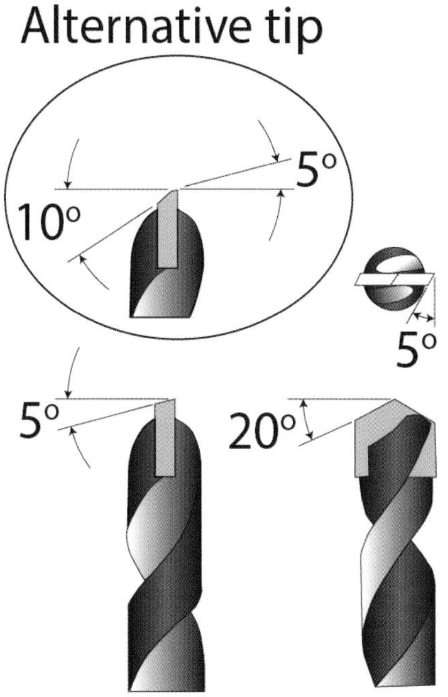

Fig. 498: Typical geometry on a masonry drill reground for drilling metal.

Grinding the sides of a spade or masonry drill

It is not always necessary, or desirable, to grind the sides of a drill, because the sides of the drill tip set the diameter of the hole, and grinding the sides will reduce the diameter of the drill. When the drill is rotating in a hole, its sides will steady the drill in the hole. However; rubbing will generate heat, so it is common to grind a clearance behind the edge. Because of the flat face, the side cutting edges are above the centre line of the drill, so the rake angle is effectively negative (Fig. 499), and the edge will tend to scrape rather than cut, in many materials. The clearance angle on the sides is typically the same as for the front cutting edge, at 5 to 7 degrees.

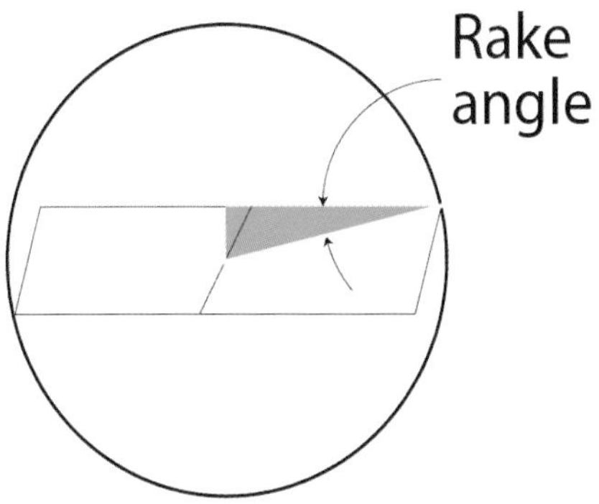

Fig. 499: Because the flat face of a drill is above the centre line, the Major face rake angle of each side cutting edge is negative. The yellow line is radial.

- Mount a flat-faced wheel such as a type 6 cup wheel. Set the axis of the drill holder and the axis of traverse parallel to the face of the wheel (Fig. 500).

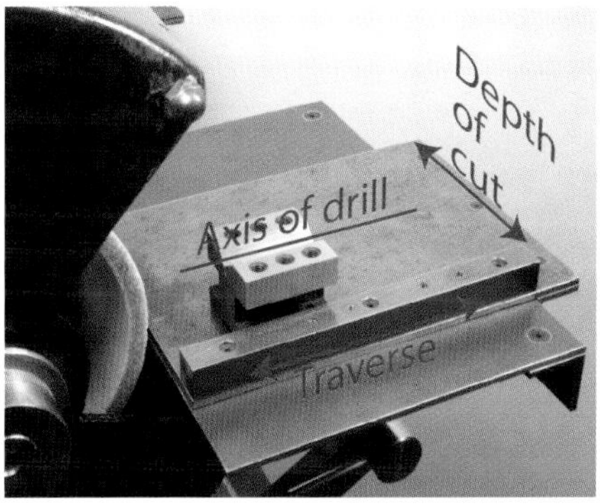

Fig. 500: Initially, set the drill holder and the axis of traverse parallel to the face of the wheel.

- Mount the drill in the workholder and rotate the drill 5–7 degrees, to create the clearance angle (Figs 486 and 501). Add a square indexing collar.
- Feed sideways until the first side just touches the face of the wheel. Traverse clear; apply a cut; traverse parallel to the face of the wheel, and retract. Rotate the drill half a turn, and grind the second cutting. Repeat, increasing the cut as necessary, then finish with a single cut on both sides without altering the feed.
- Measure the diameter of the tip; adjust the feed if necessary; and repeat until the drill is of the desired diameter.

Fig. 501: Rotate the spindle clockwise 5 to 7 degrees to create the side clearance.

Relieving the centre of a spade drill

Create, or re-form, the central groove between the cutting edges of a spade drill by using the face of a narrow type 1 wheel of 1–3mm thickness dressed to a square edge, a vee or a semi-circle.

- Put a rod in the workholder, and set it against the side of the wheel (Fig. 502).
- Retract, and move to the side half the rod diameter plus half the thickness of the wheel, to centre rod and wheel.

Fig.502: Place a bar against the side of the wheel; traverse clear; then move sideways half the rod diameter plus half the thickness of the wheel. The shank of the drill is used here, as the bar.

- Mount the drill in place of the rod, and set its flat tip horizontal (Fig. 503). Grind by plunging directly into the wheel. For a wider groove, move to one side and plunge, then repeat on the other side of the groove.

Fig. 503: Use a thin type 1 wheel to create the central groove between the cutting edges of a spade drill.

Grinding the cutting edges of a spade or masonry drill

- Set the axis of the drill at right angles to the axis of traverse. Set the cutting edges horizontal.
- If the cutting edges lie in a straight line (typically on a spade drill), set the height of the rest to create the front clearance (Fig. 504).

Fig. 504: Set the axis of the drill horizontal and at 90 degrees to the axis of traverse. Set the height of the rest, to create the front clearance.

- *Masonry drill*: swing the drill clockwise to create the half-angle between the cutting edge and the shank of the drill (Fig. 505). The included angle between the cutting edges is typically 140 degrees so the drill should be swung through 90 minus the half-angle, or 90 – 70 = 20 degrees (Figs 486 and 505).

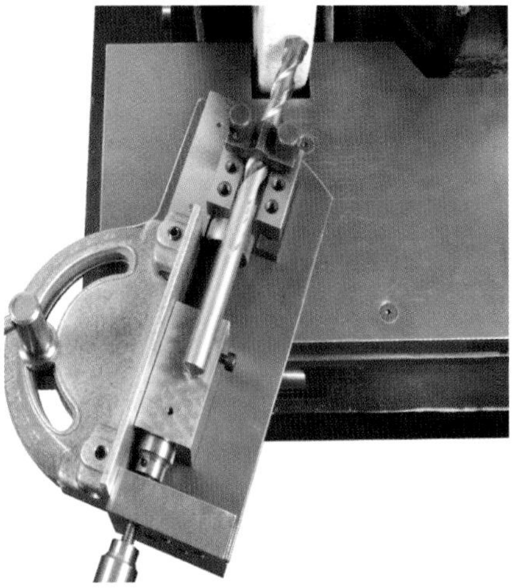

Fig. 505: Swing a masonry drill clockwise to set the approach angle of the cutting edge, before setting the height of the rest to create the clearance at the cutting edge.

- Set the height of the rest to create the front clearance.
- With the drill clear and to one side of the wheel, advance the drill to create a cut. *Spade drill*: traverse across the face of the wheel, stopping when the edge of the wheel reaches the centre of the drill. *Masonry drill*: traverse across the wheel face.
- Rotate the drill through half a turn to bring the other cutting edge into the same position, and repeat for that side.

After grinding each cutting edge, examine the Major flank, looking for a uniformly flat surface leading to a sharply defined cutting edge. The corner between the Major flank and the side of the tool should be well defined.

Checking a masonry drill for symmetry

It is essential that the lengths of the cutting edges on a masonry drill are equal. Use a gauge (Fig. 481 or Fig. 506) to measure or compare the lengths, or a pointer to compare the positions of the corners (Fig. 489) and grind the shortest cutting edge, adjusting the angles or the depths of cut on either cutting edge until the lengths are equal

Fig. 506: A home-made 140 degree gauge may be used to measure the included angle of the drill point.

Fig. 507: For each rear corner, set the axis of the drill horizontal and at 45 degrees to the face of the wheel.

and the corners are directly opposite one another. Standard commercial cutting edge gauges are most commonly made for a typical twist drill angle of 118 degrees, but the simple sheet metal gauge shown in Fig. 506 allows comparison with the point angle of a masonry drill, although it does not measure lip lengths.

Chamfering the corners of a spade bit

To chamfer the rear corners of a spade drill, set the axis of the drill horizontal and at right angles to the wheel face, then swing through 45 degrees (Fig. 507). Fully grind one corner, and note the depth of feed. Rotate the drill a half-turn about its axis, and grind that second corner, in stages, to the same depth. The front corners should be positioned horizontal and at 45 degrees to the wheel face (Figs 508 and 509). The front chamfers are cutting edges, so the height of

Fig. 508: For each front corner, set the axis of the drill horizontal and at 45 degrees to the face of the wheel. Adjust the rest height to create the clearance angle. This angle guide traverses parallel to the wheel face.

the rest must be set to create the clearance angle (5–7 degrees). Grind both chamfers to the same depth, (which need not necessarily be the same depth as the front chamfers). Take care with the direction of the angles.

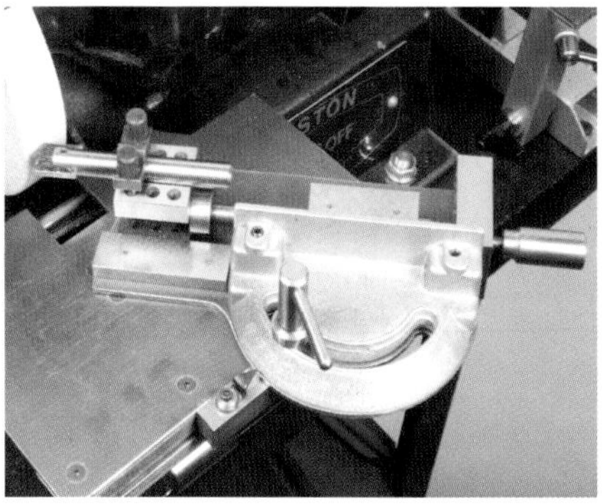

Fig. 509: A screw feed gives more accurate control.

Relieving the tip of a masonry drill

If the cutting edges of a converted masonry drill have been reground several times, the metal around the inserted tip will be close to the top of the tip (Fig. 510), and may need to be relieved. Use a type 1 wheel with a curved face for this operation. Fig. 511 shows a drill with its axis set at right angles to the face of the wheel, and the cutting edges set vertical. The workhead is tilted through 90 – half-angle (90 – 70 = 20 degrees for an included angle of 140 degrees), so that the top of the upper cutting edge is approximately at right angles to a radial line at the point of contact.

Fig. 510: The tip of a masonry drill is brazed into the body of the drill. The braze line is highlighted in red.

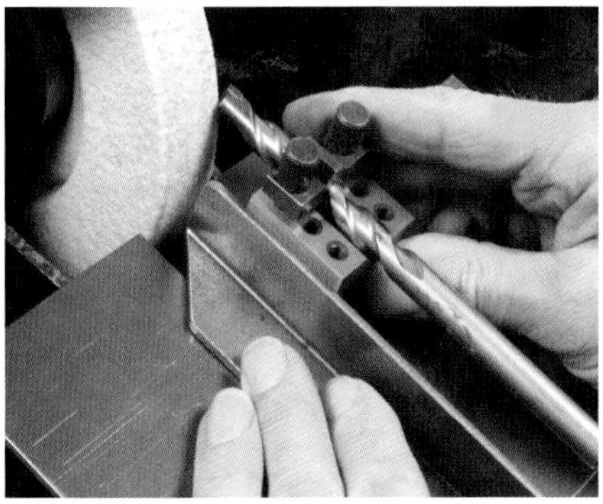

Fig. 511: Set the drill with its axis at right angles to the face of the wheel, and the cutting edges vertical. The top of the upper cutting edge should be approximately at right angles to a radial line at the point of contact.

Adjust the left-to-right movement of the workhead carriage so that the side of the wheel will just touch the Major face of the upper half of the drill, then lock the carriage, perhaps by setting right and left stops against the central fixed stop finger. Feed forward to remove material from the tip of the drill, at the side of the insert (Fig. 512). Removing material weakens the bond between insert and drill body, so grind just enough to create space for chips.

Fig. 512: Grinding creates additional space at the tip.

Spear-point drills

Spear-point drills (Figs 493 and 513) are a traditional tool bit, originally used with an Archimedes hand drill (Fig. 514).

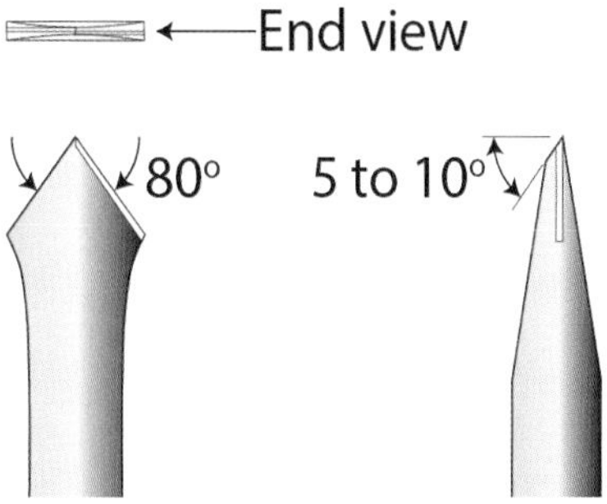

Fig. 513: Spear-point drills are forged from square-section bar, and are flared at the tip.

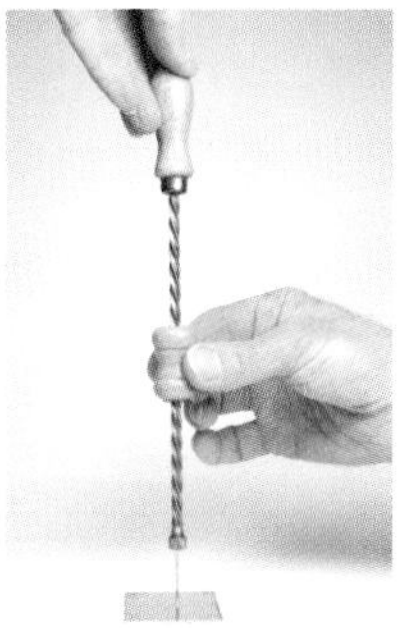

Fig. 514: When using an Archimedes hand drill, pulling the central block downwards forces the spiral shaft, collet chuck and drill bit to turn.

The tip is forged from square-section bar, and flared at the end to form the diamond-shaped tip. Cutting takes place at the sides of the vee, and, in the as-supplied condition, there is no clearance behind those cutting edges, so the drill rubs as much as it cuts. The action can be improved by grinding 5–10 degrees clearance behind each cutting edge, as well as making sure the tip is symmetrical. The tips are usually made from a carbon steel, and are not suitable for drilling in steel, but are traditionally used by clock and watch makers for drilling in brass. Although largely superseded by twist drills, existing spear-point bits can be sharpened in the same way as for masonry drills; or by hand, using an abrasive stone.

The square shank is best held in a 4-segment collet of the type found in many multi-tools. Fig. 515 shows a collet turned on the end of a 16mm diameter shaft so that it can be held in a small workhead. The nose cap (collet closing nut) is a standard spare part, supplied with a set of collets, and it requires a 9/32" x 40TPI thread.

Fig. 515: A collet socket turned on the end of a 16mm diameter shank, with a commercially-available collet nut and collets.

Fig. 516 shows a spear-point bit held in a collet in a workhead. The workhead provides swing, tilt and rotate movements. The spindle has a graduated collar at the end, to provide basic indexing facilities.

Fig. 516: A spear-point drill held in a collet in a workhead. The graduated collar can be used to control rotation and provide indexing.

These bits are small, and the tip is some distance from the collet, so this is not a particularly rigid setup. To minimize the forces involved, use a fine-grained wheel and small feeds while grinding. There is no guarantee that the head of the drill bit has been forged centrally in relation to the square shank, but it is as well to grind the bit as symmetrically as possible.

Inspecting the drill point

With such a small drill point, inspection requires high magnification. This is best carried out using a microscope or high magnification loupe. Inspect the spear point for symmetrical cutting edges, and check that grinding has completely formed the cutting edges and clearances (Fig. 517).

Fig. 517: Inspect the spear point for a central tip and corners at the same height.

Sharpening using an abrasive stone

- Select a medium grade abrasive stone.
- Mount the spindle in a graver honing plate (Fig. 518) and set the flat sides of the tip vertical. Add a square-sided collar some distance back from the plate, for adjustment later. Set the side of the collar vertical, and lock it in place.
- Loosen the plate collar lock, then, using a template as an aid, adjust the protrusion of the drill bit while keeping the side of the rear sleeve vertical (Fig. 519). Tighten the lock on the plate collar.
- Loosen the square-sided sleeve and slide it up to the plate collar. Hold the side of the sleeve vertical, and tighten it in place (Fig. 520).

The graver honing plate provides tilt and rotation, but no swing movement. Setting the protrusion of the drill places the cutting edge along the horizontal, but creating an angled clearance face behind the cutting edge requires that the drill tip is tilted to the side. Unfortunately, rotating the drill in its holder will not produce the desired effect, because the end point will remain in contact with the horizontal surface while the wings (the ends of the cutting edges) arc outwards and upwards, changing the angle of the cutting edges and any clearance created behind those edges. The solution is to angle the whole horizontal plane. That plane will be an abrasive stone, so tilting the whole stone at right angles to the cutting edge will act exactly like a tilt. Fig. 521 shows a board carrying a sharpening stone. The white plastic is slipped under the edge of the stone, tilting it to the clearance angle. A pencil line marks the position where the edge of the stone is at the same level as the board under the honing plate roller.

Fig. 518: Set the flat sides of the tip vertical. Add a square-sided collar some distance away from the fixed sleeve in the plate, and set one side vertical.

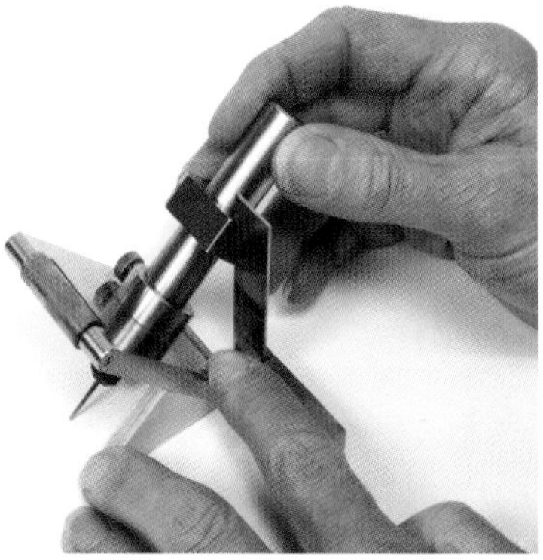

Fig. 519: Using a template, adjust the protrusion of the drill bit, keeping the side of the rear sleeve vertical.

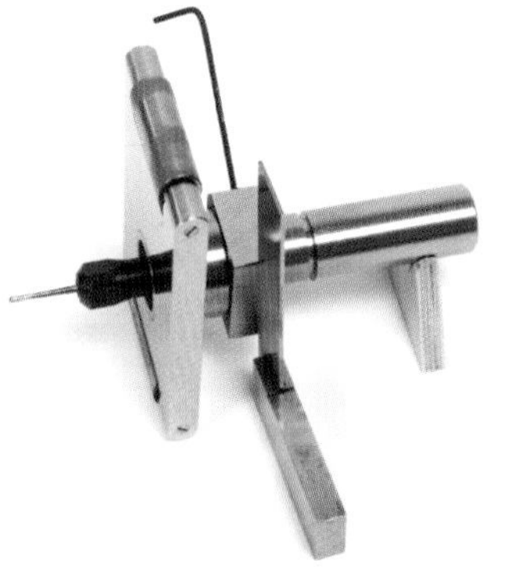

Fig. 520: Loosen the square-sided collar and slide it fully forward. Reset one side vertical, then re-tighten.

Fig. 521: The white plastic sits a little under the edge of the stone, setting the clearance angle. Draw a guide line where the left board is at the same level as the angled side of the block. Roll backwards and forwards in line with the guide line.

- Roll the tool backwards and forwards along the stone, aligned with the pencil line, to form, or re-form, the clearance face and sharpen the cutting edge.
- Loosen the lock on the plate collar, and rotate the spindle half a turn, setting the square-sided collar vertical; then lock the plate collar.
- Inspect the point frequently, until both cutting edges are sharp, and the point of the drill is central, with wing tips level, indicating that the lengths of the cutting edges are equal.

TWIST DRILLS

Twist drills (Fig. 477) are commonly used for creating holes, but they have an interesting and surprisingly complex geometry. Drills are rotary cutting tools and, compared to, say, lathe tools, where the lathe tool remains stationary and the work revolves, drills revolve while the work remains stationary. There are exceptions to those arrangements, but the relative motions of tool and work remain essentially the same. BS 328-1 (1993) and ANSI/ASME B94.11M-1993 specify the features of twist drills and define terms used to refer to the various geometric features of standard twist drills (Fig. 477). Most manufacturers produce sets of jobber drills, stub drills, long series, and extra long series drills as well as drills which have their geometry fine-tuned for cutting particular materials such as stainless steel, hard steel, aluminium or titanium effectively. The most commonly available drills are the "jobber" series. The term "jobber" refers to a notional length of flute compared to the diameter of the drill. There is some variation, but for drills between 0.2mm and 20mm diameter, the flute length should be between seven and thirteen times the diameter, with smaller drills having proportionately longer flute lengths. The typical sets of drills presented in cases show the variation in overall length and flute length quite neatly (Fig. 522). That variation in flute length and overall length may complicate the construction of drill sharpening jigs.

Fig. 522: Variation in the lengths of jobber drills from 6 to 10mm diameter.

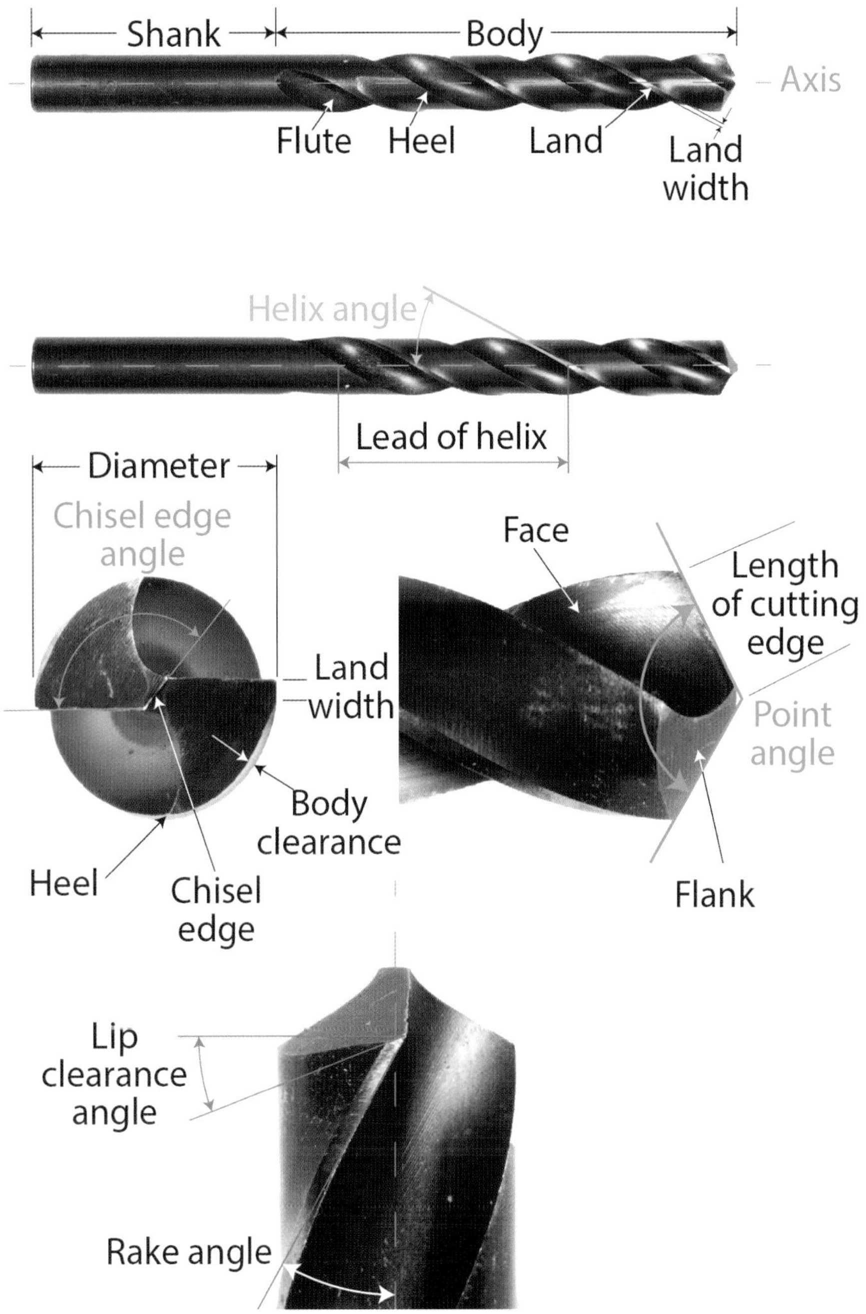

Fig. 523: Features of a typical twist drill.

Fig. 523 shows the main terms and related angles on a jobber drill. The point angle is commonly 118 +/− 3 degrees, but that is a compromise and the angle may be varied to suit the material being drilled, with values typically in the range 90 (soft plastics) to 140 (hard steel). The lip clearance angle is typically between 5 and 15 degrees, 11 degrees being a common compromise. The size of the chisel edge angle is not important, and is a consequence of the other angles. For a conventional jobber drill with point angle 118 degrees and clearance angle of 10–12 degrees the chisel edge angle is likely to be around 105 degrees. Cutting takes place along the lips of the drill, and the chisel edge doesn't cut, but scrapes as it forces its way into the work. That accounts for much of the pressure needed to force the drill into the work, particularly when the drill is creating an initial hole. There are solutions to this, but the standard jobber drill simply has a chisel edge formed as a consequence of the shape of the rest of the drill tip, particularly the lip relief (*see* later). The chisel edge represents the top of the web, so a thinner web would result in a shorter chisel edge. A thinner web would result in a weaker drill, more inclined to break under pressure, while a thicker, stronger web would result in a longer chisel edge requiring more pressure to force the chisel edge and the web through the work. So the thickness of the web is a compromise, and the length of the standard chisel edge is the result.

The cutting edges at the lips act in a similar way to lathe tool cutting edges, and require the equivalent of top rake and a front clearance angle. Top rake is formed between the flutes and the lips, so is fixed for a given drill although it is possible to modify this in the area immediately behind the lips while leaving the basic helix angle unchanged along the remainder of the flutes. In their as-supplied form, straight flute drills have no top rake and the clearance angle takes the form of the lip relief angle.

If the drill tip was a simple conical shape, it would be easy to grind by holding the drill at an angle to the wheel and rotating it about its own axis (Fig. 524). However; that would not produce any clearance on the curved surface formed behind the cutting edges at the lips, so the drill tip would rub and the cutting edges would not be able to penetrate further into the work. That clearance may be formed in different ways, each of which has an influence on the performance of the drill, but, on a standard jobber drill the geometry of the single surface behind the lips can be reproduced by making use of the properties of an offset cone. This means

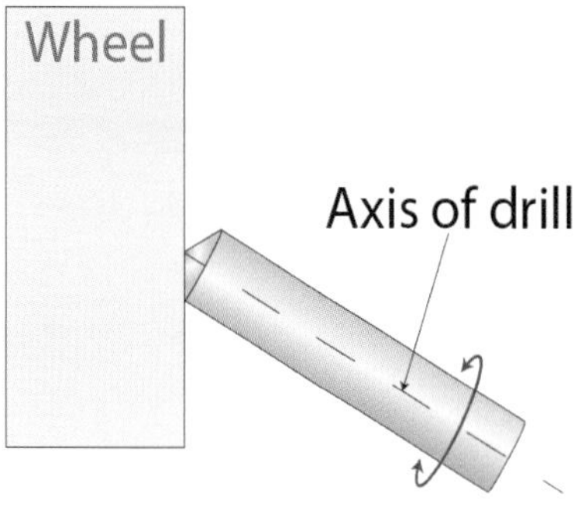

Fig. 524: A conical tip can be produced by holding the drill with its axis at an angle to the flat face of a wheel, and rotating the drill about its long axis.

the basic geometry is a little more difficult to visualize, but it also means that if the geometry is set up carefully, drill sharpening is quick and easy, and can reproduce the original geometry of the drill point. This is not the only approach to the geometry, but it is a tried and tested method. Alternative methods of forming clearance have become more common in recent years, and some suppliers now provide drills with alternative point geometry, such as "four facet" or "six facet" shapes based on flat faces. These alternative geometries have some advantages, under some circumstances, but the traditional jobber drill performs well, particularly when drilling into a smaller pilot hole. Where a good jig is available and properly set up, a jobber drill may be sharpened more quickly than alternative shapes.

An insightful analysis by Van Royen (L. A. Van Royen, *The Model Engineer and Electrician*, 14th August 1913, p.153–157) suggests there are two stages in thinking about how to create clearance on a standard twist drill.

The first stage is to create an imaginary cone with the lip of the drill lying along its surface, on a line from the tip of the cone (Figs 525 and 526). The angle of the lip of the drill is produced by the intersection of a rotating cylinder (the drill) and the surface of the cone (Fig. 526). There is a single line of contact between the surface of the cone and the tip of the drill (Figs 526 and 527). The angle between the lip and the axis

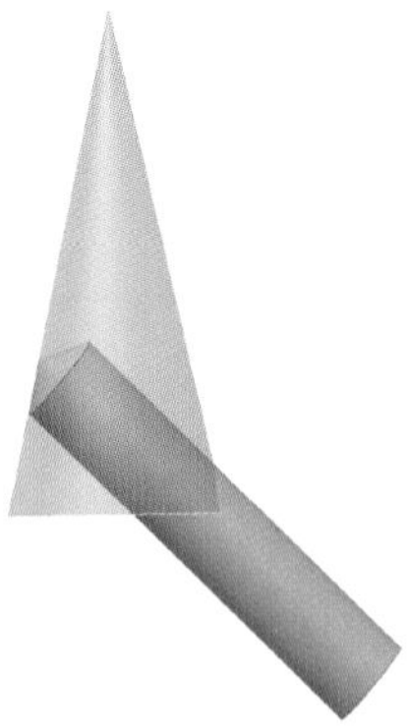

Fig. 525: A drill tip lying against the inner surface of a cone. Rotating the drill about its own axis creates a conical tip. Rotating the drill about the axis of the cone will not change that shape.

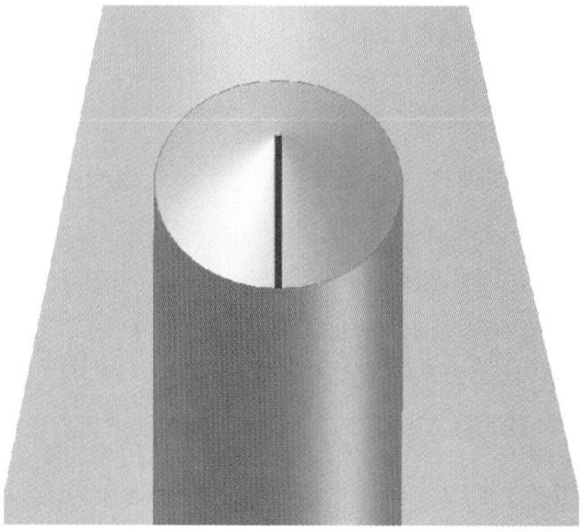

Fig. 526: A front view looking through the surface of the cone, showing (in red) the single line of contact between cone and drill.

of the drill depends on the angle between the axis of the drill and the line of contact, or, in effect, the angle between the lip and the face of the wheel (Fig. 527). The drill can be swung around the axis of the cone without changing the shape ground on its end, because the distance from the drill to the surface of the cone remains the same throughout the rotation.

The second stage involves offsetting the axis of the cone to one side of the axis through the end of the drill, parallel to the lips (Fig. 528). Part of the surface of the drill tip now sticks out beyond the surface of the cone. If the drill is now swung around the axis of the cone (stage 1), progressively more material will be removed from the area

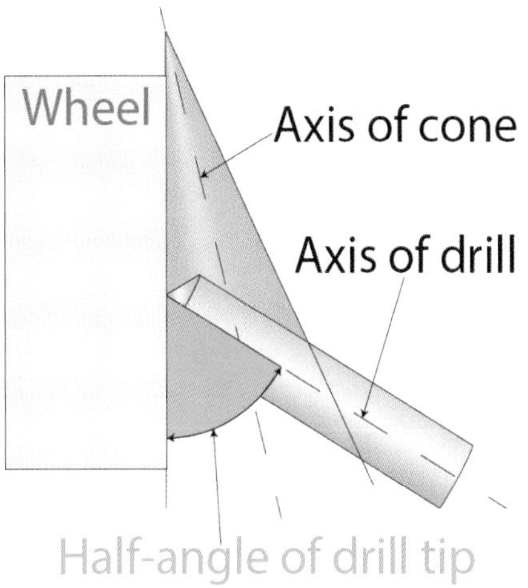

Fig. 527: If the surface of the cone lies against the flat face of a grinding wheel, the half-angle of the drill tip is the angle between the face of the wheel and the axis of the drill.

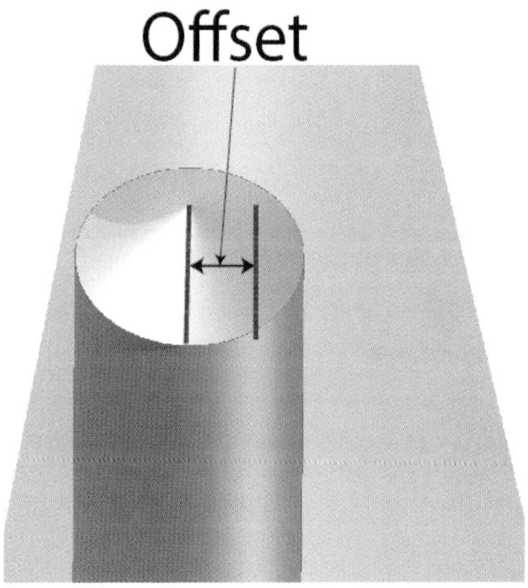

Fig. 528: Offsetting the drill to one side of the centre line of the cone creates clearance when the drill is swung around the axis of the cone.

behind the lip of the drill, creating a steadily increasing clearance. The more the offset, the greater the clearance. The distance from the point of the drill and the tip of the cone also has an effect (Fig. 529), and the smaller the distance, the greater the clearance.

Notice that the curve created at the intersection of drill and cone (i.e. the line of the material removed) sweeps downwards, then back up (visible on both the middle and bottom drills in Fig. 529). That same effect is visible on a real drill, to some extent, although the eye can easily be fooled because of the geometry.

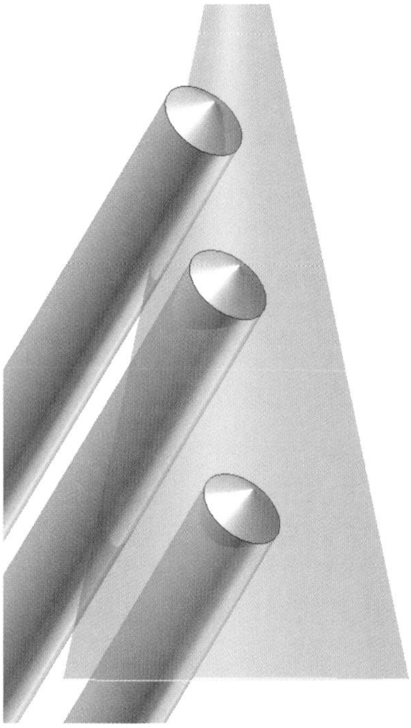

Fig. 529: This side view shows that as the drill is moved vertically closer to the tip of the cone, the clearance increases. The topmost drill has too much clearance and is not practical. The bottom drill has a small but practical, amount of clearance. The middle drill has a substantial but usable clearance.

When the drill is positioned against the wheel, there are four dimensions which need to be taken into account.

Dimension 1: the angle between the longitudinal axis of the drill and the face of the wheel should be the lip half-angle (Figs 525 and 527). That would typically be 59 degrees for a jobber drill, but could be more or less, to create the desired lip angle.

Dimension 2: The included angle of the imaginary cone (Figs 525 and 527) has been determined experimentally, and 26 degrees gives good results.

Dimension 3: The distance from the axis of the drill to the tip of the imaginary cone. This has been determined experimentally, and a suggested value for the distance is 3 x drill diameter (D), measured as shown in Fig. 530.

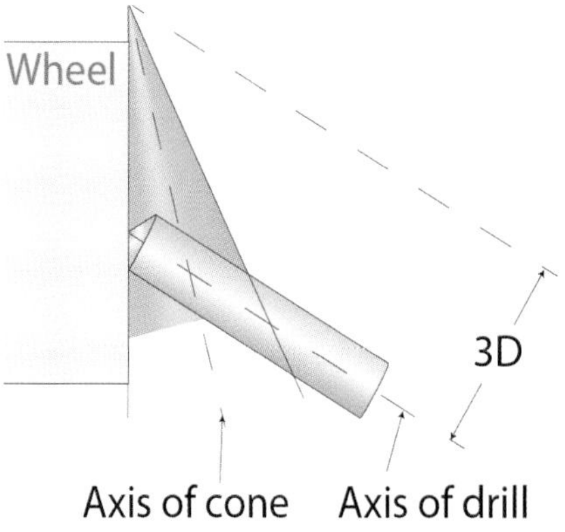

Fig. 530: The ideal distance from the tip of the cone to the axis of the drill is three times the diameter of the drill (3D).

Dimension 4: The offset distance (Fig. 528) has also been determined experimentally, and results suggest one thirteenth of the diameter of the drill (D/13). Subsequent experiments by others, in the 1950s, suggested that D/13 provided too little back-off, and that a better result could be obtained by using D/4.3, so there is some scope for variation here.

The fact that two of the dimensions depend on the diameter of the drill means a sharpening jig must be set up differently for each diameter of drill. The design of drill sharpening jigs varies considerably, but to achieve good results they should all provide the same geometric relationships, within reasonable limits. They should certainly create drill points with geometry which will allow the drill to perform efficiently, and the standard geometry of a jobber drill as supplied from the manufacturer is a good place to begin. Some jigs sharpen drills in other ways, to deliberately alter the geometry of the point (*see* later), and many of the lower priced jigs simplify the sharpening process by compromising on aspects of the geometry, but the relationships between those four basic dimensions form the basis of sharpeners recreating standard jobber point geometry.

Translating the geometry into a practical jig is a well-trodden path. Be aware, though, that while there is room for variation in the physical arrangements between drill and wheel, and a lot of creative commercial solutions, not all of those will give good results.

The geometry of a standard jobber drill represents a good working compromise between efficiency of cutting action, and durability of the cutting edges, which is perhaps why the standard geometry has remained unchanged for so long.

Fig. 523 illustrates some of the important features of a conventional twist drill such as the common jobber drill. Although the point angle is normally taken to be 118 degrees, that is for optimum performance in a volume production situation, and is not critical for less frequent use. That angle varies depending on the material being drilled, so changing the angle to 120 degrees when drilling in mild steel will make no noticeable difference to everyday performance. Other factors such as equal cutting edge length, chisel length, and clearance, have a much greater effect.

Initial shaping

Heavy damage to a drill suggests the drill requires a thorough inspection before attempting to re-shape then sharpen the point. When a drill has broken, the shank or the shaft may be bent, making the drill fit only for the scrap bin. The shank of a drill is often softer than the fluted section, and is more prone to bending, so if the fluted section has broken, roll the drill across a flat surface, and watch the behaviour of the flutes at the tip. If the tip of the drill appears to lift at any point, or if a gap appears between the outer edges of the drill and the flat surface, it should be replaced rather than repaired. In an emergency, a drill might be straightened, but its accuracy will be compromised and it may bind in a hole of any depth.

A badly damaged tip may be ground straight across, then reformed by grinding to a conical shape by holding the drill at the half-angle of the tip (Fig. 527) and rotating it against a grinding wheel. The final shape of the tip, and the clearances behind the cutting edges will be accurately ground during the sharpening stage.

Sharpening

There is a range of approaches to sharpening twist drills.

Touching-up the cutting edges

Some commercial sharpening devices are designed to sharpen the cutting edge and reform the clearances at the tip of a jobber drill. The more basic devices are suitable for quickly sharpening a drill which shows light wear but will not grind sufficiently deeply to remove badly damaged corners or flutes chipped or worn at a level below the corner of the cutting edge. The more capable devices are able to cope with greater levels of regrinding, and may also be able to resharpen masonry drills as well as thin drill webs or form spilt points (about which, more later).

Fig. 531 shows an Eclipse No. 39 Drill Sharpener (not currently available commercially). This is a hand-powered device which uses two eccentric wheels to raise and lower

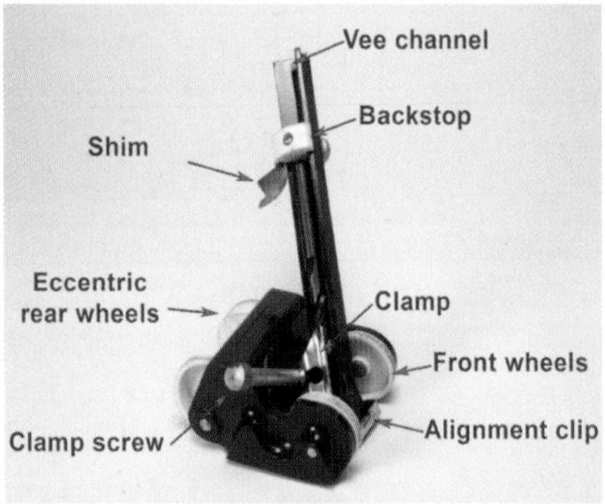

Fig. 531: Eclipse No. 39 Drill Sharpener.

the drill bit as it is dragged along with the tip of the drill rubbing against abrasive paper. Viewed from the front, Fig. 532 shows that the drill is held at an angle of 59 degrees to the vertical, forming the basic cone angle of the cutting edge being sharpened. Viewed

Fig. 532: Front view of an Eclipse No. 39 Sharpener.

from the side, Figs 533 and 534 show the eccentric wheels in their raised and lowered positions. The eccentricity causes the

Fig. 533: As it rolls along, the eccentric rear wheels lift the rear of the sharpener, tilting the drill into a more vertical position.

Fig. 534: Rolling the sharpener further causes the wheel to descend, tilting the drill backwards.

USING THE ECLIPSE NO. 39 DRILL SHARPENER

Begin with the sharpener assembled but empty.

- Undo the screw holding the backstop in position, and slide the backstop to a position near the top of the vee channel, out of the way.
- Loosen the screw holding the drill clamp to allow the clamp to open.
- Slide the drill down the vee groove, under the clamp, until the working end is more or less at the level of the wheels. Tighten the clamp to take up the slack, but leave the drill free to slide and rotate (Fig. 535). Hold the drill in position with your fingers and turn the whole jig upside down so that you can see the tip of the drill.

The little U-shaped metal clip (Fig. 536) can be adjusted to suit different drill diameters, by sliding it backwards or forwards.

- Turn the drill until one cutting edge is parallel to the protruding edge of the clip, and level with the clip (Fig. 537). Tighten the drill clamp just enough to hold the drill.
- On the backstop, swing the pivoting shim clear, then slide the backstop down to touch the end of the drill, and tighten it in that position (Fig. 538). Slide the drill down a little more, swing the shim back into the groove, and push the drill back up, against the shim, to flatten the shim against the backstop (Fig. 539). That pushes the drill down the groove a distance equal to the thickness of the shim, making it protrude just enough for sharpening. Check the cutting edge is still aligned with the end clip, then tighten the drill clamp firmly.
- Place a sheet or strip of aluminium oxide abrasive paper onto a flat surface. A whole sheet of 400 grit Wet & Dry may be glued to a sheet of glass or a piece of 18mm thick MDF or some similar flat backing. A coarser grade may be used to speed up the sharpening process, but will leave a rougher finish on the drill tip. A grade as coarse as 100 may be required to remove significant damage and 400 is fine enough for a decent working finish.
- Gripping the shaped recesses in the body of the sharpener, roll the sharpener forwards and backwards over the sheet, making sure the wheels rotate rather than skid (Fig. 540). The motion of the sharpener effectively moves the drill up and down as it slides across the abrasive surface, removing material behind the cutting edge to create clearance. After a few strokes, remove the sharpener; leave the backstop clamped and the shim in position; loosen the drill clamp; rotate the drill through half a turn; check the second cutting edge is aligned with the clip; then tighten the clamp. Repeat the rolling action to sharpen the second lip.

Both cutting edges should be sharpened so that they are of equal length and the outer corners are level with one another, but check this carefully, and give the shorter cutting edge a few more strokes, if necessary. Although this method does not provide true conical backing off, it does create clearance behind the cutting edges. The basic sharpening motion begins by abrading the cutting edge, but the cam action of the wheels tilts the drill, bringing the area behind the cutting edge into contact with the abrasive paper, removing more material from this area. Although deceptively simple, this is a cleverly designed sharpener and is an effective device which is useful for smaller drills, down to approximately 3mm. It is, however, a comparatively slow method of sharpening, and may becomes tedious for much larger drills.

Fig. 535: Place the drill in the groove.

Fig. 538: Tighten the backstop against the drill.

Fig. 536: The U-shaped clip on the underside can be adjusted to suit different drill diameters.

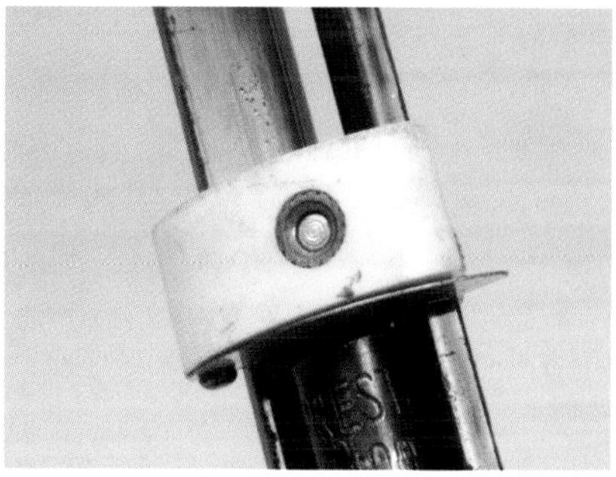

Fig. 539: Without moving the backstop, swing the shim between backstop and drill. Tighten the clamp.

Fig. 537: Align one lip with the leg of the clip.

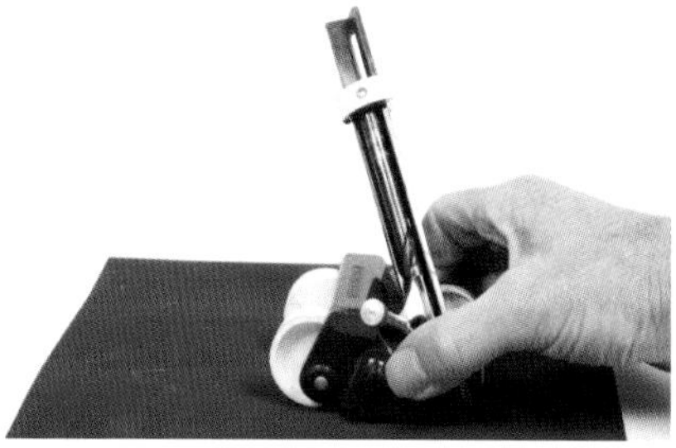

Fig. 540: Roll the sharpener over abrasive paper.

angle between the vertical and the axis of the drill to vary, providing initial clearance behind the cutting edge of 7 degrees, increasing around the tip, to 21.5 degrees. When installed in the sharpener the drill initially protrudes a little from the base, which lifts one wheel clear of the abrasive paper, ensuring the drill point contacts the paper. As material is removed from the drill, the wheel is lowered until it touches the paper, ensuring no more can be ground from the drill. If the backstop remains in the same position, both cutting edges will be sharpened equally.

Powered drill sharpeners

Fig. 541 shows a very simple low cost device consisting of a grinding wheel set at an angle to a set of vee channels. The device

Fig. 541: A simple sharpener intended to be powered by a pistol drill.

is powered by a pistol drill (not supplied) running at around 3,000rpm (or less, in the case of most battery-powered drills). The drill is placed in a channel chosen to suit its diameter, then manually pushed against the wheel, and rotated part of a turn (Fig. 542). Once one side has been sharpened, slide the drill clear of the wheel, rotate through half a turn, and grind the second side. This sharpener simplifies the geometry of the drill point, because the vee channels hold the drill below the centre height of the wheel, and the curve of the wheel creates clearance behind the cutting edge (Fig. 543). There are

Fig. 542: Push the drill against the wheel, and rotate it, but stop before grinding the second cutting edge.

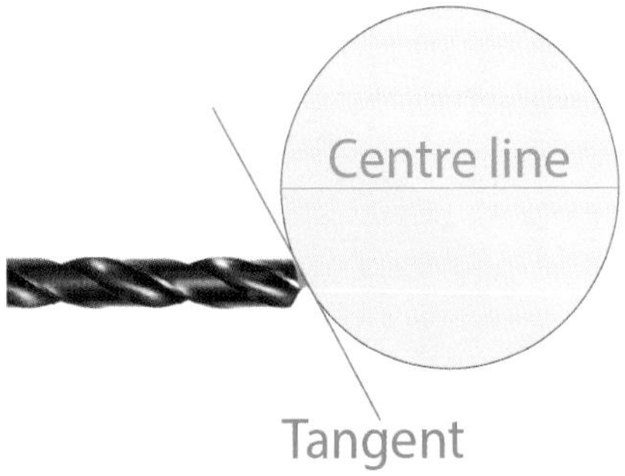

Fig. 543: The drill sits below centre, and the curve of the wheel creates the clearance.

two main difficulties in using this kind of device. The first is in ensuring that the two lips of the drill are ground to equal lengths. This can be achieved by repeatedly removing the drill and examining the tip using a drill gauge of some kind (not supplied). The second difficulty is in rotating the drill far enough that each cutting edge is ground, but not so far that the wheel damages the chisel point and cutting edge of the other side of the drill. There is no limit to the angle through which the drill can be rotated, so this depends on the judgement of the operator. The smaller the diameter of the drill, the more difficult it is to avoid collateral damage of this kind. It would be very time consuming to grind a drill sufficiently to remove significant damage, as that requires frequent re-setting of the drill as the positions of the cutting edges spiral backwards as the flutes are ground back, but it is capable of light resharpening.

Fig. 544 shows a simple and easy to use low-cost device which consists of a shaped grinding wheel, a plastic plate with a hole to suit each diameter of drill and a steel plate immediately behind the plastic plate, which limits the depth of grinding (Fig. 545). Each hole in the plastic plate has two projections

Fig. 544: A drill sharpener which has a hole for each diameter of drill, and is powered by an electric drill. Photo: JACK SEALEY LTD.

Fig. 545: The sharpener consists of a shaped grinding wheel, a plastic plate with holes for each diameter of drill, a spring to control pressure, and a tapered plug to allow the chuck jaws to provide drive.

which sit in the flutes and hold the cutting edges in the correct position in relation to the grinding wheel, so that grinding takes place along one cutting edge. The device is intended to be powered by an electric drill with a specific size of collar on the body behind the chuck.

In use, with the sharpener unpowered, put a drill into the corresponding hole and turn it until the internal projections engage with the flutes (Fig. 546). With the sharpener under power, press the drill bit further into

Fig. 546: Each drill is guided into position by a pair of protrusions inside the hole which ensure the cutting edge is correctly positioned in relation to the wheel.

Fig. 547: The grinder may be powered by an electric drill with a 42mm diameter collar.
Photo: JACK SEALEY LTD.

the hole (Fig. 547). Remove the drill, turn it through a half-turn, and repeat the process for the other cutting edge. The result should be two lightly resharpened cutting edges. Check that the cutting edges are the same length and that the tips of the outer corners are at the same height. As with all similar devices, it is easy to produce a drill which has two different lengths of cutting edges, so it is important to use a gauge to check the shape of the drill tip (*see* Fig. 481), regrinding short edges until both edges match.

The key component in this kind of sharpener is a shaped grinding wheel with an angled edge which grinds the cutting edges of the drill at an appropriate angle (usually 59 degrees half-angle and 118 degrees included angle). As the drill pushes the grinding stone back against the sprung plate, the drill twists slightly, guided by the plastic protrusions in the flutes, and that grinds clearance behind the cutting edges. One problem with some models is that although many electric drills have a suitable collar, their chucks are often too large to enter the sleeve on the body of the sharpener. However; some router collars have the correct size (Fig. 548). The drive arrange-

Fig. 548: In the absence of a suitable electric drill as a power source, or in cases where the collar is of the correct size but the chuck fouls the mounting tube, the sharpener may be powered by a router spindle which has a 42mm diameter collar by using a drive adapter.

ment for some sharpeners is unreliable and depends on the closed jaws of a drill chuck pressing into a slightly tapered hole in a plastic plug. This is not a positive drive and is inclined to slip. A better arrangement is to make a hexagonal plug with a protruding shaft (Fig. 549). The hexagon replaces the plastic plug, and the drill chuck or router collet grips the shaft. Allow just a little in-and-out freedom before clamping the collar, and keep the speed down to 2–3,000rpm.

Fig. 549: A hexagonal drive adapter may be more effective than the tapered plastic drive plug.

More robust machines can be used to carry out re-shaping of a drill bit, followed by sharpening. These machines may also be able to thin drill webs, grind facets, or create split points. Fig. 550 shows a machine designed to re-shape and sharpen drill points, as well as create split points (*see* later). Like the simpler machines for light sharpening, these more robust machines simplify the sharpening process. While some make compromises in the geometry, most will successfully sharpen a drill bit in the range 3–13mm, and some may handle larger diameter drills.

Fig. 550: A robust and versatile drill sharpening machine.

As on the cheaper, lighter, sharpeners, this heavier duty sharpener uses a shaped grinding wheel to form the basic 59 degree half-angle of the cutting edges (Fig. 551).

Fig. 551: Removing the outer casing reveals that the collars hold the drill against a shaped grinding wheel; a diamond or cBN wheel, in this case. A drill held in the front collar is rotated to form a cutting edge and the clearance behind that edge.

These machines typically hold the drill bit in a collet. The collet is then used to guide the drill as it is sharpened by a grinding wheel. The collet may also be used to position the drill against the wheel to create a split point, or to thin the web.

A typical collet will have at least six gripping jaws. An ordinary chuck, or a 3-jaw collet cannot securely and accurately hold a twist drill bit, except on the plain shank, because of the flutes and lands. The shank is often too far from the tip of the drill to provide good support near the point of contact with the grinding wheel, so the drill must be held in a collet or a close-fitting sleeve. In the model shown in Fig. 550, the drill is inserted loosely into the collet, then the collet is placed into a holder, and the projection of the tip of the drill is set against an end stop. The orientation of the cutting edges is set using two spring-loaded fingers which locate against the edges of the flutes (Figs 552 and 553). The collet is then tightened. The collet holder has projecting pegs, so the drill is in a known orientation and projects a fixed distance from the end of the collet.

The collet assembly is inserted into a sleeve, and the projecting pegs automatically set the orientation of the drill bit against a grinding wheel. Turning the collet a fixed amount, between stops, rotates the drill, grinding one cutting edge and creating the clearance behind that edge (Fig. 554). The collet assembly is then removed, rotated through half a turn, and re-inserted, to grind the other cutting edge and clearance. In practice, the collet is rotated several times in each position, to grind enough to remove all tip damage and ensure each edge is fully sharpened. In theory, the drill should be ground until it "sparks out" in each position, so that the grinding wheel will not grind any more material from either side, ensuring that each side is ground to the same size. In practice, the drill should be repeatedly removed and checked until the lips are of equal length. Where the drill requires anything more than a light resharpen, the grinding process removes some material from the end of the drill, changing the orientation of the cutting edges in relation to the flutes, so removing more material means the drill must be reset against the end stop and flute/lip guides before continuing the grinding operation.

Fig. 552: The drill is held lightly in a collet, then inserted into a collar and pushed forwards against a stop.

Fig. 553: Rotating the collet and drill allows the flutes to be set against a pair of 'fingers'. This sets the cutting edges in a known position in relation to the collet. The collet is then fully tightened.

Fig. 554: Rotating the collet back and forth sharpens the drill against the shaped grinding wheel.

Some drill sharpening machines take a different approach, using a cam to control the depth of cut and the shape of the drill behind the cutting edges, creating the clearance. The machine shown in Fig. 555 is intended to be powered by an electric drill, and is provided with a set of collets, as well as a simple way to set the projection and orientation of the drill (Fig. 556) by pushing the drill down into a vee groove while rotating the drill to locate the cutting edges against a stop (the sides of the groove). The end of the collet holder has a pair of shaped projecting lugs (Fig. 557), and the collet assembly is pushed into a tube with a shaped end (Fig. 558), located above the grinding wheel. The projecting lugs on the holder bear against the highs and lows of the end of the tube (Figs 559–562), which control the height of the tip of the drill against the type 1 grind-

Fig. 555: Intended to be driven by an electric drill, this sharpener uses a cam mechanism to create the cutting edges and clearances.

Fig. 556: The drill is gripped and guided by a collet with a built-in cam.

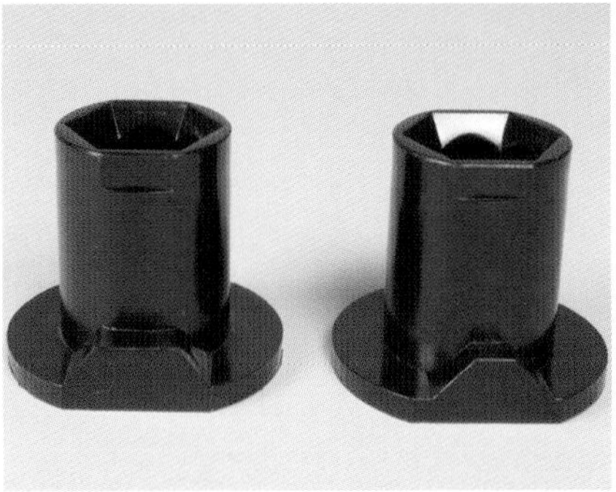

Fig. 557: Each collet has a pair of projecting lugs which may be of different heights and widths.

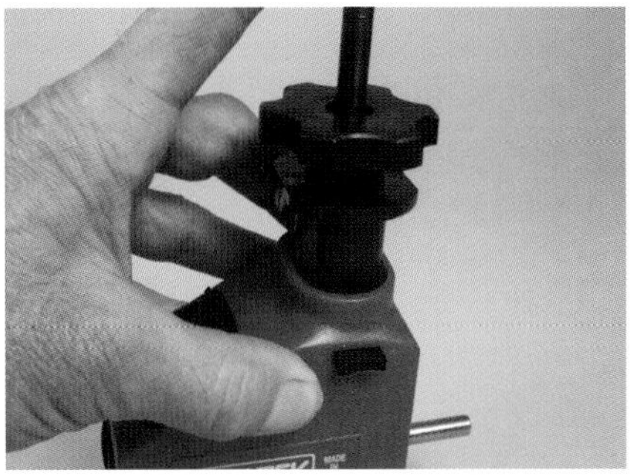

Fig. 558: The collet assembly is pushed into a tube with a shaped end, located above the grinding wheel.

Fig. 559: The projecting lugs on the collet will engage with the lugs on the collar of the sharpener.

Fig. 560: Although one side of the collar seems deeper than the other, this is an illusion caused by the tilt of the drill in relation to the wheel (see Fig. 563).

Fig. 561: The high sections of sides of the collar raise the collet assembly, grinding less deeply or not at all.

Fig. 562: The recessed sides of the collar lower the collet assembly, grinding more deeply.

ing wheel as the collet assembly is rotated. The holder on the body has two recesses and two projecting lugs, so that the collet and drill can be turned continuously. Each lug and recess creates one cutting edge and its clearance. Fig. 563 shows the wheel inside the machine, and Fig. 564 shows that the axis of the drill is held at an angle to the wheel as it is rotated, lowered and lifted, while it is being sharpened. The offset axis, and the action of the cam produce a nicely sharpened drill point with appropriate clearances. The cam operation tends to produce flats behind the cutting edges as the cam lowers the drill (Fig. 565), but practical tests confirm that this has no effect on the performance of the drill.

The collet assembly is made of plastic, so some care is required to ensure the collet is sufficiently tight without the thread disengaging or the upper knob bending.

The important principles underpinning the design of this sharpener form the basis of other devices such as end mill sharpeners. This cam-controlled method avoids the need to swing the drill around the axis of a cone. The use of a collet, and the provision of a simple method of setting the projection and orientation of the drill also simplifies the sharpening task.

Fig. 563: The type 1 grinding wheel is mounted on a spindle inside the sharpener.

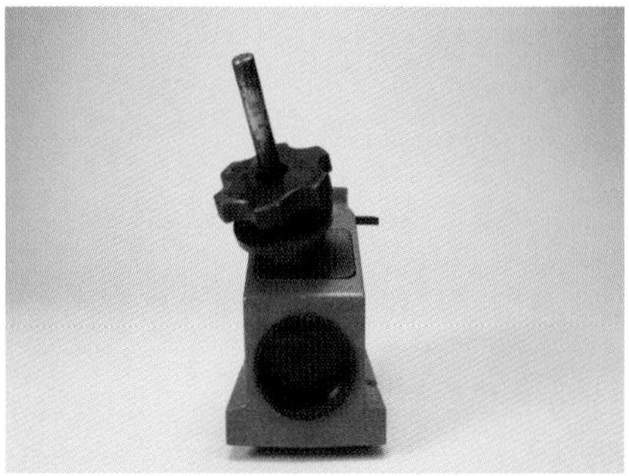

Fig. 564: The axis of the collet and drill assembly is held at an angle to the wheel.

Fig. 565: The result of the sharpening operation is a primary clearance behind the cutting edge, and further secondary clearance facets behind that. The resulting surface is a set of flats rather than a continuous curve but the clearance is perfectly adequate, because the secondary facets will not be in contact with the work.

Classic conical point sharpening devices

The geometry of a conical jobber-style twist drill point can be reproduced using a commonly available jig which swings the drill against a grinding wheel (Fig. 566). These devices have been widely available for many years, and they work well, subject to two provisos. The first is that the geometry of the jig is correct. Sadly, this is not the case with some of the currently available copies. Secondly, the drill must be set up with the correct projection from the front of the jig, and with the cutting edges correctly orientated in relation to the grinding wheel. The amount of projection, and method of orientation varies depending on the design of the jig, so it is important to follow the manufacturer's instructions (Table 14). The design of these jigs is based on Van Royen's work on the geometry required to form the cutting edges and the continuous clearance behind those edges, but simplified to reduce the complexity of the setting up process. Van Royen's four essential dimensions (*see* page 127) are set as follows:

Fig. 566: Two designs of swing sharpeners: Reliance on the right, and Picador-style on the left.

- Dimension 1 is the half-angle of the cutting edges. Usually fixed at 59 degrees, some jigs provide an adjustable pivot and an angular scale (Fig. 567).
- Dimension 2 is the half-angle of the imaginary cone around which the drill is swung (Fig. 568). This is normally fixed at 13 degrees.

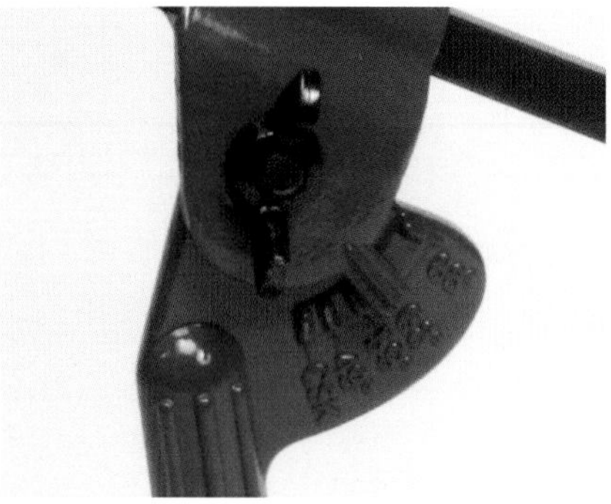

Fig. 567: The half-angle of the cutting edges may be fixed, but may be adjustable, as indicated by the pivot and scale on this sharpener.

Fig. 568: On the Reliance sharpener, the vee guide is set at the cone half-angle to the axis of the pivot.

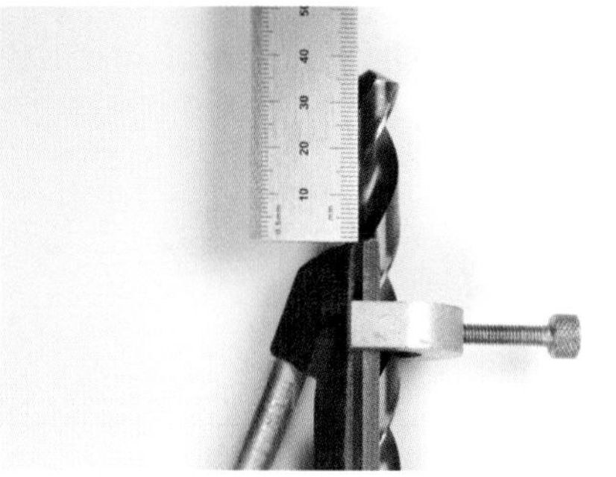

Fig. 569: The projection of the drill is measured from a point specified by the sharpener manufacturer.

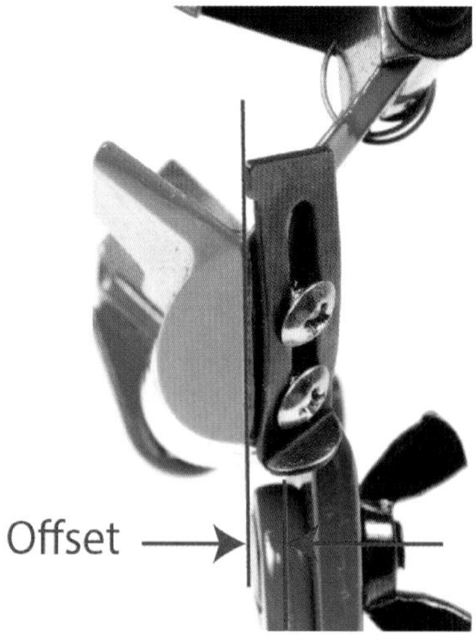

Fig. 570: In most simple jigs, the sideways offset of the axis of the drill cannot be adjusted by the user.

'Picador' sharpener drill projection distances	
Drill diameter (mm)	**Projection (mm)**
Up to 6.35	0.8
6.35 to 12.7	2.4
Over 12.7	3.2

Table 14: Drill projection distances for the 'Picador' sharpening jig.

- Dimension 3 is the height of the top of the cone above the axis of the drill (Fig. 569), and that varies according to the diameter of the drill. Measuring that directly is difficult, but it can be set by altering the projection of the drill in front of the axis of the cone. The axis of the cone is unlikely to be exactly at the front of the vee guide in which the drill sits, so the manufacturer of the jig will state the point from which the distance should be measured (usually the front of the vee guide), as well as the factor used to calculate the distance. This is often 3xD, but sometimes 1.5xD or 1.4xD; and sometimes a fixed distance between 0.8 and 3.2mm as shown in Table 14.
- Dimension 4 is the sideways offset of the axis of the drill (Fig. 570). That varies according to the diameter of the drill. Van Royen suggests this is D/13 (but note the comments on page 127 that other values of offset may be more effective) and, for a small range of drills, there is not much variation in the offset. For a drill of 3mm, the offset would be 3/13 = 0.23mm, and for 13mm it would be 13/13 = 1mm. In the simplified jigs, the offset is usually fixed at manufacture, often by offsetting the axis of the vee guide from the axis of the swing by 5 or 6mm (Fig. 570). On some sharpeners, the vee guide is set at an angle to the pivot axis so the centre of the drill moves to one side as the projection increases, increasing the offset.

The result of all of this is that only dimension 3 needs to be set according to the diameter of the drill. Everything else is fixed.

Van Royen refers to a practical jig which allows adjustment of cone height and offset (dimensions 3 and 4). A version of this jig was formerly manufactured as the Potts Drill Grinding Jig, and a kit of parts can currently be obtained from Hemingway Kits. It is, however, a more complex jig than the popular swing jigs, and is more complex to make. The drill itself is used to make the basic settings.

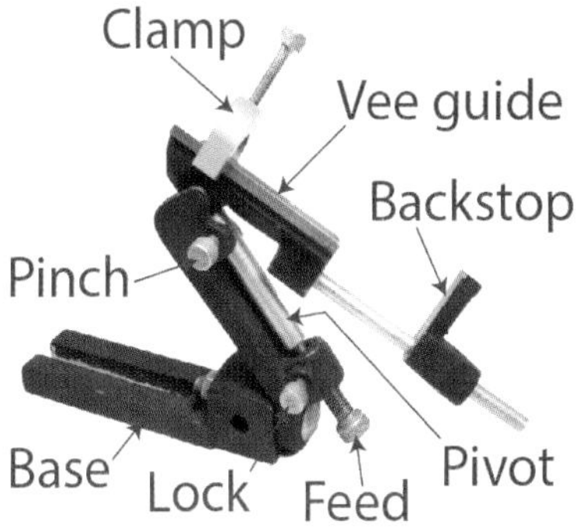

Fig. 571: The key parts of the Reliance sharpener. The vee guide is removable.

The Reliance jigs (Figs 566 and 571) simply require the projection of the drill to be set manually, by measurement, but produce good results. The projection is set at three times the diameter of the drill, so: calculate the projection, then place the drill in the vee guide, and adjust the end stop to position the tip of the drill that distance from the front of the guide. The orientation is set by looking at the front of the jig (Fig. 572) and rotating the drill so that the lower cutting edge is aligned parallel to the line engraved on the front of the vee guide. The Reliance jig has a lock screw to hold the swinging arm so that the drill is in its uppermost position for the next operation.

Figs 573 and 575 show a simple setup for drill grinding using a Reliance jig. The wheel is a flat-faced cup wheel, on a bench grinder with modified guards. The jig is fixed at right angles to the face of the wheel, and is secured by a bolt and washer in the slotted

Fig. 572: On the Reliance, the drill cutting edge is aligned parallel to a line on the front of the vee guide.

Fig. 573: A simple setup for drill grinding using a Reliance sharpening jig.

Fig. 574: A bar against the side of the base maintains alignment as the sharpener moves in or out.

base, with a steel guide bar running along the outer edge of the base to maintain alignment of the jig (Fig. 574). Slackening the bolt and sliding the jig forwards or backwards allows the setup to cope with small or large drills, which, on the Reliance requires a corresponding small or large projection of the tip of the drill from the vee guide.

The jig can be fitted with a simple

Fig. 575: A platform on a bar can be mounted in the jig, to allow a dresser to be used to true the wheel.

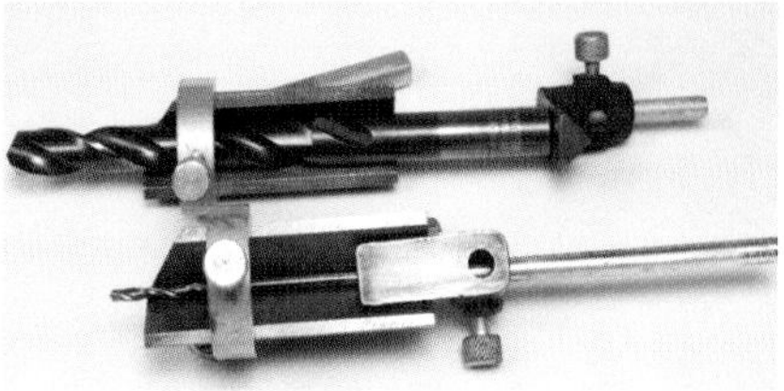

Fig. 576: The adjustable vee guide backstop can be turned over to provide a long 'finger' for short drills.

platform mounted on a bar, so that a conventional dresser can be used to true the surface of the wheel (Fig. 575). Fig. 576 shows that the adjustable vee guide backstop can be mounted in alternative positions to suit the length of the drill.

With the grinder switched off, and the swinging arm set so that the drill is in its uppermost position, slide the jig towards the wheel, at right angles, stopping just as the drill is about to touch the wheel. Clamp the base of the jig in that position. Undo the lock screw to allow the arm to swing. Start the grinder, and repeatedly swing the arm from its central starting position, over to the right and back again, using the feed screw to move the drill slowly forwards until the face has been ground satisfactorily. Remove the drill and vee guide assembly; release the clamp screw; then rotate the drill in the vee guide to bring the opposite cutting edge parallel to the engraved line. This re-alignment process can be simplified by aligning the first cutting edge and tightening the clamp, then attaching a square collar and projecting screws to the shank of the

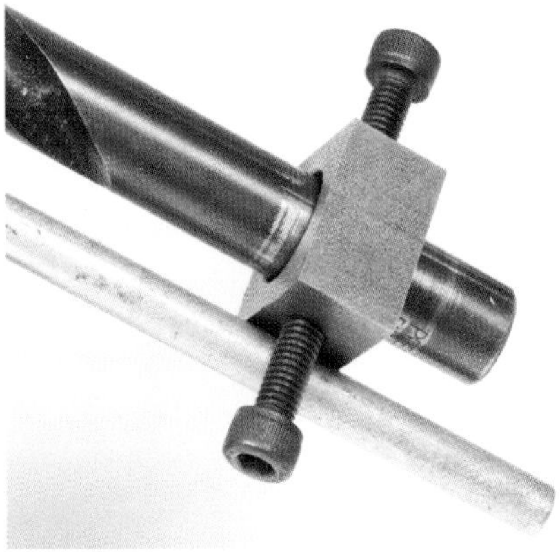

Fig. 577: Attach a collar with projecting screws to the shank of the drill, with one screw resting against the backstop rod.

drill, resting one screw against the backstop guide rod before tightening both screws (Fig. 577). To align the second cutting edge, remove the vee guide and turn the drill so that the other screw rests against the rod. Then tighten the main clamp. Reassemble, and repeat the grinding action for the second cutting edge and face. The instructions recommend that the feed screw position is not moved after grinding the first cutting edge and face, but this can make it difficult to lower the drill and vee guide assembly as the wheel is turning. The essential requirement is that the drill is ground symmetrically, and that the two cutting edges are of the same length, so that the chisel point is central and the tips of the cutting edges are aligned level with one another. As with other jigs, some care is required to achieve this, but the drill and vee guide assembly can be removed and the drill tip compared to a gauge during the operation. Removing substantial amounts of material changes the orientation of the cutting edge because of the twist in the flute. That will result in the need to reset the drill in the guide as grinding proceeds. Grind both cutting edges to an equal extent before resetting the drill projection, to maintain the correct geometry, and reset the drill before a final light grind on each cutting edge, to complete the operation.

This kind of jig can usually sharpen drills down to 3mm diameter, or a claimed 1.5mm on some models. However; a projection of three times the drill diameter may not provide full support for a smaller diameter drill, and some jigs are designed so that the measured projection is much less (1.0, 1.4 or 1.5 times the diameter, on some models). This is done by effectively extending the projection of the vee guide in front of the axis of the pivot. It is important that the required drill projection is stated in the manufacturer's instructions. Altering the amount of projection affects the amount of clearance behind the cutting edges (sometimes referred to as "backing off'), and it has some effect on the strength of the cutting edges. Reducing the projection increases the clearance, and vice versa. If the figure is not known, start with 1.5 times the diameter; sharpen a drill; then inspect the amount of backing off (clearance) around the periphery of the drill.

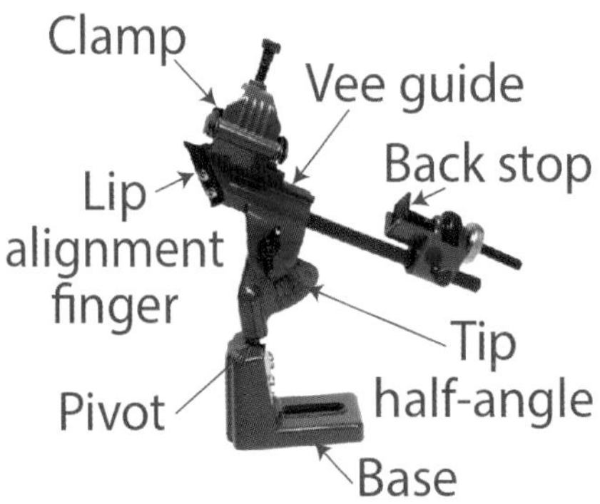

Fig. 578: The key parts of a Picador-style drill sharpening jig.

The Picador jig (Fig. 578) has an adjustment for the half-angle of the point, but it has the same swinging action. The projection is measured from the same position at the front of the vee guide, but is much smaller than for the Reliance jig (Table 14). The drill is aligned by resting a cutting edge against the locating plate fixed to the front of the vee. If the clearance is too small, increase the projection. If the clearance seems too great, reduce the projection.

Sharpening small drills

Drills of less than 3mm (1/8 inch) diameter are more awkward to sharpen because they are more difficult to hold close to a grinding wheel, and their faces are much smaller and more difficult to measure. When using a standard Reliance-style swinging sharpener, the corner of the drill holder may foul the wheel. In addition, it is difficult to clamp the small drills in the trough, never mind aligning their small cutting edges with the engraved line on the holder.

Continuous conical clearance

The Wishbone sharpener (Fig. 579) can be used to hand-sharpen drills 3mm (1/8 inch) and smaller. This is a version of a swinging sharpener, but made to grip and sharpen small drills. Insert the drill into one of the four collets, and lightly tighten. Align the cutting edges with the arms of the sharpener (Fig. 580). Then use the setting gauge

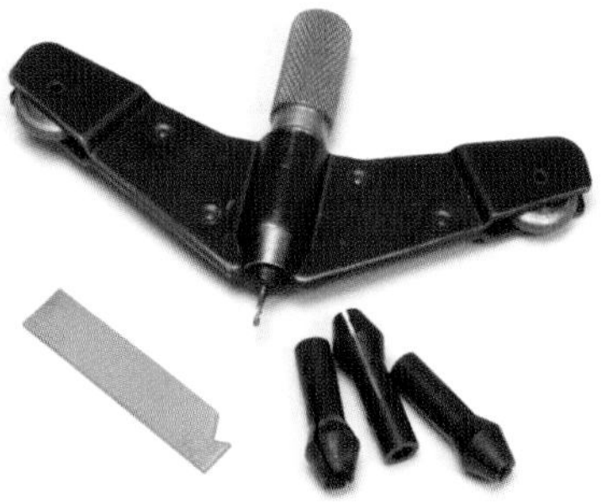

Fig. 579: The Wishbone sharpener is used by hand, to sharpen drills of 3mm or smaller diameter.

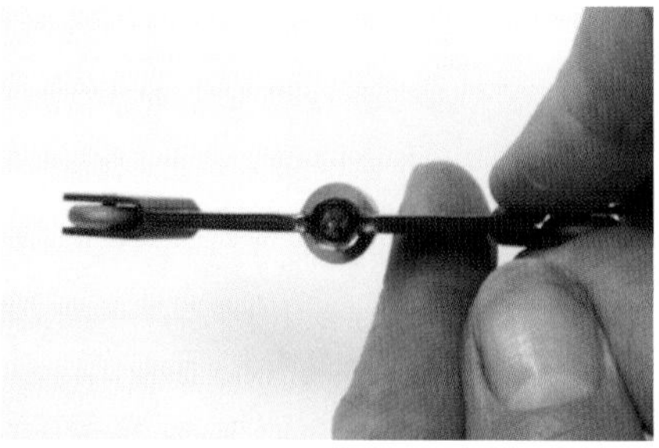

Fig. 580: Align the cutting edges with the arms of the sharpener.

to set the protrusion of the drill (Fig. 581). Hold the sharpener upright, with the drill tip and the front wheel contacting the sharpening stone (Fig. 582). Simultaneously push forwards and tilt sideways, as shown in Fig. 583. Lift the drill point clear of the stone and return to the start. Repeat this sequence 3 or 4 times. Swap ends, and repeat three or four times, to sharpen the other cutting edge. Then examine the point under high magnification. The cutting edges should be of equal length, and the corners of the tip should be level with one another. Remedy any differences with a few strokes on one side. The main challenge with this sharpener is in aligning the cutting edges initially. This should be done under high magnification. Although the Wishbone sharpener is no longer offered for sale, plans for constructing this relatively simple device have been published on several occasions (*see* Further Resources).

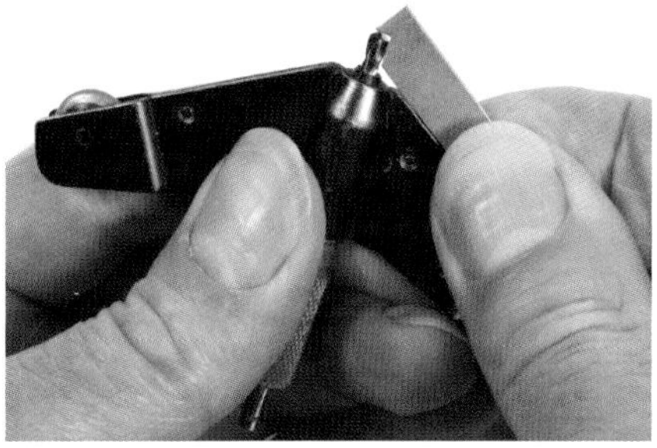

Fig. 581: The tip protrusion is set using a gauge which is normally supplied with the sharpener.

Fig. 582: Begin with the sharpener upright; the drill tip and the rear wheel in contact with the stone.

Fig. 583: Simultaneously push forwards and tilt to sharpen the cutting edge and form the clearance.

Flat clearance facets

For small drills, a single clearance facet is enough to allow the drill to cut, and that simplifies the geometry of the drill, requiring only a flat face behind each cutting edge. The position of each facet involves two moves: first, holding the drill vertical, then tilting it through 59 degrees to rest on one cutting edge; and second, tilting it at right angles to the cutting edge, approximately 10 degrees, to lie at 90 – 10 = 80 degrees (Fig. 584). This places the drill in a similar position to the end of a pass in a Wishbone sharpener. The drill can then be rubbed against a horizontal grinding stone to sharpen the cutting edge and reform the clearance flat. A second clearance flat could then be formed behind the first, by tilting the drill a little more.

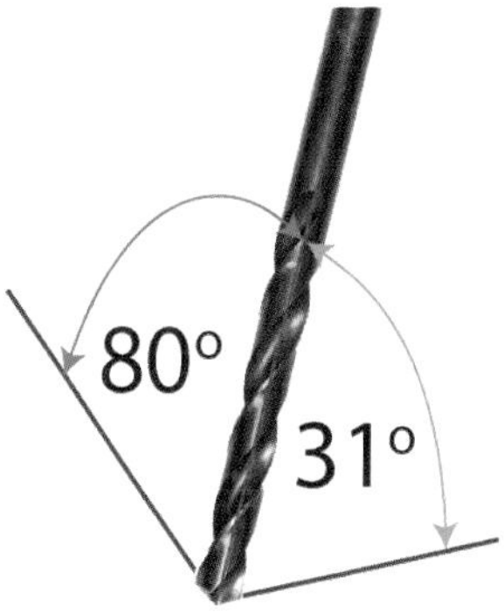

Fig.584: Holding a drill at a compound angle allows a single flat to be ground behind a cutting edge.

Fig. 585: A modified version of a sharpener designed by D.A.G. Brown; made by John Moran. Photo: JOHN MORAN at www.gadgetbuilder.com

Fig. 585 shows a modified version of the D.A.G. Brown design of hand-powered four-facet sharpening device for small diameter drills. This uses collets mounted in a square-bodied holder to grip the drills. The collet holder sits in one of two square holes machined at a compound angle in a block of steel. Both holes lie at an angle of 59 degrees from the vertical in one plane. One hole lies at 10 degrees from the vertical in a plane at right angles to the first (the primary clearance angle to provide clearance immediately behind the cutting edge), and the other lies at 25 degrees (the secondary clearance angle). The drill is sharpened with one 25 degree facet on each cutting edge, by sliding the jig backwards and forwards across a diamond plate. After sharpening one cutting edge, the square collet is removed, turned through 180 degrees, and replaced, so that the second cutting edge can be sharpened. The primary 10 degree facet is then produced in the same way, using the other square hole. The positions of the chisel edge and the tips are inspected using a magnifying lens, and any remedial work is easy to carry out by giving a few additional strokes on one face. The original device slid on rails, but this modified version uses ball races as wheels.

Further Information

BOOKS

Hall, H. (2006) *Tool and Cutter Sharpening*, Dorset, Special Interest Model Books LTD.

Lie-Nielson, T. (2004) *Taunton's Complete Illustrated Guide to Sharpening*, Newtown CT, USA, The Taunton Press.

MAGAZINE ARTICLES

Bradley, I., (1961), 'For Honing Small Drills', *Model Engineer*, vol. 125, issue 3151, 30 November, pp. 653–654

Bradley, I., 1961, 'Putting the Device to Use', *Model Engineer*, vol. 125, issue 3153, 14 December, pp. 624 - 725

Brown, D., 'Sharpening Small Drills: The End of a Boring Problem', *Model Engineer*, vol. 184, issue 4119, 5 May 2000, pp. 518 - 520

Meek, G. (2016). 'Perfectly Ground Twist Drills Every Time', *Engineering in Miniature*, vol. 37, no. 9, March, pp. 318 - 319, cont'd
April 2016, vol. 37, no. 10, pp. 345 - 347
May 2016, vol. 37, no. 11, pp. 382 - 383
June 2016, vol. 37, no. 12, pp. 405 - 407

Wilding, J., 2000, 'A Honing Jig for Small Drills: Part 1', *Model Engineer*, vol. 185, issue 4136, 29 December, pp. 652 - 654

Wilding, J., 2001, 'A Honing Jig for Small Drills: Part 2', *Model Engineer*, vol. 186, issue 4138, 26 January, pp. 83 - 85

Contributors' websites

Accu-Finish® Grind-R-Table.	www.accu-finish.com
Arc Euro Trade LTD. Suppliers of tools including collet blocks, vee blocks, and toolposts.	www.arceurotrade.co.uk
Bowland Trading LTD. Suppliers of new and used machines.	www.bowlandtrading.com
DMT Diamond Machining Technology. Suppliers of diamond coated abrasive stones, cones, the Diamond Wave Sharpener, and a knife sharpening system.	www.dmtsharp.com
Gränsfors BRUK AB. Handforged axes.	www.gransforsbruk.com
GRS. Power Hone sharpening system..	www,grs.com
Horotec SA. Watchmaker's tools.	www.horotec.ch
Jack Sealey LTD. Tools and workshop equipment.	www.sealey.co.uk
John Moran's extensive site includes useful sections on drill sharpening machines and techniques.	www.gadgetbuilder.com
Lansky Sharpeners. Knife sharpeners.	www.lansky.com
Lee Valley Tools LTD. A wide range of tools including grinder rests.	www.leevalley.com
Lindsay Engraving. Manufacturer of Lindsay AirGravers, hand engraving tools and resources.	www.lindsayengraving.com www.airgraver.com
Howard buys and sells hobby lathes, mills, cutter grinders, tooling and all live steam items.	www.myford-lathes.com
Niels Machines. Pre-loved machines.	www.nielsmachines.com
SpyderCo. Knife sharpening system.	www.spyderco.com
Tinker grinding jig, books, plans, accessories..	www.lautard.com
Tormek AB. Bench grinders and accessories.	www.tormek,com
VersaLab Inc. Suppliers of the VersaLab sharpener for watchmakers' screwdrivers.	www.versalab.com/WATCH.html
Warco (Warren Machine Tools LTD). Suppliers of bench grinders, vee blocks and abrasives.	www.warco.co.uk

Material	***Description***
Arkansas stone	Natural stone (Novaculite – a form of quartz) available in several grades. From coarsest to finest: Washita, soft, hard, black hard and hard translucent. Arkansas stone is found in Arkansas, Oklahoma and Texas.
Water stone	Naturally occurring rock, but nowadays is more often a synthetic material. Used to sharpen tools. These stones may be called water stones if water is used to lubricate the stone during the sharpening process. Lubrication is optional, but reduces friction and slows the cutting process, as well as carrying away abraded particles of stone and metal. Synthetic stones are often made of aluminium oxide held in a soft binder, which sheds grains easily and provides fast cutting.
India stone	Aluminium oxide. Brand name of Norton Abrasives (a division of Saint-Gobain).
Crystolon	Silicon carbide. Brand name of Norton Abrasives.
Silicon carbide	A synthetic abrasive which is a compound of silicon and carbon, known as carborundum (not to be confused with corundum which is a form of aluminium oxide). Moissanite is a naturally occurring form of silicon carbide, but is very rare, which is why most silicon carbide is synthetic, and most of that is produced in China. Silicon carbide stones are fast-cutting and ideal for initial shaping and sharpening, but India and Arkansas stones produce a finer finish and sharper edge. Norton Crystolon is one popular brand name for silicon carbide stones.
Aluminium oxide	The term aluminium oxide refers to several related oxides of aluminium. May also be called alumina, aloxite or alundum. Naturally occurring corundum is the most common form of aluminium oxide, and is the abrasive most commonly used in grinding wheels.
Coticule	Naturally occurring non-porous stone quarried in the mountainous Ardennes region of Belgium.
Belgian Blue whetstone	Naturally occurring non-porous stone (a form of coticule).
Ceramic stone	Ceramic materials are formed from metallic atoms and non-metallic atoms combined to form a non-metallic solid material. Ceramics include items made from fired clay, such as tiles, but engineering ceramics have specific properties and ceramic abrasives are very hard.
Sandstone	Natural stone. Normally quite soft.
Oilstone	A whetstone which is lubricated by oil in a similar way to a water stone. Oil is optional, and, like water, it reduces friction and slows the sharpening process while helping to carry away particles of abrasive and abraded metal.
Emery	Naturally occurring rock (corundite) which is mainly aluminium oxide (corundum), but may include small quantities of other materials.
Diamond	Diamond is a naturally occurring mineral and is a form of carbon. Synthetic diamonds are formed from carbon under very high pressure and high temperatures. Typically, the hardness of synthetic diamond is second only to naturally occurring diamond, and some forms of synthetic diamond are harder than natural diamond. Synthetic diamond is widely used as an abrasive.
cBN (often spelt CBN)	Cubic boron nitride. A synthetic material with a hardness only exceeded by synthetic diamond. CBN wheels run cool and can withstand a greater amount of heat than diamond, making them ideal for grinding hardened steel, nickel-based superalloys and other hard materials.
Borazon	Borazon is a type of cBN. Borazon was invented and developed by R. H. Wentorf Jr at the General Electric Company (GEC) which adopted the trade name Borazon in 1969. GEC first perfected a method of manufacturing diamonds from graphite, then went on to develop sintered cubic boron nitride. CBN is relatively inert and, compared to diamond, does not react with iron, nickel or cobalt, making it more useful than diamond, and able to withstand higher temperatures.
Rotten Stone (Tripoli)	A fine, soft polishing powder made from crushed rock containing weathered limestone and silica. Formerly mined in South Wales (UK) it is now mined in Arkansas (USA).
Corundum	The most common naturally occurring form of aluminium oxide, with chemical formula AL_2O_3. Corundum is almost as hard as diamond, making it an important abrasive. Corundum is the most common abrasive used in grinding wheels.
Whetstone	Any natural or synthetic stone used for sharpening, usually by hand.

Table 1: Common abrasive materials.

Index

Other Metalworking Titles from Crowood

ISBN: 978 1 84797 566 9

ISBN: 978 1 84797 512 6

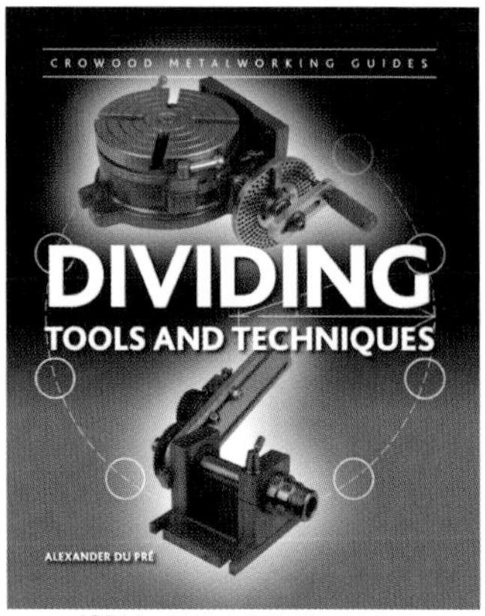

ISBN: 978 1 84797 838 7

ISBN: 978 1 78500 250 2

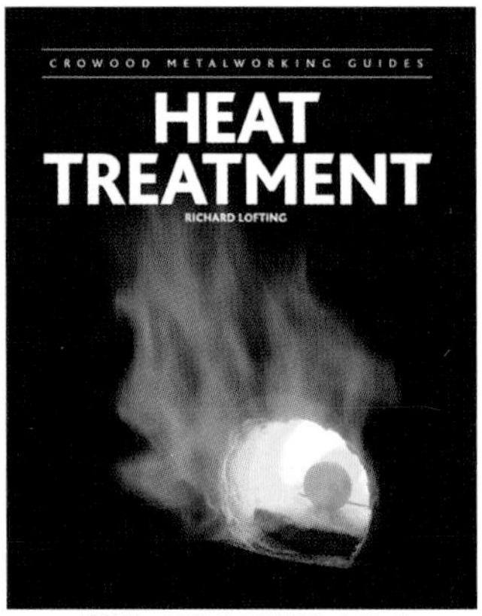

ISBN: 978 1 78500 441 4

ISBN: 978 1 84797 774 8

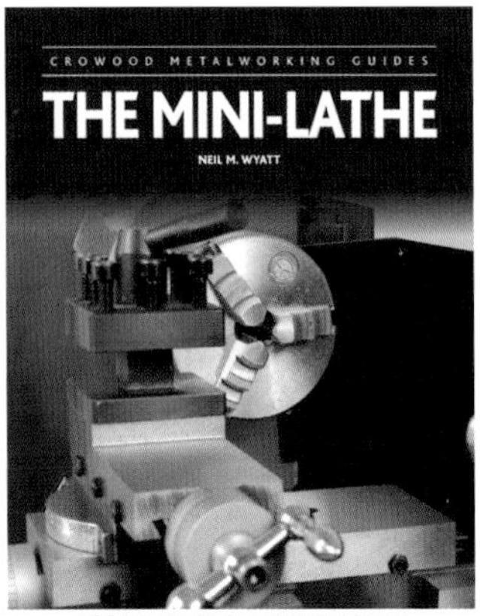

ISBN: 978 1 78500 1 284

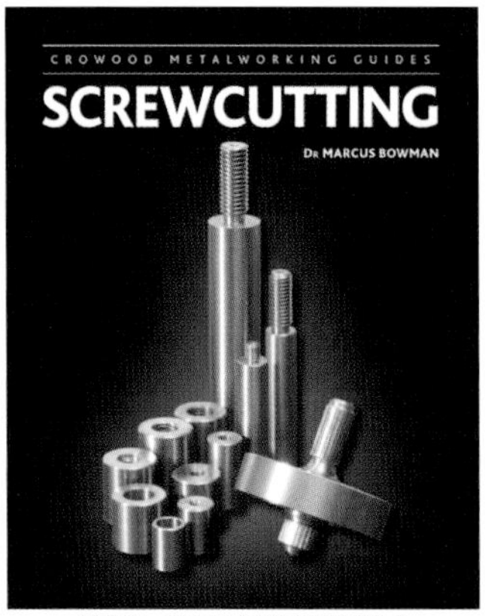

ISBN: 978 1 84797 999 5

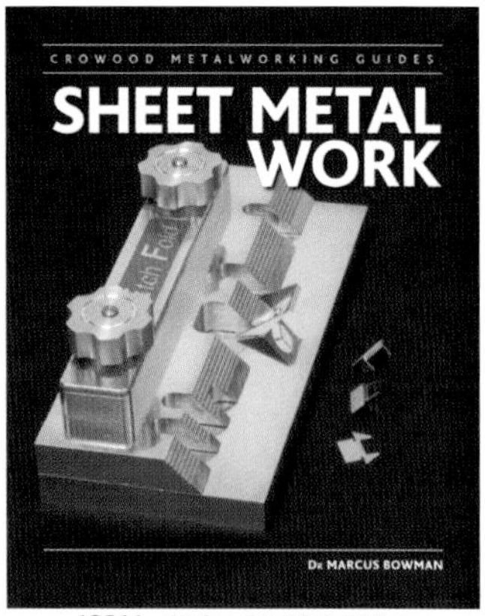

ISBN: 978 1 84797 778 6